WRITING
Making Your Mark

Edited by
EWAN CLAYTON

BRITISH LIBRARY

First published 2019 by
The British Library
96 Euston Road
London NW1 2DB

On the occasion of the British Library exhibition
Writing: Making Your Mark

British Library Cataloguing in Publication Data
A catalogue record for this publication is available from the British Library

ISBN 978 0 7123 5253 6 (hardback)
ISBN 978 0 7123 5248 2 (paperback)

Title page image: Christine de Pizan, Christine, *The Book of the Queen*. Manuscript (parchment). Paris (France), *c*.1410–*c*.1414. British Library: Harley MS 4431 fol. 103v

Note on the type
FF Scala, FF Scala Sans, Albertus

Designed by Karin Fremer
Picture research by Sally Nicholls

Printed and bound in Italy by Printer Trento

Note on caption text
Script names are included in many captions. Examples such as 'Mayan glyphs' and 'early Chinese characters' are self-explanatory. From Chapter 2 onwards, however, the naming is more complex. This is because descriptive systems for script names have yet to be harmonised. Currently they reflect the usage of scholars from different fields, and terminology from different language groups, eras, places of origin or peoples. Descriptions of individual scripts can be found within the chapters.

CONTENTS

Similiter autem necesse est et de loco physicum sicut et de infinito cognoscere, si est aut non, et quomodo est et quid est. Et enim omnes quae sunt opinantur esse alicubi; quod enim non est, nusquam est; ubi enim est hircocervus aut sphinx? Et motus qui communis maxime et maxime proprius, qui secundum locum est, quam vocamus lationem. Habet autem multas dubitationes quid forte sit locus; non enim idem videtur speculantibus ex omnibus quae insunt. Amplius autem neque habemus nihil ab aliis neque praedubitatum neque praeexpositum de ipso. Quod quidem igitur sit locus, videtur manifestum esse ex transmutatione: ubi enim nunc est aqua, hinc exeunte sicut ex vase, iterum aer inest; aliquando autem alterum aliquod corpus eundem locum hunc detinet. Hoc autem ab aliis qui fiunt et transmutantur alterum ab omnibus esse videtur; in quo enim nunc aer est, in hoc prius erat aqua; quare manifestum quod erat locus aliquid et receptaculum alterum ab utrisque, in quod et ex quo mutatum est. Amplius autem locorum motiones simplicium corporum, ut ignis et terrae et talium, non solum ostendunt quod est aliquis locus, sed quod habet quandam potentiam. Fertur enim unumquodque

in suum locum non prohibitum, hoc quidem sursum, illud autem deorsum; haec autem sunt loci partes et species, sursum et deorsum et reliquae sex distantiae. Sunt autem huiusmodi non solum ad nos dextrum et sinistrum, sursum et deorsum; nobis quidem enim non semper idem, sed secundum positionem, ut utique vertamur, fit, unde et multotiens dextrum et sinistrum, sursum et deorsum, ante et retro. In natura autem determinatum unumquodque seorsum. Non enim quodcumque contingit sursum est, sed ubi fertur ignis et leve; similiter autem et deorsum non quodcumque contingit, sed quo gravia et terrea feruntur; tamquam non positione differentia solum sed et potentia. Ostendunt autem et mathematica; cum enim non sint in loco, tamen secundum positionem ad nos habent dextrum et sinistrum, ut solum dicitur secundum positionem, non habentia natura horum unumquodque. Amplius qui vacuum affirmantes esse locum dicunt; vacuum enim utique locus erit privatus corpore. Quod quidem igitur sit aliquid locus praeter corpora, et omne corpus sensibile esse in loco, per haec aliquis suscipiat. Videtur autem utique et Hesiodus recte dicere faciens primum chaos. Dicit enim: Omnium quidem primo chaos factum est, postea autem terram latam, tamquam indigeret primum esse receptaculum his quae sunt, eo quod opinatur, sicut multi, omnia esse alicubi et in loco. Si autem sit

LIST OF CONTRIBUTORS

EWAN CLAYTON is Professor in Design at the University of Sunderland and external advisor to the exhibition *Writing: Making Your Mark.* He is a core faculty member of the Royal School of Drawing, and is a calligrapher. His book on the history of writing, *The Golden Thread,* was published by Atlantic in 2013.

ADRIAN S. EDWARDS is Head of the Printed Heritage Collections team at the British Library, where he has worked for over twenty-five years. He is the lead curator of the exhibition *Writing: Making Your Mark,* and previously curated the exhibitions *Evolving English: One Language, Many Voices* (2010–11) and *Comics Unmasked: Art and Anarchy in the UK* (2014).

MICHAEL JAMES ERDMAN is the curator of Turkish and Turkic Collections at the British Library. In 2018 he obtained a doctorate of philosophy for his dissertation on the writing of history in Turkey and the Soviet Union in the early twentieth century. Previously Michael worked as a Management and Consular Officer for Global Affairs Canada in the Middle East and Latin America. He has contributed chapters to *The First World War and its Aftermath: The Shaping of the Modern Middle East* (2015), and upcoming volumes on Kyrgyz history and on Arabic in the Ottoman Empire.

EMMA HARRISON is curator of Chinese collections at the British Library. She holds a degree in Oriental Studies from the University of Oxford and began work at the British Library in 2012 as part of the International Dunhuang Project. She has previously co-curated an exhibition entitled *Beyond Paper: 3000 Years of Chinese Writing* (2015–16). Her interests include traditional Chinese book culture, the development of Chinese script and the mechanics of humour and wordplay.

STAN KNIGHT is the author of *Historical Scripts: From Classical Times to the Renaissance* (A&C Black and Oak Knoll 1984, 1998, 2003) and *Historical Types: From Gutenberg to Ashedene* (Oak Knoll 2012). He is a past chair of the Society of Scribes and Illuminators in London, and has had a career as a teacher of design in the UK and USA. He contributed a survey of the roman alphabet to *The World's Writing Systems* (Oxford University Press 1996).

ANDREW ROBINSON is the author of books on writing, scripts and decipherment. They include: *The Story of Writing: Alphabets, Hieroglyphs and Pictograms; Writing and Script: A Very Short Introduction; Lost Languages: The Enigma of the World's Undeciphered Scripts;* plus two biographies, *The Man Who Deciphered Linear B: The Story of Michael Ventris,* and *Cracking the Egyptian Code: The Revolutionary Life of Jean-François Champollion.*

PETER TOTH is curator of ancient and medieval manuscripts at the Western Heritage Collections of the British Library. He studied Classics and Egyptology, and earned a PhD in Classics. His main interest is in cultural interaction in Late Antiquity and the Middle Ages via translations of texts and ideas from one language and tradition to the other.

ANGELA WEBB is a psychologist specialising in the academic needs of children with Developmental Coordination Disorder. Until recently, she worked at a group practice in Central London and lectured part-time at the Institute of Education, now University College, London. For twelve years she has been chair of The National Handwriting Association, a charity which advises and supports health and education professionals in their work with children. Her research explores the relationship between handwriting competence and the quality of the written compositional content.

OPPOSITE Main text: gothic quadrata. Marginal notes in cursive secretary hands. Aristotle, *Libri Naturalis*. Manuscript (parchment). Oxford? (England), around 1265–70. British Library: Harley MS 3487, fol. 22v

INTRODUCTION

Ewan Clayton

Writing is one of humanity's greatest achievements. This book aims to help us think about the role it plays in our lives and society at large, learn more about different writing systems across the globe, appreciate the beauty of writing where functionality and aesthetics meet, and feel empowered to enter the debate about its future.

Full writing systems developed, apparently independent of one another, in at least four cultures around the world. The first evidence is from Mesopotamia around 3300 BC, then from Egypt a little over a century later. In China a fully formed system was already in existence from 1300 BC, and in Meso-America from about 900 BC. These writing systems enabled their societies to begin to communicate across stretches of space and time that an individual alone could not hope to reach. Writing has since helped build societies and collaborative organisations, economies, and literary and conceptual structures that an oral tradition might not have achieved.

By the end of the twentieth century writing had become a skill that many practise, almost inconsequentially, every day. Today we write digital messages on phones and laptops; we read printed information in books, on screens and in magazines; we handwrite 'to do lists', greetings cards and exam papers, and sign our names. There is writing in our streets and homes and places of work. Indeed, it is so ever-present that often we scarcely notice the sheer amount of written materials that surround us.

OPPOSITE Mayan glyphs. Stela, Late Classic Maya Period. Carved limestone. Pusilhá (Belize), AD 600–800. British Museum: Am1928,Q.79

Yet, once upon a time, writing was a skill confined to the elite in a society. In ancient Egypt's Old Kingdom (2575–2150 BC), when the population of the country stood at around 1 million, it is estimated that at the very most just 1 per cent of the population could either read or write.[1] That percentage remained stable until the Graeco-Roman period (from 332 BC onwards), when it began to rise.

Today, in England, the level of functional literacy is around 85 per cent of the adult population.[2] This figure represents a paradigm shift in aspiration; we believe that, where possible, all members of society should have a certain degree of literacy. 'Functional' means the ability to write, read, converse and use simple numeracy to a level that allows participation in a group's everyday literary life. In Europe high literacy rates are the result of several centuries of campaigning for universal access to education. As recently as the nineteenth century in Europe there was still discrimination against women being taught to write to the same level as men.

The landscape of writing continues to shift. More and more writing is being made electronically. With over 7 billion people on the planet there are, at a conservative estimate, around 5 billion mobile/cell phone accounts. More than half the planet has access to the World Wide Web, with a quarter of a billion users being added in 2017.[3] So vast in scale does this change seem to be that some are asking what is the future for writing? Are video and audio poised to take over many of the functions that writing once had? Yet in 2018, in one average Internet minute, it is calculated that 187 million emails, 18 million text messages and 38 million WhatsApp messages were sent and 3.7 million Google enquiries were made.[4] At this moment in the history of writing, when so many conventions are in a state of flux, it may be useful to challenge ourselves to think further about the role we want writing to play in our lives, both on a personal and a social level.

Throughout the centuries, in every society where writing has been present, writing evolved in response to human needs. The earliest uses appear to have been to name and count things, to make claims of ownership, to carry a voice into the afterlife and to remember things. Writing spread into different areas of social life as groups pressed it into service in the legal world, the marketplace, learning, religion, politics and storytelling; each use subtly reshaped the forms and nature of the artefacts that were produced. This continues to happen today as writing and its artefacts are configured to be mined for big data by large global corporations.

There have also been internal ergonomic, human kinaesthetic and aesthetic factors involved in the way writing has evolved. In certain eras and places writing can come to seem less functional than it once was because the pace of life speeds up and one has to write more quickly. So, hand, pen and brush began to take shortcuts around the forms (this is how lower-case roman letters evolved out of roman capitals), or letters started to merge and join with one another creating ligatures between forms (the ampersand, for example, developed from joining **e** and **t**: *et* is the Latin word for 'and'). These kinds of factors lie behind the way many script systems develop. The script styles in use in China by the end of the fourth century – seal script, regular script (*kai shu*), clerical script (*li shu*), running script (*xing shu*) and cursive script (*cao shu*) – each reflect a different balance of formality and cursiveness.

It can also happen that there are times when faster forms are taken as a new standard. They again become more formal, aesthetically self-conscious structures: perhaps upright instead of leaning; or a previously cursive, ligatured script separates out afresh into individual unjoined letters (as with italic letters when they moved over from handwriting into type during the Italian Renaissance).[5] It happened also to Arabic writing in the tenth century AD when 'Alī Ibn Muqla, vizier to three Abbasid caliphs, envisioned a newly proportioned script structured around a system of rhomboid dots. A rather loose and informal number of scripts were then potentially shaped up into systematic designs.

Changes in form and usage can also result from the introduction of new technologies and materials. Writing has seen many technologies come and go, and there have been several major shifts in the materials upon which we write (the substrates). In China writing materials that included bone, bronze, bamboo strips and wood had been supplemented with paper by at least the first century AD. In Roman culture, during the early Christian centuries, there was a significant move away from using papyrus in scroll form towards making book-shaped artefacts with pages of papyrus, thin wooden sheets and specially prepared animal skins (vellum). These notebooks eventually developed into grand illuminated manuscripts, and then, in the later Middle Ages, vellum gave way to paper. Each substrate and its marking agent carries a different range of potential qualities: some are more durable than others (stone and bronze); or are easier to transport (paper and electronics); or are more straightforward to replicate (the digital on screens and in print). The kinds of text and designs they carry respond to these possibilities.

Printing as a method for making large numbers of identical copies of written artefacts was an important innovation. In the Far East, since at least the eighth century AD, printing from carved wooden blocks

OPPOSITE *Qur'an* with commentary and two systems of vocalisation. Manuscript, copied in the Eastern Kufic style. Iraq or Iran, 11th–12th century. British Library: Or.6573, fol. 211r

إخوانهن أو بني أخواتهن أو نسائهن
أو ما ملكت أيمانهن أو التابعين غير
أولي الإربة من الرجال أو الطفل
الذين لم يظهروا على عورات
النساء ولا يضربن بأرجلهن

containing whole pages of text, potentially closely integrated with illustration, proved a reliable low-cost method for reproducing multiple copies of books and other documents. Five hundred years ago in Europe the use of movable type opened up different opportunities that were seized upon by a hungry readership. The availability of written texts went hand in hand with a transformation in the self-understanding of many people in European countries that in turn affected their exploration of the world around them.

It is undeniable that today we are living through another of those seismic shifts in the 'order of the written word'. It feels like a revolutionary time. One of the triggers has been the development of a new technology, but of course it has not ended there. Electronic writing, using keyboards and screens, has made another kind of writing possible. Writing can now happen faster, is more easily reproduced and distributed, and its distribution systems are very accessible. Because writing has a 'social life', in other words it is about actions and creates and binds together human communities, the impact of these changes has been huge. Almost all the institutions and areas of life that are involved with the written word are in some form of identity crisis: libraries, publishing, copyright, advertising, the world of finance, and our understanding of privacy and authenticity – that you can 'trust someone's word'. These challenges affect writing systems across the globe and the worldwide nature of this impact is a further reason for our current transformation being unprecedented.

In an era such as ours we will certainly underconceive what writing is if we simply identify its story with that of a single letter or script system; or reduce the discussion to binary debates as to whether we should use pens or keyboards; or even try and sum the situation up in the fate of just one totemic object, like that of the printed book or a social media website, or the reliability of the news with which we engage. It is probably more useful to think of writing as a kind of ecology, a finely tuned complexity of forms, conventions, tools and technologies, and social organisations that bring order to the human urge to communicate – and all of these elements help shape the current order of things.

To date, our analysis of these changing times has measured poorly against the scale of the task at hand or in making sense of the huge changes we see around us. Some have mourned a system that has already passed. The death of writing has been proclaimed. Others have had a reaction wrapped up in a kind of romanticism for the 'missing ink', the glory days of fine writing instruments and stationery. Yet others cannot see there is anything to worry about at all: we should just get on with our new digital futures as fast and as immersively as possible.

However, as writing is such a vast subject, encompassing not only many script systems but also much more besides, for the purposes of a book, or an exhibition of around 100 objects, it is necessary to limit the scope.

In English the word 'writing' has several meanings. It can be a system for recording language using conventional marks, the actual process of bringing those marks into being, the marks themselves on the writing surface, a creative piece of 'writing' (a book, a blog) and a professional occupation. If we dig a bit further into the language we also discover the word 'wright', as in shipwright, meaning to make, and 'rite', meaning a ritual or ceremony that changes us in some way. These coincidences can suggest to the imaginative mind the idea of writing being a kind of making that has the power to transform things. Here we are in the realm of spells and powerful declarations.

The primary focus of this book is everything to do with the activity of making the marks themselves, the formation of letters and characters, how these forms come to be as they are, how they work within a writing system, and the tools and materials that support this. Having said that, these things themselves can be viewed as windows through which we can observe many aspects of our humanity and indeed the long backstory of the various societies in which we live.

The common-sense definition of writing in Europe is that it has something to do with recording speech, but it is hard to find a definition that works in all cases. Many early forms of writing in the Middle East included what today we would call the consonants and no vowels at all, and this remains true for some systems today. They were, in effect, an account of how we interrupt the sounds from our throats by partially narrowing or stopping the flow of air using the architecture of the tongue, teeth and mouth. When the signs were read aloud they were supplied with an additional vowel sound produced by the reader to form a spoken syllable, but often no written evidence of that vowel sound survives. So although they 'record' speech it would be impossible for a non-native speaker to pronounce the writing in question correctly. For this reason, we do not know how ancient Egyptian sounded when spoken. It was the Greeks who introduced a way of also writing down the vowels, and at that point writing and speech acquired an equivalence in the sense that all sounds could be noted and the writing itself could be read aloud and make perfect sense as speech.

Aristotle (384–322 BC) was the first to make this connection with speech part of his definition of writing; as a Greek it would have made sense to him. Nonetheless, it obscures the fact that even alphabetic writing may contain many signs that do not relate to speech at all: numbers, for instance, and some aesthetic aspects that also carry meaning, like colours, or changes of styles of lettering, from roman to italic or gothic.

Writing does both more and less than speech. It does more in that it can contain vast stretches of text, far more than a speaker could stand and produce, and it can provide information in graphic forms that speech cannot do: tables and comparative charts, diagrams and indexes, for instance. It can detach itself from a speaker and travel over time and distances far greater than our lifespan allows and, in terms of distance, it can now travel amazingly fast. A page of text, even a book, can be downloaded in any city around the world in an instant. On the other hand, what we lack in writing is everything associated with the physical presence of the speaker: tone and gesture, speeds of speech, and the small inflexions of voice and facial expression that give us a context for the words they utter. A calligraphic rendering of a text is one way of making up for some of this loss. Here the marks are expressive in their own right and can convey an additional sense of voice or emotional intensity, but it remains a poor substitute for a living presence.

The other problem with definitions is that over time writing has carried different cultural meanings. In ancient Greek and Roman society oratory was accorded greater respect than the written word. It was unusual to read silently, everyone read aloud, so reading written text involved lending your vocal apparatus to another person (the writer) who you allowed to speak through you. This was not a well-regarded thing to do in a society where your spirit was thought to reside in your breath; it was as if you had permitted someone else to take possession of this vital element. Some of the Greek and Roman metaphors for reading are the same as those used for prostitution. Writing was bound up not only with sound but also with breath. Reading and writing were something educated slaves were employed to do. The realm of the free man was the spoken word.

In China writing evolved from different roots: from divination practices. Oracle bones from the Late Shang Dynasty (1300–1050 BC) contain up to 6,000 symbols, many of which can be identified as the ancestors of characters still employed in Chinese writing today. The bones were used in a ceremony. The earliest diviners, going back to at least 3000 BC, studied the cracked marks appearing in the scorched remains of cattle and turtles in order to discern the direction in which events were moving, and often they had specific questions in mind. Would this soon-to-be-born child be a boy or a girl? Would this raid on nearby barbarians be successful? By the Late Shang period both questions and answers were written on the bones. Although it was the cracks on the bones that were read by diviners and the inscriptions simply record this exchange, characters and cracks alike were believed to originate with natural phenomena. They were not arbitrary marks but signs of nascent realities, living traces of a kind of natural force at work in the universe. This is one reason why calligraphers have understood themselves to be participating in the spontaneously unfolding activity of *qi*, or 'life movement', whenever they write. When structuring the characters, calligraphers are expected to be in tune with the phenomena that arise within nature and to make the characters move and grow and hang together as a result of similar forces realising themselves within the writer. To write, to be a calligrapher, is to swim in the emerging flow of existence. It was therefore presumed that calligraphers would be long-lived, for they cultivate and channel the energy of life itself. This was partly why the art form *shu fa* was accorded the highest respect.

From the first century AD onwards, writing in China was explicitly recognised as an art and from the eighth century a critical literature developed debating the qualities of different inks, the merits of brushes and papers, and the role of personal expression in writing. In ancient China writing not only represented sounds but the symbols themselves were forces of nature. For writers in the ancient Greek and Roman worlds personal expression does not seem to have been an important consideration, and nor would it be when the ancient classical world was superseded by early Christian Europe where the majority of writers were anonymous scribes working for the greater glory of God in religious communities. It is for reasons like these that the linguist Florian Coulmas has written that 'every attempt at a single universal definition of writing runs the risk of being either ad hoc or anachronistic, or informed by cultural bias'.[6]

The widest definition for the accomplishments of a full writing system is perhaps that offered by the

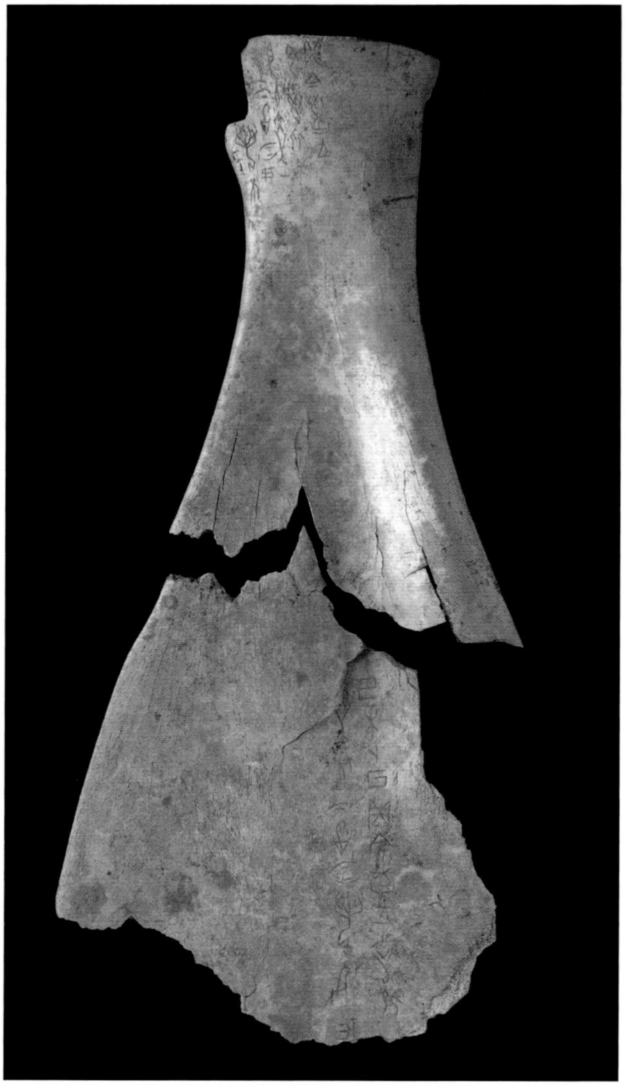

ABOVE Early Chinese characters. Inscribed oracle bones, Shang Dynasty. Animal bone. China, 1300–1050 BC. British Library: Or.7694/1554 and 1592

OPPOSITE Cang Jie, legendary creator of the Chinese script. China, 19th century. British Library: Or.2262, fol. 13

sinologist John DeFrancis when he describes writing as 'a system of graphic symbols that can be used to convey any and all thought' or by Ignace J. Gelb: 'a system of intercommunication by means of conventional marks'.[7] For the sake of this book we think of writing as primarily tied to speech, but not exclusively so. Andrew Robinson writes more about this in the opening chapter and David Levy adds his comments in Chapter 5, noting how every definition is to some extent a political choice, favouring one or other aspect of our behaviour.

There have been a number of other graphical notation systems developed for aspects of human creativity that are nothing at all to do with language or speech. Dance notation is one of them; there are systems that go back to the eighteenth century. Musical notation is another and here systems date back more than 1,000 years. While acknowledging the existence of these notation systems, this is not something that is covered in this book. They are a subject in their own right, as are codes and ciphering, shorthand (although we touch on it when discussing notetaking), and mathematical and algebraic writing conventions.

✧✧✧

Myths and stories about the origin of writing in various cultures support an understanding of writing that goes back a long way in human history. Even 4,000 years ago, when writing was young by our standards, most civilisations had lost contact with its origins. In China the invention of writing was attributed to Cang Jie, the mythical soothsayer of the deity known as the Yellow Emperor, who had four eyes and double sight, gazing towards both heaven and earth simultaneously. In one version of the myth, which comes from the first half of the eighth century AD, so penetrating was his vision that he could observe the movements of the constellations, the tracks of birds and nature in its dynamic whole; he distilled its essential movements into the characters for writing. In our illustration on page 15 he is depicted more prosaically as an official.

In Egypt writing was thought of as an invention of the gods, specifically the ancient, ibis-headed god of wisdom, Thoth. His daughter (or perhaps consort), the female deity Seshat, had writing, record-keeping and measuring specifically in her care. In Mesopotamia the earliest deity associated with writing was also a woman, the agrarian goddess of grain, Nisaba, who became goddess of writing and record-keeping and acted as 'scribe to the gods'. For the Mayan civilisation the legend of the *Popol Vuh* tells us that the gods of the scribes were the two monkey-men gods, rivals of the sons of heaven, and also Pawahtuun, an ancient god who presided over the end of each calendar year and upheld heaven and earth. While the legends around Mesopotamia's goddess of grain do hint at the agrarian accounting system that may have been the original stimulus for record-keeping

ABOVE Drawing of a scribe at work. John of Salisbury, *Polycraticus*. England, last quarter of 12th century AD. British Library: Royal MS 12 F VIII, fol. 73v (detail)

OPPOSITE Ganesh, Hindu patron of writing and scribe of the *Mahabharata*. From 61 paintings illustrating the *Adhyatma Ramayana*. Watercolour on paper. 1803–4. British Library: MSS Eur C116/1

in the 'land between two rivers', it is the Greek stories that perhaps come closest to the truth of their system's origins. The Greeks attributed the arrival of writing to a heroic individual, Cadmus, who brought the seed of writing out of Egypt via Phoenicia.

Clearly writing's origins are ancient; its roots lie deep in prehistory and somehow they are bound up in our species' ability to use the visual as a means of human communication and expression, and to employ gesture in a similar way. The oldest decorative mark-making that we know of comes from Indonesia and dates from some 500,000 years ago, from the time of *Homo erectus*. The first known decorative work by *Homo sapiens* dates to 100,000 years ago and was found in Blombos Cave in South Africa. The artworks of the cave complex at Lascaux in France are less than 20,000 years old. The repertoire of marks in this pattern-making, a mixture of geometric forms and drawings of animal life, is similar to the graphic vocabulary of early writing.

✧ ✧ ✧

Many individuals have taken up the challenge of inventing their own writing systems for fictional use. For example, Thomas More (Lord Chancellor to Henry VIII) composed an alphabet for the society he described in his book *Utopia* (1516). In more recent times J. R. R. Tolkien created mythologies around the many scripts he devised, the most famous of which is Tengwar, used for Elvish languages. It is Tengwar script that appears on the ring in his epic adventure *The Lord of the Rings* (1954). In the *Star Wars* movies (1977 onwards) calligraphic inscriptions in books and on clothing are written in Aurebesh, a squarish angular script for transcribing Galactic Basic, one of the most frequently used languages in the galaxy.

Yet some societies have also thrived without writing and even invented record-keeping systems on an entirely different basis. The Inca empire of Andean South America used a system of knotted strings, for example. The *quipu* was a highly effective device. These string bundles recorded not only financial information, such as taxes collected and owed, but also may have acted as memory devices for sacred poems and chronologies. The strings were read by special *quipu* tellers, of which most large settlements had a few, who looked at the way they were joined one to another, at the knots that ran along their length, the sequence and type of knot, the way the cords themselves were twisted and the colours that were in the thread. The bundles could weigh up to 3 kilograms each and throughout the Inca kingdom there were more than 3,200 kilometres of roads, with runners in post-houses roughly every 40 kilometres apart, for the rapid transport of the bundles and messages from place to place. Writing, as we know it, is not inevitable even in complex extended societies.

✧ ✧ ✧

Writing surrounds us in the modern world, but how did it develop into the systems we use today and, given the developments of the twenty-first century, what does its future hold? These were the questions at the forefront of our minds as we drew together this book and an exhibition that had writing as its focus.

As far as possible the featured works are from the British Library's own collections. Through a little over 100 objects we trace the story of writing from its first occurrence in Mesopotamia and Egypt more than 5,000 years ago. We celebrate the diversity of the world's writing systems in scripts that range from ancient Egyptian hieroglyphs to Inuktitut from modern northern Canada. Two-thirds of the globe today has alphabetical systems for writing. Systems as diverse as Arabic, Hebrew and Cyrillic, and most probably Devanagari, Tibetan and Thai, all have their origins in writing originally devised in the south-eastern Mediterranean. We trace their roots to developments in the use of Egyptian hieroglyphs some 3,800 years ago. We also look at the roman alphabet employed in Britain today and the many stylistic variations it has taken in the past. From this wide variety of forms come the templates for the letters we have now.

This book is not a comprehensive history of the world's writing systems. For this we refer readers to the British Library's *A History of Writing* (1992) by Albertine Gaur. Our publication does, however, examine the tools and technologies that have served writing. We look at pens and quills, tablets and styluses, ancient and modern. One of our key messages is that so far new writing technologies, although rapidly evolving, have added to the range of choices available to us rather than deprived us of choice.

Our selection of objects is the result of more than a year of discussion among a small group of curators: the lead curator Adrian S. Edwards, manager Western Printed Heritage Collections (1450–2000); Michael James Erdman, Curator, Turkish and Turkic Collections; Emma Harrison, Curator, Chinese Collections; Peter Toth, Curator, Ancient and Medieval Manuscripts; and Ewan Clayton, historian, calligrapher and Professor in Design at the University of Sunderland, academic adviser to the project and editor of this book. Punctuating the space between chapters each curator elaborates on one object from the collection that particularly fascinates them.

The writers who have contributed to this book include Andrew Robinson, an author and scholar of ancient writing. Andrew describes the significant times and places in human history where writing systems have evolved, the nature of those systems and the major systems employed today. Stan Knight, a calligrapher and historian of roman lettering and type, describes the different stylistic variations that written and printed roman letters have taken. Ewan Clayton looks at the material basis of writing, as well as its social dimensions. The future of writing is the topic discussed in Chapter 5, when Ewan Clayton interviews David Levy, Professor in the Information School at the University of Washington and Brody Neuenschwander, a text artist and calligrapher who lives in Belgium.

Concluding the main section of the book Dr Angela Webb, an educator and researcher, examines writing as a cognitive and muscular task and discusses the latest evidence for how we learn to write and how we use writing in our daily lives. This is a resource for teachers and learners of writing today, including those who struggle with writing. Adrian S. Edwards, lead curator of the project for the British Library, contributes an afterword outlining the Library's work for researchers in this area.

1

THE ORIGINS OF WRITING

ANDREW ROBINSON

1535 B

A man has departed: his corpse is in the ground.
His contemporaries have passed from the land.
But writing will preserve his memory
In the mouth of a person who speaks it.
A book is better than a built house,
Better than the tombs constructed in the West.
It is more beautiful than a well-built villa,
More beautiful than a stela in a temple.

(Lines from an ancient Egyptian papyrus of the Nineteenth Dynasty [that of Ramesses II], c.1190 BC, *exhorting the reader to become a scribe.)*[1]

Without writing, there would have been no permanent recording, no history and, of course, no books. The creation of writing permitted the command of a ruler and his seal to extend far beyond his sight and voice and even to survive his death. If the Rosetta Stone did not exist, for example, the world would be virtually unaware of the nondescript Egyptian king, Ptolemy V Epiphanes (reigned 205–180 BC), whose priests promulgated his decree upon the Stone on 27 March 196 BC in three different scripts: hieroglyphic, demotic and (Greek) alphabetic.

How did writing begin? The favoured explanation, until the Enlightenment in the eighteenth century, was divine origin. Today many – probably most – scholars accept that the earliest writing evolved from accountancy. Inventories and calculations are certainly crucial in the written records of ancient Mesopotamia and also ancient Crete, although they are puzzlingly little to be seen in the surviving writing of ancient Egypt, India, China and Meso-America (which does not preclude the possible earlier existence of commercial record-keeping on perishable materials, such as bamboo, in these early civilisations). In other words, some time in the late fourth millennium BC, in the cities of Sumer in Mesopotamia – the 'cradle of civilisation' – the complexity of trade and administration reached a point where it outstripped the power of memory among the governing elite. To record transactions in an indisputable, permanent form became essential.

Some scholars believe that a conscious search for a solution to this problem by an unknown Sumerian individual in the city of Uruk (biblical Erech), *c.*3300 BC, produced writing. Others posit that writing was the work of a group, presumably of clever administrators and merchants. Still others think it was not an invention at all, but an accidental discovery. Many regard it as the result of evolution over a long period, rather than a flash of inspiration. One particularly well-aired theory (championed by the archaeologist Denise Schmandt-Besserat) holds that writing grew out of a long-standing counting system of clay 'tokens'. Such 'tokens' – varying from simple, plain discs to more complex, incised shapes whose exact purpose is unknown – have been found in many Middle Eastern archaeological sites, and have been dated to 8000–1500 BC. The substitution of two-dimensional symbols in clay for these three-dimensional tokens was a first step towards writing, according to this theory. One major difficulty is that the 'tokens' continued to exist long after the emergence of Sumerian cuneiform writing (for almost two millennia); another is that a two-dimensional symbol on a clay tablet might be thought to be a less, not a more, advanced concept than a three-dimensional clay 'token'. It seems probable that 'tokens' accompanied the emergence of writing, like tallies, rather than giving rise to writing.

Apart from the 'tokens', numerous examples of what might be termed 'proto-writing' exist. They include the Ice Age symbols found in caves in southern France, which are probably 20,000 years old. A cave at Pech Merle, in the Lot, contains a lively Ice Age graffito showing a stencilled hand and a pattern of red dots. This may simply mean 'I was here, with my animals', or perhaps the symbolism is deeper. Other prehistoric

PREVIOUS PAGE Early Chinese characters. Inscribed oracle bones, Late Shang Dynasty. Animal bone. China, 1300–1050 BC. British Library: Or.7694/1535

OPPOSITE Handprint and dots. Red ochre. Pech Merle cave (France), 20,000–16,000 BC

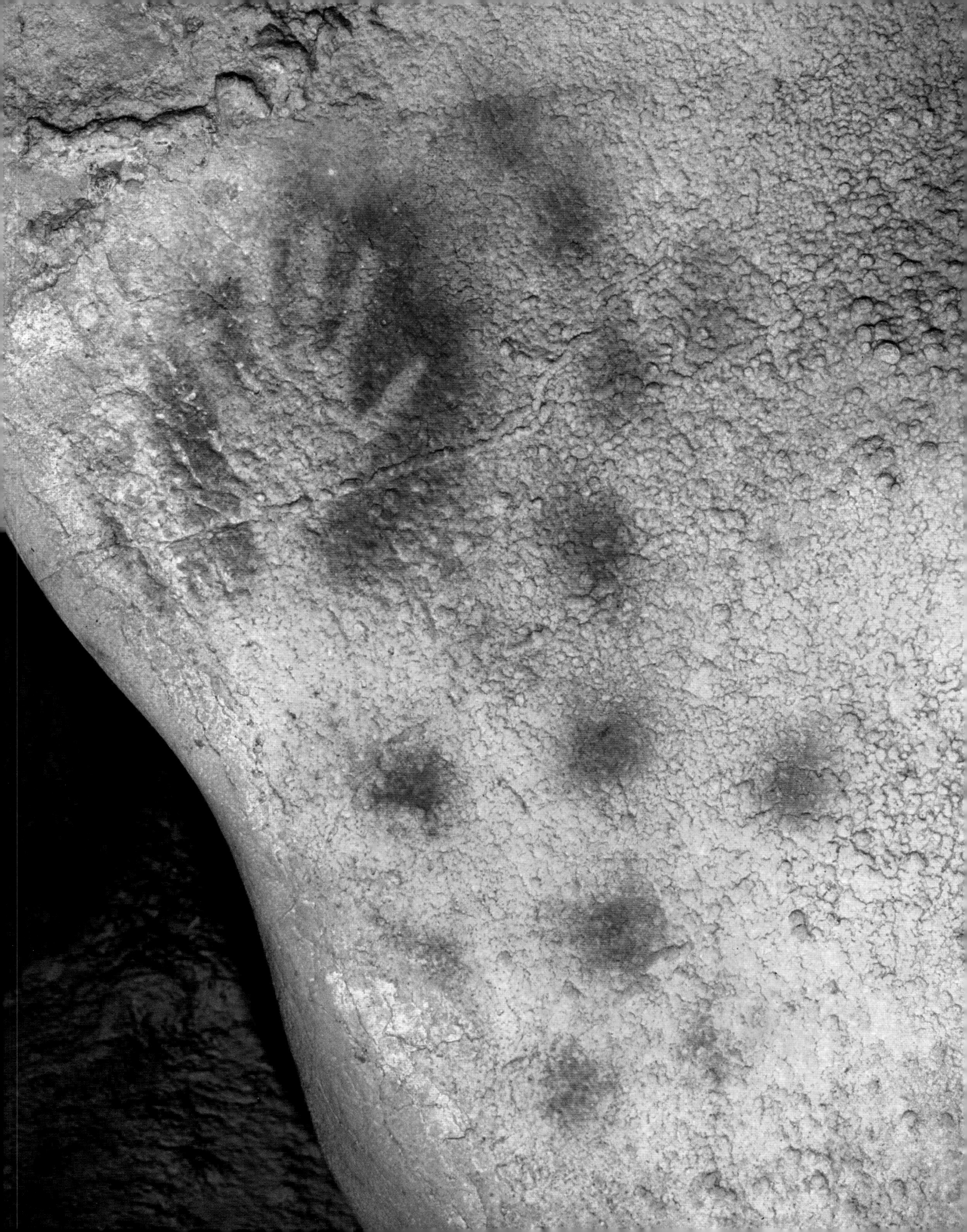

images show animals such as horses, bison and a stag's head, overlaid with signs; and notched bones have been found that apparently served as lunar calendars.

'Proto-writing' is not writing in the full sense of the word. A scholar of writing, the sinologist John DeFrancis identified 'full' writing as a 'system of graphic symbols that can be used to convey any and all thought': a concise and influential definition.[2] According to it, 'proto-writing' would include not only Ice Age cave symbols and Middle Eastern clay 'tokens', the Pictish symbol stones of Scotland and tallies like the fascinating knotted Inca *quipus* of Andean South America, but also contemporary sign systems such as international transportation symbols, highway code signs, computer icons, emojis, and mathematical and musical notation. None of these ancient or modern systems is capable of expressing 'any and all thought', but each is good at specialised communication.

To express the full range of human thought requires a writing system intimately linked with spoken language. For, as the founder of modern linguistics, Ferdinand de Saussure, wrote in 1983, language may

ABOVE Early cuneiform writing. Administrative record, Late Uruk Period. Clay tablet. Mesopotamia, 3300–3100 BC. British Museum: 1989,0130.3

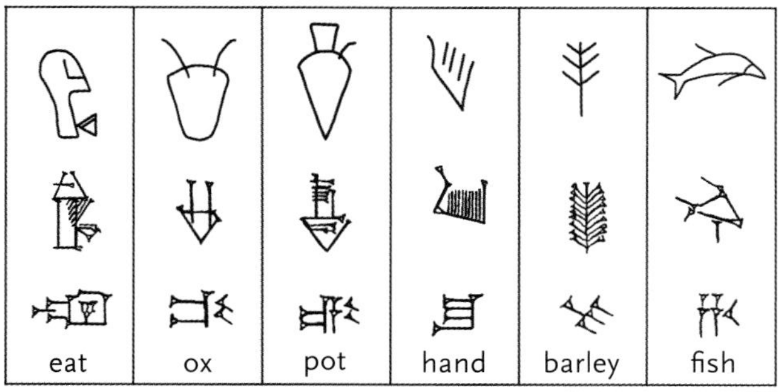

be compared to a sheet of paper: 'Thought is on one side of the sheet and sound on the reverse side. Just as it is impossible to take a pair of scissors and cut one side of the paper without at the same time cutting the other, so it is impossible in a language to isolate sound from thought, or thought from sound.'[3]

The symbols of what may have become the first 'full' writing system are generally thought to have been pictograms: iconic drawings of, say, a pot, a fish or a head with an open jaw (representing the concept of eating). These have been found in Mesopotamia and Egypt dating to the mid-fourth millennium BC, in the Indus Valley (Pakistan/India) dating to the third millennium and in China dating to as early as the fifth millennium, according to the claims of some Chinese archaeologists. In many cases, their iconicity soon became so abstract that it is barely perceptible to us. The chart above shows how Sumerian pictograms developed into the cuneiform signs inscribed on clay tablets that went on to dominate Middle Eastern writing for some 3,000 years.

Yet pictograms were insufficient to express the kinds of words, and their constituent parts, that cannot be depicted. Essential to the development of 'full' writing, as opposed to limited, purely pictographic, 'proto-writing', was the discovery of the 'rebus principle'. This radical idea, from the Latin word *rebus* meaning 'by things', enables phonetic values to be represented by pictographic symbols. Thus in English, a picture of a bee beside the number four might (if one were so minded) represent 'before', and a bee with a picture of a tray might stand for 'betray', while an ant next to a buzzing bee hive might (less obviously) represent the personal name 'Anthony'. Egyptian hieroglyphs are full of rebuses; for instance the 'sun' sign, pronounced /R(a)/ or /R(e)/, is the first symbol in the hieroglyphic spelling of the pharaonic name Ramesses. In an early Sumerian accounting tablet the abstract word 'reimburse' is represented by a picture of a reed, because 'reimburse' and 'reed' shared the same phonetic value, *gi*, in the Sumerian language.

Once writing of this 'full' kind, capable of expressing the complete range of speech and thought, was invented, accidentally discovered or evolved, did it then diffuse throughout the globe from Mesopotamia? It appears that the earliest such writing in Egypt dates from 3100 BC, that in the Indus civilisation (undeciphered sealstones) from 2500 BC, that in Crete (the undeciphered Linear A script) from 1750 BC, that in China (the oracle bones) from 1200 BC, and that in Mexico (the undeciphered Olmec script) from 900 BC: all dates are approximate and subject to new archaeological discoveries. On this basis, it seems reasonable that the idea of writing, but not the signs of a particular script, could have spread gradually from culture to distant culture. After all, 600 or 700 years were required for the idea of printing to reach Europe from

ABOVE The development of Sumerian pictograms (top row), *c.*3000 BC, into wedge-shaped cuneiform signs.
RIGHT Indus script. Engraved burnt steatite seal. Indus river valley, 2600–1900 BC. Metropolitan Museum of Art: 49.40.1

China (if we discount the isolated and enigmatic Phaistos Disc of *c.*1700 BC, found in Crete in 1908, which appears to be 'printed'), and even longer for the idea of paper to spread to Europe: why should writing not have reached China from Mesopotamia over an even longer period?

Nevertheless, in the absence of solid evidence for transmission of the idea (even in the case of the physically much more proximate civilisations of Mesopotamia and Egypt), most scholars prefer to think that writing developed independently in the major civilisations of the ancient world. The optimist, or at any rate the anti-imperialist, will emphasise the intelligence and inventiveness of human societies; the pessimist, who takes a more conservative view of history, will tend to assume that humans prefer to copy what already exists, as faithfully as they can, restricting their innovations to cases of absolute necessity. The latter is the favoured explanation for how the ancient Greeks (near the beginning of the first millennium BC) borrowed the alphabet from the Phoenician culture of the eastern Mediterranean, adding in the process signs for the vowels not written in the Phoenician script. Another well-known example of script borrowing is the Japanese taking of Chinese characters in the first millennium AD and incorporating them into a highly complex writing system that mixes several thousand Chinese characters (known in Japan as *kanji*) with slightly fewer than 100, much simpler, syllabic symbols of Japanese origin (*hiragana* and *katakana*). If ever the Rongorongo script of Rapa Nui (Easter Island) in the south-eastern Pacific Ocean – the most isolated inhabited spot on earth – is deciphered, it may shed light on the intriguing question of whether the Rapa Nui people borrowed it from Europeans who first visited Rapa Nui in the eighteenth century, brought the idea of writing from Polynesia in their canoes or invented Rongorongo independently. If Rongorongo, once deciphered, could be proved to have been created unaided on Rapa Nui, this would at last guarantee that writing must have had multiple origins, rather than radiating from a single source (presumably in Mesopotamia).

Decipherment has, of course, always been key to the understanding of ancient writing systems – hence the worldwide fame of the Rosetta Stone. The term was first used by an Englishman, Thomas Herbert, in 1677, with reference to the cuneiform inscriptions of the Persian king Darius engraved *c.*500 BC at Persepolis, a wonder of the world that was then almost entirely mysterious. Herbert called them 'well worthy the scrutiny of those ingenious persons that delight themselves in the dark and difficult Art or Exercise of deciphering'.[4]

In ordinary conversation, to decipher someone's 'indecipherable' handwriting is to make sense of the meaning; it does not imply that one can read every single word. More technically, as applied to ancient scripts, 'deciphered' means different things to different scholars. At one extreme, everyone acknowledges that the Egyptian hieroglyphs have been deciphered, because all trained Egyptologists would make the same sense of virtually every word of a given hieroglyphic inscription (although their individual translations would still differ, as do all independent translations of the same work from one language into another). At the other extreme, scholars generally agree that the script of the Indus civilisation, exquisitely engraved on steatite sealstones, is undeciphered, because no one can make sense of its seals and other inscriptions to the satisfaction of anyone else. Between these extremes lies a vast spectrum of opinion. In the case of the Mayan hieroglyphic writing of Meso-America, for example, most scholars concur that a high proportion, as much as 85 per cent, of the inscriptions can be meaningfully read, and yet there remain large numbers of individual Mayan glyphs that are contentious or obscure. No shibboleth exists by which a script can be judged to be either deciphered or

OPPOSITE Japanese *katakana* syllabary. *Nanatsu iroha.* Printed book. Kyōtō (Japan): Hon'ya Kyūbē, 1688. British Library: Or.75.h.4.(1.), fol. 10v

ヱ je	ア a	ヤ ja	ラ ra	ヨ	チ tsii	イ i
ヒ fi	サ ssa	マ ma	ム mu	タ ta	リ ri	ロ ro
モ mo	キ ki	ケ ke	ウ u	レ re	ヌ nu	ハ fa
セ se	ユ ju	フ fu	井 i	ソ so	ル ru	ニ ni
ス su	メ me	コ ko	ノ no	ツ tsu	ヲ wo	ホ fo
京	ミ mi	エ je	オ o	子 ne	ワ wa	ヘ fe
	シ si	テ te	ク ku	ナ na	カ ka	ト to

undeciphered; we should instead speak of degrees of decipherment. The most useful criterion is that a proposed decipherment can generate consistent readings from new samples of the script, preferably produced by persons other than the original decipherer.

In this sense, the Egyptian hieroglyphs were deciphered in the 1820s by Jean-François Champollion and others; Babylonian cuneiform in the 1850s by Henry Creswicke Rawlinson and others; Mycenaean Linear B in 1952–3 by Michael Ventris; and the Mayan hieroglyphs by Yuri Knorosov and others in the 1950s and after – to name only the most important of the successful decipherments. This leaves a number of significant undeciphered scripts, such as the Etruscan script from Italy, the Indus script from Pakistan/India, Linear A from Crete, the Meroitic script from Sudan, the Proto-Elamite script from Iran/Iraq, Rongorongo from Rapa Nui, and the Olmec, Zapotec and Isthmian scripts from Mexico. These may be resolved into three basic categories: an unknown script writing a known language, a known script writing an unknown language and an unknown script writing an unknown language. The Mayan hieroglyphs were until their late-twentieth-century decipherment an example of the first category, since the Mayan languages are still spoken, and the Zapotec script may be, too, if it writes a language related to modern Zapotec; Etruscan writing is an example of the second category, since the Etruscan script is basically the same as the Greek alphabet, but the unknown Etruscan language is not related to Indo-European languages such as Greek and Latin; and the Indus script is an example of the last category, since the script bears no resemblance to any other script and the language of the Indus civilisation does not appear to have survived (unless, as some scholars speculate, the now-extinct Indus language was related to the Dravidian languages of south India, such as Tamil).

In each undeciphered case, the techniques used in successful decipherments have been applied, with varying results. Ventris – perhaps the most ingenious of all the decipherers, since he alone had no help from a bilingual aid like the Rosetta Stone – gave a masterly summary of the science and art of decipherment just after announcing his decipherment of Linear B as writing an ancient form of classical Greek, in 1952–3:

> Each operation needs to be planned in three phases: an exhaustive analysis of the signs, words, and contexts in all the available inscriptions, designed to extract every possible clue as to the spelling system, meaning and language structure; an experimental substitution of phonetic values to give possible words and inflections in a known or postulated language; and a decisive check, preferably with the aid of virgin material, to ensure that the apparent results are not due to fantasy, coincidence or circular reasoning.[5]

As Ventris's collaborator, classicist John Chadwick, reflected in 1983:

> The achievement of the decipherment ... required painstaking analysis and sound judgement, but at the same time an element of genius, the ability to take a leap in the dark, but then to find firm ground on the other side. Few discoveries are made solely by processes of logical deduction. At some point the researcher is obliged to chance a guess, to venture an unlikely hypothesis; what matters is whether he can control the leap of the imagination, and have the honesty to evaluate the results soberly. Only after the leap has been made is it possible to go back over the working and discover the logical basis which provided the necessary springboard.[6]

Linear B, which was used from 1450 to 1200 BC, turned out to be a syllabic writing system, unlike the later writing system of classical Greece, an alphabet invented *c.*800 BC, in which the signs stand for vowels

OPPOSITE Mayan glyphs. Carved limestone lintel. Yaxchilan (Mexico), AD 725. British Museum: Am1923,Maud.5

and consonants, not syllables. How are writing systems classified? Europeans and Americans of ordinary literacy must recognise and write around fifty-two alphabetic signs (twenty-six capital letters and their lower-case equivalents) and sundry other signs, such as numerals, punctuation marks and 'whole-word' semantic signs, for example +, =, &, %, £ and $, which are generally called logograms. Japanese readers, by contrast, are supposed to know and be able to write some 2,000 signs, and, if they are highly educated, must recognise 5,000 signs or more. The two situations, in Europe/America and in Japan, appear to be poles apart. But, in fact, the different writing systems resemble each other more than first appears.

Contrary to what many people think, all scripts that are 'full' writing (in the sense defined by DeFrancis above) operate on one basic principle. Both alphabets and the Chinese and Japanese scripts use symbols to represent sounds (that is, phonetic signs); and all writing systems mix such phonetic symbols with logographic symbols (that is, semantic signs). What differs between writing systems – apart from the forms of the signs, of course – is the proportion of phonetic to semantic signs. The higher the proportion of phonetic representation in a script, the easier it is to guess the pronunciation of a word. In English the proportion is high; in Chinese it is low. Thus English spelling represents English speech sound by sound more accurately than Chinese characters represent Mandarin speech; but Finnish spelling represents the Finnish language better than English spelling represents spoken English. The Finnish script is highly efficient phonetically, while the Chinese (and Japanese) script is phonetically seriously deficient, as indicated in the upper diagram opposite.

Hence there is no such thing as a 'pure' writing system, that is, a 'full' writing system capable of expressing meaning entirely through alphabetic letters, syllabic signs or logograms: all 'full' writing systems are a mixture of phonetic and semantic signs. How best to classify writing systems is therefore a controversial

ABOVE Linear B tablet. Record of grain rations for women workers. Burnt clay. Knossos (Crete), *c.*1400–1375 BC. Ashmolean Museum: AN1910.214

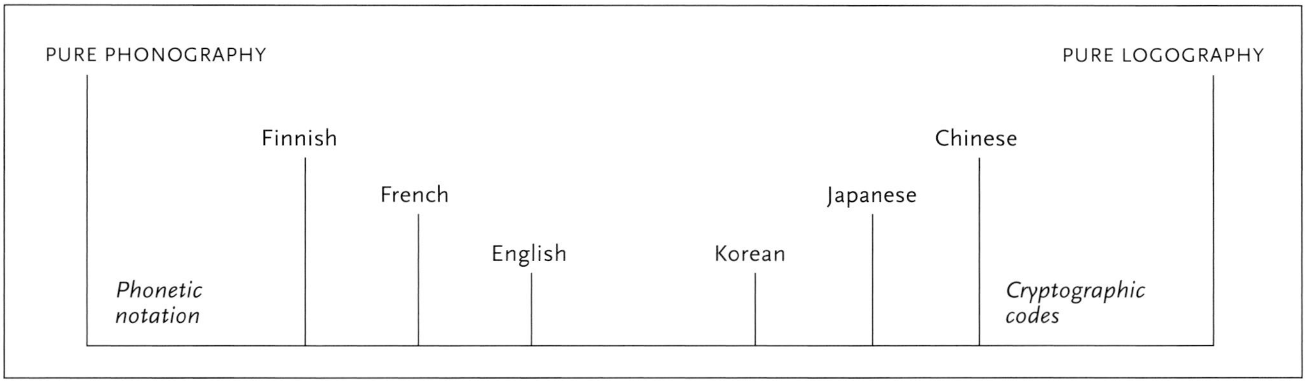

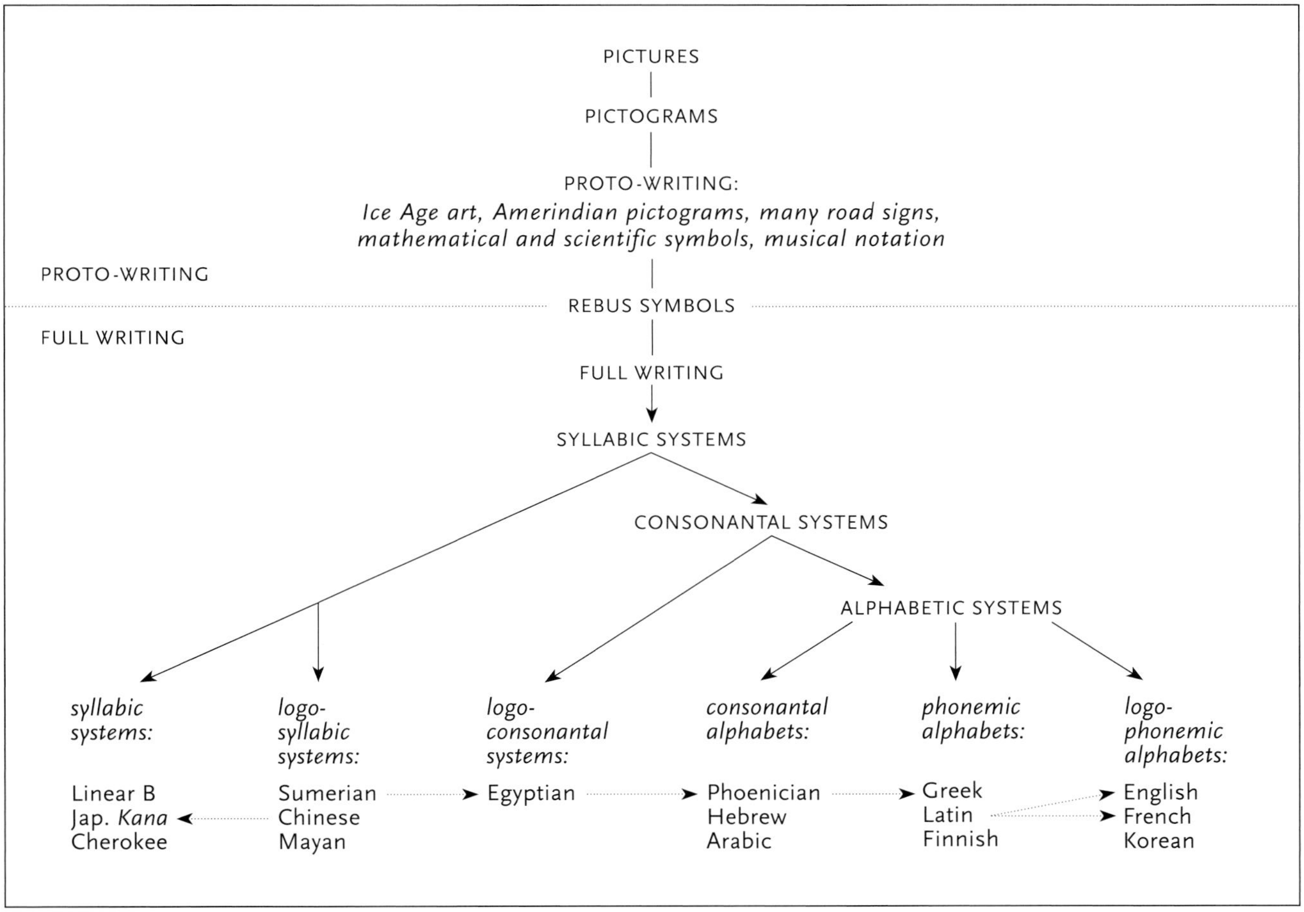

ABOVE All writing systems are a mixture of phonetic and logographic (semantic) signs, but the proportion of each varies. Finnish is the most phonetically efficient script, Chinese script the least

BELOW Writing systems are grouped in this diagram according to their nature (not their age, nor how one writing system may have given rise to another historically). The dashed lines indicate possible influences of one system upon another

matter. For example, some scholars deny the existence of alphabets prior to the Greek alphabet, on the grounds that the Phoenician script marked only consonants, not vowels (like the early Arabic script). Nevertheless, classifying labels are useful to remind us of the predominant nature of different systems. The tree shown in the lower diagram on the previous page divides writing systems according to this criterion, not according to their age; it does not show how one writing system may have given rise to another historically. (The dashed lines indicate possible influences of one system upon another, for example Chinese characters, *kanji*, on the Japanese syllabic *hiragana* and *katakana*.) Thus, the Phoenician script is labelled a 'consonantal alphabet', with the emphasis on its consonants and without significant logography, in contrast to the 'logo-consonantal' system of Egyptian hieroglyphs, where logography dominates but there is also a phonetic element based on the consonants: twenty-four hieroglyphic signs, each representing a consonant. The tree's terminology is self-explanatory, except perhaps for 'phonemic': the phoneme is the smallest contrastive unit in the sound system of a language, for example the English vowel phonemes /e/ and /a/ in 'set' and 'sat', and the consonantal phonemes /b/ and /p/ in 'bat' and 'pat'.

If the emergence of writing is full of riddles, then the enigma of the first alphabet is even more perplexing. That the alphabet reached the modern world via the ancient Greeks is well known – the word 'alphabet' comes from alpha and beta, the first two of the twenty-five Greek letters – but we have no idea of exactly how and when the alphabet appeared in Greece; how the Greeks thought of adding letters standing for the vowels as well as the consonants; or how, even more fundamentally, the idea of an alphabet occurred to the pre-Greek societies at the eastern end of the Mediterranean during the second millennium BC. The first well-attested alphabets belong to ancient Ugarit, today's Ras Shamra on the coast of Syria, where a thirty-sign cuneiform alphabet was used in the fourteenth century BC, and to the Phoenicians in Canaan in the late second millennium, who used twenty-two consonantal letters.

Scholars have devoted their lives to these questions, but the evidence is too scanty for firm conclusions. It is not known whether the alphabet evolved from the scripts of Mesopotamia (cuneiform), Egypt (hieroglyphs) and Crete (Linear A and B), or whether it struck a single unknown individual 'in a flash'. Nor is it known why an alphabet was thought necessary. It seems most likely that the alphabet was the result of commercial imperatives. In other words, commerce demanded a simpler and quicker means of recording transactions than, say, Babylonian cuneiform or Egyptian hieroglyphs, and also a convenient way to record the babel of languages of the various empires and groups trading with each other around the Mediterranean. If so, then it is surprising that there is no evidence of trade and commerce in the early alphabetic inscriptions of Greece. This, and other considerations, have led a few scholars to postulate, controversially, that the Greek alphabet was invented to record the oral epics of Homer in the eighth century BC.

In the absence of proof, anecdote and myth have filled the vacuum. Children are often evoked as inventors of the alphabet, because they would not have had the preconceptions of adult writers and their elders' investment in existing scripts. One possibility is that a bright Canaanite child in northern Syria, fed up with having to learn the complexities of Babylonian cuneiform and Egyptian hieroglyphs, borrowed from the hieroglyphs the familiar idea of a small number of signs standing for single consonants and then invented some new signs for the basic consonantal sounds of his own Semitic language. Perhaps the child first doodled the signs in the dust of some ancient street: a simple outline of a house, Semitic 'beth' (the 'bet' in 'alphabet'), became the sign for **b**. In the twentieth century, Rudyard

Kipling's child protagonist in 'How The Alphabet Was Made', Taffimai, designs what she calls 'noise-pictures'. The letter **A** is a picture of a carp with its mouth wide open like an inverted **V** and its barbel forming the cross-stroke of the **A**; this, Taffimai tells her father, looks like his open mouth when he utters the sound /ah/. The letter **O** matches the egg, or stone, shape and resembles her father's mouth saying /oh/. The letter **S** represents a snake, and stands for the hissing sound of the reptile. In this somewhat far-fetched way, a whole alphabet is created by Taffimai.

To quote an earlier poet, William Blake, writing in *Jerusalem*: 'God ... in mysterious Sinai's awful cave/To Man the wond'rous art of writing gave'. A small sphinx in the British Museum at one time seemed to show that Blake was right, at least about the origin of the alphabet. The sphinx was found in 1905 at Serabit el-Khadim in Sinai, a desolate place remote from civilisation, by the famous Egyptologist Flinders Petrie. He was excavating some old turquoise mines that were active in ancient Egyptian times. Petrie dated the sphinx to the middle of the Eighteenth Dynasty (1550–1295 BC); today, its date is thought to be *c.*1500 BC, but may be as early as *c.*1800 BC. On one side of it is a strange inscription; on the other, and between the paws, there are further inscriptions of the same kind, plus some Egyptian hieroglyphs that read: 'beloved of Hathor, mistress of turquoise'. Similar inscriptions were written on the rocks of this remote area.

Petrie guessed that the unknown script was probably an alphabet, because it comprised fewer than thirty signs (out of a much larger number of text characters); and he thought that its language was probably Semitic, since he knew that Semites from Canaan – modern Israel and Lebanon – had worked these mines, in many cases as slaves of the Egyptians. Ten years later, another distinguished Egyptologist, Alan Gardiner, studied the 'proto-Sinaitic' signs and noted resemblances between

LEFT Early Phoenician inscription. Bronze arrow-head. Phoenicia, 11th century BC. British Museum: 1989,0409.1

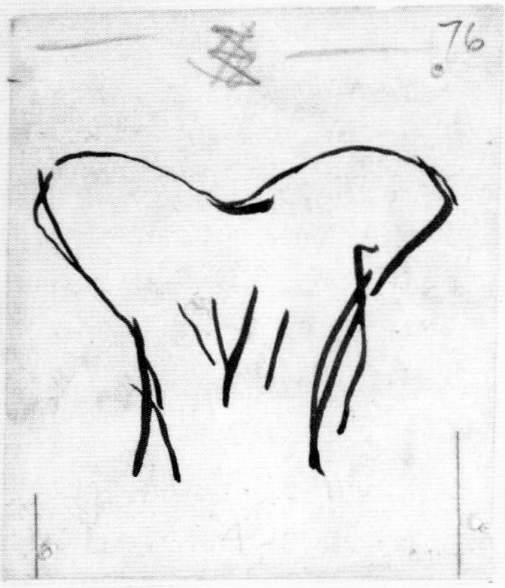
76
4

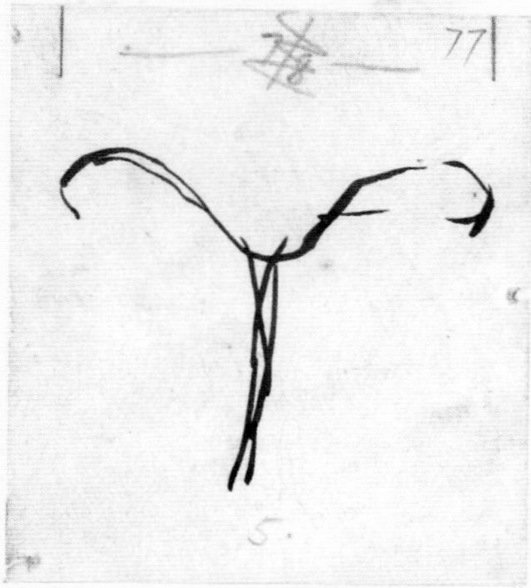
77
5.

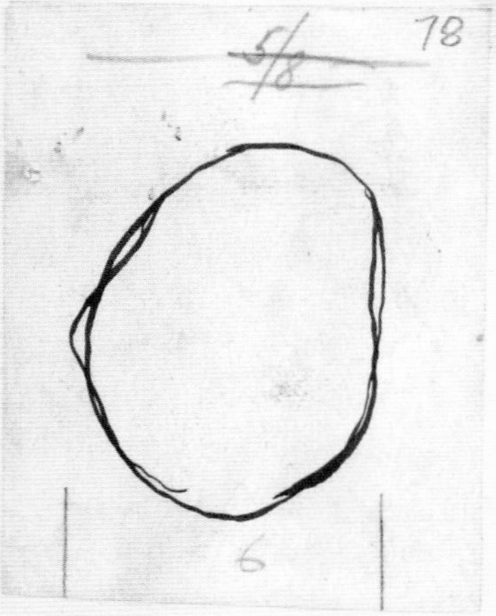
78
6

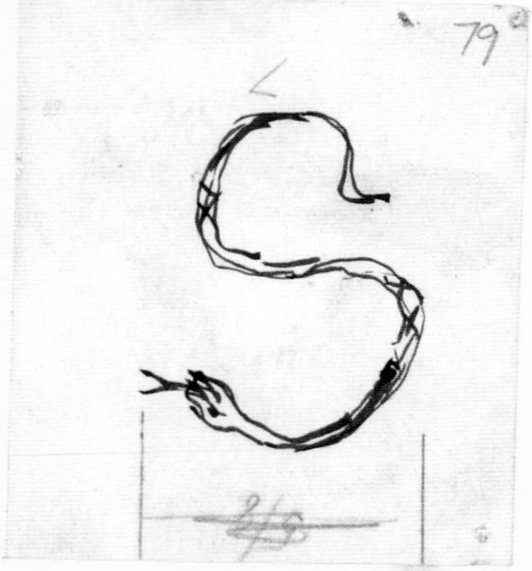
79

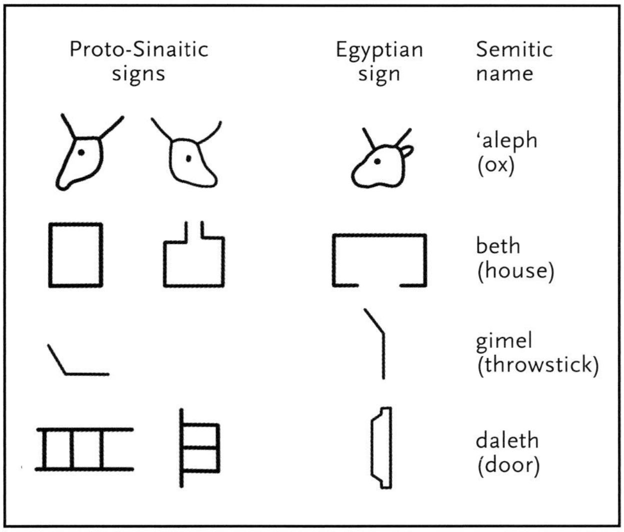

some of them and certain pictographic Egyptian hieroglyphs. Gardiner now named each sign with the Semitic word equivalent to the sign's meaning in Egyptian (the Semitic words were known from biblical scholarship), such as 'beth' for 'house' and 'gimel' for 'throwstick' (see diagram above). These Semitic names are the same as the names of the letters of the Hebrew alphabet: a fact that did not surprise Gardiner, since he knew that the Hebrews had lived in Canaan in the late second millennium BC. However, although the names are the same, the shapes of the Hebrew letters are different from the proto-Sinaitic signs, suggesting that any link between them cannot be a straightforward one.

Gardiner's hypothesis enabled him to translate one of the inscriptions that occurred on the sphinx from Serabit el-Khadim as 'Baalat': in an English transcription, with the vowels spelt out. (Hebrew and other Semitic scripts do not indicate vowels; readers guess them from their knowledge of the language, as explained later.) Gardiner's reading made sense: Baalat means 'the Lady' and is a recognised Semitic name for the goddess Hathor in the Sinai region. So the inscription on the sphinx seemed to be an Egyptian-Semitic bilingual. Unfortunately no further decipherment proved tenable, mainly because of lack of material and the fact that many of the proto-Sinaitic signs had no hieroglyphic equivalents. Scholarly hopes of finding the story of the Exodus in these scratchings were scotched. Nevertheless, it is conceivable that a script similar to Petrie and Gardiner's proto-Sinaitic script was used by Moses to write the Ten Commandments on the tablets of stone.

It is still not known whether Gardiner's 1916 guess was correct, plausible though it is. For some decades after Petrie's discoveries in Sinai, the inscriptions were taken to be the 'missing link' between the Egyptian hieroglyphs and the cuneiform alphabet at Ugarit and the Phoenician alphabet. But it seems unconvincing that lowly – and presumably illiterate – miners in out-of-the-way Sinai should have created an alphabet; prima facie, they seem to be unlikely inventors. Subsequent discoveries in Lebanon and Israel have shown the Sinaitic theory of the alphabet to be a romantic fiction. These inscriptions, dated to the seventeenth and sixteenth centuries BC – a little earlier than the proto-Sinaitic inscriptions – suggest that the people then living in the land of Canaan were the real inventors of the alphabet, which would be reasonable. They were cosmopolitan traders at the crossroads of the Egyptian, Hittite, Babylonian and

OPPOSITE Rudyard Kipling, 'How the Alphabet was Made'. Autograph manuscript. England, 1902. British Library: Add MS 59840, ff. 76r
ABOVE 'Proto-Sinaitic' inscription. Sandstone sphinx; known as the Serabit Sphinx. Sinai (Egypt), 1800-1500 BC. British Museum: 1905,1014.118
BELOW Some 'Proto-Sinaitic' signs resemble pictographic Egyptian hieroglyphs

Cretan empires; they were not wedded to an existing writing system; they needed a script that was easy to learn, quick to write and unambiguous. Although unproven, it is probable that the (proto-)Canaanites were the first to use an alphabet.

In the late 1990s, however, the picture was further complicated by new discoveries in Egypt itself, and a revised version of the Gardiner theory now seems plausible. In 1999 two Egyptologists, John and Deborah Coleman Darnell, announced that they had found examples of what appeared to be alphabetic writing at Wadi el-Hol, west of Thebes, while they were surveying ancient travel routes in the southern Egyptian desert. The date of the inscriptions is *c.*1900–1800 BC, which places them considerably earlier than those from Lebanon and Israel and makes them the earliest-known alphabetic writings.

The two short inscriptions are written in a Semitic script and, according to the experts, the letters were most probably developed in a fashion similar to a semi-cursive form of the Egyptian script. The writer is thought to have been a scribe travelling with a group of mercenaries (there were many such mercenaries working for the pharaohs). If the Darnell theory turns out to be correct, then it looks as if the alphabetic idea was, after all, inspired by the Egyptian hieroglyphs and invented in Egypt, rather than in Canaan. However, the evidence is by no means conclusive and the search in Egypt for more alphabetic inscriptions continues.

From its unclear origins on the eastern shores of the Mediterranean, writing employing the alphabetic principle spread: westwards (via Greek) to the Romans and thence to modern Europe, which uses roman letters to write many of its languages; eastwards (via Aramaic, most likely) to India and thence to Southeast Asia. By the twentieth century, as a consequence of Europe's colonial empires, most of the world's peoples except the Chinese and Japanese were writing in alphabetic scripts. These employ on average between twenty and thirty basic signs; the smallest, Rotokas, used in Papua New Guinea, has twelve letters, while the largest, Khmer, used in Cambodia, has seventy-four letters.

The western alphabetic link between the Greeks and the Romans was Etruscan, as is clear from the early Greek letterforms inscribed on Etruscan objects dating from the sixth century BC, which were then borrowed by early Latin inscriptions. (The transference of the script occurred despite the dissimilarity of the Indo-European Greek and Latin languages to the non-Indo-European Etruscan language mentioned above; see page 29). This early Roman acquisition from Greek accounts for the differences between some modern European letterforms and the modern Greek letters, which are based on a later Greek alphabet known as Ionian that became standard in Greece in 403–402 BC.

The eastern alphabetic link is indicated by the remarkable fact that in Mesopotamia, by the fifth century BC, many cuneiform documents carried a notation of their substance in the twenty-two letters of the Aramaic alphabet, inked onto the tablet with a brush. From the time of Alexander the Great (356–323 BC) onwards, cuneiform was increasingly superseded by Aramaic; it eventually fell into disuse around the beginning of the Christian era, with the last cuneiform inscription dated AD 75. In Egypt, fairly soon after that, the Coptic alphabet (consisting of twenty-four Greek letters plus six letters borrowed from Egyptian demotic script) supplanted Egyptian hieroglyphs; the last Egyptian hieroglyphic inscription is dated AD 394.

The Aramaic script is the ancestor of modern Arabic and of modern ('square') Hebrew script, as used in Israel. (A second Hebrew script, known as 'old Hebrew', evolved from the Phoenician script and disappeared from secular use with the dispersion of the Jews in the sixth century BC.) The first independent Arab kingdom, that of the Nabataeans centred on Petra in modern Jordan, spoke a form of Arabic but wrote in the Aramaic script. The presence of certain distinctively Arabic forms and words in these Aramaic inscriptions eventually gave way to the writing of the Arabic language in Nabataean Aramaic script. This was the precursor of the Arabic script, which arose during the first half of the first millennium AD and replaced the Aramaic script.

Both the Arabic and Hebrew scripts write only the consonants, not the vowels, in their respective Semitic languages, using twenty-eight letters in Arabic and twenty-two in Hebrew. Thus the three letters in modern Hebrew that stand for **sfr** or **spr** can take the following meanings: *sefer* (a book), *safar* (counted, as in 'he counted'), *sapar* (a barber), and even *sefar* (border, frontier or fringe). In practice, however, various additional signs have been developed to aid the reader in pronouncing the 'missing' Arabic and Hebrew vowels. The commonest of these is a system of dots placed above and below a letter, referred to as *niqqudot* (dots) in Hebrew. A separate, historically much earlier system, known as *matres lectionis* – Latin for 'mothers of reading' – used three semi-vowels, w, y and ' (aleph), to denote long vowel signs instead of their consonant values.

OPPOSITE Early Euboean Greek inscription. Aryballos (flask). Cumae (Italy), 670 BC. British Museum: 1885,0613.1
ABOVE Etruscan inscription. Burnished black Bucchero kantheros. Italy, *c.*600 BC. British Museum: 1953,0426.1

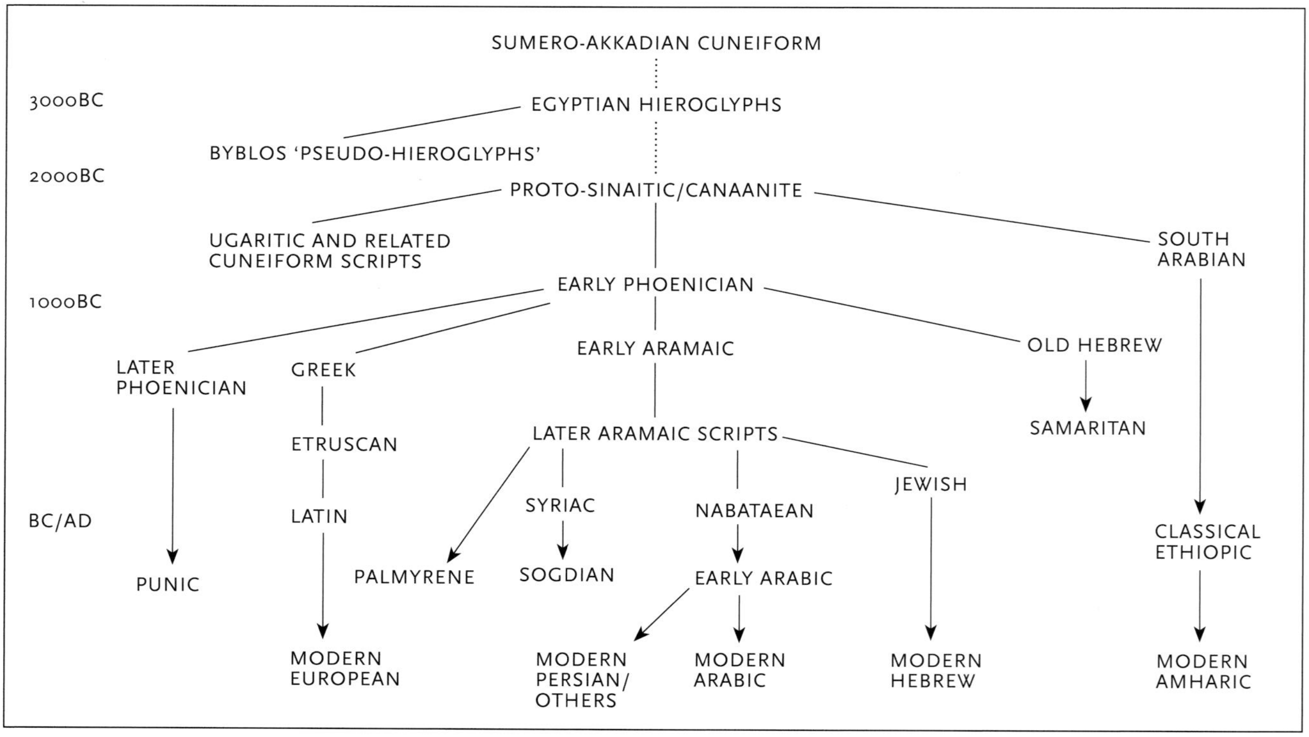

The time chart above shows the main lines of emergence of the modern alphabetic scripts from the Proto-Sinaitic/Canaanite scripts of the second millennium BC. It does not include the Indian scripts and their Southeast Asian derivatives, since their connection with Aramaic is problematic and, strictly speaking, unproven. (The earliest Indian scripts, leaving aside the undeciphered Indus writing of the third millennium BC, are Kharosthi and Brahmi, used in the rock edicts of the Emperor Ashoka in the mid-third century BC.) Nor does the chart show later alphabets such as the Cyrillic alphabet used in Russia, which was adapted from the Greek alphabet in the ninth century AD, the Korean Hangul alphabet, invented by King Sejong in Korea in 1443, or the so-called Cherokee alphabet (really a syllabary), devised by a Native American, Chief Sequoyah, in the USA in 1821. Also excluded are runes, since the origin of the runic alphabet, in the second century AD or earlier, although clearly influenced by the roman alphabet, is not known.

The undoubted worldwide triumph of alphabetic writing, except in China and Japan, has encouraged a mystique of the alphabet. It is often said that the alphabet was necessary for the growth of democracy; its very simplicity enabled numerous people to become literate and politically aware. Others have claimed that the West's global dominance in the second millennium AD, particularly in science, was largely the result of a so-called 'alphabet effect'. They contrast the West with China and its characters: while both developed science, the West went on to produce the analytical thinking of, say, a Newton or an Einstein, and left China far behind, because these thinkers were nurtured on the letter-by-letter principle (inherent in the alphabet). Put at its crudest, alphabets are alleged to promote reductionist thinking; Chinese characters holistic thinking.

ABOVE The evolution of the main alphabetic scripts according to an approximate time-scale (after John F. Healey, *The Early Alphabet*)

The first suggestion, about democracy and the alphabet, has a kernel of truth. But did the alphabet help democracy to grow, or did a nascent European desire for democracy give rise to the invention of the alphabet? The ancient Egyptians, in a sense, invented the alphabet in the third millennium BC when they created twenty-four signs for their consonants. But instead of using this simple system to write their language, the Egyptians chose to write in hieroglyphs with many hundreds of signs. Perhaps they felt no urge for democracy in their pharaonic political system?

The second suggestion, about science, appealing as it may be to some, is a fallacy. It is quite conceivable that the Chinese writing system, as a result of its enormous complexity, retarded the spread of literacy in China, but it is ludicrous to connect a deep cultural trend, a supposed dearth of Chinese analytical thinking, with the predominance of logograms over phonetic signs. To explain profound cultural differences, we need to look at cultures in the round, not single out one aspect, such as a culture's writing system, however important this may appear to be. After all, if Isaac Newton and Albert Einstein could understand gravity and relativity, they could surely have mastered an education imparted in Chinese characters or, for that matter, in Egyptian hieroglyphs or Babylonian cuneiform.

Chinese characters also enjoy a mystique. The complexity of Chinese writing encourages the notion that it operates differently from other modern writing systems. The obscurity of its origins – which may or may not have involved foreign stimulus from, for example, Mesopotamian writing – reinforces its apparent uniqueness. The antiquity of the modern Chinese characters, many being recognisable in the Shang oracle bone inscriptions of about 1200 BC, further reinforces this view, abetted by national pride in the system's exceptional longevity, which exceeds that of Babylonian cuneiform and equals that of the Egyptian hieroglyphs.

The most important claim is that Chinese characters are 'ideographic': a word now generally avoided by scholars in favour of the more specific 'logographic'. That is, the characters are thought to be capable of communicating ideas without the intervention of phoneticism or indeed spoken language. This claim is seemingly supported by the fact that speakers of different Chinese dialects, such as Mandarin and Cantonese, who may not be able to understand each other fully when speaking, may still write using the same characters. Even Chinese and Japanese speakers are sometimes able to achieve some level of mutual understanding through the use of characters common to both their scripts. This, of course, would be inconceivable for English, French, German and Italian monoglots, even though they share one (roman) script.

The claim is, however, false. No 'full' writing system, as already explained, can be divorced from the sounds of a spoken language. The majority of Chinese characters are composed of both a phonetic and a semantic component, which readers must learn to recognise. The phonetic component gives a clue to the pronunciation of the character, the semantic component to its meaning. These two components are generally characters in their own right, with their own pronunciation and meaning. For example, the simple character 羊 is pronounced *yáng* in Mandarin and means 'sheep'. This provides the phonetic component of the compound character 洋, which is also pronounced *yáng* and means 'ocean'. The three-stroke sign on the left side of 洋 is a semantic component, which means 'water' and provides a broad category of meaning for the character. In dialects other than Mandarin, this simple character and this compound character still have the same meanings and share a common phonetic value. A Cantonese speaker, for example, would know that these two characters mean 'sheep' and 'ocean' (while pronouncing them both as something other than *yáng*). In order to communicate with a Japanese speaker using characters, a Chinese person would have to hope that the particular characters he or she is using are not only used in Japanese but also that they have retained the same form and meaning in modern Japanese as in Chinese. (The characters for 'sheep' and 'ocean' are identical in Chinese and Japanese.)

The Japanese language differs greatly from the Chinese, phonologically, grammatically and syntactically. Even so, the Japanese based their writing system on the Chinese characters, as already discussed. When they first adopted Chinese characters during the early centuries of the first millennium AD, the Japanese applied their own pronunciations, sometimes based on native Japanese words and sometimes adapting an original Chinese pronunciation to the sounds of the Japanese language. (Indeed *kanji*, the Japanese word for Chinese character, is a rendering of a term which in modern Mandarin is pronounced *hanzi*, meaning 'Han characters'.) Gradually, over time, they developed two fairly small sets of supplementary phonetic signs, the syllabic *kana* (now standardised as forty-six *hiragana* and forty-six *katakana*) – the forms of which are actually simplified versions of the Chinese characters – in order to make clear how the characters were to be pronounced in Japanese and how to transcribe native (that is, Japanese) words and grammatical endings. It would have been simpler, one might reasonably think, if the Japanese had used only these invented signs and had abandoned the Chinese characters altogether, but this would have entailed the rejection of an ancient writing system of huge prestige. (From the 1980s, it is true, certain words written in *katakana* began to be written in the roman alphabet, as so-called *romaji*, which were considered to be fashionable, especially by the Japanese advertising world, but there is no possibility of *romaji* supplanting the native script altogether.) Just as a knowledge of Latin was until quite recently a *sine qua non* for the educated European, so a familiarity with Chinese has always been considered essential by the Japanese literati.

✧ ✧ ✧

As the sixth millennium of recorded civilisation opened in 2000, Mesopotamia was again at the centre of historical events. Where once, at the birth of writing, the statecraft of absolute rulers like Hammurabi and Darius was recorded in Sumerian, Babylonian, Assyrian and Old Persian cuneiform on clay and stone, now the Iraq wars against Saddam Hussein generated millions of mainly alphabetic words on paper and on the World Wide Web written in a babel of languages.

But although today's technologies of writing are immeasurably different from those of the third millennium BC, its linguistic principles have not changed very much since the composition in cuneiform during the second millennium BC of the epic about the legendary Sumerian king, Gilgamesh. However, the seismic impact of electronic writing and archiving on information distribution, research and communications has polarised the debate about the correct definition of 'writing'. Must 'full' writing depend on a spoken language, as maintained in this chapter? Or can it float free of its phonetic anchor? If so, the world could theoretically become open for universal written communication, without barriers of language.

While some people persist in thinking that the digital revolution since the 1990s has made little or no difference to what happens in their minds when they actually read, write and think, others as stoutly maintain that the digitisation of writing is radically altering our absorption of knowledge and will at last usher in the ideographic utopia imagined by the philosopher Gottfried Wilhelm Leibniz in the 1690s: 'As regards signs, I see ... clearly that it is to the interest of the

'British Library':

大英圖書館
(written in Chinese)

大英図書館
(written in Japanese)

ABOVE Can a Chinese speaker and a Japanese speaker communicate in writing without knowing the other's language? To some extent they can, as suggested by the Chinese and Japanese spellings of 'British Library'.
BELOW Thoth, Egyptian god of writing. Carved and painted relief. Temple of Ramesses II, Abydos (Egypt), 1279–1213 BC

Republic of Letters and especially of students, that learned men should reach agreement on signs.'[7] Moreover, this faith in the increasing intelligence of computers – with their ubiquitous pictographic and logographic icons – chimes with many scholars' growing respect for the intelligence behind ancient scripts. Down with the monolithic 'triumph of the alphabet', they say, and up with Chinese characters, Egyptian hieroglyphs and Mayan glyphs, with their hybrid mixtures of pictographic, logographic and phonetic signs. This conviction has in turn encouraged a belief in the need to see each writing system as enmeshed within a whole culture, instead of viewing it simply as a technical solution to a problem of efficient visual representation of the culture's language. Although one may or may not share the belief in the hidden power of digitisation, and one may remain sceptical about the expressive virtues of logography, this holistic view of writing systems is surely a healthy development that reflects the real relationship between writing and society in all its subtlety and complexity.

Perhaps this relationship is captured best in a story told by the ancient Greek philosopher Socrates (who famously never published a word of his thoughts in writing), which was recorded by his student, Plato, in a dialogue in the fourth century BC. Socrates talks of the Egyptian god Thoth, the inventor of writing, who came to see the Egyptian king seeking the royal blessing on his enlightening invention. However, the king was ambivalent about the new invention. He told Thoth:

> You, who are the father of letters, have been led by your affection to ascribe to them a power the opposite of that which they really possess ... You have invented an elixir not of memory, but of reminding; and you offer your pupils the appearance of wisdom, not true wisdom, for they will read many things without instruction and will therefore seem to know many things, when they are for the most part ignorant.[8]

In a twenty-first-century world drenched with written information and surrounded by information technologies of astonishing speed, convenience and power, these cautionary words about writing recorded 2,500 years ago surely have a surprisingly contemporary ring.

2

THE ROMAN ALPHABET

STAN KNIGHT

EFFICIUNT AUT UMBRA NOCENT PATER IPSE COLENDI
HAUD FACILEM ESSE VIAM VOLUIT PRIMUSQUE PER ARTEM
MOVIT AGROS CURIS ACUENS MORTALIA CORDA
NEC TORPERE GRAVI PASSUS SUA REGNA VETERNO
ANTE IOVEM NULLI SUBIGEBANT ARVA COLONI
NE SIGNARE QUIDEM AUT PARTIRI LIMITE CAMPUM
FAS ERAT IN MEDIUM QUAEREBANT IPSAQUE TELLUS
OMNIA LIBERIUS NULLO POSCENTE FEREBAT
ILLE MALUM VIRUS SERPENTIBUS ADDIDIT ATRIS
PRAEDARIQUE LUPOS IUSSIT PONTUMQUE MOVERI
MELLAQUE DECUSSIT FOLIIS IGNEMQUE REMOVIT
ET PASSIM RIVIS CURRENTIA VINA REPRESSIT
UT VARIAS USUS MEDITANDO EXTUNDERET ARTIS
PAULATIM ET SULCIS FRUMENTI QUAERERET HERBAM
UT SILICIS VENIS ABSTRUSUM EXCUDERET IGNEM
TUNC ALNOS PRIMUM FLUVII SENSERE CAVATAS
NAVITA TUM STELLIS NUMEROS ET NOMINA FECIT
PLEIADAS HYADAS CLARAMQUE LYCAONIS ARCTON
TUM LAQUEIS CAPTARE FERAS ET FALLERE VISCO
INVENTUM ET MAGNOS CANIBUS CIRCUMDARE SALTUS

The original manner in which the Latin language was written down was devised well over 2,000 years ago. Since then, what we call the 'roman' alphabet has been used not only for Latin texts but also for the majority of the world's written languages. Although the history of the roman alphabet is ancient, geographically widespread and intriguingly complex, fundamentally little has changed. The capital letters that we use today are recognisably similar to the carved letterforms of classical Roman times, and our lower-case letters are almost indistinguishable from those of Carolingian scripts written at the time of Charlemagne, 1,200 years ago.

ANCIENT EUROPE

The first known examples we have of those roman letters are 'epigraphic' (carved in stone) or scratched on pottery, some dating from the sixth or even seventh century BC. Early roman letters were 'monoline' capitals (without thick and thin strokes), with consistent and legible forms, derived from previous Greek models. Sometimes the text was 'retrograde' (that is, it was written and read from right to left).

However, by the first century AD the carved capitals of ancient Rome had developed such an extraordinary level of sophistication that they have endured virtually unaltered to this day. Their careful letter proportions, the balance of their thin and thick strokes and their subtle serifs (tiny endings added to the letter strokes) were all probably derived from letters that were first written on the stone with a square-edged brush before they were carved. Similar brush-written letters can be seen in 'advertising' notices painted on walls at Pompeii. The popular modern font called Trajan, designed by Carol Twombly, is a copy of 1,900-year-old inscriptional letters on Trajan's Column in Rome, and required little or no alteration to make it perfectly legible for us today.

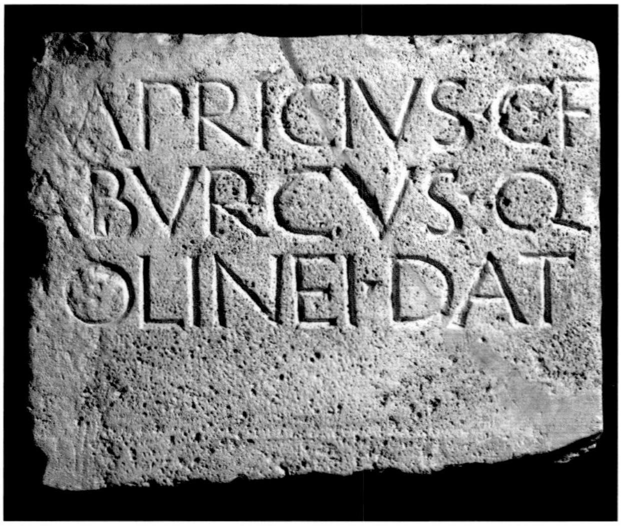

The scripts of Roman times can be classified according to their use and their character. The informal styles adopted for less important documents and the everyday handwriting of the intelligentsia are called 'cursive' scripts. They were generally written with a blunt, pointed pen on papyrus or with a stylus on wax tablets. More formal scripts are known as 'calligraphic' or 'book' scripts, and were written by professional scribes, usually for formal documents in scroll or book form. These scripts were written with a specially cut, square-edged pen (often a reed, but later a quill), which produces their characteristic thick and thin strokes.

PREVIOUS PAGE Roman square capitals. Virgil, *Georgics*, known as *Codex Augusteus*. Manuscript book (parchment). Italy, 4th century AD. Vatican Library: Ms. Vat. Lat. 3256, fol. 3r

ABOVE Republican Roman monoline capitals. Stone inscription dedicated in Latin to Apollo by Umbricius Caburcus. Viterbo (Italy), around 2nd century BC. British Museum: 1867,0508.67
BELOW Roman imperial capitals. Inscription in marble from the base of Trajan's Column (detail). Rome, AD 113.
OPPOSITE New Roman cursive. Record of a sale of property in Rimini, in Latin (detail). Papyrus scroll. Ravenna (Italy), AD 572. British Library: Add MS 5412

[illegible]

domni [illegible]

[illegible]

[illegible]

[illegible]

[illegible]

[illegible]

[illegible]

[illegible]

[illegible]

[illegible]

[illegible]

[illegible]

[illegible]

[illegible]

Ancient cursive scripts

The oldest handwritten Latin document we know of can be traced to the first century BC. The scripts we now term old Roman cursive undoubtedly date from some time before that and they persisted into the third century AD (see above). Old Roman cursive bears some features of the earliest Latin carved inscriptions; but since it was written quickly (cursive means 'running'), and not always consistently, there is some loss of legibility – especially for us. The final word 'consulatus' in Papyrus 730 (above) has an A with no cross bar and long diagonal extensions to the L and the top of the S. This script was ideally suited for the stylus and wax tablets, or the pen and wooden tablets like those found at Vindolanda near Hadrian's Wall, and can even be seen in the graffiti on the walls of Pompeii.

A process of evolution of old Roman cursive, part natural, part conscious reform (completed by the fourth century AD), resulted in the group of administration and correspondence scripts of Late Antiquity, which we now call new Roman cursive (see illustration on p. 45). This was a rapidly written script. The speed of writing and a greater use of ligatures and cursive flourishes make it hard to read. New Roman cursive, however, was widely employed and played an important part in the development of later, more formal scripts, like half-uncials.

Ancient formal scripts

The earliest fully developed Latin book script was rustic capitals and we know of examples from the first century AD. It was written with a square-cut pen held at a very steep pen angle (the edge of the pen held at almost 90 degrees to the writing line) and the resulting capital letters are narrow. Much of its character was taken from the contemporary old Roman cursive script. The **A** often lacks a crossbar, **E** and **F** are very narrow, the **M** is widely spread and the bowl of **R** overlaps the vertical stem. Despite its unsophisticated name, this was a mature calligraphic script, later selected for many deluxe manuscripts (see opposite). These capitals continued to be used in manuscripts up to the onset of the Gothic period for 'display' purposes: that is, for headings, opening pages and prefaces.

The term 'uncial' covers a major category of ancient book scripts that were in very common use from the fourth to the eighth centuries for copying the text of books. Most of the earliest surviving uncial manuscripts actually have their origins in northern Africa. The oldest datable uncial script is from Hippo Regius (modern-day Annaba, Algeria) and was written sometime between AD 396 and 426. Later, uncials were used in Italy (particularly in Rome), mostly for biblical texts; through missionary activity the script spread to almost every part of the Roman Empire, from the southern Mediterranean to northern Britain. In Northumbria it reached a very high level of accomplishment.

The original form of uncials used a slanted, natural pen angle, perhaps evolving from old Roman cursive

ABOVE Old Roman cursive. Receipt for goods, in Latin. Papyrus fragment. Alexandria (Egypt), 167 AD. British Library: Papyrus 730
OPPOSITE Rustic capitals. Virgil, *Eclogues*, known as *Codex Romanus*. Manuscript book (parchment). Rome, second quarter of 5th century AD. Vatican Library: Ms. Vat. Lat. 3867, fol. 9r

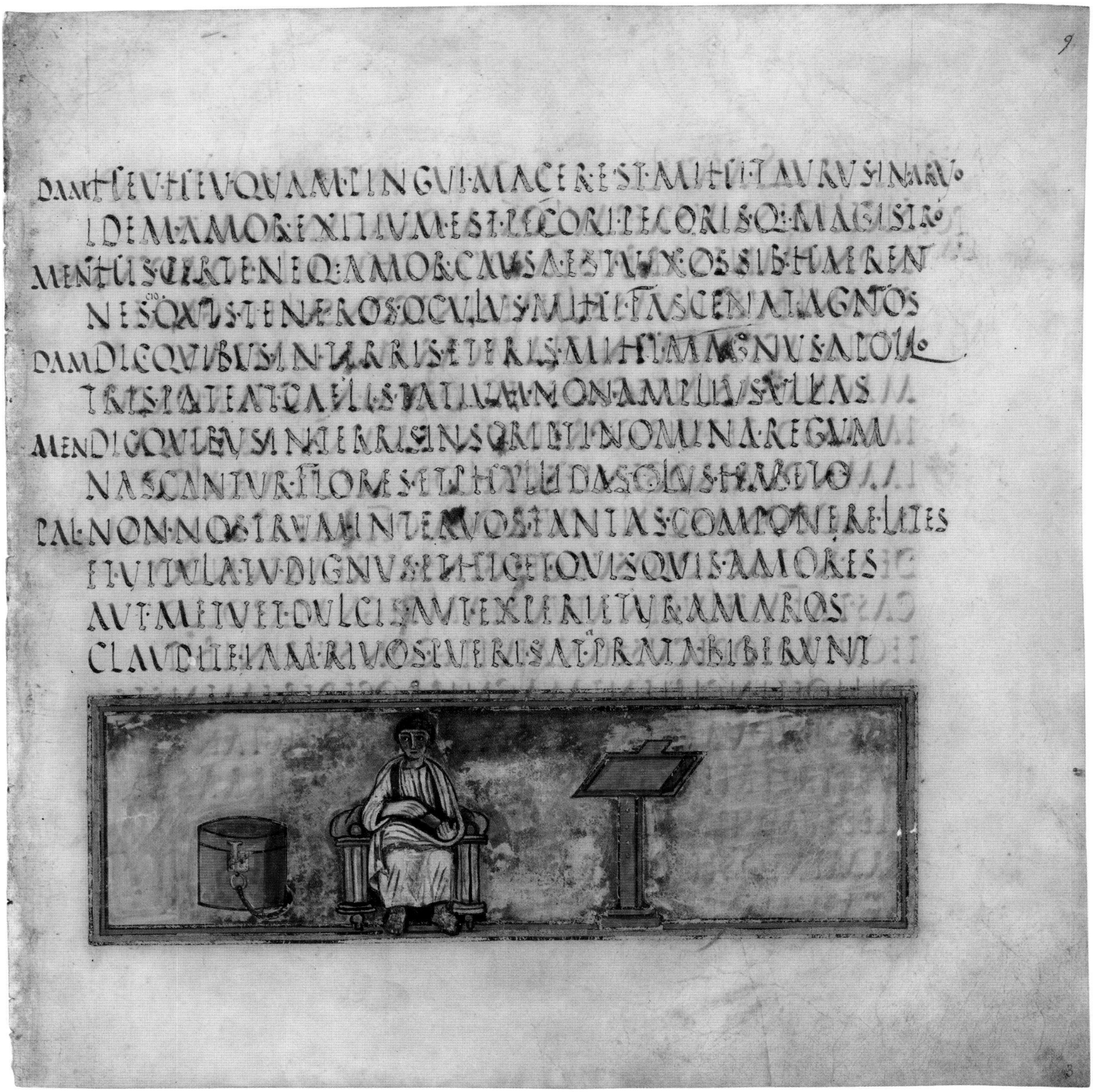

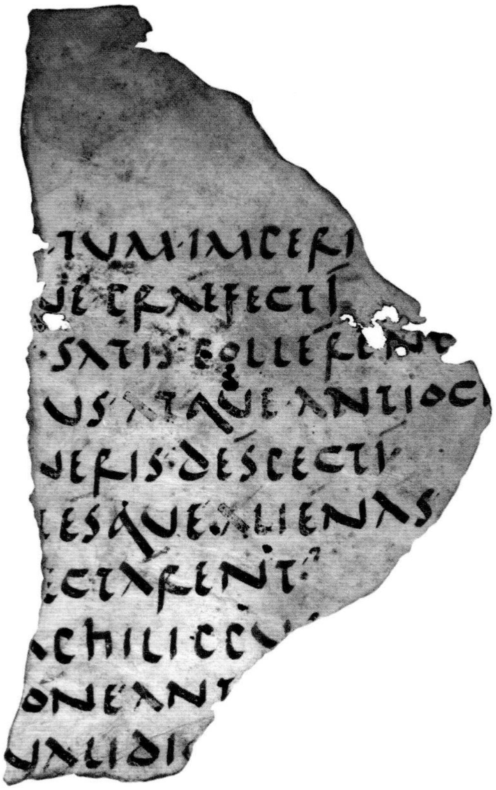

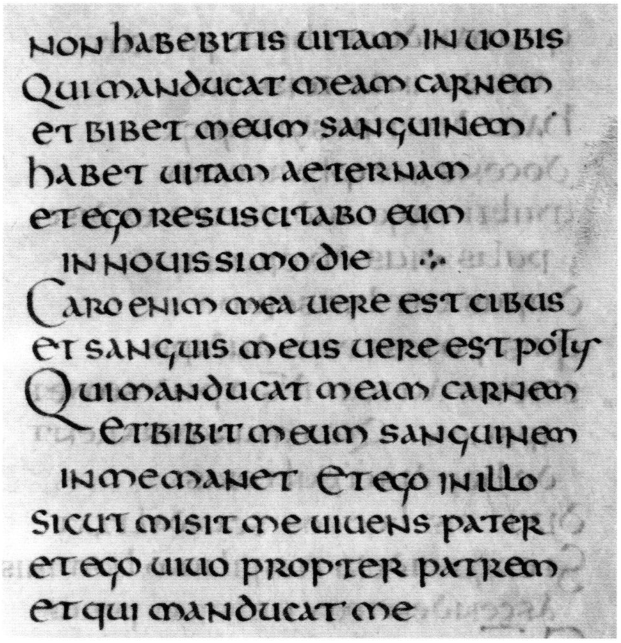
non habebitis uitam in uobis
Qui manducat meam carnem
et bibet meum sanguinem
habet uitam aeternam
et ego resuscitabo eum
in nouissimo die
Caro enim mea uere est cibus
et sanguis meus uere est potus
Qui manducat meam carnem
et bibit meum sanguinem
in me manet et ego in illo
Sicut misit me uiuens pater
et ego uiuo propter patrem
et qui manducat me

ABOVE Literary version of old Roman cursive. *De Bellis Macedonicis*. Manuscript book fragment (parchment). Egypt, 2nd century AD? British Library: Papyrus 745
BELOW Uncial. Gospel of St John, known as the *St Cuthbert Gospel*. Manuscript book (parchment). Wearmouth-Jarrow (England), early 8th century. British Library: Add MS 89000, fol. 29r (detail)

scripts, and then became more formalised in the manner of the *De Bellis Macedonis* fragment (written perhaps as early as AD 100; see upper left). This shows a mixed script with discernible uncial characteristics. Some have claimed that uncials developed directly from rustic capitals, but rustics are constructed differently, with a much steeper pen angle: compare the forms of **A**, **D**, **E** and **R**. The particular characteristics of uncial scripts include **A** with a bowl, rounded forms of **D**, **E**, **H** and **M**, ascenders for **D**, **H**, **K** and **L**, and descenders for **F**, **G**, **P** and **Q** (see lower left).

Later forms of uncial developed a more formal aspect than the earlier examples and employed a more complex method of letter construction (see lower illustration opposite). Palaeographers sometimes refer to these as 'Roman uncials', indicating their origins. The pen angle was flattened (the edge of the pen held almost parallel to the writing line) and there was extensive use of pen 'manipulation' (for example, some twisting of the pen in the formation of the serifs, stem endings and rounded strokes). The corner of the pen must have been used for the hairline strokes and some serifs.

Half-uncial scripts were first given that name in the mistaken idea that they were a degenerate form of uncials. But early half-uncials, which initially appeared in the fourth century, probably evolved from new Roman cursive scripts, eventually leading to more formal manuscripts written with a square-edged pen, like the fragment of Livy's *Epitome* from the beginning of the third century AD (see opposite above). Both the *Epitome* script and half-uncials used a flattened pen angle (the edge of the pen held almost parallel to the writing line). The characteristics of half-uncials are long ascenders (letters like **b**, **d**, **f**, **h** and **l**) and descenders (letters like **g**, **p**, **q** and long **s**); round forms of **a** and **t**; **g** shaped a little like a figure 5; **m** with a straight first stroke and curving end stroke; and the capital form of **N**. Many of these letters can also be seen in the later half-uncial hands of Anglo-

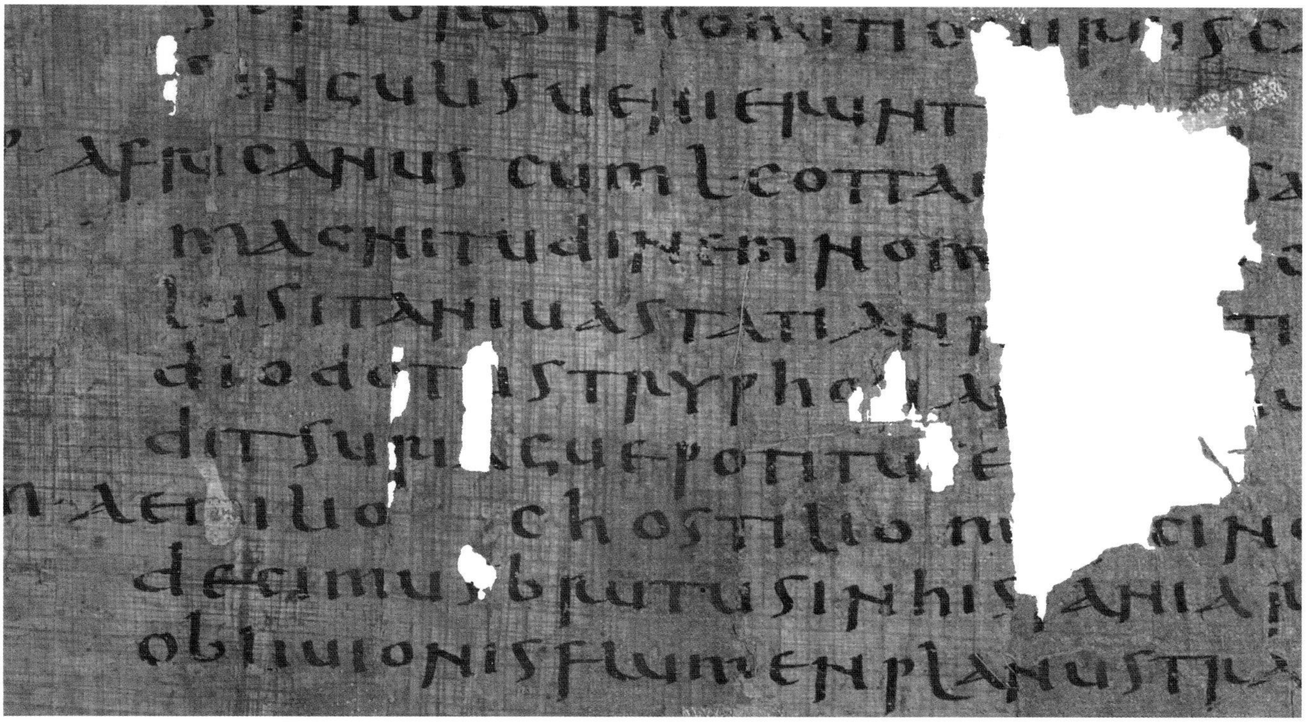

ABOVE Proto Roman half-uncial. *Epitome of the Histories of Livy*. Fragment (papyrus), Egypt, early 3rd century? British Library: Papyrus 1532v (detail)
BELOW Uncial. Book of gospels, known as the *Harley Gospels*. Manuscript book (parchment). Northern Italy, late 6th century. British Library: Harley MS 1775, fol. 223v (detail)

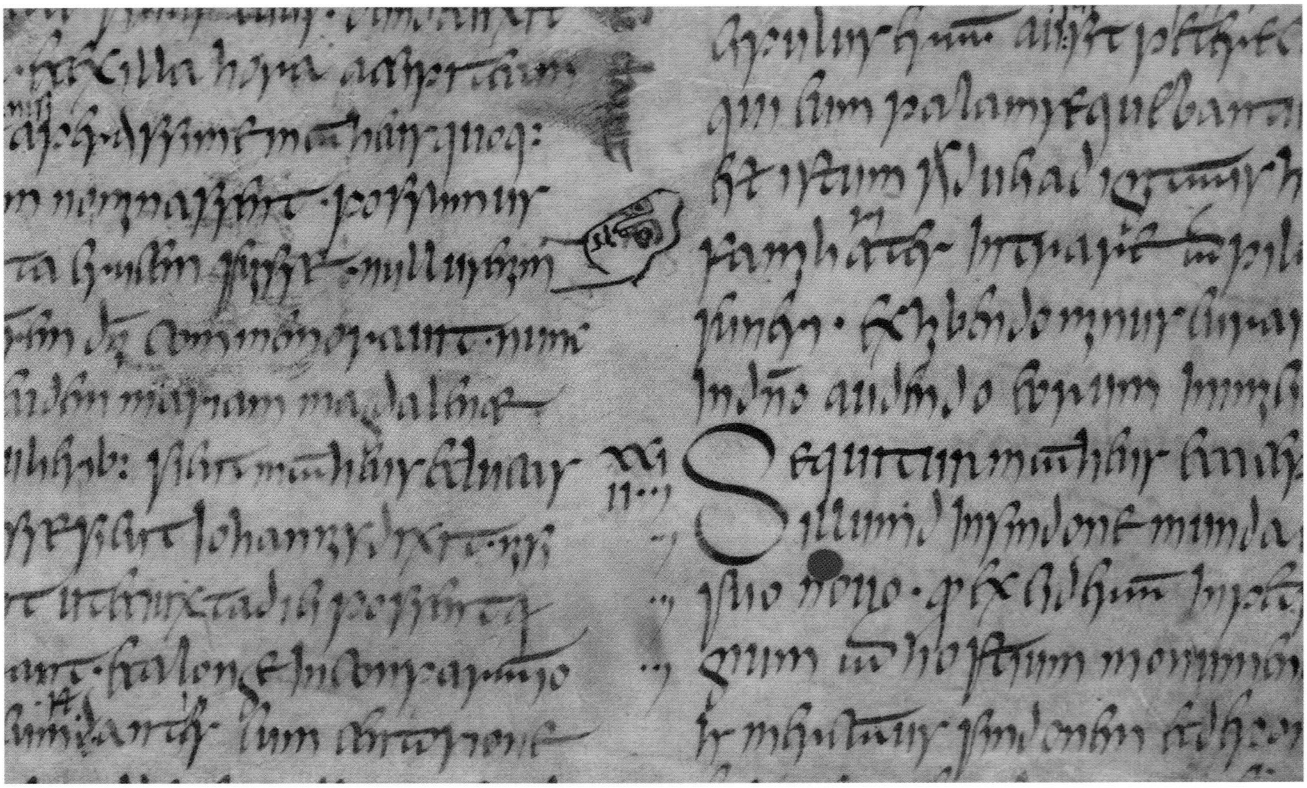

Saxon England (see opposite) and Ireland which developed from these Roman roots.

For the text of prestigious manuscripts of Virgil in the fourth and fifth centuries AD, scripts were employed that followed the forms and generous letter spacing of classical Roman inscriptional letters. They are generally known as 'written square capitals'. Copying such detailed carved letterforms with the pen must have been extremely difficult for the scribe and would have slowed down the writing process considerably. Prof. T. J. Brown (1923–1987), an eminent palaeographer, rightly regarded the use of such capitals for lengthy manuscript texts as 'a late idea and a bad one'.[1]

In fact, only two ancient square capital manuscripts survive, both in fragments: *Codex Sangallensis* (St Gallen, Stiftsbibliothek, Ms. Cod. 1394, pp. 7–48) and *Codex Augusteus* (four folios in the Vatican, Vat. Lat. 3256 – see p. 43 – and three folios in Berlin, Staatsbibliothek, Cod. Lat. Fol. 416).

MEDIEVAL EUROPE

Following the decline of the Roman Empire in Europe many distinctive local scripts emerged in the various centres of scribal activity. These generally flourished from the fifth century AD onwards, but in certain more isolated areas survived well into the Gothic period. One important group is the scripts from the British Isles.

Insular scripts

The term 'insular' refers to scripts of the British Isles up to the mid-ninth century and is often used when

ABOVE Anglo-Saxon cursive minuscule. Augustine of Hippo, *De consensu evangelistarum*. Manuscript fragment (parchment). Northumbria? (England), late 8th century. British Library: Cotton MS Cleopatra A iii/1, fol. 1v (detail)

OPPOSITE Main text hand: Insular half-uncial. Anglo-Saxon gospel book, known as the *Lindisfarne Gospels*. Manuscript book (parchment). Lindisfarne (England), *c*.700. British Library: Cotton MS Nero D IV, fol. 203v

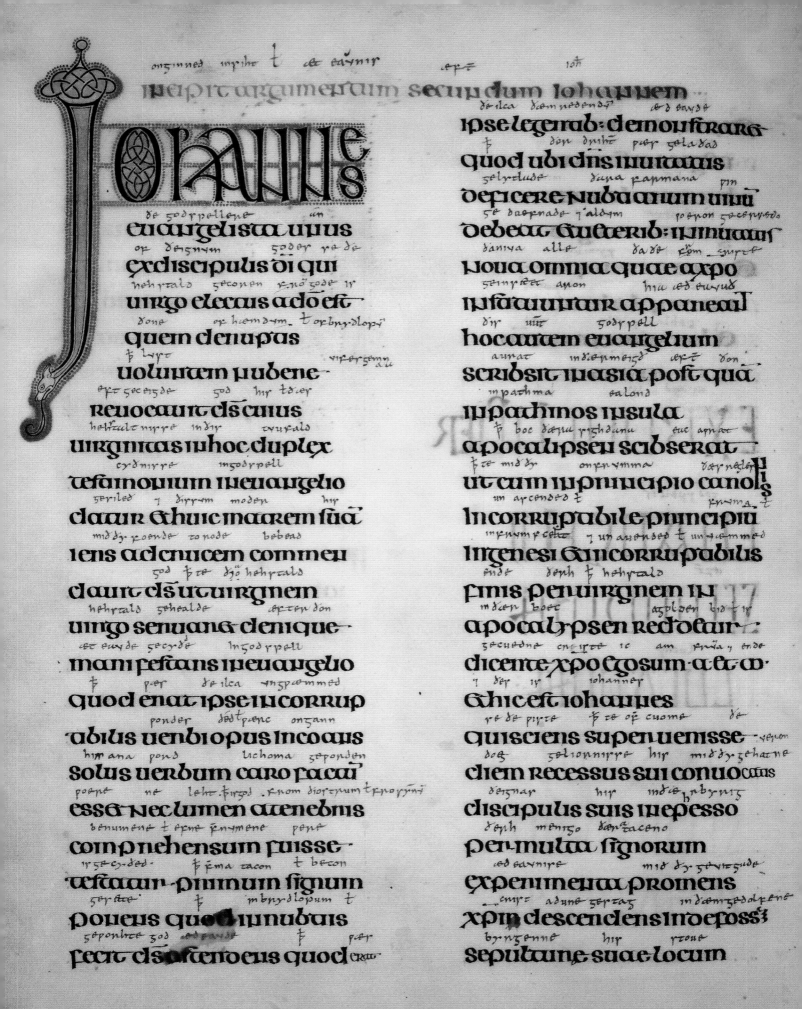

INCIPIT ARGUMENTUM SECUNDUM IOHANNEM

IOHANNES
euangelista unus
ex discipulis di qui
uirgo electus a do est
quem de nuptiis
uoluntatem nubere
reuocauit ds cuius
uirginitas in hoc duplex
testimonium in euangelio
datur et hic matrem suã
iens ad crucem commen
dauit ds ut uirginem
uirgo seruans denique
manifestans in euangelio
quod erat ipse incorrup
tibilis uerbi opus inchoans
solus uerbum caro factũ
esse nec lumen a tenebris
conprehensum fuisse
testatur primum signum
ponens quod in nuptiis
fecit ds ostendens quod erat
ipse legentib: demonstraret
quod ubi dns inuitatus
deficere nuptiarum uinũ
debeat et ueterib: inmutatis
noua omnia quae a xpo
instituuntur appareant
hoc autem euangelium
scribsit in asia post quã
in pathmos insula
apocalipsen scibserat
ut cum in principio canonis
incorruptibile principiũ
in genesi et incorruptibilis
finis per uirginem in
apocalypsen redderetur
dicente xpo ego sum a et ω
et hic est iohannes
qui sciens superuenisse
diem recessus sui conuocatis
discipulis suis in epheso
per multa signorum
experimenta promens
xpm descendens in defoss[um]
sepulturae suae locum

Anglo-Saxon or Irish origin is uncertain. As the Romans departed from Britain, there developed an extensive and coherent pattern of scripts in Christian Ireland based on the writing of the late Roman world. Vigorous Irish missionary activity took the scripts to northern England and eventually to many parts of Europe. Later, fine versions of Roman uncials were incorporated into insular manuscripts (but never in Ireland).

A system of insular minuscule scripts, deriving from such everyday cursive hands as that of St Boniface (*c.*657–754), by the eighth century reached a mature enough form to be used for fine manuscript books (see p. 50). The letter **d** is 'open'; **c** and **e** are tall (especially in ligature); **p**, **r** and **s** all have descenders and are very similar in appearance. Overall, the aspect is of a compressed letterform written with a steeply slanted pen.

The characteristic formal insular book script, usually labelled 'insular half-uncial', probably originated in Ireland as a modification of the earlier Roman half-uncial. One of the earliest known Irish manuscripts, *c.*600, reveals a script somewhere between the two.

The majestic script of the Gospels, written between 698 and 721 by Eadfrith, Bishop of Lindisfarne, shows insular half-uncial at its most developed stage (see p. 51). These are heavy, rounded letters written with a flattened pen angle. The characteristic forms are **a**, **b**, **g**, **l** and **D**. Alternative uncial forms of **A**, **D**, **N**, **R** and **S** occur, perhaps due to the influence of the nearby Wearmouth-Jarrow scriptoria and their magnificent uncial scripts. The 'gloss' (the writing between the main lines of text) in the Lindisfarne manuscript was added in the mid-tenth century in Anglo-Saxon cursive and is the earliest surviving 'English' translation of the Gospels.

Carolingian minuscule

The reforms of Charlemagne (*c.*742–814), in the late eighth and early ninth centuries, encouraged the use of a legible (and, incidentally, beautiful) book script that

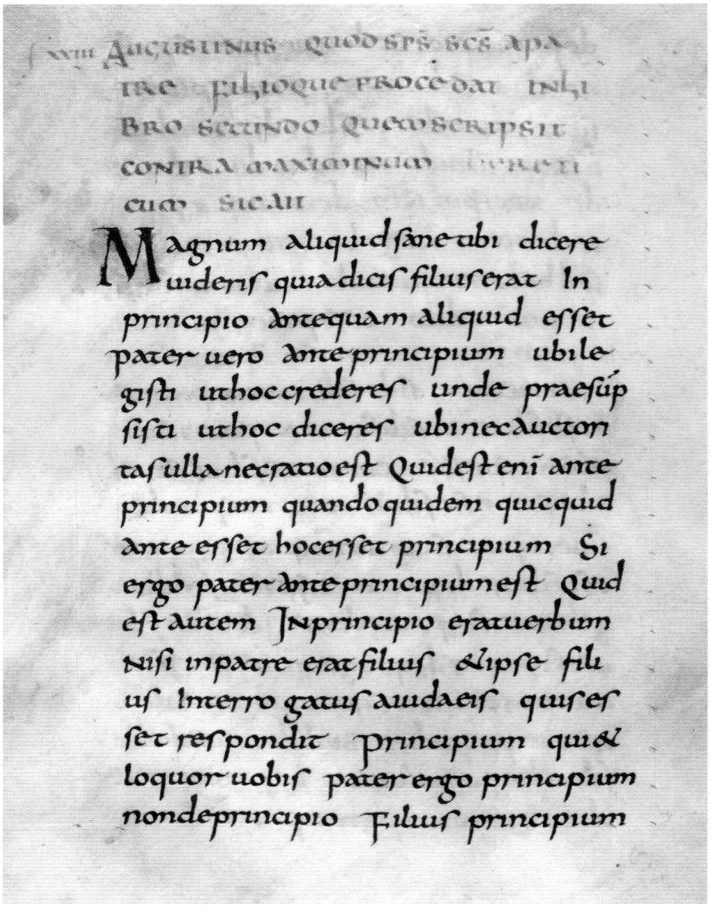
XVIII AUGUSTINUS QUOD SPS SCS A PA
TRE FILIOQUE PROCEDAT IN LI
BRO SECUNDO QUEM SCRIPSIT
CONTRA MAXIMINUM
CUM SIC AIT
Magnum aliquid sane tibi dicere
uideris quia dicis filius erat In
principio antequam aliquid esset
pater uero ante principium ubi le
gisti ut hoc crederes unde praesump
sisti ut hoc diceres ubi nec auctori
tas ulla nec ratio est Quid est eni ante
principium quando quidem quicquid
ante esset hoc esset principium Si
ergo pater ante principium est Quid
est autem In principio erat uerbum
nisi in patre erat filius & ipse fili
us interrogatus a iudaeis qui esses
set respondit Principium qui &
loquor uobis pater ergo principium
non de principio Filius principium

emerged in the calligraphic centres under his influence in France, most notably at the Abbey of Tours. This Carolingian (or Caroline) minuscule evolved from the ancient Roman half-uncial script and incorporated certain features from local minuscule scripts. Early manuscripts from Corbie Abbey show how half-uncial could be modified to a more minuscule form. In the Grandval Bible certain sections are written in a half-uncial style of minuscule (see left-hand column in the illustration opposite).

Compared to the many, barely readable and over-elaborate cursive regional scripts, the mature Carolingian minuscule (see p. 53) was a disciplined and

ABOVE Heading: uncials. Main text: Carolingian minuscule. Theodulf of Orléans, *De Spiritu Sancto*. Manuscript book (parchment). Orléans (France), 809–16. British Library: Harley MS 3024, fol. 33r

OPPOSITE Headings: Roman capitals and uncials. Main text: Carolingian minuscule. Latin Bible, known as the *Moutier Grandval Bible*. Manuscript book (parchment). Tours (France), 834–43. British Library: Add MS 10546, fol. 410r

INCP ARGVMTV HIERNM IN EPLA AD ROMANOS.

Epistolae ad romanos causa haec est ecclesiam e duobus populis. id est de iudaeis et gentilibus congregatam exaequat meritis ut causas ei auferat simultatis quae de uoluntatem praelationis mutuae nascebantur. Ergo ut pace inter se et caritate iungantur ostendit pares conditione dum peccatis fuisse obnoxii comprobantur. qui aeque salutem per fide xpi sint et gratiam consecuti. Nam neq: iudaeis profuisse legem incustoditam docet. nec gentiles posse legis ignoratione defendi. quos ratio et ad di notitiam perducere poterat et ab omni uitae prauitate reuocare.

Scito qui legis non expositione continua esse dictorum. sed subnotationes breues singulis uersibus ac uerbis apposita.

Pauli apostoli epistolae. numr. XIIII.
Ad romanos. I. Ad corinthios. II.
Ad galathas. I. Ad ephesios. I.
Ad philippenses. I. Ad colosenses. I.
Ad thessalonicenses. II. Ad timotheu. II.
Ad titum. I. Ad philimonem. I.
Ad hebraeos. I. Omnis textus uel numerus epistolarum ad unius hominis perfectionem proficiunt.

Cum romanis ita agit apostolus paulus quasi cum incipientibus qui post gentilitatem ut initia fidei sortiantur et perueniant ad spem uitae aeternae. Multa de physicis rationibus insinuat. multa de scripturis diuinis. Ad corinthios prima consecutos iam fidem non recte conseruantes obiurgat. Secunda ad corinthios. Contristatos quidem sed emendatos ostendit. Galathas in fide ipsa peccantes et ad iudaismum declinantes exponit. Ephesios quia incipiunt et custodiunt laudat quod ea quae acceperant seruauerant.

Philippenses quod in quo crediderunt seruantes ad fructum peruenerunt.

Colosenses conlaudat quia uelut ignotis scribit. et accepto nuntio ab epafra custodisse euangelium gratulatur.

Thessalonicenses in opere et fide creuisse gloriatur. In secunda praeterea quod et persecutionem passi in fide perseuerauerint quos et scos appellat ut illos qui in iudaea xpm confessi persecutiones fortiter tolerarunt.

Ad hebraeos ad quorum similitudinem passi sunt. Thessalonicenses ut in mandatis perseuerantes persecutiones prumptissime patiantur.

Omnes ergo epistolae pauli sunt numero XIIII. Ad romanos. ad corinthios. II. Ad galathas. ad ephesios. ad philippenses. ad colosenses. ad thessalonicenses. II. Ad hebraeos quos hortatur ad similitudinem thessalonicensium. haec in canone non habetur. Reliquae ad timotheum. Primam quemammodu agat ecclesia. Ad timotheum. II. quemammodum se ipsum agat. Ad titum ut creditam sibi ecclesiam cretae ordinet. Ad philimonem de onesimo seruo. qui emendatus melior factus est.

EXPLT ARGVMENTVM.

IT EIUSDE ARGUMTU.

Primum quaeritur quare post euangelia quae supplementum legis sunt et in quib: nobis exempla et praecepta uiuendi plenissime digesta sunt uoluerit apostolus has epistolas ad singulas ecclesias destinare.

Haec aut causa factum uidetur scilicet ut initia nascentis ecclesiae nouis causis existentib: et praesentia atq: orientia resecaret uitia et post futuras excluderet quaestiones exemplo prophetarum. Qui post edita lege moysi in qua omnia mandata di legebantur Nihilominus tamen doctrina sua rediuiua semper populi compressere peccata. Et propter exemplum libris ad nostram etiam memoriam transmiserunt. Deinde quaeritur cur non amplius quam decem epistolas ad ecclesias scribserit. Decem sunt enim cum illa quae dicitur ad hebraeos. Nam reliquae quat

D ignare dn̄e die isto
sine peccato nos custodire
M iserere nr̄i dn̄e. miserere nr̄i
F iat misericordia tua dn̄e
sup̄ nos. quemadmodum
sperauimus inte
I nte dn̄e speraui. non confun
dar in aeternum

HYMNUS TRIUM PUERORUM.

B enedicite om̄ia opera dn̄i dn̄o
laudate & super exaltate
eum in secula
B en̄ angeli dn̄i dn̄o. b̄ celi dn̄o
B en̄ aquae om̄s quae sup̄ celos
sunt dn̄o. b̄ om̄s uirtutes dn̄i dn̄o
B en̄ sol & luna dn̄o
benedicite stellae celi dn̄o
B en̄ om̄is imber & ros dn̄o

formal script, capable of maintaining legibility even at extremely small sizes. It employs a slightly slanted pen angle (rather than the flattened angle of the half-uncial) and has a more defined body height. Certain letterforms were improved: uncial **a** soon replaced the half-uncial form; a distinctive looped **g** replaced the 'figure 5' form.

The emergence of the Carolingian minuscule is one of the most important developments in the history of Western calligraphy. It became an international script and was copied and adapted in succeeding centuries by scribes all across Europe. A modern typeface, Silentium Pro, designed by Jovica Veljović, is based directly on this 1,200-year-old script and yet it is perfectly legible for modern readers.

English Carolingian minuscule

Following ecclesiastical reforms in the mid-tenth century, English scribes wrote a very distinctive version of Carolingian minuscule (see opposite). While it was generally reserved for Latin texts it lasted to the end of the eleventh century. Larger in scale and more formal in structure than the French Carolingian minuscule, it nevertheless maintains many of the features of the earlier script: uncial **a** and **h**, looped **g**, long **s** and half-uncial **ɪ**. The use of **&** to represent *et* ('and') within a word seems peculiar to Anglo-Saxon manuscripts.

English Carolingian minuscule at its best is a supremely legible and calligraphic script. The English scribe and teacher, Edward Johnston (1872–1944), recognised that 'This extremely legible MS. would form an almost perfect model for a modern formal hand'.[2]

Italian minuscule

Carolingian minuscule arrived in Italy at an early stage. It was used for Italian books and documents from the ninth to the end of the thirteenth century, alongside Beneventan minuscule and other regional more cursive scripts.

Italian Carolingian minuscule reached its peak in the twelfth century and rivals the achievements of English tenth-century scribes. The round, upright letters are quite heavy, but they were well constructed and confidently written. Discreet serifs were added to the base of the first stems of **m** and **n** (see p. 56).

This is the script that was later revived by Renaissance scholar/scribes and so became a model for the first printers' types in Italy. Their influence has lasted until the present day: our modern-day roman fonts hardly differ from the late fifteenth-century types of Nicolas Jenson or Aldus Manutius.

THE 'GOTHIC' PERIOD

The term 'gothic' is often used to describe the character of art and architecture, including manuscript 'styles', of the late twelfth to late fifteenth centuries. It was originally coined in sixteenth-century Italy as a term of derision for what was perceived as the 'barbaric' art of northern and Western Europe. The features of fully developed gothic book scripts from the end of the twelfth century are heavy weight, sharp angularity of form and lateral compression (narrow letter shapes).

The rise of the secular universities and the expansion of the monastic system in the twelfth century prompted the need for many more books. A large number of different grades of scripts were employed at this time to cope with the demand.

Gothic cursive scripts

This period saw a revival of true cursive scripts, introduced first in England at the end of the twelfth century. Many of them incorporated impressive calligraphic flourishes and other decorative features. The secretary script, as its name implies, was primarily employed for correspondence and other informal documents (see the marginal notes in the illustration on p. 6). It has an

---

OPPOSITE Heading: Rustics. Main text: English Carolingian minuscule. Latin psalter, known as the *Ramsey Psalter*. Manuscript book (parchment). Winchester or Ramsey? (England), fourth quarter of 10th century. British Library: Harley MS 2904, fol. 201v

OVERLEAF (LEFT) Italian Carolingian minuscule. Homiliary: sermons and homilies. Manuscript book (parchment). Central Italy. Second half of 12th century. British Library: Harley 7183, f.119v

OVERLEAF (RIGHT) Secretary hand. Jean Creton, *Histoire rimée de Richard II (La Prinse et mort du roy Richart)*. Manuscript book (parchment). Paris. 1401–c.1405. British Library: Harley 1319, fol. 50r

in conspectu templi sci infructuosus: sed
offer munus tuū · ad illū eñi te hoc di-
ctum nos ammonet: omīs loquens:
ut et nos dona et munera nra non tene-
amus apud nos · sed reddamus deo no-
stro · maxime cū de aliqua liberamur ·
tribulatione · Offer inquit munus tuū ·
Quare: ut omīs qui uident te portare
et offerre: credant his mirabilib; : et magnificent dnm q misertus est tui: et in
fidelib; per hoc increpatio · et testimonium duritie cordis ipsorū fiet · Sic
et illū triginta et octo annis iacentē
in infirmitatem erigens a languore ·
iussit portare grabattū suū et ire in
domū suā · ut hunc ipsum lectū por-
tatus abeo p mediā ciuitatē clamas-
et laudando. set saluantē se inuocando · Sic et illū
cecū in natatoria syloe misit · ut uiden-
tes eum ambulare illuc euntem cecū ·
et iterū remeantē mirati et obstupe-
scentes crederent: huic talia mirabilia
facienti · Post hec que superius dicta
sunt cū introisset capharnaū in ciuita-
tem galilee · Sic cognominata ē caphar-
naum in qua sepius dns uirtutis sue
magnificentiā demonstrauit · Ingre-
diente in eo capharnaū · Capharnaū
namq; interpretatur ager · uel uilla
consolationis · Cum ager quod in eo
aliquid agatur · uel uilla a circū ualla-
tione limitis · hoc ē munitione custo-
die nomē acceperint · Congrua dispen-
satione carnis illo ingressus asseritur
dns quo p deitatis sue potentiā circum
dando attrahens ad credulitatē incre-
dulos · et sanitatis miraculū erat actu-
rus · Accessit centurio exter nue generatio-
ne · sed mente domesticus · militum
princeps · sed plus anglorū gaudium ·
Accessit ad eū centurio · Increpatio hic
nempe illorū ostenditur ascendentiū
quondā ad heliā in carmelo quinqua-
genariorū · q manentes in fidelitate:
celesti sunt igne consūpti · iste uero ex
infideli particeps fidei factus · in sinu
ilico deputatus ē abrahe · Accessit ad
eum centurio: rogans eū et dicens · Dñe:
puer mīs iacet in domo paraliticus et
male torquetur · Multi illo tēpore
pro diuersis rogabant infirmitatib; · nul-
lus tam p seruo · nisi iste solus · Et hoc
ei ad augmtū beatitudinis et coronā
glē erat · Quid eñi in mentis abdito di-
gnum uoluens iudiciū centurio iste age-
bat · michi hic seruus ē et ego creatoris ·
iste me sup terrā: et ego magnū in celis
habeo dnm · Si ego ei ñ misereor quomō
ille michi miserebitur: Si ego huic ñ
subuenio · quomodo michi ille subue-
niet: Sic debent omīs qui famulos habent et famulas cogitare · sic misereri
et condolere eis supplicare et curam
habere de seruis uel ancillis suis: sicut
et ille beatus centurio fecit · Puer mīs
inquit iacet in domo · Non in una rē
tantū miserabilis quod iacet · sed in
alia quod paraliticus · tertia quod male torquetur · Omnia eñi ista dolorē
cognominauit · et iacentē paraliticū
et dure detentū · ideo ut sue anime an
gustias demonstraret · et dnm cogno-
uisset quatenus illius cruciatū mon-
straret · et dñi beniuolentiā inuitaret ·
Puer mīs iacet in domo · Et huc quare
non attulisti eū: ideo ait · qa non opus
est illi ostendere omīa uidenti · ñ opus
est in conspectu afferre eis · cuius potentia ñ terminatur · nec includitur nec
excluditur · Iacet in domo paraliticus
et male torquetur · Quid ergo uis: uel
cupis · seu desideras: Non multum loquor ait · scio eñi quod ad omīa cogno-
scentē loquor · ñ uerbosor · Scio enim
quod ad omīa prescientē respondeo ·
ideoq; iste agnoscens corda respondēs
dicit · ego ueniā et curabo eū: ego ad
abraham ueniens · senilē sare sanaui
uterū in senectute eius · ysaac filiū do-
nans · Ego ueniens et nunc ad te curabo eū · Et quomodo pmittis dñe ad
uentū tuū huic nec querit · nec petit ·
sciens quod ñ acceptabile sit ei · ut ueniens in domū eius · ob hoc ut uos pre
ualeatis et eius fidei similetis uel cogno
scatis · quis iste sit · uel qualis in eo fidei
thesaurus habeatur occultus · Iam eñi
et primitus abraham tēptaui · non pro
hoc ut cognoscerē que ipse sciebam:
sed ut uos ei similes in omī tēptatione:

14

Beau cousin de lancastre vous soiez le tresbien venu lors
respondi le duc henry enclinez assez bas a terre.
Monseigneur je suis venu plus tost que vous ne mavez
mande la raison pourquoy je le vous diray La
commune renommee de vostre peuple si est telle que vous
les avez par lespace de xx ou xxii ans trop
mauvaisement et trop rigoreusement gouvernez et
tant quilz nen sont pas bien content Mais sil plaist
a nostre seigneur je le vous aideray a gouverner mieulx
quil na este gouverne le temps passe Le roy richart
lui respondi alors Beau cousin de lancastre puis
quil vous plaist il nous plaist bien Et sachiez de certain

[illegible]

gas ac defendas. Tribue ei q̄s
dn̄e diuitias grē tuę cōple
in bonis desideriū ei9. corona
eū in miscdia tua. tibiq; dn̄o
pia deuotione iugiter famu-
letur. p. Cum datur anulus.

Accipe regię dignitatis anu-
lum. & p hunc in te catho-
licę fidei signaculū. quia ut
hodie ordinaris. caput & pn-
ceps regni ac popli. ita pse-
uerabis auctor ac stabilitor

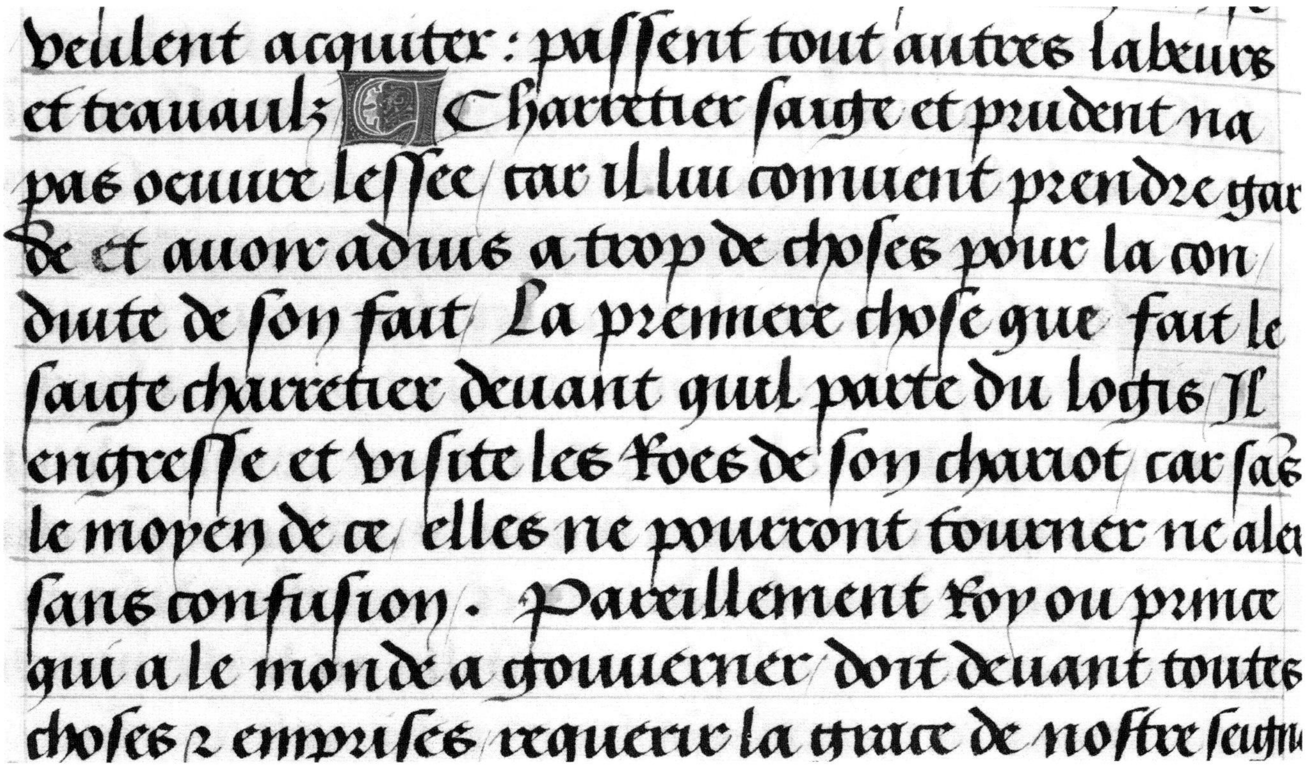
veulent acquiter: passent tout autres labeurs
et travaulz. Chartretier saige et prudent na
pas oeuure lessee car il luy comuient prendre gar
de et auoir aduis a trop de choses pour la con
duite de son fait La premiere chose que fait le
saige charretier deuant quil parte du logis Il
engresse et visite les roes de son chariot car sas
le moyen de ce elles ne pourront tourner ne aler
sans confusion. Pareillement roy ou prince
qui a le monde a gouuerner doit deuant toutes
choses et emprises requerir la grace de nostre seign

angular, pointed look with mannered pen flourishes and a swelling applied to certain tall letters (especially **f** and long **s**), the result of pressing down to widen the slit of the pen. From the end of the thirteenth century, cursives were accepted for use as book scripts, especially those intended for universities (see p. 57).

The formalised book script evolving from secretary, gothic *bâtarde*, is particularly associated with the royal court at Burgundy in northern France (see above). It retains many of the vanities and peculiar letterforms of the secretary script (for example, **r** and short **s**;), while having the formality and texture of other gothic book scripts. It was written with a very flexible pen; the heavy **f** and long **s** are again the result of pen pressure.

Formal gothic scripts

The formal Gothic scripts developed directly from Carolingian minuscule. The period of transition from the mid-eleventh century through to the end of the twelfth produced scripts of increasing compression and angularity, which are sometimes referred to as proto-gothic scripts. These letterforms, also called transitional gothic, are characteristically narrow and heavy, with a hint of angularity (see opposite). The serifs at the 'waistline' are heavy and the ends of strokes at the baseline are more elaborate than before.

Gothic *prescissus* scripts are high-grade, sophisticated scripts whose letter stems (for example, **m** and **n**) are cut off square at the baseline (see p. 60). Numerous alternative forms were used: **d** in both round and upright forms, **r** in both 'branching' and 'figure 2' shapes, and **s** both round and long. Additional details include the usual use of the 'figure 2' **r** (when following **o** and other curved letters) and the sharing of stems

OPPOSITE Proto-gothic minuscule. Latin Office Book of Episcopal Rites. Manuscript book (parchment). Canterbury (England), *c.*1150–60. British Library: Cotton MS Tiberius B VIII/1, fol. 95v (detail)
ABOVE Gothic *Bâtarde*. Hugues de Lannoy, *Imaginacion de Vraye Noblesse*. Manuscript book (parchment). Ghent or Bruges (Belgium), *c.*1496. British Library: Royal Ms 19 C viii, fol. 43v (detail)

tutes domini domino.

Benedicite sol ⁊ luna domino: bene
dicite stelle celi domino.

Benedicite ymber ⁊ ros domino: be
nedicite omnes spc dei dño.

Benedicite ignis ⁊ estus domino: be
nedicite frigus ⁊ estas domino.

Benedicite rores ⁊ pruina domino.
benedicite gelu ⁊ frigus dño.

Benedicite glacies ⁊ niues dño: be
nedicite noctes ⁊ dies dño.

Benedicite lux ⁊ tenebre dño: benedi

(called 'biting') of certain letters (for example, **b**, **d** and **p** with the letters **e** or **o**).

Another sophisticated series of gothic scripts, *quadrata*, have consistently angled baseline terminations (see upper right). The letter **i**, for example, was made in three distinct movements. That **i** shape was repeated as part of so many letters that it resulted in the 'picket fence' effect that is highly characteristic of later gothic scripts.

Fifteenth- and sixteenth-century versions of this script became even more compressed and heavier, giving rise to the description *textura*, meaning 'woven'. The baseline terminations were invariably made with elaborate, overlapping lozenge-shaped strokes (see illustration upper right). Here the narrowness, heavy weight and angularity of the letters are at their extreme. The rigidity of the uniformly spaced strokes enhances the overall decorative appearance but, to our modern eyes, makes it very difficult to read (see p. 62).

In Spain and Italy, rigidly angular gothic scripts were largely avoided. Instead, a book script evolved in the thirteenth century (continuing in places until the eighteenth century) that was truly gothic, but more rounded (see lower right). Gothic *rotunda* was widely used for liturgical texts, ranging from tiny, personal Books of Hours to enormous ceremonial manuscripts (often with musical notation).

This script has the texture and heavy appearance of the northern gothics, but it maintains the roundness of the Carolingian minuscule. The letters **d** and **h** take uncial form. Both forms of **r** and **s** are used (round **s** is reserved for word endings). The unusual form of **g** is unique to gothic *rotunda*. Like all gothic scripts, *rotunda* is written with a slanted pen angle, the square baseline terminations being completed with a corner of the pen.

A new gothic script emerged in Germany early in the sixteenth century, which we now call *fraktur* (indicating its 'broken' letter strokes, especially its curves). Although

OPPOSITE Gothic *prescissus*. Psalter, known as the *Queen Mary Psalter*. Manuscript book (parchment). London, *c*.1310–20. British Library: Royal MS 2 B vii, fol. 294v

ABOVE Gothic *quadrata*. English psalter, known as the *Gorleston Psalter*. Manuscript book (parchment). Gorleston-on-Sea (England), 1310–24. British Library: Add MS 49622, fol. 133r (detail)
BELOW Gothic *rotunda*. Book of Hours, known as the *Sforza Hours*. Manuscript book (parchment). Milan (Italy), 1490–1521. British Library: Add MS 34294, fol. 14v

In vigilijs mortuo[rum]

Ant. Placebo.

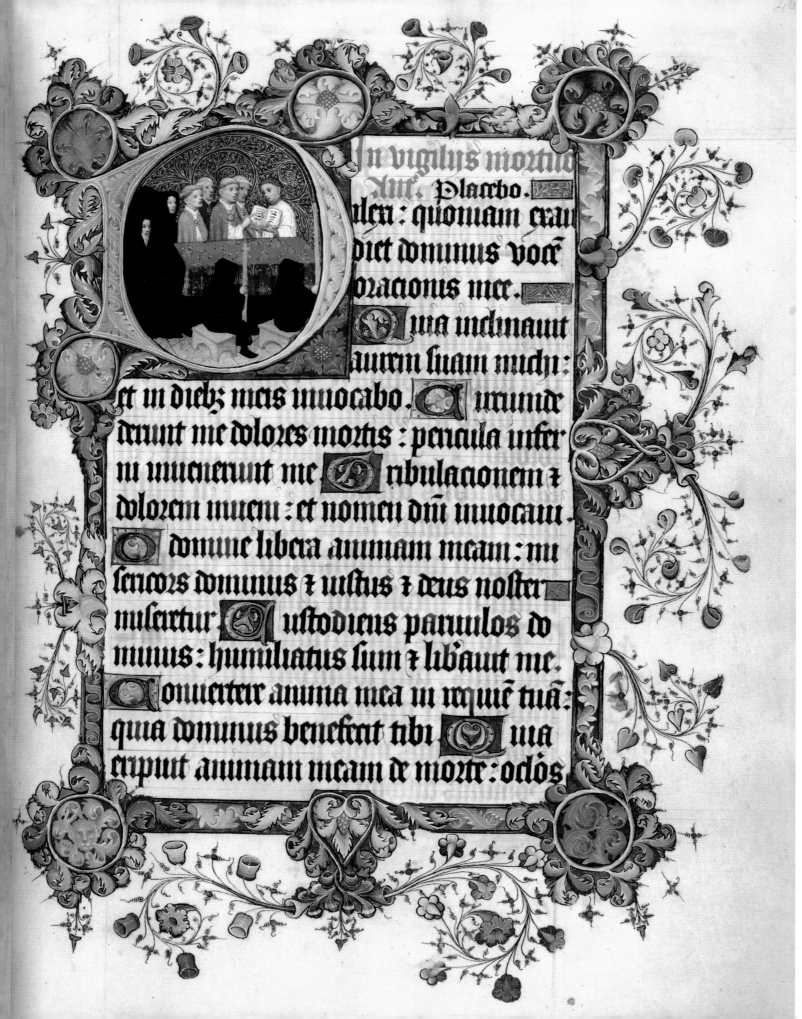

Dilexi: quoniam exau-
diet dominus vocē
oracionis mee. Quia inclinauit
aurem suam michi:
et in diebz meis inuocabo. Circumde-
derunt me dolores mortis: pericula infer-
ni inuenerunt me. Tribulacionem ꝛ
dolorem inueni: et nomen dñi inuocaui.
O domine libera animam meam: mi-
sericors dominus ꝛ iustus ꝛ deus noster
miseretur. Custodiens paruulos dominus: humiliatus sum ꝛ liberauit me.
Conuertere anima mea in requiē tuā:
quia dominus benefecit tibi. Quia
eripuit animam meam de morte: oclōs

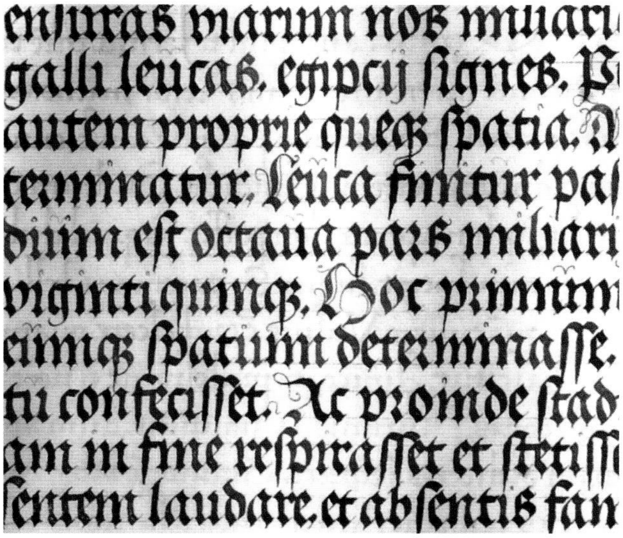

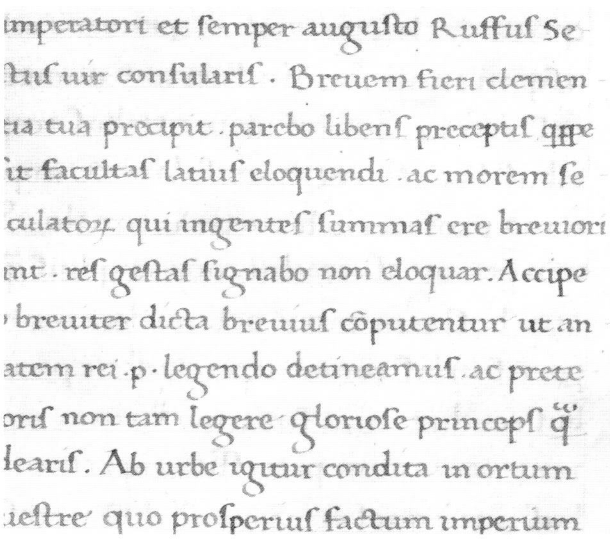

confined to areas of German-speaking influence, this would become an extremely important and well-used type style for hundreds of years.

As far as is known, the earliest form of *fraktur* is that shown in a book of 100 sample scripts skilfully handwritten by a monk of Augsburg, Leonhard Wagner (d. 1522), and dated 1508 (see above left). Six years later Emperor Maximilian I commissioned a new Prayer Book from the Augsburg printer Johannes Schönsperger (the Elder). Parts of this *Gebetbuch* were set in a type very similar to the *fraktur* scripts of Wagner. During the sixteenth century, other scribes and printers followed with their own versions of *fraktur* and this style of type became extraordinarily popular. *Fraktur* remained in use, in German-speaking countries, until the 1940s.

RENAISSANCE EUROPE

At the beginning of the fifteenth century Renaissance scholars and scribes began a reformation of scripts in a conscious effort to improve legibility and elegance in book design. That approach was deliberately in opposition to the prevailing gothic style of northern Europe.

Humanist scripts

Poggio Bracciolini (1380–1459) of Florence has been credited with the revival of the Carolingian minuscule script in the fifteenth century. The earliest known example is a manuscript copied by Poggio around 1402–3 of *De Verecundia* by Coluccio Salutati (1331–1406). Basing his minuscule on twelfth-century Italian manuscripts, Poggio undoubtedly worked in collaboration with others, like the scholar-politician Salutati and scholar Niccolò Niccoli (1364-1437).

Humanist minuscule was usually written small, with lengthened ascenders and descenders (see above right). Carolingian characteristics were retained: rounded **h**, long **s**, and **ct** and **st** ligatures. Later Humanist minuscule manuscripts included short **s** at word endings.

A quickly written form of Humanist minuscule was probably first devised by Niccolò Niccoli. Copies of classical texts made by this Renaissance scholar around 1420 were written in a new, more cursive script. This innovative book script, which we now refer to as italic, was written swiftly with narrow letterforms, a strong forward slant and some joining letters (see p. 64).

Formal versions of this cursive script were developed

OPPOSITE Gothic *quadrata*. Book of Hours, known as the *Bedford Hours and Psalter*. Manuscript book (parchment). London, 1414–22. British Library: Add MS 42131, fol. 46r
ABOVE LEFT Gothic *Fraktur*. *Proba Centum Scripturarum*, a model book of 100 scripts. Manuscript book (parchment). Augsburg (Germany), 1507–17. Augsburg, Ordinariatsbibliothek: Hs 85a, fol. 12v (detail)

ABOVE RIGHT Humanist minuscule. Rufus Festus, *Breviarium*. Manuscript book (parchment), in the hand of Dominicus Casii de Narnia. Florence? (Italy), *c*.1440. British Library: Burney MS 255, fol. 1r (detail)

dissputatum est. Reliqua deinceps
persequemur.

M. TVLLII CICE RONIS OFFICIO RVM. LIB. TERTIV

P SCI PIO NEM MAR CE FILI, EVM

Aphricanus.

Cato.

qui primum Aphricanus appellatus est
dicere solitum scripsit Cato: qui fuit
fere eius aequalis: numq̃ se minus &
ociosum ee q̃ cum ociosus: nec minus

by papal chancery scribes, like Ludovico Vicentino degli Arrighi (d. ?1527). The names they gave to these scripts varied from scribe to scribe. The writing master Bernardino Cataneo, whose Copybook was completed in 1545, distinguished two major types: *cancellaresca formata*, with rounded arches on **m** and **n** and seriffed ascenders; and *cancellaresca corsiva*, with narrower, more pointed arches and hooked ascenders.

THE PRINTED WORD

Up to the middle of the fifteenth century, almost every document and book was written by hand, letter by letter, and each was a unique artefact. With the 'invention' of a fully integrated system of printing from reusable type, the process of book-making was revolutionised. It enabled the much wider dissemination and preservation of knowledge and information, and made possible the multiplication of books with identical texts.

Documentary and circumstantial evidence is now overwhelmingly in support of the long-held traditional view that Johannes Gutenberg of Mainz (*c.*1400–1468) was indeed the first in Europe to print a substantial work by means of movable type (metal letters formed in a mould, which could be assembled into pages of text, used for printing, cleaned and then returned to a storage tray for further use).

The earliest printed documents closely imitated the form and style of contemporary manuscripts. They had the same codex structure (folded pages gathered into sections, and sewn together), the same page layout (often with narrow columns of text and wide margins) and in particular the same letterform style. Some were also printed on vellum (calfskin), which is excellent for writing, but difficult to print on.

Gothic types

The indulgence document printed by Gutenberg must be one of the very first to have been printed with movable type. More than thirty copies of this indulgence are known (see p. 105), and all were purchased between October 1454 and April 1455. Spaces were left in the printed text for the name of the donor and the date to be inserted by hand. Two styles of type were employed that match contemporary manuscript hands. The *textura* of the heading was the same as that used for the text of the 42-line Bible. The smaller gothic type is unusual, with its rounded form of **a** and **d**, square **g**, uncial **h**, and cursive forms of **f** and long **s**. Numerous ligatures were included following manuscript precedents.

Gutenberg's famous 42-line Bible (called this because most copies have columns of forty-two lines of text, and to distinguish it from a later Bible with just thirty-six lines) was the first substantial book ever printed in Europe, most probably completed before the end of 1455 (see p. 66).

Gutenberg selected fine vellum and paper, he developed an excellent ink for printing, and his typesetting and presswork gave a crisp, clear impression. The 42-line Bible was printed in a *textura* gothic letterform used in contemporary manuscripts, and followed other scribal practice by incorporating a multitude of abbreviations and ligatures. And like contemporary illuminated manuscripts, the Bible was sold unbound, as loose gatherings, with spaces left in the text for an illuminator to decorate and a rubricator to inscribe the coloured initials and headings.

Despite the fact that the *Mainz Psalter* was printed just two years after the completion of Gutenberg's Bible it was an extremely elaborate production (see p. 106). The intricately decorated initials used at the beginning of each Psalm were made up of several tightly 'nesting' metal engravings that would have been lifted out of the forme (the frame holding all the type together), each part inked separately and replaced for each printing. Even the text matter was printed in three colours. The

OPPOSITE Heading: Humanist roman capitals. Text: Humanist italic cursive. Marcus Tullius Cicero, *De Officiis*. Manuscript book, in the hand of Bartolomeo Sanvito. Rome, 1498. British Library: Harley Ms 2692, fol. 104v

OVERLEAF, LEFT Medieval gothic *textura quadrata* type. Latin Bible, known as the *Gutenberg Bible*. Printed book. Mainz (Germany): Johannes Gutenberg, *c.*1455. British Library: C.9.d.3-4, vol. 1, fol. 293r

OVERLEAF, RIGHT Italian Renaissance roman type. Marcus Tullius Cicero, *Epistolae ad Brutum*. Printed book. Venice: Nicolas Jenson, 1470. British Library: 167.f.11, fol. 1r

de hebreis voluminibꝫ additū noue-
rit eque usqꝫ ad duo pūcta · iuxta theo-
dotionis dumtaxat editionē: qui sim-
plicitate sermonis a septuaginta inter-
pretibus nō discordat. Hec ergo et vo-
bis et studioso cuiqꝫ fecisse me sciens.
nō ambigo multos fore · qui uel invi-
dia uel supercilio malent contemnere
et videre preclara quam discere: et de
turbulento magis rivo quam de pu-
rissimo fōte potare. Explicit prologꝰ.

Incipit liber ympnorū vl' soliloquiorū

Beatus vir qui nō
abiit in cōsilio im-
piorū: et in via pec-
catorum nō stetit:
et in cathedra pesti-
lēcie nō sedit. Sed
in lege domini volūtas eius: ⁊ in lege
eius meditabit die ac nocte. Et erit
tamq̄ȝ lignū quod plātatum est secus
decursus aquarū: qd fructū suū dabit
in tpe suo. Et foliū eius nō defluet: ⁊
omnia quecūqꝫ faciet prosperabūtur.
Non sic impii nō sic: sed tanq̄ȝ puluis quē proicit ventus a facie terre. I-
deo nō resurgūt impii ī iudicio: neqꝫ
peccatores in cōsilio iustorū. Quoniam novit dominus viā iustorꝫ: ⁊ iter
impiorum peribit. Psalmus david

Quare fremuerūt gētes: et ppli me-
ditati sunt inania? Astiterūt
reges terre et principes cōvenerunt in
unū: adūsus dnm ⁊ adūsus xpistū eiꝰ.
Dirumpamꝰ vincla eorꝫ: ⁊ piciamꝰ
a nobis iugū ipsorꝫ. Qui habitat ī celis irridebit eos: ⁊ dns subsānabit eos.
Tunc loquet ad eos in ira sua: ⁊ in
furore suo cōturbabit eos. Ego autem cōstitutꝰ sum rex ab eo super syon
montem sanctū eiꝰ: pdicās preceptū
eius. Dominus dixit ad me filius
meus es tu: ego hodie genui te. Po-
stula a me et dabo tibi gentes heredi-
tatem tuā: et possessionē tuā terminos
terre. Reges eos ī virga ferrea: ⁊ tan-
q̄ȝ vas figuli cōfringes eos. Et nūc
reges intelligite: erudimini q̄ iudica-
tis terrā. Servite dño ī timore: et ex-
ultate ei cū tremore. Apprehendite di-
sciplinam: ne quādo irascatur dominus ⁊ pereatis de via iusta. Cum ex-
arserit in brevi ira eius: beati omnes
qui confidunt in eo. Psalmus david
cū fugeret a facie absolon filii sui.

Domine qd multiplicati sunt qui
tribulāt me: multi insurgūt ad-
versum me. Multi dicūt anime mee:
nō est salus ipsi in deo eius. Tu aūt
dne susceptor meꝰ es: gloria mea ⁊ ex-
altās caput meū. Voce mea ad do-
minū clamavi: ⁊ exaudivit me de mō-
te sācto suo. Ego dormivi ⁊ soporatꝰ
sum: ⁊ exsurrexi quia dns suscepit me.
Non timebo milia populi circūdan-
tis me: exurge dne salvū me fac deus
meus. Quoniam tu pcussisti omes
adūsantes michi sine causa: dentes
peccatorū cōtrivisti. Domini est salꝰ:
et super populū tuum benedictio tua.
In finem in carminibus · psalmꝰ david

Cum invocarē exaudivit me deus
iusticie mee: ī tribulatione dila-
tasti michi. Miserere mei: et exaudi o-
rationē meā. Filii hominū usqꝫ quo
gravi corde: ut quid diligitis vanita-
tem et queritis mēdacium? Et scitote
quoniā mirificavit dns sāctum suū:
dns exaudiet me cū clamavero ad eū.
Irascemini et nolite peccare: qui di-
citis in cordibus vestris in cubilibus
vestris compungimini. Sacrificate
sacrificiū iusticie ⁊ sperate in domino:
multi dicunt qs ostendit nobis bona.

CLODIVS TRIBV. PLE. DESIGNATVS ualde me diligit: uel ut dicã ualde me amat: quod cum mihi ita psuasũ sit non dubito (bene enim me nosti) quin illum quoq; iudices a me amari. Nihil eĩm mihi minus hoĩs uidet: q̃ nõ respõdere in amore his a qbus prouocere. Is mihi uisus est suspicari nec sĩe magno meo qdẽ dolore aliqd a suis uel p suos potius iniquos ad te esse delatum: quo tuus aĩus a se ess& alienior. Nõ soleo mi Brute (quod tibi notum esse arbitror) temere affirmare de altero. Est enim periculosũ propter occultas hominum uoluntates multiplicesq; naturas. Clodii animum pspectũ habeo: cognitũ: iudicatũ. multa eius iudicia: sed ad scribendum non necessaria. Volo eĩm hoc testimonium tibi uideri potius: q̃ epistolã. Auctus Antonii beneficio est: eius ipsius beneficii magna pars a te est. Ita eum saluis nobis uellet saluũ. In eum autem locum rem adductam ĩtelligit (est enim ut scis minime stultus) ut utriq; salui esse nõ possĩt. Itaq; nos mauult. de te uero amicissime & loquit̃ & sentit. Quare si quis secus ad te de eo scripsit: aut si coram locutus est: peto a te etiã atq; etiã: mihi ut potius credas: qui & facilius iudicare possum: q̃ ille nescio qs & te plus diligo. Clodiũ tibi aĩcissimũ existima: ciuemq; talem: qualis & prudentissimus & fortuna optĩa esse deb&.

SCripta et obsignata iã epistola litteræ mihi redditæ sũt a te: plenæ rerum nouarũ maximeq; mirabiles: Dolobellam quiq; cohortes misisse in chersonesum. Adeone copiis abũdat: ut is qui ex asia fugere dicebatur: europam appetere conetur? Quinq; autem cohortibus quid se nam facturum arbitratus est: cum tu eo quĩque legiones optimum equitatum maxima auxilia haberes: quas quidem cohortes spero iam tuas esse: quoniã latro ille tam fuit demens: & tuũ consiliũ uehemẽter laudo: q nõ prius tuum exercitũ Apollonia Dyrrachioq; mouisti: q̃ de Antonii fuga audisti: Bruti eruptione: populi romani uictoria. Itaq; q scribis postea statuisse te ducere exercitũ in chersonesũ: nec pati scelera- tissimo hosti ludibrio esse imperiũ populi roãni: facis ex tua dignitate & ex re. pu. Quod scribis de seditiõe: quæ facta est in legione quarta de antoniis: quod dicam in bonam partem accipias: magis mihi probatur militũ seueritas: q̃ tua. Te beniuolentiã exercitus equitũq; expertũ esse uehementer gaudeo. De Dolobella ut scribis siquid habes noui facies

magnificent *textura* typeface was huge (equivalent to modern 42-point type), yet a colophon by the printers Peter Schoeffer (*c.*1425–1503) and Johannes Fust (*c.*1400–1456) at the end of the Psalter is at pains to emphasise that, although it has all the characteristics of a manuscript, it has been 'given the form artificially by means of a contrivance for printing and inscribing without the use of the pen'.

Roman types

In Mainz, printers had quite naturally taken current German manuscript hands as the basis for their typeforms, so it is not surprising that when the art of printing arrived in Italy, the typefounders there copied the handwriting of contemporary Italian manuscripts.

The letterforms of Nicolas Jenson of Venice (*c.*1420–1480) bear great similarity to the Humanist minuscule script of his day (see p.63, upper right), and are one of the earliest examples of what we now call roman type (see p. 67). His lower-case letters have an unmistakable calligraphic character. The strokes of a square-edged pen can be sensed underlying many of Jenson's forms, for example **a** and **d**, and seen in the natural scribal axis for the rounded forms, like **d**, **e** and **o**. His capitals follow classical roman inscriptional letter shapes and proportions. The design of Jenson's roman type has been greatly admired. It is perfectly legible for us (long **s** excepted) some 550 years after its creation.

Aldus Manutius (*c.*1451–1515) is one of the most honoured names in typographic history. He is considered to be *the* scholar-printer of the Italian Renaissance, although he probably never operated a printing press himself. Aldus moved to Venice in 1490, which was by then a flourishing centre of printing. He established a printing company with the primary aim of publishing Greek classics, but he also printed some magnificent books in Latin, employing delicate roman types cut for him by Francesco Griffo of Bologna (1450–1518). The books printed by Aldus were beautifully designed, with elegant typesetting and wide margins, and were sometimes decorated with engraved woodcuts of remarkable high quality (see p. 139).

However, they mainly attract our attention now because of Griffo's roman typeforms, which reached a peak of refinement that has hardly been improved upon to this day. His letters were lighter in weight than Jenson's and there seems less dependence on the pen strokes of the scribe. For better balance, his capitals were cut slightly shorter than the ascenders (a practice still followed today in more sophisticated font designs). These types of Griffo became the inspiration for the new types of the French printers Simon de Colines (d. 1546) and Robert Estienne (d. 1559), and even the famous punchcutter Claude Garamond (d. 1561), now often known as Garamont. In the 1920s, as a mark of esteem for the types used in the books of Aldus, the Monotype Corporation also issued 'copies' of them – Bembo and Poliphilus – and they are still available today as fonts for our laptops.

The first appearance of an italic typeface, in a work by Virgil published by Aldus Manutius in 1501, was a remarkable innovation (see opposite). The cutting of an italic letter (with its sloping letters and flowing extenders) to fit on the rectangular body of the metal pieces of type was in itself a technical triumph. But this type is tiny, less than 4 millimetres high. In the colophon of this book Aldus pays tribute to the engraver of the type, which was 'cut by the skilled hands of Francis of Bologna' (that is, Francesco Griffo).[3] Aldus deliberately used small italic type to condense the size of the book. He explained this was done 'so that you may carry it conveniently with you'. They were the very first printed 'pocket books'. Despite the size of the type Griffo manages to capture many of the cursive features of the Chancery script of the time. Ludovico Vicentino degli Arrighi, a professional scribe in the Vatican chancery

---

OPPOSITE Main text: Italian Renaissance italic type. Virgil, *Works*. Printed book. Venice: Aldus Manutius, 1501. British Library: C.19.f.7, fol. A2r

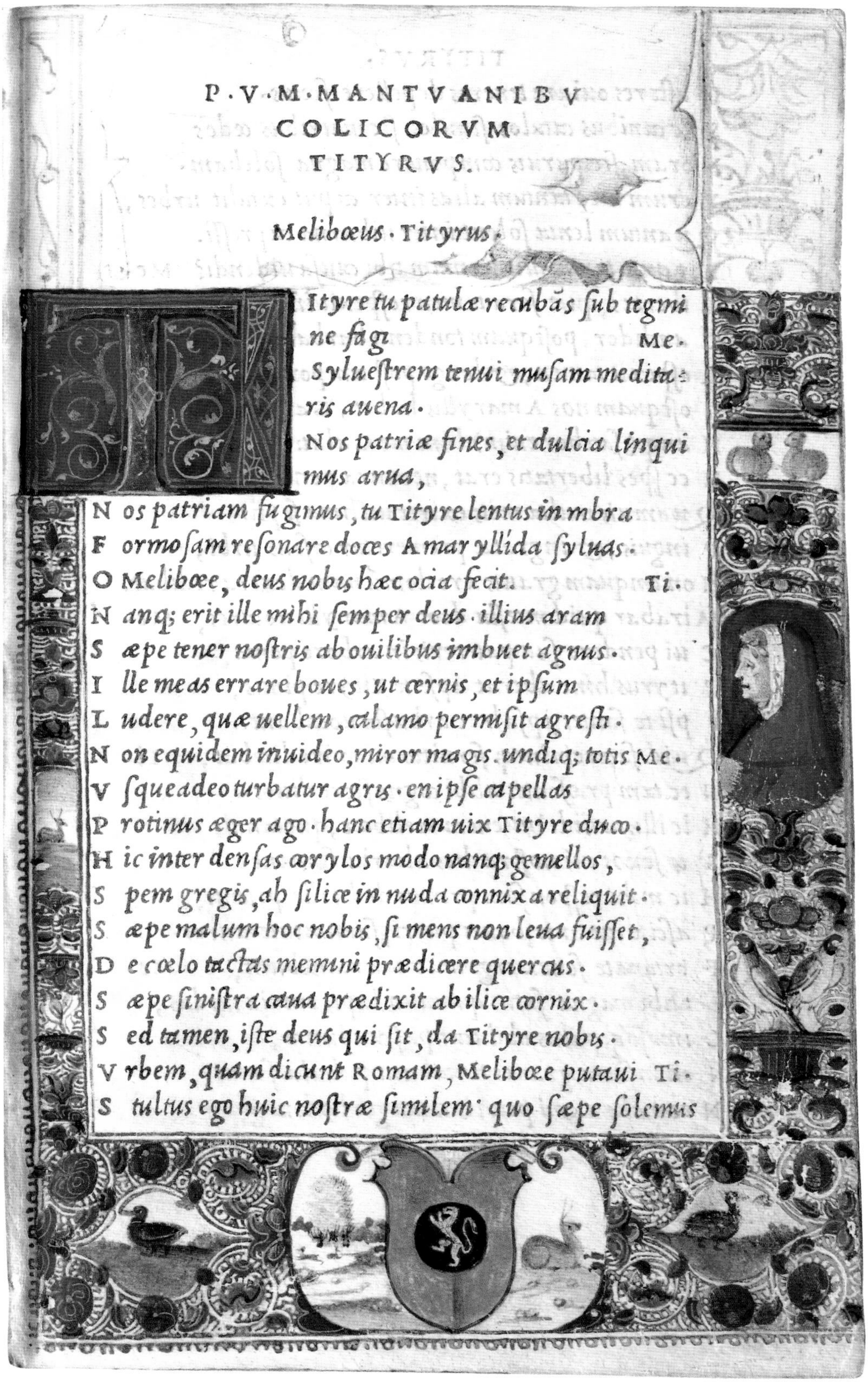

P·V·M·MANTVANI BV
COLICORVM
TITYRVS.

Melibœus · Tityrus.

Ityre tu patulæ recubãs sub tegmi
ne fagi   Me.
Syluestrem tenui musam medita-
ris auena.
Nos patriæ fines, et dulcia linqui
mus arua,
N os patriam fugimus, tu Tityre lentus in mbra
F ormosam resonare doces Amaryllida syluas.
O Melibœe, deus nobis hæc ocia fecit.   Ti.
N anq; erit ille mihi semper deus. illius aram
S æpe tener nostris ab ouilibus imbuet agnus.
I lle meas errare boues, ut cernis, et ipsum
L udere, quæ uellem, calamo permisit agresti.
N on equidem inuideo, miror magis. undiq; totis Me.
V sque adeo turbatur agris. en ipse capellas
P rotinus æger ago. hanc etiam uix Tityre duco.
H ic inter densas corylos modo nanq; gemellos,
S pem gregis, ah silice in nuda connixa reliquit.
S æpe malum hoc nobis, si mens non leua fuisset,
D e cœlo tactas memini prædicere quercus.
S æpe sinistra caua prædixit ab ilice cornix.
S ed tamen, iste deus qui sit, da Tityre nobis.
V rbem, quam dicunt Romam, Melibœe putaui Ti.
S tultus ego huic nostræ similem: quo sæpe solemus

PETIT CANON.

S'ils diſent, Vien auec nous, tendons des embuſches pour tuer: aguettons ſecretement l'innocent encores qu'il ne nous ait point fait le pourquoy. Engloutiſſons-les comme vn ſepulcre, tous vifs, & tous entiers cõme ceux ꝗ deſcendent en la foſſe. Nous trouuerons toute precieuſe cheuance, nous remplirons nos maiſons de butin.

ITALIQVE PETIT CANON.

Tu y auras ton lot parmi nous, il n'y aura qu'vne bourſe pour nous tous. Mon fils, ne te mets point en chemin auec eux: retire ton pied de leur ſentier. Car leurs pieds courent au mal, & ſe haſtent pour reſpandre le ſang.

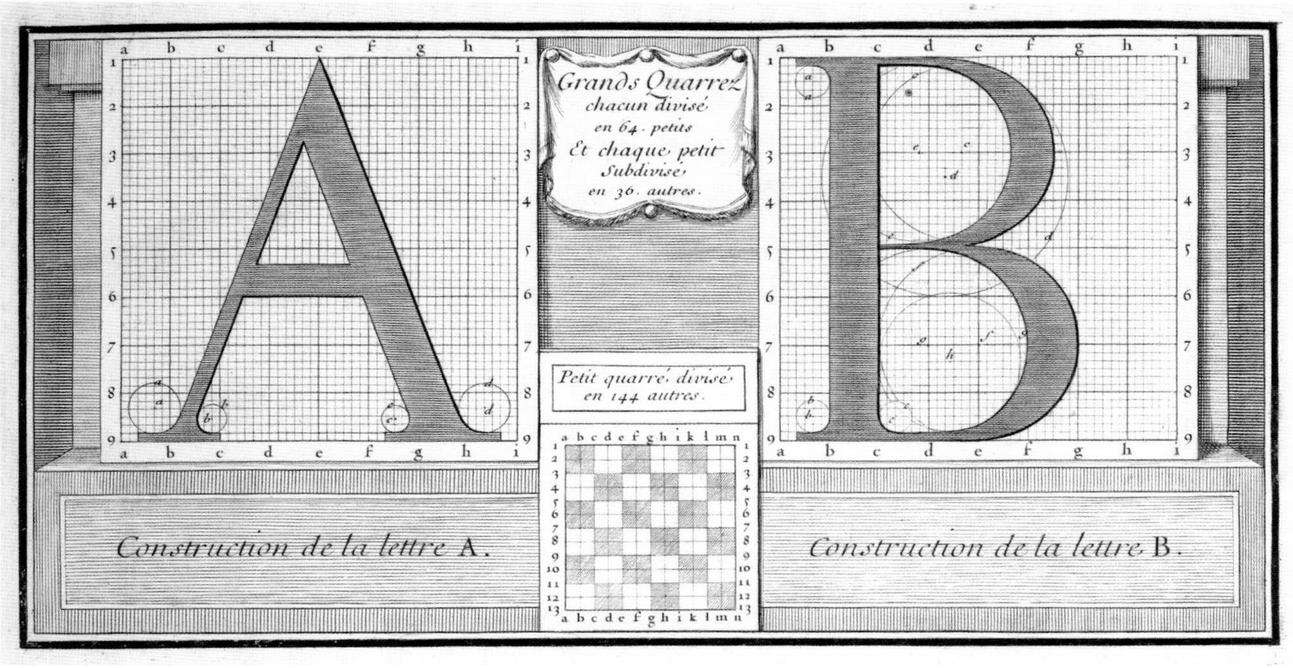

(the scribal office), also set up a printing establishment in Venice in 1522, later moving it to Rome. Arrighi printed more than thirty titles and, significantly, his beautiful italic types were a skilful adaptation of his own Chancery cursive calligraphy (see p. 127).

Innovations in roman type from the sixteenth century onwards

The italic types of Aldus were used as an independent alternative to roman letterforms. Later in the sixteenth century italics were employed as an auxiliary to roman type, occurring in the same book but usually in separate sections. Today, roman and italic types are normally designed together, and have a complete affinity with each other. They deliberately have the same body size, the same baseline, the same x-height and also have compatible weights.

In the *Introduction* to his type specimen, printed in 1621 (see opposite), Jean Jannon (1580-1658) says that he had created many typefaces in different sizes 'and *their* italics'(author's emphasis). Clearly Jannon's intention was to produce a compatible series of roman and italic types in a range of sizes, and he was probably the very first to do so. However, his letterforms deviate considerably from those of the previous, sixteenth, century. They are more delicate, quite light in weight and have a certain 'prickly' sharpness.

In 1693 a Commission of the French Académie des Sciences, under the direction of Jean-Paul Bignon, began to document 'all the techniques used in the practice of the arts'. They started with printing, 'the Art which preserves all others'.[4] One consequence of this study was a series of complex geometrically constructed letters all devised by the Commission and exquisitely engraved on copper plates by Charles-Louis Simonneau (1654–1727). The more complicated capitals are drawn on a grid of 8 × 8 squares, each subdivided 6 × 6, a total of 2,304 squares in all (see above). A further

OPPOSITE Baroque roman and italic type. The 1621 specimen of Jean Jannon, edited in facsimile with an introduction by Paul Beaujon. Printed book. London: Chiswick Press for Stanley Morison, 1927. British Library: C.98.f.13
ABOVE Charles-Louis Simonneau, *Designs for a series of geometrically constructed types.* Collection of engravings. Paris, 1695–1716. British Library: 61.g.15, Plate 11 (detail)

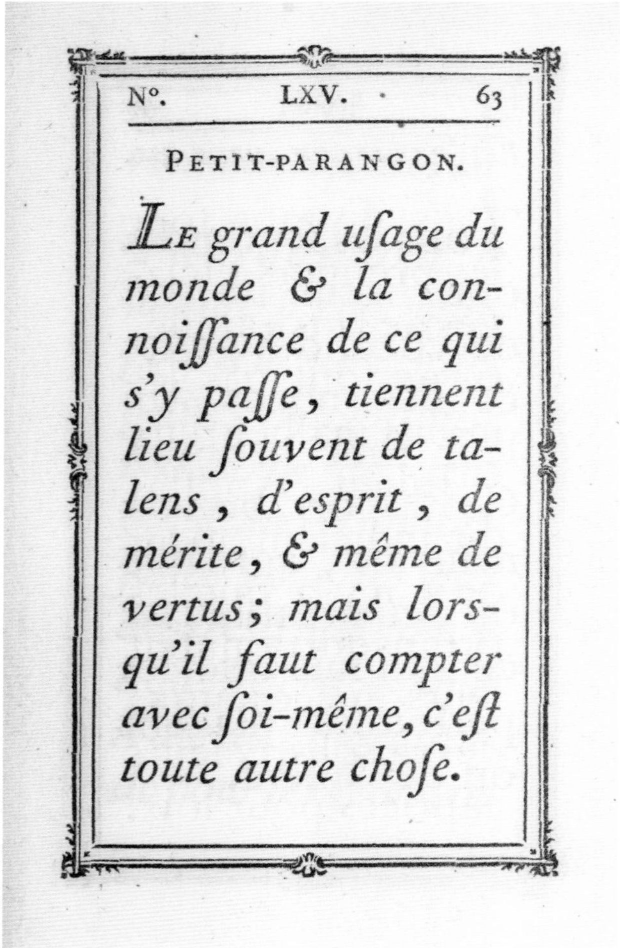
N°. LXV. 63

PETIT-PARANGON.

LE grand uſage du monde & la connoiſſance de ce qui s'y paſſe, tiennent lieu ſouvent de talens, d'esprit, de mérite, & même de vertus; mais lorsqu'il faut compter avec ſoi-même, c'eſt toute autre choſe.

development of the Commission's work was a series of printing types, intended for the exclusive use of the Imprimerie royale, initially cut by Philippe Grandjean (1666–1714), and eventually given the name *romain de roi* ('the King's roman'). Grandjean's type has a certain geometric flavour, and represents a deliberate move away from previous roman types (his letter strokes have a stronger thick and thin contrast, and all his curved letters have a horizontal axis), yet it has much more personality than the rather sterile geometric letters of the Commission.

ABOVE Neoclassical italic type. Pierre-Simon Fournier, *Manuel typographique*. Printed book. Paris: P.-S. Fournier, 1764–66. British Library: 51.b.22-23, vol. 2, p. 63

Pierre-Simon Fournier (1712–1768) was the most distinguished of a remarkable family of French type-founders. His typefaces were widely admired, but he was also an energetic scholar of printing. His type designs demonstrate a further move away from earlier styles, especially his italics (see left). He intended to reform the italics 'by bringing them a little closer to our style of writing'.[5] A writing manual by Alais de Beaulieu (d. 1689), *L'Art d'Ecrire* published in Paris in 1680, shows a script that is very similar to Fournier's italic type. In contrast to the 'pointed' chancery italics of Griffo and Arrighi, the italic of Fournier is rounder and perhaps less cursive. It has more of a 'sloped roman' character (like an upright letter that has been pushed forward to the right).

John Baskerville (1707–1775) claimed that his letterforms were original: 'My letters are not (one of them) copyed [*sic*] from any other; but are wrought from my own Ideas only.'[6] His italic type in particular has many features to be expected of an accomplished penman (he was a writing master earlier in his life); however, his punches were undoubtedly cut for him by his foreman, John Handy (d. 1792).

To achieve the best possible impression of his delicate types, Baskerville meticulously improved his paper, his ink and also his printing press, turning it into a precision instrument. And he never reused his types: 'It was Mr Baskervills [*sic*] custom to melt the Types when they had completed One Book so that he always printed with a new letter'.[7]

Most of his books were what we would now call 'limited editions'; many were sold by private subscription (see opposite). They were not only carefully printed, but also beautifully designed. The type, set in its hierarchy of various sizes, was allowed to 'speak for itself', without additional ornament. The lines of text were widely spaced and aligned perfectly with the lines on the reverse page, the capitals in the headings were

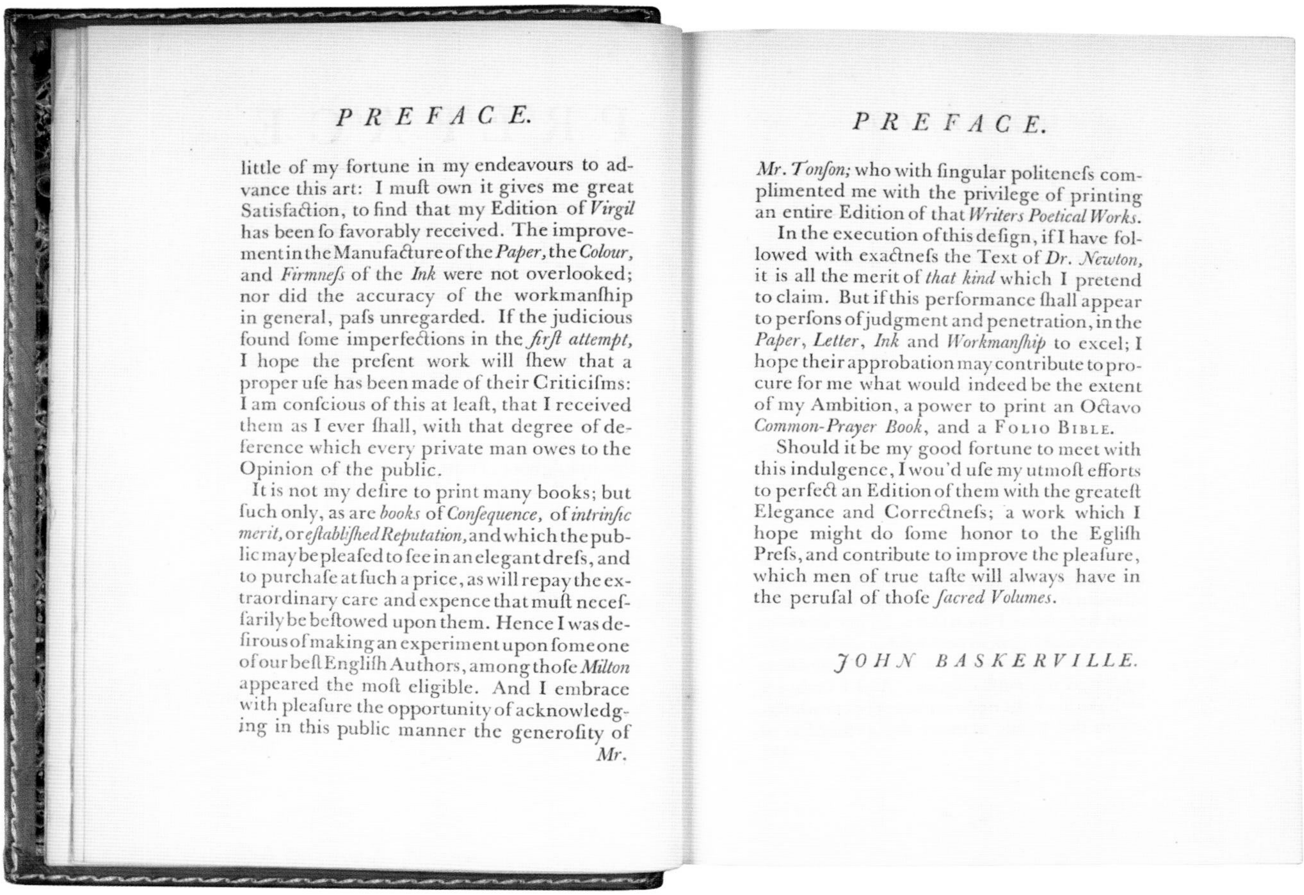

PREFACE.

little of my fortune in my endeavours to advance this art: I muſt own it gives me great Satisfaction, to find that my Edition of *Virgil* has been ſo favorably received. The improvement in the Manufacture of the *Paper*, the *Colour*, and *Firmneſs* of the *Ink* were not overlooked; nor did the accuracy of the workmanſhip in general, paſs unregarded. If the judicious found ſome imperfections in the *firſt attempt*, I hope the preſent work will ſhew that a proper uſe has been made of their Criticiſms: I am conſcious of this at leaſt, that I received them as I ever ſhall, with that degree of deference which every private man owes to the Opinion of the public.

It is not my deſire to print many books; but ſuch only, as are *books* of *Conſequence*, of *intrinſic merit*, or *eſtabliſhed Reputation*, and which the public may be pleaſed to ſee in an elegant dreſs, and to purchaſe at ſuch a price, as will repay the extraordinary care and expence that muſt neceſſarily be beſtowed upon them. Hence I was deſirous of making an experiment upon ſome one of our beſt Engliſh Authors, among thoſe *Milton* appeared the moſt eligible. And I embrace with pleaſure the opportunity of acknowledging in this public manner the generoſity of

Mr.

PREFACE.

Mr. Tonſon; who with ſingular politeneſs complimented me with the privilege of printing an entire Edition of that *Writers Poetical Works*.

In the execution of this deſign, if I have followed with exactneſs the Text of *Dr. Newton*, it is all the merit of *that kind* which I pretend to claim. But if this performance ſhall appear to perſons of judgment and penetration, in the *Paper*, *Letter*, *Ink* and *Workmanſhip* to excel; I hope their approbation may contribute to procure for me what would indeed be the extent of my Ambition, a power to print an Octavo *Common-Prayer Book*, and a FOLIO BIBLE.

Should it be my good fortune to meet with this indulgence, I wou'd uſe my utmoſt efforts to perfect an Edition of them with the greateſt Elegance and Correctneſs; a work which I hope might do ſome honor to the Egliſh Preſs, and contribute to improve the pleaſure, which men of true taſte will always have in the peruſal of thoſe *ſacred Volumes*.

JOHN BASKERVILLE.

letter spaced and the whole was enhanced with huge margins. Baskerville's books may be appreciated as self-conscious works of fine art.

The books and typography of John Baskerville were admired in Europe, but not especially in Britain. Jean-Pierre Fournier thought them 'veritable masterpieces of clarity',[8] and Giambattista Bodoni (1740–1813) in Parma emulated many of the features of Baskerville's printing in his own books. Bodoni excelled in all aspects of the printing process. He cut punches with exacting precision and provided a huge variety of weights, widths and x-heights within each size of type, as can be seen in his *Manuale Tipografico* of 1818. Bodoni's letterforms exemplify what used to be described as the 'Modern' group of historical types. The contrast between the thick and thin letter strokes is very strong, the axis on the curves is firmly horizontal and the serifs are mere 'hairline' strokes.

The page designs of Bodoni's books, clearly in imitation of Baskerville, have monumental simplicity (see p. 74). His books are larger than usual, but their immense margins, wide interlinear spaces, open letter spacing and deliberate lack of decoration all draw attention to his sharply printed types. Opening a Bodoni book can be breathtaking.

'Modern' typefaces, typified by those of Bodoni,

ABOVE Neoclassical roman and italic type. John Milton, *Paradise Lost*. Printed book. Birmingham (England): John Baskerville, 1758. British Library: 680.e.9

Pectore verba puer; nunc te melioribus offer.
Quo semel est imbuta recens, servabit odorem
Testa diu. Quod si cessas, aut strenuus anteis;
Nec tardum opperior, nec praecedentibus insto.

EPISTOLA III.

AD IVLIVM FLORVM.

Iuli Flore, quibus terrarum militet oris
Claudius Augusti privignus, scire laboro.
Thracane vos, Hebrusque nivali compede vinctus;
An freta vicinas inter currentia turres,
An pingues Asiae campi, collesque morantur?
Quid studiosa cohors operum struit? hoc quoque curo.
Quis sibi res gestas Augusti scribere sumit?
Bella quis, et paces longum diffundit in aevum?
Quid Titius, Romana brevi venturus in ora,
Pindarici fontis qui non expalluit haustus,
Fastidire lacus, et rivos ausus apertos?
Vt valet? ut meminit nostri? fidibusne Latinis
Thebanos aptare modos studet, auspice Musa?
An tragica desaevit, et ampullatur in arte?
Quid mihi Celsus agit? monitus, multumque monendus,

became the fashionable norm for nineteenth-century printing, despite their rather austere, even 'unfriendly', character. But commercial printers found that their thin strokes and hairline serifs wore out quickly and needed frequent replacement. The London-born punchcutter Richard Austin (1756–1832) designed new types in 1812 and 1813 for two Scottish foundries, in which, as he said later in an 'Address to Printers', he deliberately combined 'the utmost durability united with the most elegant shape'.[9] His types were still quite heavy in weight, but had rounded forms, carefully balanced thin strokes and robust, bracketed serifs. Austin's types were later imported into the USA where these 'Scotch Faces' were praised for their quality, durability and cheapness. So it was that types derived from those of Richard Austin became known as 'Scotch Roman'.

Typography in the nineteenth century was greatly influenced by the growing needs of commercial advertising for large, bold letters. Type foundries responded with heavy 'Egyptian' letters, which had square slab or slab-bracketed serifs similar to today's Linotype Clarendon or Monotype Rockwell fonts (see right). Alternatively, they gave outrageous thick-thin contrast to the 'Modern' letterforms and called them 'Fat Faces' (see p. 76, top left). A modern example would be Linotype Thorowgood. A third category was sans-serif letters, often confusingly labelled in America, 'Gothic' and in Britain, 'Grotesque' – hence ITC Franklin Gothic.

Letters without serifs have been used since the earliest times, but their incorporation into types for printing has been comparatively recent. The first sans-serif types, capitals only, are seen on a Caslon Company specimen, dating from about 1816. From the 1830s many such types appeared, used for posters, flyers and other ephemeral printing. Lower-case letters were added to the capitals in a proliferation of weights, widths, shapes and sizes. An 1865 specimen from the George Bruce New York Type Foundry even shows sans-serif types in small text sizes.

In the twentieth century, however, sans-serif typefaces grew in importance. Edward Johnston's innovative design for the London Underground Railway (1916) produced letters of great clarity and distinction. At first they were used for large station signs and posters, and later they were turned into types for printing. Johnston Sans remains the defining typeface of Transport for London to this day, although his letters have been modified several times since it was first released, most thoroughly in the 1970s by Eiichi Kono working for the design studio Banks and Miles, and then most recently in 2016 by Monotype (at London

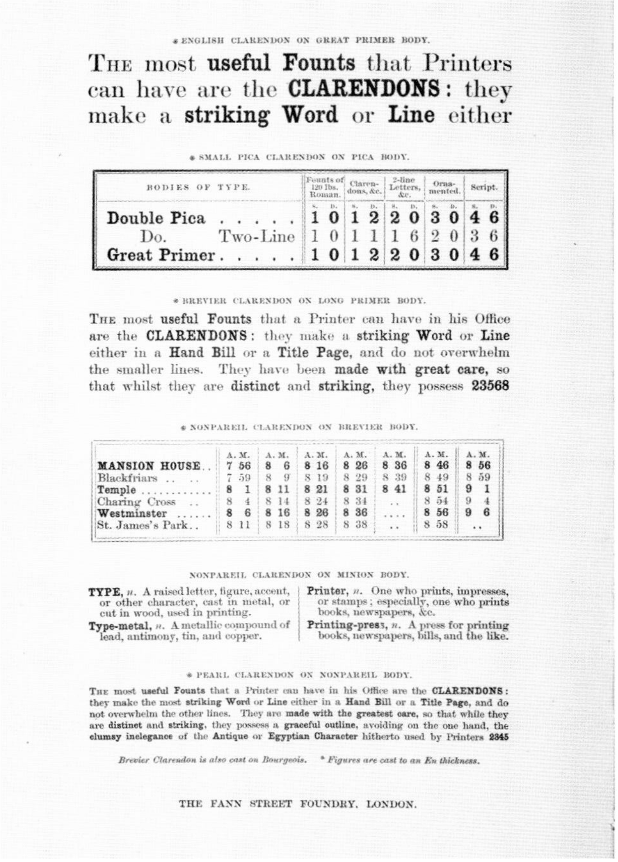

* ENGLISH CLARENDON ON GREAT PRIMER BODY.

THE most **useful Founts** that Printers can have are the **CLARENDONS**: they make a **striking Word** or **Line** either

* SMALL PICA CLARENDON ON PICA BODY.

BODIES OF TYPE.	Founts of 120 lbs. Roman.		Claren-dons, &c.		2-line Letters, &c.		Orna-mented.		Script.	
	s.	d.	s.	d.	s.	d.	s.	d.	s.	d.
Double Pica	**1**	**0**	**1**	**2**	**2**	**0**	**3**	**0**	**4**	**6**
Do. Two-Line	1	0	1	1	1	6	2	0	3	6
Great Primer	**1**	**0**	**1**	**2**	**2**	**0**	**3**	**0**	**4**	**6**

* BREVIER CLARENDON ON LONG PRIMER BODY.

THE most **useful Founts** that a Printer can have in his Office are the **CLARENDONS**: they make a **striking Word** or **Line** either in a **Hand Bill** or a **Title Page**, and do not overwhelm the smaller lines. They have been **made with great care**, so that whilst they are **distinct** and **striking**, they possess **23568**

* NONPAREIL CLARENDON ON BREVIER BODY.

	A. M.	A. M.	A. M.	A. M.	A. M.	A. M.	A. M.
MANSION HOUSE . .	**7 56**	**8 6**	**8 16**	**8 26**	**8 36**	**8 46**	**8 56**
Blackfriars	7 59	8 9	8 19	8 29	8 39	8 49	8 59
Temple	**8 1**	**8 11**	**8 21**	**8 31**	**8 41**	**8 51**	**9 1**
Charing Cross . .	8 4	8 14	8 24	8 34	. .	8 54	9 4
Westminster	**8 6**	**8 16**	**8 26**	**8 36**	. . . .	**8 56**	**9 6**
St. James's Park . .	8 11	8 18	8 28	8 38	. .	8 58	. .

NONPAREIL CLARENDON ON MINION BODY.

TYPE, *n.* A raised letter, figure, accent, or other character, cast in metal, or cut in wood, used in printing.

Type-metal, *n.* A metallic compound of lead, antimony, tin, and copper.

Printer, *n.* One who prints, impresses, or stamps; especially, one who prints books, newspapers, &c.

Printing-press, *n.* A press for printing books, newspapers, bills, and the like.

* PEARL CLARENDON ON NONPAREIL BODY.

THE most **useful Founts** that a Printer can have in his Office are the **CLARENDONS**: they make the most **striking Word** or **Line** either in a **Hand Bill** or a **Title Page**, and do not overwhelm the other lines. They are **made with the greatest care**, so that while they are **distinct** and **striking**, they possess a **graceful outline**, avoiding on the one hand, the **clumsy inelegance** of the **Antique** or **Egyptian Character** hitherto used by Printers **2345**

Brevier Clarendon is also cast on Bourgeois. * *Figures are cast to an En thickness.*

THE FANN STREET FOUNDRY, LONDON.

OPPOSITE Modern rational roman type. *Horace*. Parma (Italy): G. Bodoni, 1791. British Library: General Reference Collection 74.k.1, p. 289

ABOVE *Clarendon* Roman types. Sir Charles Reed & Sons, *Specimens of printing types, ornaments, &c.* London: Charles Reed, 1897. British Library: RB.23.a.28300

2 LINE GREAT PRIMER ROMAN, No. 4.

The Fann Street Letter Foundry will be carried on with the same spirit and liberality as before, by W. THOROWGOOD. £1234567890.

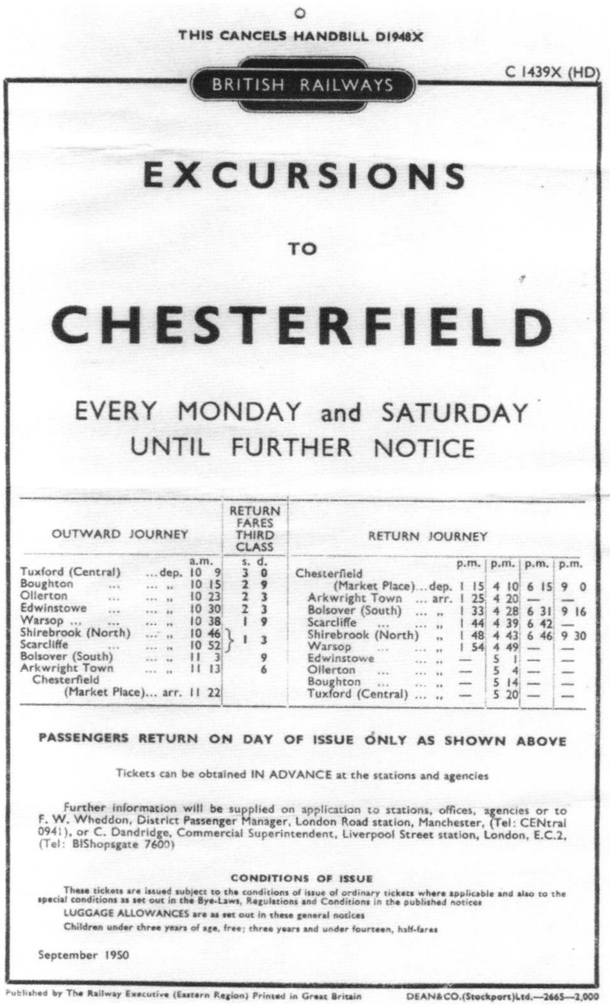
THIS CANCELS HANDBILL D1948X

C 1439X (HD)

BRITISH RAILWAYS

EXCURSIONS

TO

CHESTERFIELD

EVERY MONDAY and SATURDAY
UNTIL FURTHER NOTICE

OUTWARD JOURNEY		a.m.	RETURN FARES THIRD CLASS s. d.
Tuxford (Central)	...dep.	10 9	3 0
Boughton ...	... ,,	10 15	2 9
Ollerton ...	... ,,	10 23	2 3
Edwinstowe ...	... ,,	10 30	2 3
Warsop	... ,,	10 38	1 9
Shirebrook (North)	... ,,	10 46	1 3
Scarcliffe ...	... ,,	10 52	(1 3)
Bolsover (South)	... ,,	11 3	9
Arkwright Town	... ,,	11 13	6
Chesterfield (Market Place)...	arr.	11 22	

RETURN JOURNEY		p.m.	p.m.	p.m.	p.m.
Chesterfield (Market Place)...	dep.	1 15	4 10	6 15	9 0
Arkwright Town ...	arr.	1 25	4 20	—	—
Bolsover (South) ...	,,	1 33	4 28	6 31	9 16
Scarcliffe	,,	1 44	4 39	6 42	—
Shirebrook (North)	,,	1 48	4 43	6 46	9 30
Warsop	,,	1 54	4 49	—	—
Edwinstowe ...	,,	—	5 1	—	—
Ollerton	,,	—	5 4	—	—
Boughton	,,	—	5 14	—	—
Tuxford (Central) ...	,,	—	5 20	—	—

PASSENGERS RETURN ON DAY OF ISSUE ONLY AS SHOWN ABOVE

Tickets can be obtained IN ADVANCE at the stations and agencies

Further information will be supplied on application to stations, offices, agencies or to F. W. Wheddon, District Passenger Manager, London Road station, Manchester, (Tel: CENtral 0941), or C. Dandridge, Commercial Superintendent, Liverpool Street station, London, E.C.2, (Tel: BIShopsgate 7600)

CONDITIONS OF ISSUE

These tickets are issued subject to the conditions of issue of ordinary tickets where applicable and also to the special conditions as set out in the Bye-Laws, Regulations and Conditions in the published notices

LUGGAGE ALLOWANCES are as set out in these general notices

Children under three years of age, free; three years and under fourteen, half-fares

September 1950

Published by The Railway Executive (Eastern Region) Printed in Great Britain DEAN&CO.(Stockport)Ltd.—2665—2,000

ABOVE Fat face roman type. William Thorowgood, *A Specimen of the printing types in the Fann-Street Letter Foundery, London*. Printed catalogue. London: W. Thorowgood, 1828. British Library: 11898.cc.19
BELOW Sans-serif romans. Eric Gill. Gill Sans typeface. Railway Handbill. England, 1950

Transport's request) resulting in Johnston 100. It was a tribute to the centenary of the type and reintroduced several original Johnston features including a slightly more asymmetric lowercase g. Although his letters have been modified several times since, Johnston Sans remains the defining typeface of Transport for London to this day (see top right, p. 140).

Eric Gill (1882–1940), the letter carver and sculptor, was persuaded by the Monotype Corporation to design a sans-serif type. Gill Sans, which first appeared in 1928, was in essence a refinement of the Johnston letters (see lower left). Like Johnston, Gill based his capitals on classical roman forms, allowing much more variation of width in them than the earlier 'gothic' forms of sans, and the lower-case letters followed the proportions of traditional seriffed typeforms more closely.

At the same time in Germany, under the influence of the Bauhaus School, Paul Renner (1878–1956) designed a sans-serif with a more geometric look (see upper image, opposite). Futura has a small x-height, thus allowing long ascenders, and the letters give the appearance of being drawn with compass and ruler, although in fact their construction is much more subtle.

A third type of sans-serif emerged in the late 1950s. In 1957 the Swiss-born type designer Adrian Frutiger (1928–2015) refined and expanded the nineteenth-century 'gothic' style of sans. His typeface Univers was an extraordinary family of twenty-one fonts, providing a complete range of weights, widths and italics in a set of totally matching, compatible types, with a simple, unique coding system to identify each one (see lower image, opposite). A few years later a very similar font, designed by Max Miedinger (1910–1980), was issued by the Stempel foundry in Germany and called Helvetica. This became so frequently used by graphic designers, and in particular for public signage, that it earned the nickname of the 'Airport Type'. Helvetica was eventually adopted, in the late 1980s and early 1990s, as the

FUTURA light
NEXT MEETING
Graceful Methods
10 Point 25 A 48 a
STILE. MODERNISM IS NOT A WAYWARD
enthusiasm. It is not exemplified at its best in the many
grotesque creations that one encounters everywhere
ADVERTISING
Manufactured
12 Point 22 A 43 a
WHILE IT MIGHT BE CONSIDERED A
rebellion against conventions and traditions,
it is not totally destructive. In fact, this new
FURNITURE
West Indies
14 Point 19 A 37 a
FEELING WHICH HAS COME UPON
art has clearly demonstrated a worthy
and commendable seriousness of intent
Umbrella
16 Point 15 A 32 a
PROVINCIAL GARDEN SUBURB
Stock of Cheviots and Worsteds
Photography and Printing Presses
Sublime
18 Point 12 A 22 a
SPECIAL MOTION PICTURE
Resources of Central America
Mediterranean Cruises de Luxe
Roman
24 Point 8 A 15 a
EMINENT DESIGNERS
Graphic Arts Expositions

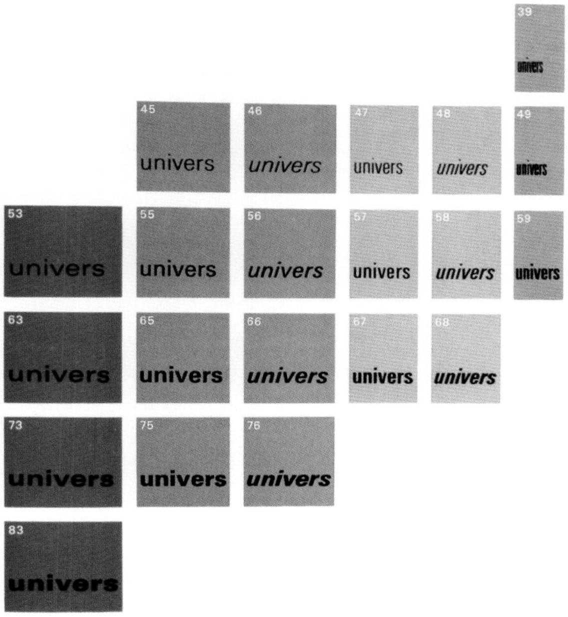
39
45 univers
46 univers
47 univers
48 univers
49 univers
53 univers
55 univers
56 univers
57 univers
58 univers
59 univers
63 univers
65 univers
66 univers
67 univers
68 univers
73 univers
75 univers
76 univers
83 univers

ABOVE Sans-serif romans. Paul Renner. Futura Light typeface specimen. Bauer Type Foundry, Frankfurt and New York, 1930s
BELOW Sans-serif romans. Adrian Frutiger. Univers chart issued by Deberny & Peignot (Paris), probably 1957 when Univers was launched.

standard letterform for the whole of the New York subway system. This replaced the previous bewildering visual chaos of numerous different lettering styles and colours, and provided order and clarity for passengers.

These typefaces proved extremely popular and paved the way for the greater acceptance of sans-serif types by graphic designers and typographers. Nevertheless, there is a long-standing resistance to setting long, continuous text in sans-serif fonts, so very few books can be found that are typeset throughout in sans-serif. There are exceptions, but they are usually books about typography. It is generally conceded that seriffed type is less tiring on the eyes and that the serifs themselves make the text easier to read.

Magazines and journals in the twenty-first century are not so reticent. Many employ sans-serif fonts for all their typesetting, and nowadays they do have plenty to choose from. One website, Identifont, currently lists 7,800 different sans-serif typefaces. Maybe sans-serifs are destined to define the type of the future?

However, we must remember that technology has revolutionised typography and printing in dramatic ways in recent years. Type is now designed both by traditional drawing and directly using software on the screen. Today type designs may have to be made to work across a variety of media from traditional print, to laptops and mobile phones, all using different resolutions. Type can be 'animated'. Some designs are made solely for use on electronic devices and morph to fit the format and space available. Given these new possibilities it is difficult to predict how the roman alphabet will evolve from here.

Focus One

CAXTON'S FIRST PRINTING OF *THE CANTERBURY TALES*

Adrian S. Edwards

The King's Library Tower stands at the heart of the British Library. Behind the security glass, its shelves are filled with antiquarian books originally collected by King George III. Dozens of these volumes might easily be described as treasures, but only a handful have the power to catch your breath as you appreciate their beauty and the stories they tell about the development of writing. Among these is William Caxton's first printing of *The Canterbury Tales* by Geoffrey Chaucer: the first major book printed in England.

William Caxton (*c*.1422–1492) was a businessman. He is often described as England's first printer, but in truth he was more of a publisher, editor and translator who employed skilled workers from continental Europe. He seems to have learned the art of printing while living in Cologne, before returning to his earlier base in Flanders and setting up a printing business there. His first publication was – perhaps unexpectedly – a work in English, the *Recuyell of the Historye of Troye* (1473–4).

The winter of 1475–6 saw Caxton leave Flanders and return to England. He set up shop within the precincts of Westminster Abbey and over the next two years issued a series of nine short pamphlets. At the same time he seems to have been working on his *Canterbury Tales*. No date is given in the final publication, but bibliographers are generally settled on 1476–7.

The high quality of workmanship in this 374-leaf volume suggests that Caxton was using the talents of skilled compositors and pressmen brought over from the continent. He also continued to use the same set of type that he had recently begun using in Flanders (known to printing historians as 'Caxton Type 2'). Its design was based on the kind of scribal handwriting seen in the best Flemish manuscripts, and known as a *bâtarde*. Researchers have established that it was created by Johan Veldener, a punch cutter and printer who is thought to have worked with Caxton on a variety of projects. Notable features visible on the first page shown here include two distinct forms of upper case **I** (both can be seen in Line 20) and flourishes on the tail of **d** when at the end of a word (as seen wherever a line begins *And*). Toward the end of Line 2, there is also an instance of the word *the* written with a small **e** above a character similar to a **y**. This is a late variant of the Anglo-Saxon character þ or *thorn*, still then used in English handwriting for the sound /th/. As with many other early publications, there are also small 'guide letters' indicating where a rubricator is expected to insert large red initials by hand.

It is not known how many copies of the book were printed, but a figure of around 600 seems probable. Thirty-eight copies survive in major research libraries around the world, but almost all are fragments often comprising just one, two or three leaves. The copy in George III's collection is one of the few that is still complete, which just adds to the magical quality of this particular volume.

OPPOSITE Geoffrey Chaucer, *The Canterbury Tales*. Printed book. Westminster (England): William Caxton, 1476-7. British Library: 167.c.26, fol. 2r

Whan that Apprill with his shouris sote
And the droughte of marche hath pcid ye rote
And badid every veyne in suche licour
Of whiche vertu engendrid is the flour
Whanne zepherus eke with his sote breth
Enspirid hath in every holte and heth
The tendir croppis and the yong sonne
Hath in the ram half his cours y ronne
And smale foulis make melodie
That slepyn al nyght with opyn ye
So prikith hem nature in her corage
Than longyng folk to gon on pilgremage
And palmers to seche straunge londis
To serve halowis couthe in sondry londis
And specially fro every shiris ende
Of yngelond to Cauntirbury thy wende
The holy blissful martir forto seke
That them hath holpyn when they were seke
And fil in that seson on a day
In Suthwerk atte tabard as I lay
Redy to wende on my pilgremage
To Cauntirbury with devout corage
That nyght was come in to that hosterye
Wel nyne & twenty in a companye
Of sondry folk be aventure y falle
In feleship as pilgrymys were they alle
That toward Cauntirbury wolden ryde
The chambris and the stablis were wyde
And wel were they esid atte beste

A woman is best pitte
full than a man more
Envious then a serpent
and mor malycious
then a tyrant more
deceytfull then ye devyl

Anthony

[illegible]

3

WRITING TOOLS AND MATERIALS

EWAN CLAYTON

透火焙乾

From the first human marks on the walls of caves, or scored lines on pieces of bone, how was it that a simple repertoire of forms became the sophisticated writing systems we know today? This chapter approaches that question by looking at four different strategies for mark-making: incising or scratching into surfaces, writing with ink, printing, and digital mark-making. It concludes with a more theoretical discussion about the roles that tools and materials play.

Incising and scratching

While the oldest writing from many cultures is incised and scratched, one does not know to what extent this is merely a matter of survival. Could there have been less durable materials employed at the same time? Contemporary with the first rock engravings in Egypt we find forms similar to those later used in hieroglyphs painted with brush and coloured clay on pottery vessels from Upper Egypt. Alongside some of the early oracle bone inscriptions in China there are a few fragments of writing that appear to have been written on the bones with brush and ink. Could this ink calligraphy go back further into Chinese history?

It is clear we have lost much material. Glimpses of painted lettering on stone monuments from the Greek world indicate that many blank panels and pediments may once have held painted inscriptions. Fragments of painted roman lettering from Pompeii and Herculaneum show this may also be true of the Roman world. In Central America, records of the Spanish conquistadores reveal that large numbers of handwritten and painted multi-leaved books existed; today there are just four late survivals.

It seems likely that the earliest material that humans used to write upon was clay: the simplest of substrates and needing little modification before use. It was readily available in Mesopotamia, the 'land between two rivers', where alluvial silts had made a wide fertile plain. Damp clay could be formed into a tablet in the hand and then drawn into with a stylus. The tablets could be baked to make them permanent. The consensus is that the first stylus was probably a cut reed. Close examination of some of the surfaces of incisions seems to support this, with one side appearing smooth (as if the outer edge of the reed formed this facet) and the other showing rough striations (as if the internal grain of the reed's stem had been exposed). Furthermore, the rounded shape of some signs (for example, for the number ten) and other scooped shapes would have been easily created by simply upending a reed and impressing its circular section into the clay.

From around 2900 BC pictograms became more stylised. This was encouraged by the adoption of a slightly different technique for writing. Instead of drawing the edge of a pointed reed through the clay to make incised lines, scribes began to use the quicker and cleaner process of impressing the long edge of the reed directly into the clay, producing the wedge-shaped marks that came to be known as 'cuneiform' (from the Latin *cuneus*, meaning wedge). Over the next 600 years, curves were eliminated and the direct connection between the look of symbols and their original object of reference was lost. Sometime during this same period cuneiform came to be read left to right in horizontal lines and in keeping with this the signs were rotated by 90 degrees anti-clockwise. This change seemed to make pressing the signs into the clay tablet easier. Both hands worked continuously, rotating the reed and the tablet into different orientations as the characters were built up. The tablet was not held fixed in one position. The movement from a distance might look like the practised manipulation of a Rubik's cube.

The script also acquired a self-aware aesthetic during this period and this continued into the second millennium in formal stone inscriptions such as the law code of Hammurabi of *c.*1754 BC. Here the use of contrasting

PREVIOUS PAGE Sheets of handmade paper being dried. Illustration of papermaking from Song Yingxing, *Tian gong kai wu*. Facsimile of a 1637 print. Shanghai: Zhonghua shu ju, 1959. Volume 2 (of 3) pp. 76–77. British Library: 15226.b.19

movements in the region. Nonetheless, clay tablets have proved durable documents: fire, which destroys paper, simply hardens the clay and hundreds of thousands of the tablets still survive today.

From 3200 BC onwards Egyptian hieroglyphs appeared in an incised form on small ivory tablets used as labels for grave goods in the pre-dynastic tomb of King Scorpion at Abydos and then in low relief on ceremonial cosmetic palettes, such as the Narmer Palette. Recent discoveries by Yale archaeologist John Darnell of large-scale incised ceremonial scenes at the rock art site of El-Khawy in Egypt date to around 3250 BC. They show affinities with these early hieroglyphic forms, and some of the rock-carved signs are nearly half a metre in height.

line lengths in the make-up of characters elevated the writing from simple utility into an artistic practice with rhythmical patterning that was both visual and tactile.

Over the centuries the gradual process of abstraction, a phenomenon shared with many writing systems, led to marks that were schematically simpler and capable of great compression. Experiments with making multifaceted tablet shapes produced almost sculptural writing artefacts, such as tall octagonal standing cylinders, that could contain more substantial lengths of text. Later in history, during the reign of the Assyrian King Ashurnasirpal II (reigned 883–859 BC), cuneiform was used in large architectural displays of writing across low-relief stone sculpture in palace murals, a practice that survived until at least the end of the Assyrian Empire some 250 years later. Among the best preserved are those from Nineveh (modern-day Mosul, Iraq) in the care of the British Museum in London. The use of cuneiform, which had been adopted for a number of languages in the Middle East, began to decline from the sixth century BC, overtaken by significant cultural

ABOVE Sumerian administrative record in cuneiform, Third Dynasty of Ur. Clay tablet. Mesopotamia, *c.*2100–2000 BC. British Museum: 1895,0329.2
RIGHT 18th Dynasty Egyptian stela. Carved limestone. Egypt, *c.*1400–1351 BC. British Library: Talbot Stela 4

Over the next 500 years hieroglyphs would become one of the great inscriptional writing systems of world history. They were carved in low relief; modelled in plaster; sunk *en creux* into stonework, where they are usually infilled in blue or green paint; drawn in silhouette, where they are painted in solid black or blue; or cut deeply with finely carved and chased interiors.

The chased writing on the soft gold interior coffin of Tutankhamun (*c*.1342–1327 BC) ripples slightly in the direction in which the engravers' tools moved. One can see how a form was carved (that is, stroke number, order and direction) and from this one can understand that even the most formally executed hieroglyphs have not just a visual appeal but also, to the maker, a tactile and choreographic sense of flow.

Probably because writing often appears in the context of carved and painted narrative pictures, hieroglyphs became even more carefully painted and coloured as time went by. Exquisite polychrome colouring can be found in the tombs of Ramesses I, II and III of the Eighteenth Dynasty (1550–1295 BC). The Theban tomb of Rekhmire, vizier to Tuthmosis III and Amenhotep II of the same dynasty, has some of the most exquisitely coloured inscriptions of any in the history of the world's writing systems. In these craftsmen's hands writing had become an art form.

The first evidence of alphabetical writing is also inscriptional and dates to around 1850 BC in graffiti on the cliffs within the Wadi el-Hol valley in Egypt. Similar forms occurred in the Sinai Peninsula some 200 years later and they appear to have provided the basis for shapes for what came to be known as the Phoenician alphabet, which today we also find in carved inscriptions, moulded in clay or cast in metal. By 1100 BC a version of this alphabet had moved to Cyprus, where it displaced an earlier system, and then to Greece; from Greece it arrived in the Italian Peninsula around 800 BC.

In China the first examples of incised oracle bone script date to 1300–1050 BC. Most of the signs reflect objects drawn from the natural world. From about 1100 BC onwards a new style of script known as Bronze script appeared, incised and cast into bronze vessels and weaponry. The lines are lively and seem to reflect the freedom of a brush more than the constraints of an inscription. Yet inscriptional influence returned around 500 BC with the development of a formally majestic group of writing styles that would become known as seal scripts, due to their widespread use in seals, characterised by a more even distribution of space throughout the characters. Small seal script was adopted and standardised under the First Emperor (221–210 BC).

Another application of the impressed or incised approach to writing was the use of wax tablets. Entering the Greek and Roman world via Egypt they became one of the most commonly available writing materials, with the last recorded use coming from France in the nineteenth century. The tablets were fashioned from wood (or precious materials like ivory) and carved out with a recessed surface filled with beeswax mixed with a small amount of vegetable material (10 per cent olive oil works) to make the surface more pliable. If you try writing in 100 per cent beeswax you will soon find that the hard, whitened shavings kicked up by the stylus get in the way of legibility. This form of tablet was the notebook of the ancient and medieval world; they were employed for drafting, taking down dictation, drawing up accounts, making lists and also as exercise books for learning to write. The nature of these messages and the easily marked writing surface seems to have encouraged a less formal approach to writing. If written on and then sealed, wax tablets could serve as legal documents, but they could also be reused time and again. The pointed stylus of metal or bone usually had the non-writing end splayed out in a spatulate form. When heated, it smoothed the wax and erased the writing. It is most likely that the idea of the book form first came from

these tablets that were often hinged together with thongs to make a collection of closely fitting pages. Frescos from the ruins of Pompeii of individuals holding wax tablets reveal a lost world of gestures associated with the writing stylus, held poised in the hand or pressed, cool, against one's lips.

The consensus among scholars is that the majority of carved Greek and Roman lettering was written onto the stone first with brush and paint and then incised. Most incised work relies on light introducing a shadow to make the writing legible; sometimes pigment is rubbed into the incision (as seen in writing made with a sharp stylus on palm leaves from the Indian subcontinent). The letters may also be painted once carved, as in Roman lettering.

ABOVE Coloured inscription from the 18th Dynasty. Painting of the tomb of Rekhmire, by Charles K. Wilkinson. Thebes (Egypt), 1479–1425 BC. Tempera on paper. 1928. Metropolitan Museum of Art: 30.4.79

Until the invention of tungsten-tipped chisels in the mid-twentieth century, carving in stone with mallet and chisel involved much sharpening of the chisel's faceted edge, which was easily blunted. Stone-carved inscriptions continue to flourish today for use as foundation stones, in naming buildings, as decorative panels in gardens and domestic interiors, and for the creation of individual memorials. Stone, a permanent durable writing surface, has been pressed into service by the majority of the world's writing systems.

The stone inscriptions of Mesoamerica are the only inscriptions from one of the four originators of writing where forms were usually low relief, with characters stacked tightly like grains of corn on the cob. Rarely does stone-worked writing appear as three-dimensional as it

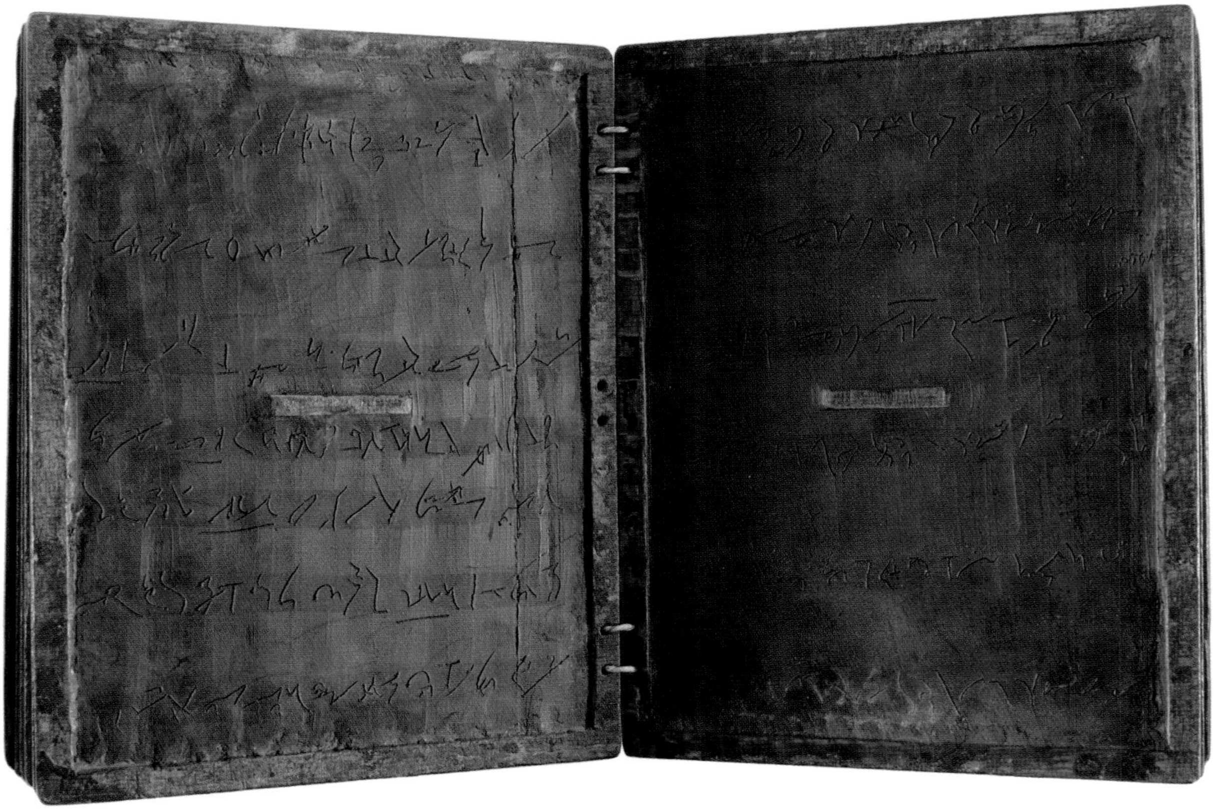

ABOVE Wax tablets with tachygraphic symbols and memoranda in Greek concerning haulage. Egypt, 3rd century BC. British Library: Add MS 33270
BELOW Fragment of a Greek inscription on augury. Carved marble. Ephesus (Turkey), 6th century BC. British Museum: BM 1867,1122.44
OPPOSITE Terentius Neo and his wife with scroll and wax tablet. Fresco. The House of Terentius Neo. Pompeii (Italy), AD 55–79. Museo Archeologico, Naples

does in the Mayan tradition, although, in hard stones such as granite, raised three-dimensional lettering is often more easily read (when using alphabetically derived shapes) than recessed forms.

Another great tradition of three-dimensional and low-relief letterforms comes from the Islamic world. Architectural inscriptions in Arabic, Ottoman and Persian are frequently made as carved ribbon-like structures sitting proud of recessed backgrounds. A simple example for Arabic is the façade of the Qula'un tomb complex in Cairo dating to 1283–5. Foliated and floriated Kufic script styles of writing flourished as relief inscriptions and stucco mouldings of great beauty and can often be seen in funerary inscriptions and madrasas: for example, the bordered Kufic inscription from the Nizamiyya madrasa at Khargird (1072–7) now in the Iran Bastan Museum in Tehran, and the first known inscription in Persian found inside the tomb at Safid Buland in Uzbekistan (1055–60). No tradition excels the Islamic in its profusion of inscribed objects.

Ink, pens, brushes and writing surfaces

Writing with ink appeared first in Egypt, almost as early as the incised hieroglyphs (3200 BC). Some have spoken of two media for writing evolving contemporaneously: carving in stone and writing with ink on materials like ivory, textiles and papyrus scrolls. Ink would become the most common way of making writing and its use would spread throughout the globe.

Essentially there are two kinds of ink. The first is a staining ink that penetrates the writing surface and dyes it: indigo, walnut inks, inks based on aniline dyes, many modern fountain pen inks and the inks within fibre-tip pens are examples. The second is ink made from a pigment, in other words coloured particles of material that lie on the surface of the 'paper' and do not go into the surface or dye the fibres. These coloured particles would rub off the surface when dry unless they are mixed with some sort of glue that will fix them in place, what an artist would call a medium. Traditionally, inks in most cultures were combined with glue made from

animal hide, a type of gelatine. Later other gums, such as gum arabic, were adopted. Eggs were another medium used for writing with coloured pigments: the yolk for warm-coloured writing fluids such as vermilion, and the white of egg (whipped up and left overnight when it re-liquefies into 'glair') for cooler colours. The red dots around letters in the *Lindisfarne Gospels* from Anglo-Saxon Britain still gleam, made glossy by the addition of egg yolk to the vermilion.

Iron gall inks are some of the most ancient inks that were used in Europe. They are made by treating salts of iron with tannic acid; the effect is to precipitate out small particles of iron. The source for the tannin can be various but the most common is oak galls, the round berry-like shapes that oak twigs exude around burrowing parasites. The galls from Aleppo were once the most highly prized having nearly 80 per cent tannin content (British galls have less than 40 per cent). A 1540 recipe from the Italian calligrapher Giovanni Battista Palatino (*c.*1515–*c.*1575) produces an excellent dark ink:

> Soak 3 ounces of galls coarsely crushed in 1 5/8 pints of rainwater. Leave in the sun 1 or 2 days. Add 2 ounces of copperas [iron sulphate, also known as green vitriol], finely crushed, stir well with a fig stick. Leave in the sun for 1 or 2 days. Add 1 ounce of Gum Arabic and leave one day in the sun.[1]

While iron gall ink can give a very fine line, unfortunately it fades over time to a lighter brownish colour and, because it is acidic, eats into the paper.

OPPOSITE Relief inscription in Arabic. Wooden screen. The Mausoleum of Sultan Qala'un. Cairo (Egypt), 1280s
ABOVE Anglo-Saxon gospel book, known as the *Lindisfarne Gospels*. Manuscript book (parchment). Lindisfarne (England), *c.*700. British Library: Cotton MS Nero D IV, fol. 19r (detail)

A more reliable ink is to be found across Asia, in India, China and Japan, based on carbon mixed with a little gum or gelatine. The black carbon particles are obtained from catching the soot given off by the flame of a burning wick floating in oil, or from the combustion of resinous pinewood. Usually used in a solid cake form, these ink sticks are reconstituted by being ground down with water on a smooth stone. Carbon inks made from similar sources were also known in the ancient world and medieval Europe. Carbon is the most stable element in the universe and so these inks will never fade.

Some of the purest carbon inks originate in Japan. Ninety per cent of the ink still manufactured comes from Nara, the ancient capital, where ink production first began in the seventh century. Only a few companies continue to make the dried sticks by hand. The carbon particles are mostly obtained by burning vegetable oils: rapeseed, linseed or, rarely, camellia oil; the highly prized resinous roots of the red pine were also used before the tree became scarce. These inks are available in all the shades of black one can see in a starling's wing, from purplish brown to cool blue. The soot is often combined with a scent – usually camphor, from ancient trees that still grow in many temple grounds – and *nikawa*, a glue made from animal hide. The ink at this stage is like a ball of dough and it is kneaded by being trodden underfoot. Small balls of the dough are torn off, weighed and pressed into engraved pearwood moulds. Once extracted from the mould, the ink sticks are slowly dried in ash from rice husks, to prevent them cracking, and are cured for a year or more before being released onto the market.

Writers can develop strong attachments to the materials they use for writing. Here is the Japanese calligrapher artist Toko Shinoda (b. 1913), now into her

ABOVE Calligraphy set. Ōsaka region (Japan), mid-20th century. Private collection second century, expressing the depth of her relationship with her inks:

> Once again, deliberating on the water and ink that are the materials of my work, I see them as the two extremes: water and fire ... The ink that results from collecting the final residue of the flame seems to me the spirit, the incarnation, the sublimation of fire. I feel in the ink the ultimate stage of life and matter. Indeed as I quietly grind the old ink known as 'highest smoke' against an inkstone, I have a strange, somehow sensual impression. It is as if the life in the highest reaches of the extinguished flame were being conveyed to me. I feel the power of the physical, the delicacy of the particles, the elegance of the order, but, too, I feel the presence of something beyond the physical. The ink that is the ultimate manifestation of flame is brought back to life by the opposite extreme, water. I may seem to exaggerate when I say this is an emotional awareness, but I somehow think that we who work with water and ink should be more in awe of them.[2]

From the sublime to the prosaic, ink research for modern pens is ongoing. The development of viscous ink used by László Bíró for his pen design of the late 1930s and '40s set off a completely new direction in pen manufacturing, leading to the many different disposable pens of today. Ink, its colours and textures (think of gels and glitter), is one of the unique selling points to which every manufacturer aspires. Pen and ink technologies, far from declining, have snowballed in recent decades.

✧ ✧ ✧

Reeds are one of the oldest writing instruments and they have been employed for several thousands of years in the Middle East, the Indian subcontinent and Europe. In India strips of bamboo have also been used. The reed that has the highest reputation is the common reed, *Phragmites australis* (once known as *Phragmites communis*), which comes from Iraq. Between cutting and distribution, when in times past it was sweated in the dark for many months, it turned a deep chocolate colour; for a good reed pen one looks for a dense internal structure and a straight shaft.

For Arabic, Ottoman, Persian and Urdu calligraphy the reed is cut with a strong, sharp knife and trimmed on an ivory cutting plate (a *maqta*); the nib is cut left oblique, the precise angle varying according to the style you wish to write. The basic Arabic script is made from twenty-nine letter shapes. Vowel marks are written above or below the consonant that precedes the vocalised vowel. There is a sign that indicates the absence of a vowel, and also diacritical marks that distinguish between otherwise identical letters. Diacritical marks and vowels are often produced just with the tip of the pen. The script is written from right to left; the nib slant is cut specifically to aid this direction of movement. In certain Muslim areas of China, varieties of Arabic are written with a brush.

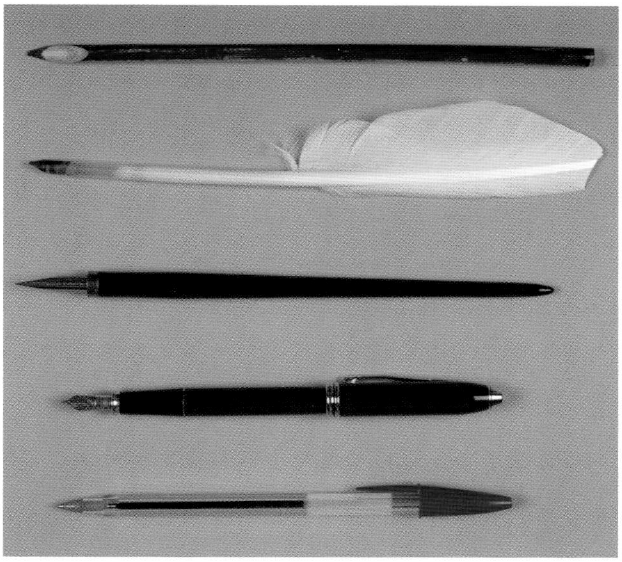

ABOVE Selection of pens: reed pen, goose quill, pointed metal nib in penholder, fountain pen and BIC Cristal ballpoint.

sicut ipsa vinea benedicta — semper est infirmius

u u intenteam dicu nobis

Ego intentem

Ego intentendiu nobis expedit nobis

expedit nobis

Ego intentem

Ego ego intentendiu

intendiu

nobis sup

milla pos fecte tem in pro incenta medie

nullit ves est

dominus noster

C. X

Si vero ... distinctione pulsantur sunt fan anglm hemem z
congresurus sunt videlicet non vincere ... ...
sunt per accepta ... imaginem ... et non sunt per ... ... forme

distinctione ...

Qui est quoq

catholica ...

regens

... dicens ... ... fuit ... sit ... fano
... distinctione ... ... sit ...
... ... sit

For roman and Greek letters the reed nib is cut in the opposite direction to the Arabic, that is, right oblique. For later Greek minuscules, however, the nib is used almost blunt, or at least with a softer edge. Of all the European scripts Greek minuscule is the most cursive, rounded and ligatured. Developed in the eighth century, it built on earlier Byzantine roman cursives. A blunt point means less catching or resistance between the nib and the writing surface, which can help speed up writing.

In Europe, during the Late Antique period, the quill pen gradually became more popular than the reed. Papyrus and supplies of reeds from the East were becoming harder to obtain. The quill had a natural synergy with vellum, a writing material produced from calf and other skins, which was increasingly favoured at this time. Both quill and vellum are made from the same substance: collagen.

Any bird feather can be used to write with but it was a goose feather that was the most popular, as it was easy to hold in the hand and readily available. But quills were difficult to use: they wore out, split unpredictably and became scratchy. They represented an obstacle to the young student learning to write.

Metal pens had been around since Roman times but serious manufacture had to wait for the Industrial Revolution. James Perry of Manchester began making metal nibs in 1819, moving his company to London in 1824. By 1835 Perry's company was stamping out nearly 5,250,000 nibs a year. Joseph Gillott, in Birmingham, who had begun life as a maker of penknives, also turned to producing steel pens in the 1820s. In the twelve months from October 1838 to 1839 his 'manufactory' turned out 44,654,702 nibs. In 1840 he was named 'steel pen maker to the Queen'.[3] Birmingham would ultimately become the centre of the trade, with pens being sent across the globe, from India to Latin America. There is a pen museum in the city today.

The goal of metal pen manufacture was a smoothly writing, flexible and reliable nib, but the holy grail was a constant flow of ink that minimised the necessity of dipping into an inkwell with the associated problems of uneven ink flow.

The first experiments with what we know as fountain pens began several centuries ago. Samuel Pepys (1633–1703), a handwriting enthusiast, had a pen with some kind of ink reservoir. The earliest forms held the

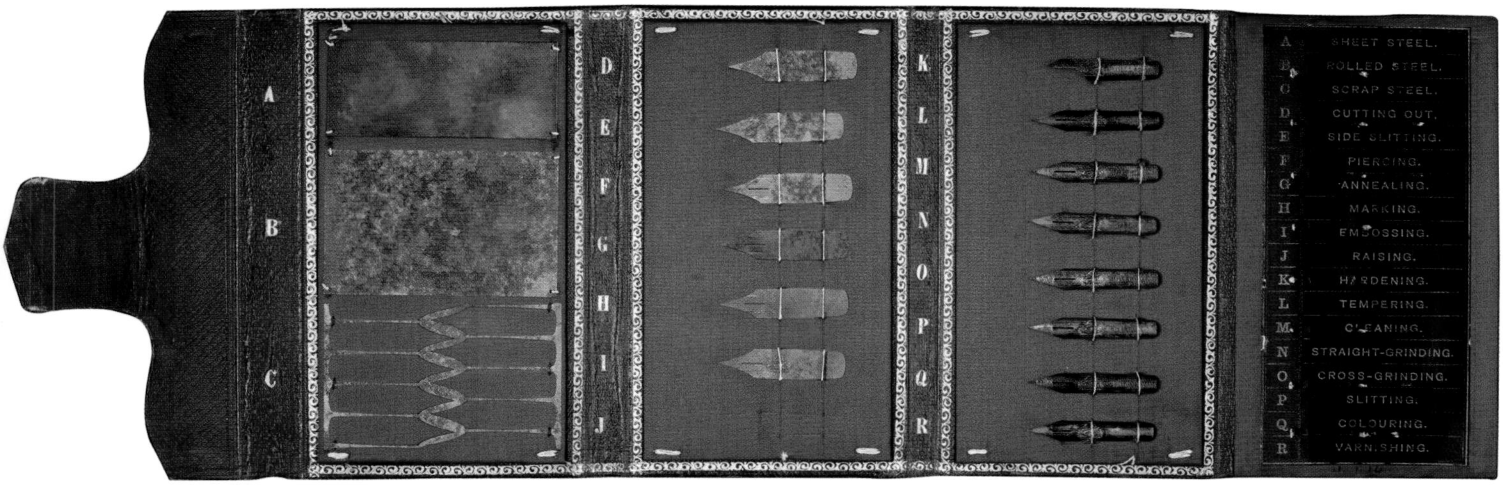

OPPOSITE Pen trials in an English devotional miscellany. Manuscript book. Norfolk (England), 13th century. British Library: Arundel MS 292, fol. 114v
ABOVE Joseph Gillott, Specimen steel nibs. In a presentation binding. Birmingham (England), 1830s. British Library: C.194.a.1407

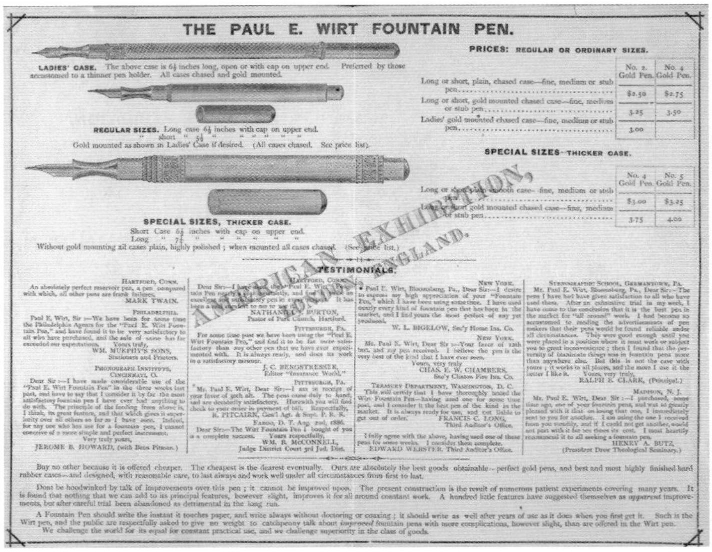

ink in sealed sections of the quill barrel within specially constructed handles. The first patents for fountain pens were awarded in 1809; by the early 1870s they were a recognised feature of the advertisement pages in many popular magazines.

✧ ✧ ✧

In the East the brush held sway: they were, and are, made from a variety of animal hair (horse, goat, weasel), each with different properties. Horse is springy and not very absorbent; weasel is exactly the opposite. But brushes can actually be made from many types of fibres, from hammered-out bamboo or even chicken feathers for those with an exotic taste in their calligraphy. The hairs are carefully grouped, gathered and shaped, tied together and fixed (usually glued) in a shaft. Brushes have the potential to be a highly expressive tool with which to write for they can carry a large charge of ink and are capable of rendering lines from the thinnest trace to a broad black sweep.

In the Chinese and Japanese tradition, and in those other countries that have followed suit, the shaft of the brush is held at right angles to the writing surface giving good ink flow and a full sense of the springiness of the brush tip. Through a series of subtle lifts and turns at stroke endings, the direction of the tip of the brush is carefully controlled when writing. In the most aesthetically pleasing brush writing there is no re-inking of the brush midway through making a character: the ink is allowed to fade as the brush dries up. Yet overall the writer carefully controls the visual weights of the characters across a composition to make a pleasing dynamic balance.

Brushes lend a responsive tactile quality to writing. Kyuyo Ishikawa (b. 1945), a calligrapher from Japan, has named this tactile reciprocity 'taction': the well-spring of calligraphic expression. In his book of that name he writes:

> every action the calligrapher undertakes *vis à vis* the medium – every contact between the brush and the paper – elicits an opposite and equal reaction. The calligrapher is continuously parrying the energy that rebounds from the medium even as he or she continues to pour energy into the medium through the brush. That continuing reciprocity of action and reaction animates the drama that unfolds as a work of calligraphy.[4]

He makes a further point (valid too for roman capital letters) that another kind of reciprocity also shapes the letters: the mutual influence between chisel and brush. Historically the evolution of brushwork and carving proceeded in parallel.

In many traditions writing tools can be treasured objects. In the Islamic world the scissors for cutting paper, burnishers for preparing it, the reed or *qalam* itself, and the knife and cutting surface for shaping its nib became things of high craftsmanship. The same is true elsewhere. In China and other East Asian calligraphic traditions the ink, the stone on which it is

ABOVE Paul E. Wirt (firm), Fountain pen advertisement. Printed sheet. Bloomsburg (Pennsylvania)?, 1887. British Library: Evan.7475
OPPOSITE Nizami Ganjavi, *Poems of Khamsah*. Manuscript. India, early 17th century. British Library: Or.12208, fol. 325v

اذر سال حلم الهی از جلوس ابد پیوند پادشاهی امید که بر صفحه
کاینات تا نام و نشان قلم و رقم باشد منشور سلطنت و
اقبال بطغرای غرای آنحضرت
سپهر بلندی باد بعترت پاکان پاک نهاد
تمت تم

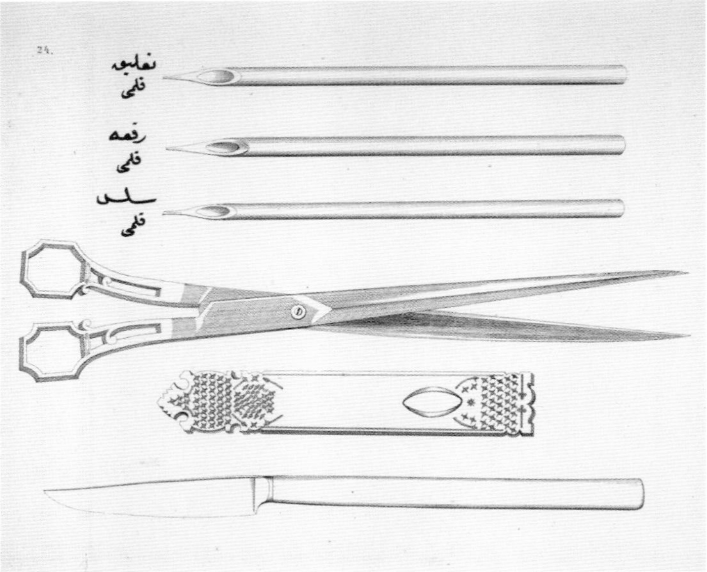

ground, the brush and the paper were known as the scholar's 'Four Treasures'. They are often objects of great beauty.

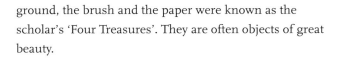

✧ ✧ ✧

The papyrus plant that grew along the banks of the Nile in Egypt provided the main writing material for the Mediterranean world for nearly 3,000 years. The oldest surviving sheet comes from Saqqara and is about 5,000 years old. The triangular stems could be sliced into strips down their length and then laid in two layers across one another. When lightly pounded together the natural sap of the plant bound the layers together. The surface has a slight grain and was sometimes lightly pumiced to smooth it. The sheets could be glued together to make scrolls. Papyrus can be recycled by being washed and scrubbed, but gradually its cellulose and lignum age and become brittle, and layers can flake off. Very little papyrus survived outside Egypt where the dry climate favoured its longevity. Scrolls of up to 10 metres are relatively easy to handle and this may to some extent have encouraged the lengths at which classical texts were composed.

Paper, which today in Europe we may think of as ephemeral, can also have an extremely long life if kept in the right conditions. The crisp, smooth paper of the Lotus Sutra scroll found in the Dunhuang caves at the edge of a desert in China dates to AD 672. Archaeological evidence of paper-making in China seems to go back to at least the first century BC, with firm documentary evidence from AD 105 onwards. Paper was made from the pounded and separated fibres (cellulose) of various plants, such as hemp, bamboo, wild mulberry, linen and cotton, and from waste textiles. The fibres were floated in water that was then strained through a perforated screen (a 'mould'). Once the water had drained out the fibres combined physically and chemically to form a closely woven mat. In the European and Islamic worlds paper was often given a further preparation that sized

ABOVE Writing materials illustrated in an Ottoman calligraphy manual. Engraved book. Istanbul, 1850s? British Library: HSL.74/671, Plate 24
RIGHT *Lotus Sutra*, with detailed colophon. Manuscript scroll. Chang'an (Xi'an, China), 17 May 672. British Library: Or.8210/S.4209

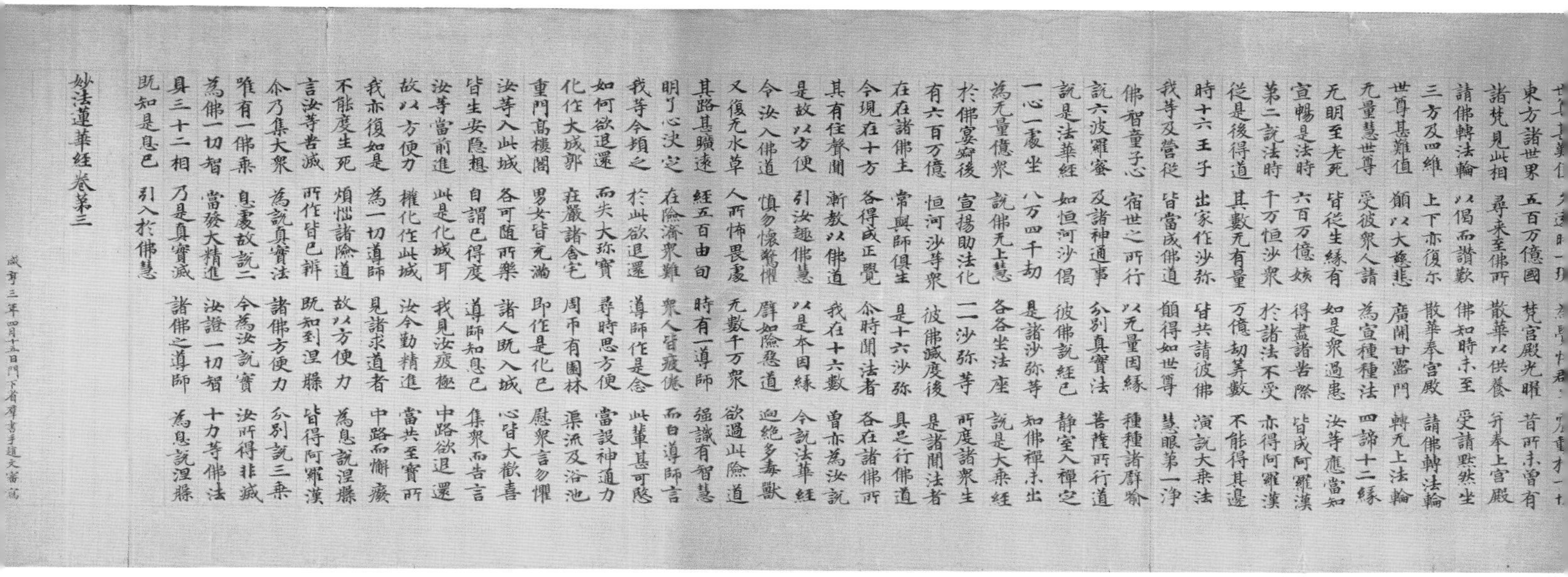

(sealed) and smoothed the surface. Gelatine size was used in the West and in Ottoman times the old practice of sizing paper with starch gave way to coating the surface with egg white and alum and then polishing it until it was smooth.

Buddhist monks and missionaries carried knowledge of paper-making to Korea, Japan and Vietnam. Such knowledge spread to the Arab world in the eighth century AD and reached Europe via the Iberian Peninsula from the tenth century. A few decades later paper arrived in West Africa via Islam, although no paper was actually made in the region until the twentieth century. Paper's earliest appeal seems to have been to merchants and bureaucrats, as it was light and affordable. From the thirteenth century it was being produced in parts of Italy. Paper-making began in Poland in 1491 and Moscow in 1578; the first paper mill in Britain was established by 1495.

Paper has played a crucial role in the spread of writing and printing across the globe; it is an inexpensive, durable and flexible surface. It has allowed correspondence and book culture to thrive. Yet the introduction of new materials has often been fraught: can they be trusted? The papal archives continued to use papyrus into the twelfth century. Durability is a renewed concern today with regard to paper made by industrial processes using wood pulp in the nineteenth century (spurred on by the huge rise in demand for paper generated by industrialisation). Its acidic content means the material is beginning to crumble and documents printed during this era may have a limited life. We are now also sensitive to the environmental damage that is sometimes caused by paper production.

Although paper-making was introduced to India by the late twelfth century, palm leaves provided the basic writing material for the majority of India's languages and script systems into the nineteenth century. This was also true in the countries influenced by India: Nepal, Indonesia, Burma and Thailand. It seems almost certain that the shape of writing in the region owes

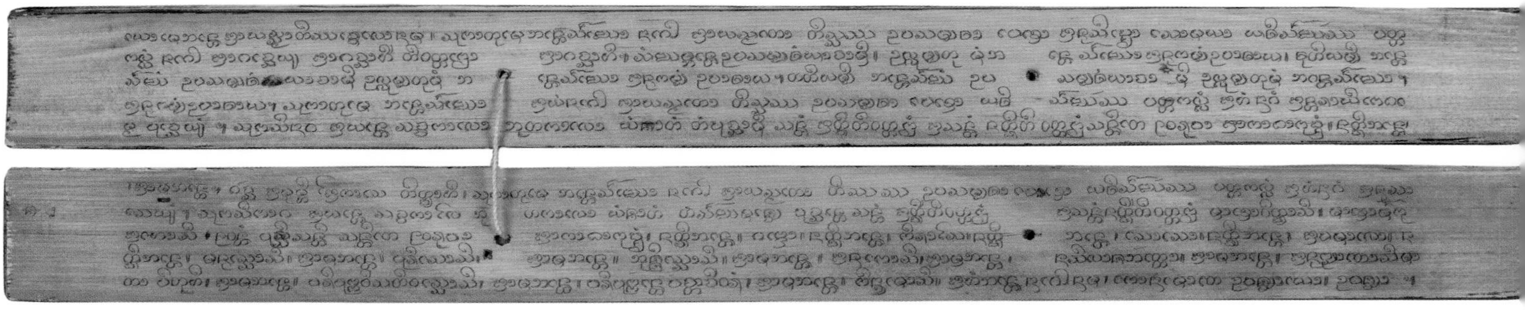

something to the challenges of writing on this material. Our best understanding (though still not a settled one) is that the scripts of the Indian subcontinent come from the original system developed in the Middle East at the end of the second millennium BC, with Brahmi being at the root of almost all contemporary Indian scripts (other than those brought in by Islam). While in the northern areas palm leaves were written on with pen and ink, in the south metal styluses were used that cut into the surface, the incisions invariably coloured in with rubbed pigment and oil. When writing with a stylus any scored lines along the grain of the leaf can cause it to split, but this is less likely to happen if lines are rounded or strokes are made to travel in a more diagonal direction. Many of the scripts from the southern regions have this rounded character, and they dispense with the joined ligatures running along the tops of letters that we find for instance in scripts such as Devanagari and Bengali.

As with vellum, palm-leaf manuscripts need to be rewritten every few centuries if a text is to be carried down to the present. While manuscripts can last at least 300 years, after that they risk becoming more fragile, although there are a few very old palm-leaf manuscripts that have managed to survive. In the University Library at Cambridge in the UK there is a richly illustrated Buddhist text (the Astasāhasrika Prajñāpāramitā, or *The Perfection of Wisdom*) written on palm leaves that is almost certainly 1,000 years old. The writing is in Sanskrit and the tool was a reed or bamboo pen. Existing manuscript fragments from central Asia and Japan are thought to go back to the second century AD.

Palm-leaf books were prepared by trimming the pages out from the leaf; the pages are landscape format and sometimes taper slightly towards each end. They are then boiled several times and burnished smooth to create the writing surface. Once written the leaves are stacked, threaded together on cords and placed as a bundle between wooden boards. These bundles are tied with cords, wrapped in cloth and stacked on shelves or placed in boxes. Beautiful stands have also been made to display pages. The pages themselves (and their book covers) can sometimes be highly decorated, glowing with colour, gold and lacquer; the majority, however, have a beige unpretentious softness.

✧ ✧ ✧

Leather and vellum have been used as writing materials for thousands of years in the Middle East. The earliest example of a document on leather comes from around 2400 BC in Egypt. Writing on vellum (prepared calfskin) was already happening in Hellenistic times. Pliny the Elder (AD 23–79) gives us the story that the city of Pergamum (or Pergamon) in Greece lent its name to the 'parchment' making process. Within the calligraphic

ABOVE Palm leaf text, inscribed and wiped with soot. Northern Thailand, 19th century. British Library: Or.13157

OPPOSITE Crafts Council of England and Wales, Royal Charter of Incorporation. Parchment (calf skin vellum) with calligraphy by Donald Jackson. London, 1983

ELIZABETH THE SECOND
BY THE GRACE OF GOD OF THE UNITED KINGDOM OF GREAT BRITAIN AND NORTHERN IRELAND AND OF OUR OTHER REALMS AND TERRITORIES QUEEN, HEAD OF THE COMMONWEALTH, DEFENDER OF THE FAITH: TO ALL TO WHOM THESE PRESENTS SHALL COME, GREETING!

Whereas it has been represented unto Us that it is expedient that We should be graciously pleased to grant a Charter of Incorporation to the unincorporated organization established in the year of our Lord One thousand nine hundred and seventy-one and known as the Crafts Council [hereinafter referred to as "the unincorporated Council"]:

Now therefore know Ye that We by virtue of Our prerogative Royal and of all other powers enabling Us in that behalf have granted and ordained and do by these Presents for Us, Our Heirs and Successors grant and ordain as follows:

1 The persons now Members of the unincorporated Council and all other persons who may hereafter become Members of the body corporate hereby constituted shall for ever hereafter be one body corporate and politic by the name of the "Crafts Council" and by the same name shall have perpetual succession and a Common Seal with power to break, alter and make anew the said Seal from time to time at their will and pleasure & by the same name shall and may sue and be sued in all courts and in all manner of actions and proceedings and shall have power to enter into contracts, to acquire, hold and dispose of property of any kind, to accept trusts and generally to do all other matters and things incidental or appertaining to a body corporate:

2 In this Our Charter unless the context otherwise requires:

(i) "the Council" shall mean the Crafts Council as hereby incorporated and shall be constituted as prescribed in the Bye-Laws;

(ii) the Bye-Laws shall mean the Bye-Laws set forth in the Schedule hereto or other the Bye-Laws from time to time of the Council;

(iii) words importing the singular number only shall include the plural number and vice versa, words importing the masculine gender only shall include the feminine gender and words importing persons shall include corporations;

(iv) references to Our Secretary of State are to Our Secretary of State for Education and Science:

3 The Object of the Council shall be to advance and encourage the creation and conservation of works of fine craftsmanship

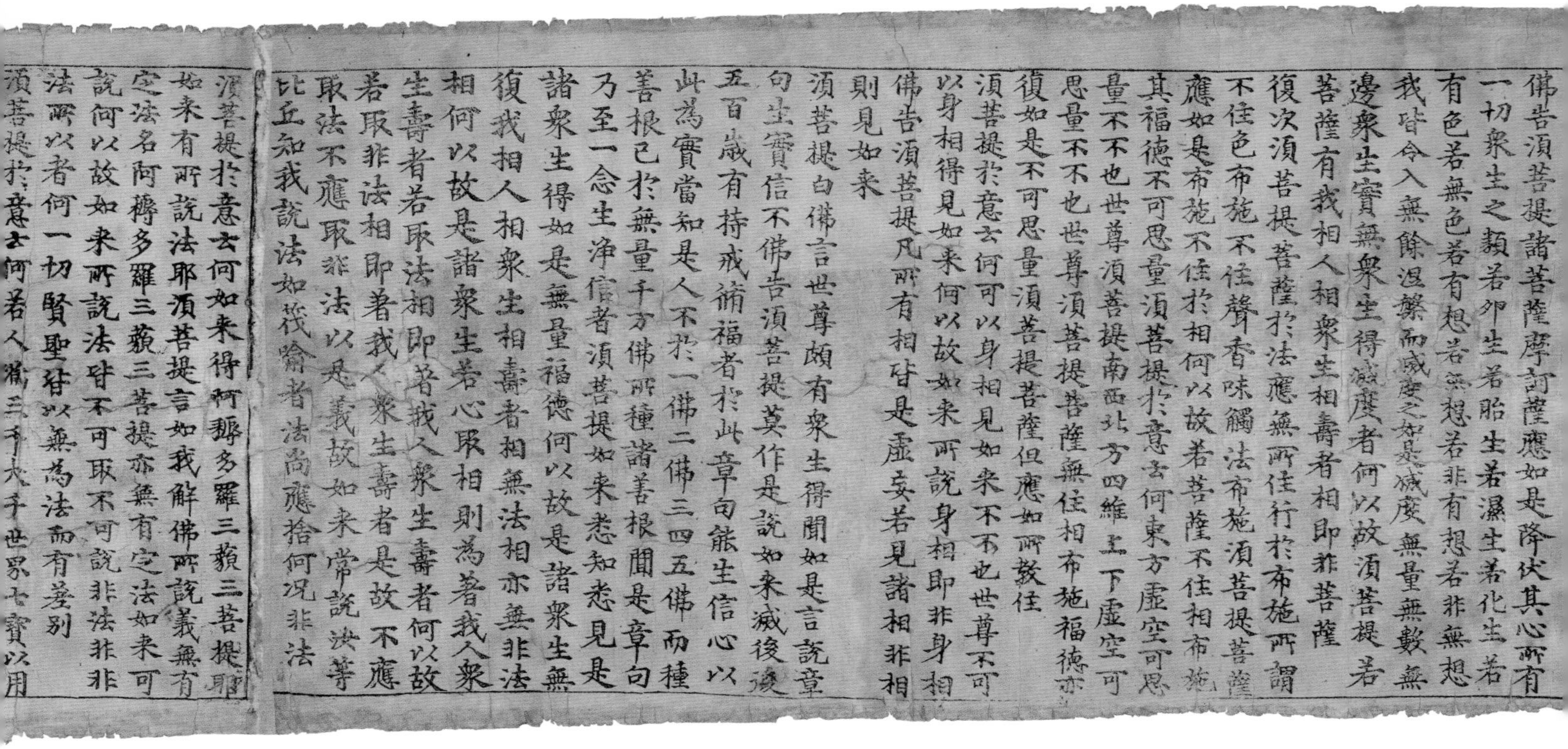

world vellum refers to calfskin and parchment to a similar product made from sheep, although parchment in particular is often used as a generic label. Vellum continues to be employed today in the UK for official and ceremonial documents. From the early sixteenth century until as recently as 2017 all British Acts of Parliament were printed on a vellum copy as it has proved the most durable material, needing very little special care under normal conditions.

Some religious documents, such as the scrolls of the Torah written in Hebrew, continue to be written on vellum, and in the profession of the *sofer*, the Hebrew religious scribe, a meticulous and highly skilled approach to this craft still flourishes in many countries.

Vellum and parchment are made by soaking skins in lime for several weeks. They are then washed and stretched and pared to provide a taut writing surface of a creamy colour. Before writing the skin is lightly abraded to raise a soft velvety knap that helps the scribe produce a controlled and sharp line. The skin can be re-scraped if mistakes are found. Sheepskin is thinner than vellum and less susceptible to scraping: in the Middle Ages some records of the English exchequer were kept on sheep parchment as it made it easier to see if any figures had been altered.

Printing

Printing, the technique of directly transferring an image from one surface onto another, is as ancient as the red ochre handprints we see in rock art, but in terms of written forms its use began with seal-making. Engraved seals were important in Mesopotamia, ancient Egypt, the Roman Empire and ancient China, where they have been in use since the Late Shang Dynasty (1300-1050

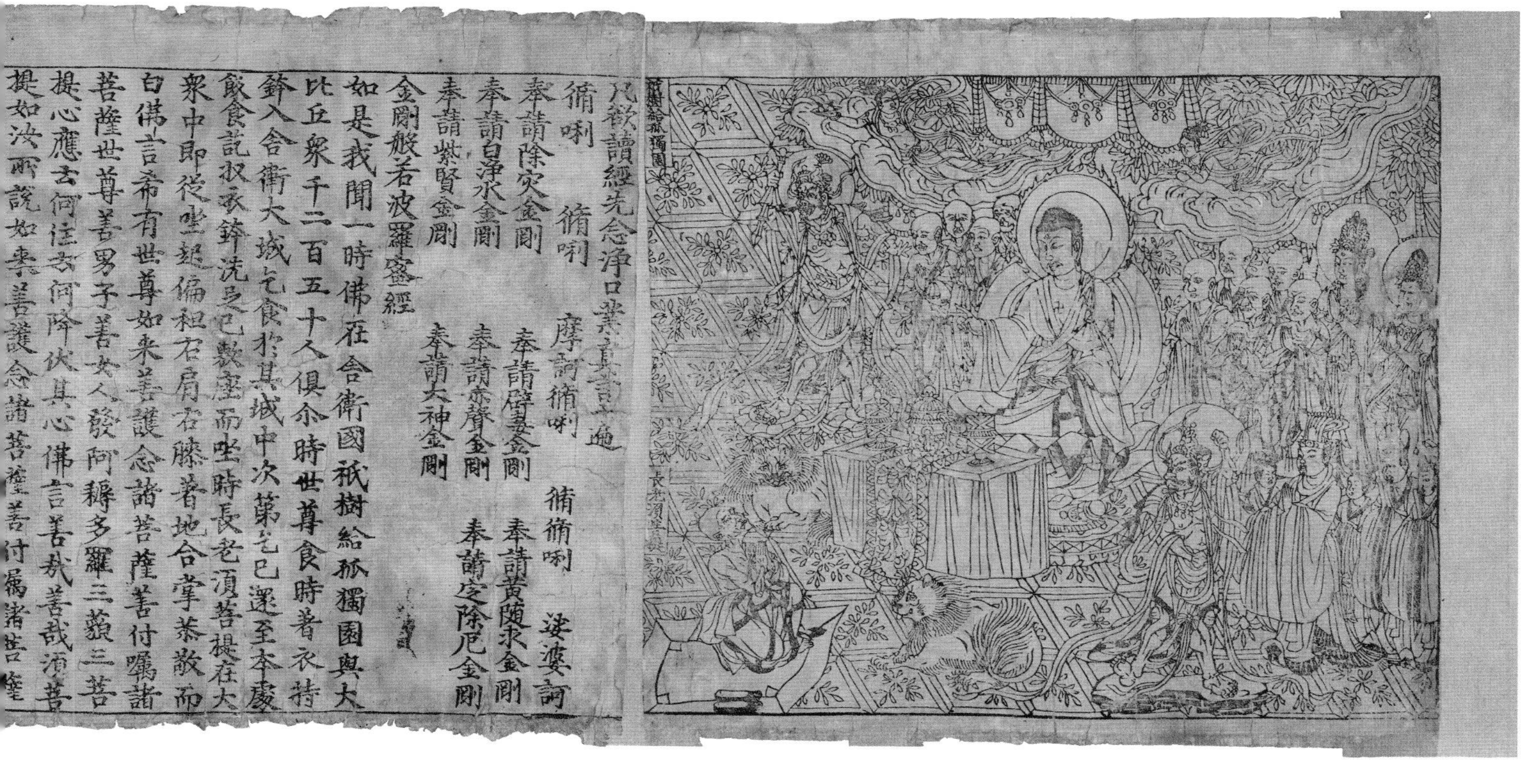

BC). It was also the practice in China from this time onwards to carve works of literature, government edicts and fine calligraphy into stone from which rubbings could be taken. When printed the writing appeared white against a black background.

By the eighth century and probably earlier the Chinese had found a way of cutting calligraphic texts into wooden blocks that could be utilised to make prints (xylography). A calligrapher wrote the text on paper that was glued to the wooden block; the paper was then either thinned by rubbing it or oiled in order to make the inked written characters clearly visible to the wood engraver, who cut away the background leaving the writing and illustrations standing proud. The printing method that involved inking the block and burnishing (or rubbing) clean paper down onto it meant that thin paper had to be used and it could only be printed on one side. The earliest woodblock print was discovered in the 1960s during the excavation of a stupa at the Pulguk-sa Temple in Korea and dates to roughly AD 704–751. From around 770, there are similar small Buddhist magical incantations printed in Japan on the orders of the Empress Shōtoku (718–770) who had ordered 1 million of them, in miniature pagodas, to be placed throughout the country for her protection. Perhaps most impressive is the scroll of the Diamond Sutra, which was found at Dunhuang in China; it is printed on paper and bears the date 11 May 868. It is the oldest dated, complete printed work in the world.

By the eleventh century in China printing using a system of movable moulded characters had been developed. Bi Sheng is recorded as using a method involving baked clay characters held by paste in an iron frame sometime between 1041 and 1048. In the Yuan

ABOVE *Diamond Sutra*. Dunhuang (China), 11 May 868. British Library: Or.8210/P.2

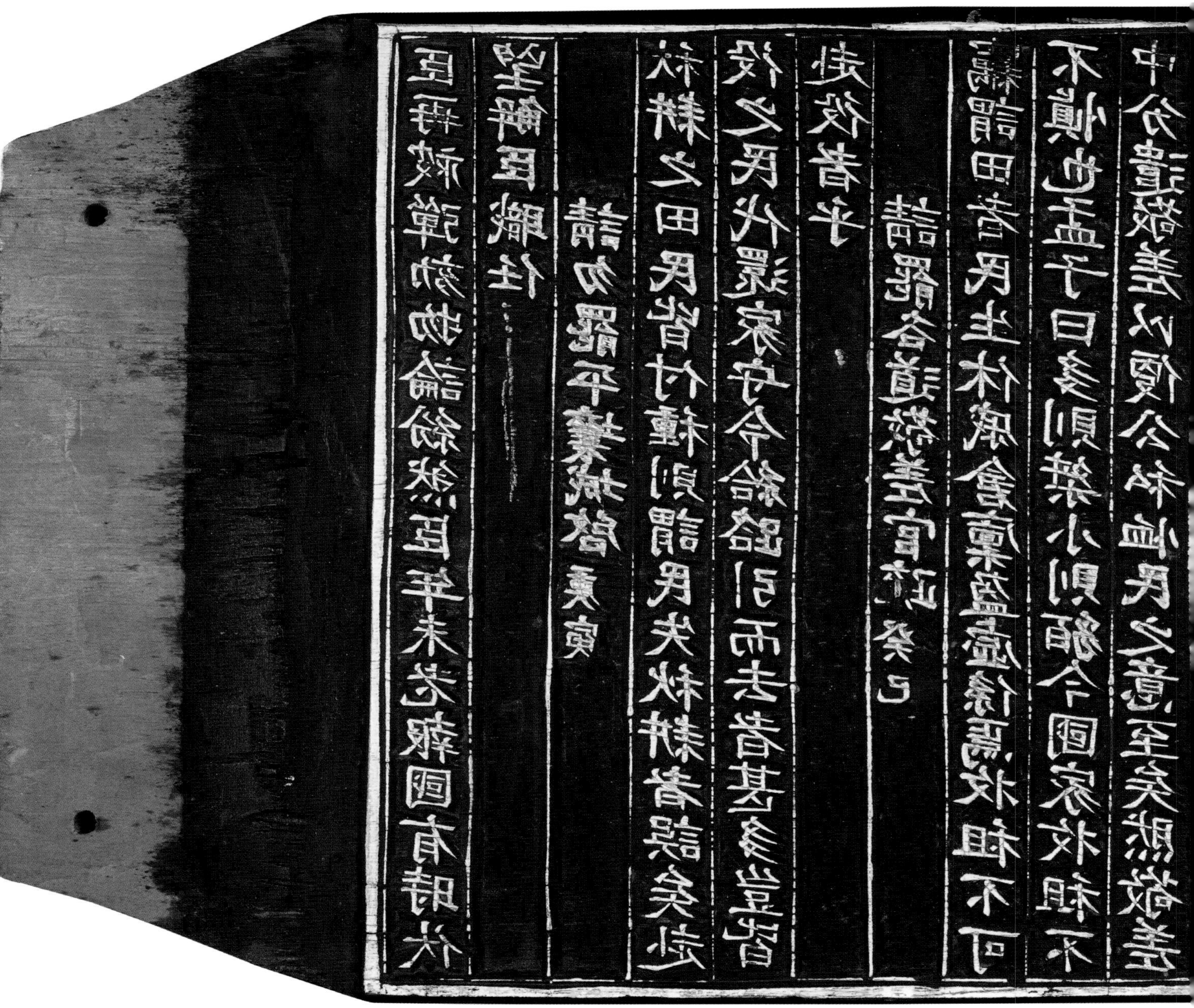

ABOVE Woodblock for printing *Panyang Sego*. Korea, 1907.
British Library: ORB Misc 121

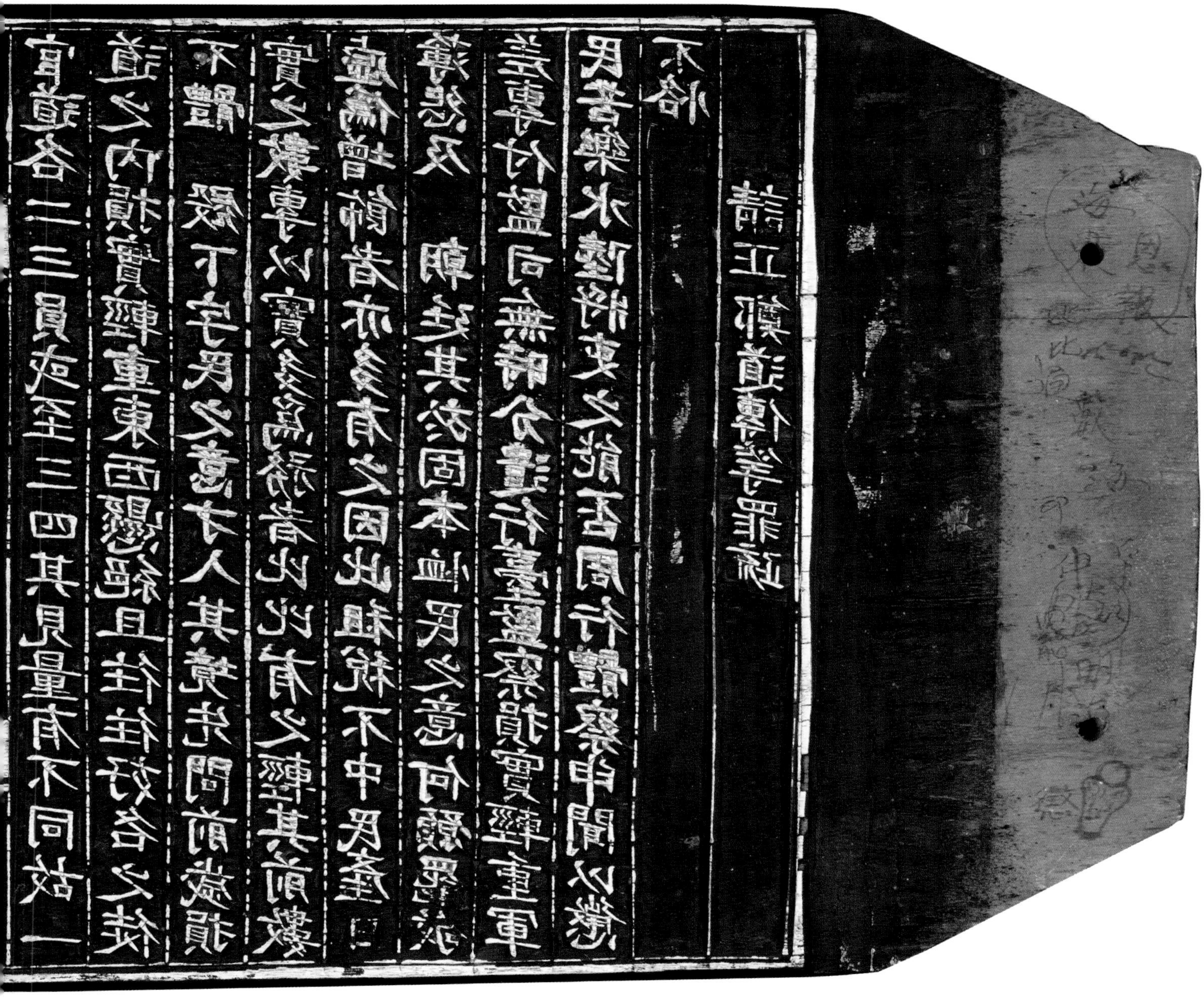

period (1279–1368) wooden type was being employed. Perhaps as early as the thirteenth but definitely by the late fourteenth century, printing from movable metal types was happening in Korea. In Japan printing with movable metal types briefly flourished during the period of contact with Portugal but then it disappeared, as did this technology in other parts of the region, until reintroduced from Europe in the nineteenth century.

Historically there were several disadvantages to working with type within the Chinese context. The sheer volume of different characters required an expensive initial outlay. There were also logistical problems with the compositing process: how do you store, select and redistribute such a vast array of type?

The traditional method of woodblock printing held a number of advantages. Although there was an initial cost in writing the calligraphy, the labour of cutting the blocks was inexpensive. When stored safely these blocks remained good for several centuries. The low-tech nature of woodblock printing meant it could be done anywhere. This form of publishing was not dependent upon a market; it could even happen in outlying areas or a scholar's home. It did not need to take place in the big centres of commerce to which European printing was forced to gravitate.

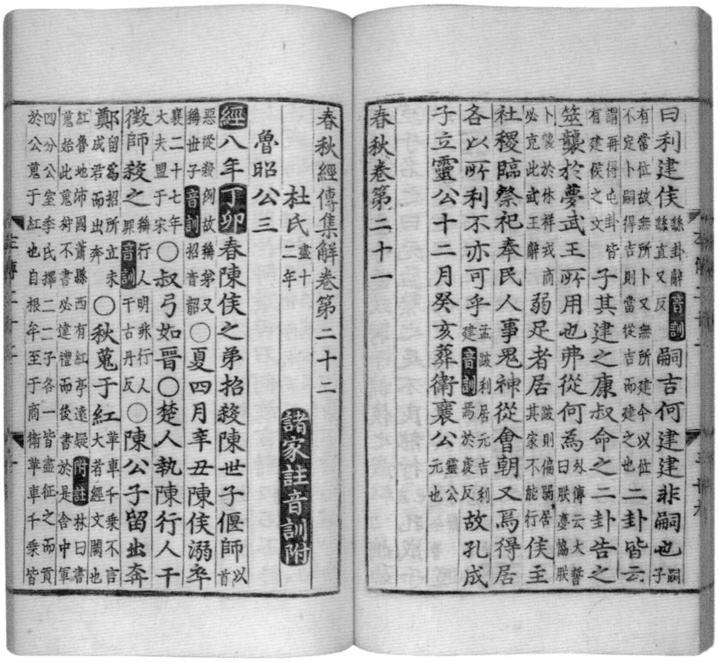

ABOVE Collected commentaries on the *Spring and Autumn Annals*. Printed book (movable type). Korea, 1442. British Library: 16015.c.3, Zuozhuan 21, f.39v – Zuozhuan 22, f.1r

The challenge with European methods of printing was that to reprint a book using type one had to start all over again and recompose every single page. So movable type encouraged the printer to create large numbers of texts in one go because the reprinting costs were high. To be profitable printers had to risk judging the market and print the maximum number of volumes they thought they could sell. Then they had to store the copies until they were sold. This required not only fine judgement but also considerable financing up front. Europe's first printer, Johannes Gutenberg (*c.*1400–1468), fell foul of this problem when his partner Johannes Fust demanded his loans back before Gutenberg had had a chance to sell the Bibles he had printed, so Gutenberg had to surrender his stock and most of his printing equipment to satisfy his creditor. With a book printed from woodblocks one could simply respond in real time to actual demand.

One further notable difference between the Chinese and the European methods of book production was that in China printed and written texts maintained a close correspondence to each other, for the original paper working sheet for every carved text was always a hand-written master.

Huge numbers of books were produced by this process, stimulated by the high respect for learning and education in Chinese society. With civil service examinations being the main established pathway to secure employment and status, and access that was not class bound (in principle, although not always in practice), education was prized at all levels of society.

In Europe Gutenberg, a goldsmith from Mainz, Germany, was the first to print with movable type. There

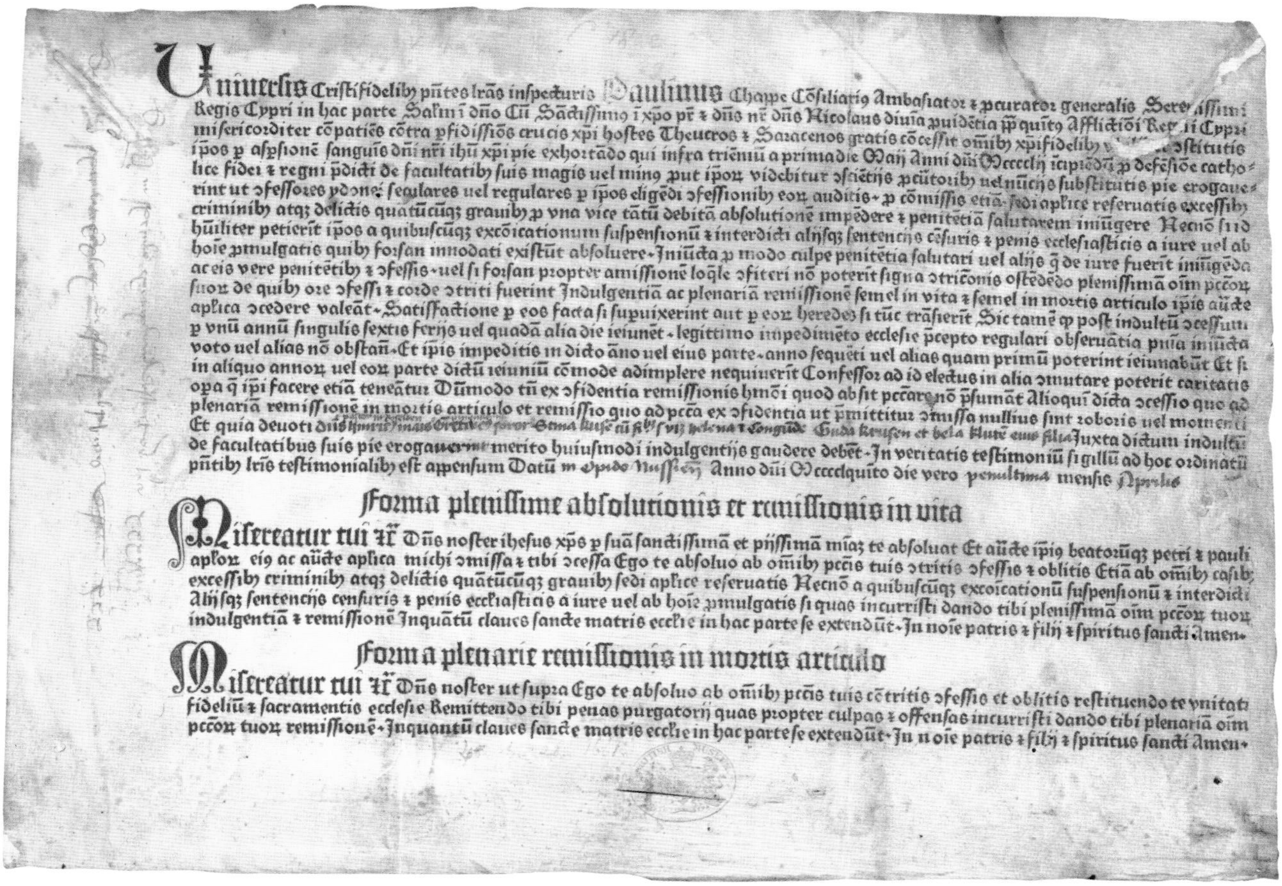
Forma plenissime absolutionis et remissionis in vita

Forma plenarie remissionis in mortis articulo

seem to be no direct connections between his invention and developments taking place slightly earlier in East Asia. He had perfected his invention over the course of around twenty years and it featured not only a system for casting and using type but also a specially modified press. As a goldsmith he was familiar with metals and casting processes. While the Gutenberg Bible of 1455 is his masterpiece, he had begun two or three years earlier with smaller projects, including a papal indulgence generally dated to 1454–5. Civil strife in Mainz in the 1460s speeded up the spread of printing to other cities in Europe as the original band of printers left to find work elsewhere. By 1480 there were presses across Europe. At least thirty cities in Germany had presses and fifty in Italy. The printing press came to Britain in 1476 when William Caxton (1422–1492) printed Geoffrey Chaucer's *The Canterbury Tales*.

In the second half of the fifteenth century the variety of printed letter shapes in use was very many, drawing on the previous century or more of calligraphy, but within the next fifty years the choices had resolved down to two broad families: roman lower and upper case, with italic and gothic black letter and *fraktur* forms.

In Europe, over the long run, the printing press and newly effective distribution systems for books led to a widespread redistribution of knowledge that had an enormous impact. During the Reformation, when the Protestant Church split from Rome, it was estimated

ABOVE Pope Nicholas V, Indulgence issued to raise funds to defend Cyprus from Ottoman attacks. Printed sheet (movable type). Mainz (Germany): Johannes Gutenberg?, 1454–5. British Library: IB.53

Dñicis diebꝫ post festū trinitatis · Inuitatoriū.

Regē magnū dñm venite adoremus. ps Venite ·
Dñicis diebꝫ post festū ephie Inuitatoriū ·

Adoremꝰ dñm qui fecit nos. Ps venite aū Seruite ·

BEatus vir qui
non abijt in — Euouae ·
consilio impiorū et in
via pctōꝝ nō stetit: ⁊ in
cathedra pestilēcie nō sedit. Sed i lege dñi vo
lūtas eiꝰ: et in lege eius meditabit die ac
nocte. Et erit tanqȝ lignū qd plātatū iuxta
decursus aqꝝ: qd fructū suū dabit in
tpe suo. Et foliū eiꝰ nō defluet: ⁊ oia qcūqȝ
faciet psperabūt. Nō sic impij nō sic sed
tanqȝ puluis quē pijcit ventus a facie terre.
Ideo non resurgūt impij in iudicio: neqȝ
pctōres in cōsilio iustoꝝ. Qm nouit dñs
viā iustoꝝ: ⁊ iter impioꝝ peribit. Gloria P

that between 1518 and 1525 in Germany alone 3 million printed pamphlets on the topic were in circulation.

Over time the shapes of books themselves changed to reflect a more competitive market. They became smaller in size and lost some of their marginal glosses, but also gained page numbers and indexes. A pared-down presentation of the text allowed for faster reading and clearer lines of argument to be flagged up. Solid text was divided up with spacing for paragraphs. Undoubtedly the spread of printing encouraged an uptake in learning reading and writing. Literacy across Europe surged upwards, particularly in the late seventeenth century when printing finally became ubiquitous and then again in the later eighteenth. The Industrial Revolution would affect printing through the introduction of metal presses and the addition of steam power. In the early nineteenth century the volume of material that could be produced on new circular cylinder presses was huge. The numbers of copies printed by *The Times* grew from 1,100 impressions an hour in 1814 to 12,000 an hour by 1848. By 1869 it was turning out 12,000 copies of an entire newspaper in an hour. Those who composed the type could scarcely keep up; in the 1890s this process, too, became automated using Linotype and Monotype hot-metal casting systems where the whole operation was controlled by the compositor pressing keys on a large typewriter-like keyboard.

Initially Arabic writing and European ways of printing were not an easy fit. While roman typography was based on units of mostly single letters, Ottoman, Arabic and Persian calligraphy developed as finely balanced connected scripts. Letters did not line up repetitively along a single base line but assimilated their forms to each other in graphic strings, though not all letters had to be connected. With no spaces between words, special adaptations of form signalled word endings. In addition, there was no apparent baseline (there is one, but every letter does not have to land on it):

ABOVE Jan Luiken, *Het Menselyk Bedryf.* Engraved book. Amsterdam: Johanneses en Cospaares Luiken, 1694. British Library: 12331.dd.1, Plate 61
OPPOSITE Latin psalter, known as the *Mainz Psalter,* p. 2 (detail). Printed book (movable type). Mainz (Germany): Johannes Fust and Peter Schoeffer, 1457. British Library: G.12216, fol. 1r

dots and vowel marks worked in layers above and below.

Early examples of books printed in Arabic script came to the Ottoman Empire from other parts of Europe in the sixteenth century, but the forms were distorted by misunderstanding of the script and perceived mechanical constraints. The Arabic-script printing press was banned by Ottoman authorities from the late 1490s. Over the ensuing centuries, experiments with Arabic type continued, largely unsuccessfully, in both Europe and the Ottoman Empire. In the 1720s however İbrahim Müteferrika, working in Istanbul, produced a typographically sophisticated response. By the late nineteenth century and early twentieth century, in the hands of Armenian Ohanis Mühendisoğlu, Ottoman type design was at a zenith. Setting the complex type (sometimes made not only of letter complexes but also individual parts of letters) required great skill: indeed a knowledge of the underlying calligraphic system. It would need today's technologies to fully realise the complexities and refinements that Mühendisoğlu had envisioned. In the twenty-first century the fluid possibilities of digital type have dovetailed with other cultural factors to produce real excitement about possibilities in this area.

In the 1790s Aloys Senefelder (1771–1834) devised a technique of writing on a surface (originally a very smooth stone) with a slightly waxy or greasy tool. The stone was then wetted. Next ink was rolled out across the stone: it would not stick to the dampened surface (which consequently remained un-inked) but it would adhere to those areas covered by the waxy writing or drawing. From this a print could be taken. Handwriting and drawing could thus be reproduced directly. and this opened up new possibilities in the field of printing. It would eventually be used as a graphic medium for artistic and commercial printing across the globe.

The number of different printing and copying systems introduced into workplaces in the twentieth century is legion. Automated composing systems, lithographic printing and many proprietary methods for copying documents were supplemented in the 1950s with photocomposition using projected images as a means of composing a page of type on a plate.

The other big development of the later part of the nineteenth century was the typewriter. Ideas for the improved mechanisation of writing had been around in Europe since the beginning of the 1700s. Although the earliest patent was granted to Henry Mills in 1714 and various pieces of equipment relating to such a machine were among his possessions at his death, there is no evidence that he actually built one. The first machine in commercial production came from Denmark. The Reverend Rasmus Malling-Hansen's (1835–1890) model was globe-shaped with a forest of keys like a dandelion's head. A pastor who ran Copenhagen's Royal Institute for the Deaf, Hansen originally invented his instrument for the pupils. It continued in production into the early 1900s, but it was the Remington typewriter released in 1872 that established the model that everyone else would follow. A QWERTY keyboard (a randomisation of keys to scatter the most popular letters across the keyboard and prevent jamming of adjacent keys) allowed the operator to depress a key and send an individual hammer carved with a letter towards an ink-impregnated ribbon that marked the paper being scrolled through the machine line by line. The idea had grown out of a machine designed to number lottery tickets and pages and was the product of Christopher Latham Sholes (1819–1890), the editor of a newspaper in Milwaukee, Wisconsin, and two friends. They sold their patent on to Remington, a company that up to this point had been a manufacturer of rifles and sewing machines.

Typewriters allowed the operator to write up to about 150 words a minute as opposed to thirty with pen and paper. By using carbon paper several copies could be made simultaneously. It was women, now benefiting from access to education, who would be the main

operatives of these machines, dramatically changing the nature of both the workforce and the workplace.

In the USA Samuel Morse (1791–1872) with his assistant Alfred Vail patented an electrical telegraph system in 1840. By the 1870s a network stretched from Britain to India, reaching Australia in 1872. In 1896 the young Italian engineer Guglielmo Marconi (1874–1937) began experimenting with radio telegraphy and in 1901 a signal was successfully sent from Land's End in the UK to St John's, Newfoundland, Canada. Postal services had also improved with the introduction of the Penny Post in 1840, which charged a standard fee for sending a letter

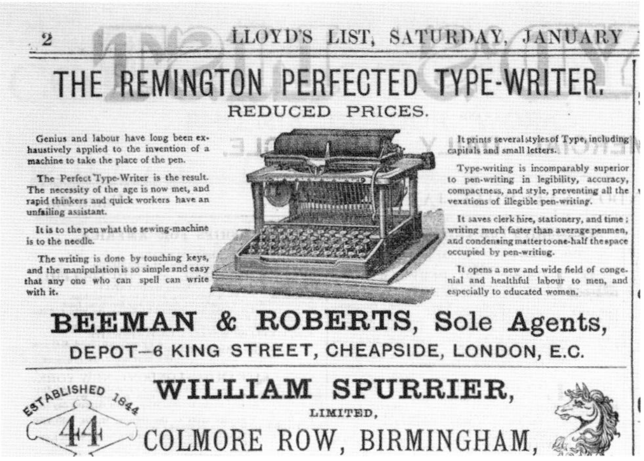

2 LLOYD'S LIST, SATURDAY, JANUARY

THE REMINGTON PERFECTED TYPE-WRITER.

REDUCED PRICES.

Genius and labour have long been exhaustively applied to the invention of a machine to take the place of the pen.

The Perfect Type-Writer is the result. The necessity of the age is now met, and rapid thinkers and quick workers have an unfailing assistant.

It is to the pen what the sewing-machine is to the needle.

The writing is done by touching keys, and the manipulation is so simple and easy that any one who can spell can write with it.

It prints several styles of Type, including capitals and small letters.

Type-writing is incomparably superior to pen-writing in legibility, accuracy, compactness, and style, preventing all the vexations of illegible pen-writing.

It saves clerk hire, stationery, and time; writing much faster than average penmen, and condensing matter to one-half the space occupied by pen-writing.

It opens a new and wide field of congenial and healthful labour to men, and especially to educated women.

BEEMAN & ROBERTS, Sole Agents,

DEPOT—6 KING STREET, CHEAPSIDE, LONDON, E.C.

ESTABLISHED 1844 44

WILLIAM SPURRIER,

LIMITED,

COLMORE ROW, BIRMINGHAM,

ABOVE Staff in the offices of George Munro, Covent Garden, London. 8 October 1919. Private collection
BELOW Advertisement for Remington typewriter. Lloyd's List, 13 January 1883

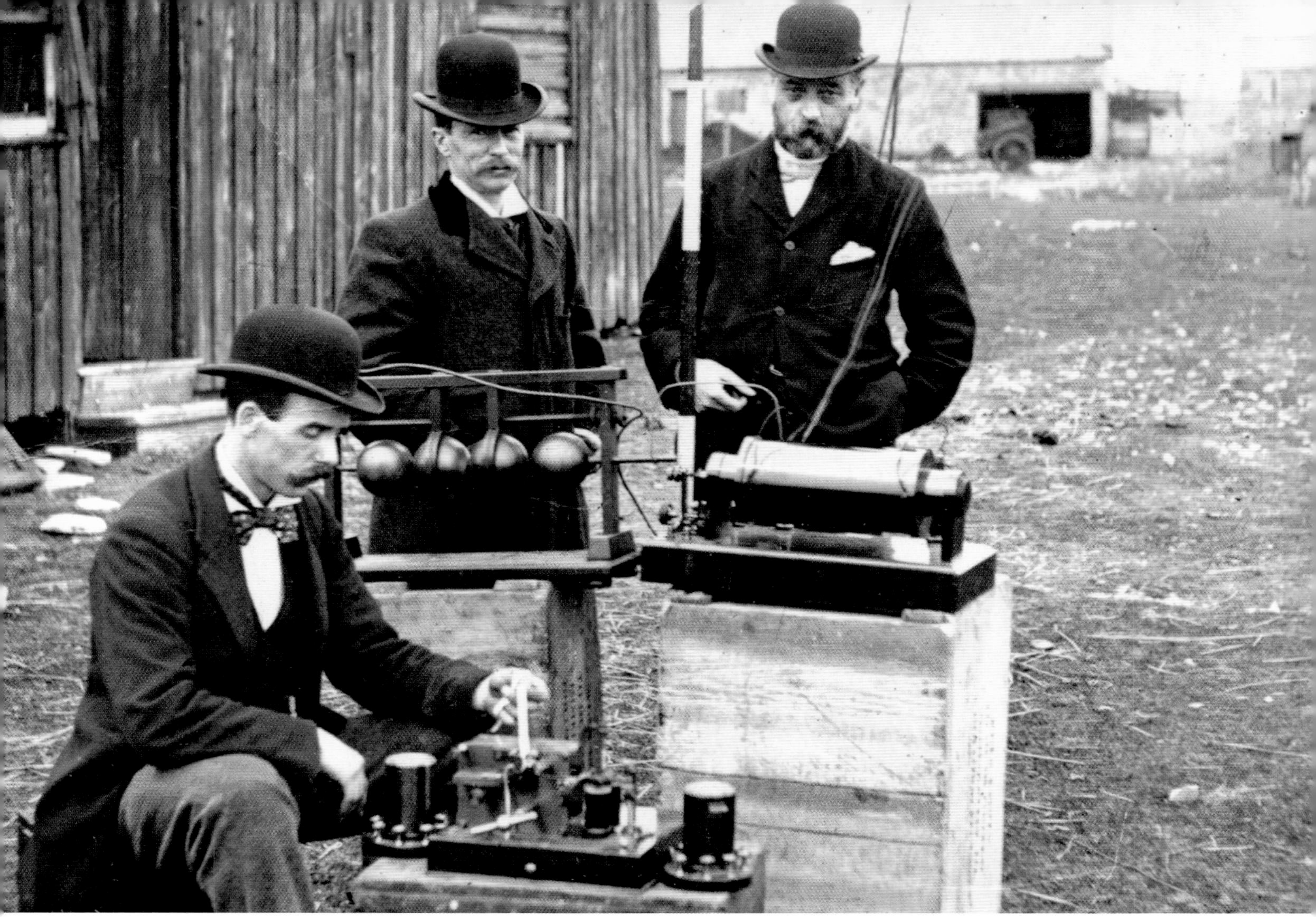

within the UK however far or near the destination. By the late Victorian period an international network of postal and telegram services working across ocean liners, the railway and undersea cables had encircled the globe.

The big leap forward to our present-day systems happened in the 1960s and '70s. From shortly after the Second World War computers had screens and keyboards attached to them for programming purposes, enabling the inputting and editing of the simple computer code of the period. But it became clear by the 1970s that this configuration could be used for writing itself: word processing, as it came to be called.

ABOVE British Post Office engineers inspect Guglielmo Marconi's wireless telegraphy (radio) equipment, during a demonstration on Flat Holm Island, South Wales, 13 May 1897. This was the world's first demonstration of the transmission of radio signals over open sea, between Lavernock Point and Flat Holm Island (a distance of 3 miles).

Furthermore, it eventually became possible to think of these tools as playing a role in shaping the layout of documents. So in the course of a couple of decades computers, once thought of as giant calculating machines that planned national economies or placed men on the moon, were reconceived as new writing tools in succession to the quill pen and the typewriter.

Soon the computer was becoming a platform that brought together a variety of technologies. This era was inaugurated first in the imagination and then in reality. The initial vision dates to 1945 and was the dream of Vannevar Bush (1890–1974), the scientist who had been in charge of the interdisciplinary research effort that the USA had initiated in response to its involvement in the Second World War. Bush had overseen the beginnings of the Manhattan Project to produce atomic weapons. As the war came to a close he dreamed of turning the efforts of his fellow scientists to a new project that would be non-destructive and beneficial to all humanity: one that would augment human memory and intelligence through harnessing the power of a variety of cutting-edge technologies. Bush's vision fired the mind of a young researcher called Douglas Engelbart (1925–2013) who made this his life's work at the Augmentation Research Center (ARC), which he established at Stanford. The kind of mathematics that he and others could draw upon was also crucial.

As early as the time of the philosopher René Descartes (1596–1650), scholars had been wondering if mathematics and geometry could provide some kind of symbolic basis for human thinking that was logical and precise. It was George Boole (1815–1864) from Lincolnshire who put flesh on this vision. Claude Shannon (1916–2001), an electrical engineer at the Massachusetts Institute of Technology, picked up his Boolean logic in the 1930s to provide the wiring patterns for the electrical circuits of a calculating machine. Eventually Shannon would write a paper describing a mathematical theory of communication. It related to signalling using the telegraph but commentators at the time noted that the theory could also be applied to letters and words, symphonic music and pictures, all of which could be mathematically and mechanically modelled.

At ARC Engelbart focused on how to make inputting, manipulating and outputting information from computers an easier task. At nearby rival centre Xerox's Palo Alto Research Center (PARC, established 1970), work proceeded on related but slightly different lines. With hindsight one can say that PARC's visionary researcher Alan Kay (b. 1940) understood, as no one else quite did, that here were not simply augmented ways of working but something much more intimate. It was a whole new medium, accessible to all. Through it we would discover new ways of being in the world.

In 1972 Ray Tomlinson (1941–2016), who worked for a contractor to the US Department of Defense, experimented with a program to send messages from one mainframe computer to another. Without realising it, he established the standard email address system we have today when he chose the @ symbol to separate the user name from the host name. At the time he thought of his experiment as a 'neat idea'. Just a few months later, when a research network within the Department of Defense decided to share software and data down telephone lines between computers in different parts of the USA, Tomlinson's program for email was piggybacked onto their new File Transfer Protocols (FTP). Having been a tool for local use, it was now being employed to communicate across sites. One year later emails comprised 75 per cent of the traffic on the network. Their popularity was a complete surprise. The release of an open architecture Transmission Control Protocol (TCP) in 1973 meant that many computer networks began to link up until, a little over a decade later, there was one global 'Internet' community through which one could transfer files and send email. The final piece of the system we know today, the World Wide Web, which runs over the Internet just as email does, fell into place in 1991. Uptake grew over the next few years and on 30 April 1993 the World Wide Web was made available free of charge to anyone who wanted to use it.

Electronic technologies have proved highly significant for writing and today this includes SMS or text messages on mobile devices as well as Internet protocol-based message services, such as Apple's iMessage, Facebook Messenger, WhatsApp, Viber, WeChat and many others. The volume of this writing is extraordinary. More writing is happening now than at any time in human history. New formats (the character limit on messages, for instance) challenge our creativity; new spellings (c u 2night) and acronyms (LOL) have been introduced. We have also seen the arrival of emoticons: pictures that stand for a variety of feelings and which can disambiguate short messages.

New digital letterforms have also become necessary for messages that must read across multiple devices in different scales and formats. New tools for digital type design have been developed and printers, too, have become sophisticated digital platforms. It was probably Adobe's software for printers that really helped desktop publishing take off in the mid-1980s.

Technological determinism

In this chapter we have seen how various tools and materials characterise different writing. But the danger today, as we experience the dramatic disruptive influence of new digital technologies, may be that we attribute too great a role to technologies in the evolution of writing and that we narrowly paint the future as one of competition between them – this would be a false choice. It may be that we need all of them.

Technological determinism in the field of writing overstates the role that technologies play in shaping what is written and the impact on society's structure and values. It is a powerful but reductionist viewpoint. Clearly technology is involved in forming writing but it interacts with existing drives and aspirations within communities of people. An example from the early world of writing illustrates the point. One theory of the origins of writing proposes that it evolved in Mesopotamia from counting, but how did it become a means for recording speech? Denise Schmandt-Besserat argues that technology had very little to do with it; rather it was related to beliefs about the afterlife and the practice of putting names and then prayers on grave goods.[5] Sumerians believed if your name continued to be spoken after your death your spirit would have life beyond the grave. Repurposing written symbols helped this. If they could stand for a sound, and not only the object to which they referred, a lot more could be done with them. It helped that Sumerian, the first language to be represented in writing, was so structured that it had many sound-alike words (homophones). In addition we can see from surviving texts about dream interpretation from ancient Sumer that Sumerians relished deriving meanings from the use of puns; the 'rebus principle', which Andrew Robinson described earlier in this book (see p. 25), was thus already alive and well in Sumerian society. What we see here, then, are juxtaposed material, social, linguistic and religious factors providing a creative context for this evolution.

Uses for multiple technologies

One of the most striking features of writing history is the variety of tools and materials employed, from wet clay to pixels of light, stone, metals, tree bark, paper, leather, textiles, bamboo and even human skin. Also striking is how many of these materials and tools have been in simultaneous use. There has never been only one writing material or tool available in any given society. The Romans carved letters in stone and etched them into metals, they wrote with reed pens and ink onto papyrus scrolls, they used metal styluses to write onto wax tablets and they painted letters on walls with brushes. They had multiple writing technologies.

One of the reasons for wanting multiple channels of technology to be available is because we often require writing to do different things in different circumstances. Some writing, like a boundary marker, we may want to be immovable and durable and capable of withstanding all weathers. Other messages may have a contrasting relationship to time: we need them to be erasable or, as in legal documents and accounts, modifiable only in very carefully controlled ways. We may wish for other correspondence to remain private: here one thinks of news stories from 2013 that the Kremlin was spending up to $200,000 on buying typewriters. In an age of electronic communications it had realised that some documents need to be offline and traceable back to source: typewriter technology fitted the bill.

Our lives are actually spent in a world of multiple intersecting writing technologies, from street signs to Google maps, subtitles to audiovisual clips, vehicle number plates and licensing documents, computers, printers and scanners. This complexity was brought home to scientists working in the area of information science (where they might expect computers alone to be sufficient) in a study of an American airport made in the late 1990s by a team from Xerox PARC.

The Palo Alto Research Center (PARC) is the research lab from which much of our modern information technology stemmed. It developed the first networked desktop computers with multifunctional software, the Ethernet, laser printers, and the look and feel of the windows desktops that we use today. The airport study came about because of a strategic error that Xerox made around this technology in the early 1980s. The scientists at PARC had invented 'the future' but Xerox executives could not see how it was relevant to what they regarded as their core business of photocopying – so they virtually gave away all this knowledge and technology. Soon they realised they had made a mistake of historic proportions. Where did we go wrong, they asked? The answer, they believed, was that they had tied their idea of the company to one individual piece of technology – the photocopy machine – without understanding that in a digital world they would need an identity that was independent of any one technology. So in searching for something that was at the core of their business but technologically independent they focused on the notion of Xerox the 'document company'. It was a brilliant idea; whatever document technology might become in the future they would continue to be the experts. Even if documents became entirely audiovisual they would still, theoretically, have a business.

But then they realised that to think about the future of documents they had to have an idea of what they actually were, how they worked now, and so informally a whole new area of research began to get under way. One of these research projects led a team of anthropologists to look at a document-rich environment: the ground-control operations room of an American airport.[6]

Ground 'operations' is in charge of everything that happens in the airport once a plane has landed and is at the gate: all the passenger and luggage movements, meals, and the refuelling of aircraft. Social scientists from Xerox PARC went in and monitored the room twenty-four hours a day; they interviewed the staff, and they watched and made notes of their daily activities. Initially they thought they would be able to view all this activity as one giant information system, but gradually they realised this was not going to be possible or desirable. The information necessary for the ground-control staff to do their jobs was coming in from so many different channels: from noisy runways, check-in desks, airport corridors, from co-workers monitoring various systems in their shared work space, from moving vehicles and aircraft. All these multiple, partial sources of information had to be read against each other in relation to an unfolding situation by the highly skilled operatives in the room. To accomplish this task ground-control staff were using multiple computer screens, computer print-outs, printed and photocopied manuals, whiteboards, notepads, telephone systems, radio-controlled walkie-talkies, 'shout outs' to the whole room, even the view through a window and much else.

The outcome of the study was not a large workstation that encompassed more and more facts about a context but a more nuanced understanding of what an information system actually is. An information system

is made up from multiple partial fragments of information resources that are read against each other in relation to an unfolding situation using a variety of tools and skills. The information system was the assemblage of artefacts together with all the tools used and work done to make sense of them. This is what writing is. It involves using assemblies of artefacts and skills. Furthermore, the multiple partial information resources may have a vital role to play in making something useful of human communication itself. Charles Goodwin (1943–2018), an anthropologist who once worked at PARC, has shown in many elegant papers that conversational analysis indicates conversations succeed not because there are no difficulties in understanding, but rather because humans have resources at their disposal to help them collaborate and repair misunderstandings.[7] In other words, we usually come to understand each other through the to and fro of conversation, and this is how meaning is actually established, which is why scripted conversations are so frustrating. Understanding something is actually a process of muddling through. It does not pass seamlessly from mind to mind like algorithms. This kind of process for understanding occurs in speech but it also happens in the way we use written artefacts themselves. Rarely are they not intended to be read against each other or some complex background context and we know, too, that it is good practice to look for multiple sources to confirm a 'story'. We collect those stories using different media in different environments and contexts employing

ABOVE Control room for operations within the city of Rio de Janeiro, 2017. Diverse data supplied by weather stations, traffic flow cameras and other information resources are gathered here.

different tools. The British television programme *Time Team* provides us with an illustration of such a process. The premise is that a team is invited in to study an archaeological site over the course of a weekend. The team's job is to 'make sense' of the site. The story of this sense-making process provides the dramatic narrative of the programme. During the course of sixty minutes lots of documentary evidence is collected, drawings made of excavations, finds examined and compared, old maps and legal documents searched for, and ground radar results and aerial photography obtained. As this all comes together during various meetings throughout the weekend, these multiple, partial sources of information send the evidence now this way and now that, through to the programme's denouement and final judgement.

For these reasons it is unsurprising that in all periods of human history, once writing systems get going, we find multiple tools and technologies in use, as well as many different kinds of material artefacts.

This chapter ends with a plea for the inclusion of all technologies in our thinking about making written artefacts, or 'documents' as we might broadly call them. There are few good reasons for one technology having to displace another; in the past they have usually just added another layer. Printing with movable type, for instance, was developed in the West in the 1450s, and it certainly triggered huge social changes, but handwriting did not disappear. In fact it became absolutely crucial to the next phase of scientific and economic development in the West. It was through handwritten letters and carefully kept notebooks of first-hand observations (in other words in handwriting) that all the new discoveries of the Age of Enlightenment (mid-seventeenth to early eighteenth centuries) were actually made and communicated. The Royal Society in London, for example, was founded as a place to meet, where international correspondence on scientific subjects could be read out to the assembled members. It was, in effect, a corresponding society. Handwriting was also crucial for the expansion of the first global corporations, the Dutch and British East India Companies. Careful documentation established their corporate nature and finances and regulated their complex overseas trading business, account books, minute books, bills of lading and share certificates. Handwriting was vital to the growth of all the distributed business operations that grew out of the Industrial Revolution. The kind of banking we know today began in handwritten promissory notes. All legal business continued to be conducted through handwritten documents into the late nineteenth century, as did personal correspondence and other writings.

A reason why one technology rarely completely displaces another is that continuity is important in systems based on widely understood conventions. There is a limit to how fast you can change without the system itself breaking down. One huge plus factor for the early uptake of the screen and printer as new writing tools in the 1990s was the development of 'Postscript', a page description language from Adobe that among other things gave us the PDF (Portable Document Format): a way of making documents on screen and in digital printers that looked like pages on paper. There was no technological reason that things had to go in this direction, but it really helped people understand how this technology could be useful to them.

All the materials and tools with which we write have rich histories that we can only briefly touch on here. Surfaces, with different weights, scale, colour, erasability, shape and availability, team up with marking processes to generate their own range of issues relating to storage, transport and reproduction. In essence, they all have very particular relationships with space and time – and thus with the human body and the various environments and concerns within which we operate. It is to these human connections that we turn in the next chapter.

Focus Two

THE DOUBLE PIGEON CHINESE TYPEWRITER

Emma Harrison

If you are not familiar with Chinese, then the concept of a Chinese typewriter may seem baffling. Even if you are, you may still find yourself at a loss trying to picture a mechanism able to deal with the realities of the Chinese script: Chinese has neither an alphabet nor a syllabary, but instead each character represents a word or concept. As a result, even basic literacy entails the ability to recognise thousands of characters, while the written language as a whole consists of tens of thousands. Thankfully, not all of these appear on a Chinese typewriter, but it would clearly take a great deal of skill, dexterity and muscle memory to operate proficiently.

In some ways, the Double Pigeon typewriter works like any other: you press a lever and a piece of type is brought up to strike a ribbon of ink, imprinting a single character on a piece of paper. In other ways, it is substantially different. Instead of a QWERTY keyboard, a lever-operated selection tool hovers over a tray bed of 2,418 'slugs' of type. In theory, these are some of the most common characters and are themselves organised into categories based on frequency of use and shared orthographic components, known as 'radicals'. But in case none of those are the character you are looking for, you are provided with two additional boxes of type each containing another 1,716 characters. Furthermore, as the type is loose within the tray bed, it is fully customisable: you can add, remove or rearrange the characters to suit your needs.

The story behind the Chinese typewriter is one of compromise. For over a century, Chinese characters were scrutinised, prioritised, categorised, fragmented, encoded, decoded and ultimately reimagined as new approaches were devised to distil thousands of characters into a system that was accessible for everyday use. Looking at a Chinese typewriter now, it is easy to forget all the quirky experiments, failed prototypes or ill-timed innovations that led to that point, but they all played their part in developing a once-fabled machine that would bring typing technology into the homes and offices of a rapidly modernising China.

As early as the 1920s and '30s, typewriters became a common fixture of workplaces around China. However, with thousands of characters to navigate it is not surprising that twenty characters per minute was considered a decent pace. The Double Pigeon was by no means China's first typewriter, nor even the first to be mass-produced, but it was in the right place at the right time and soon became the typewriter of choice in Maoist China.

Manufactured in Shanghai around 1975, this machine is full of clues that speak to its historical and political context: its characters are simplified, owing to the language reforms that took place soon after the founding of the People's Republic of China in 1949; in an area of the tray bed reserved for special category characters (for example, numbers, weights, measures and cardinal directions) are the characters used to form 人民 *renmin* 'the people' and 中央委员会 *Zhongyang weiyuanhui* 'Central Committee'; even the instruction manual reflects the values of the time, its red border framing a quote from Chairman Mao (1893–1976) himself: 'the people, and only the people, are the driving force behind the making of world history'.[1]

Typewriters played a crucial role in the democratisation of printing technologies, placing them in the hands of ordinary people more than a century before word processors and personal computers. The Double Pigeon Chinese typewriter is very much of its time, and yet oddly timeless as it embodies a single stage in an ongoing dialogue between one writing system and the everyday technology that people use to produce it.

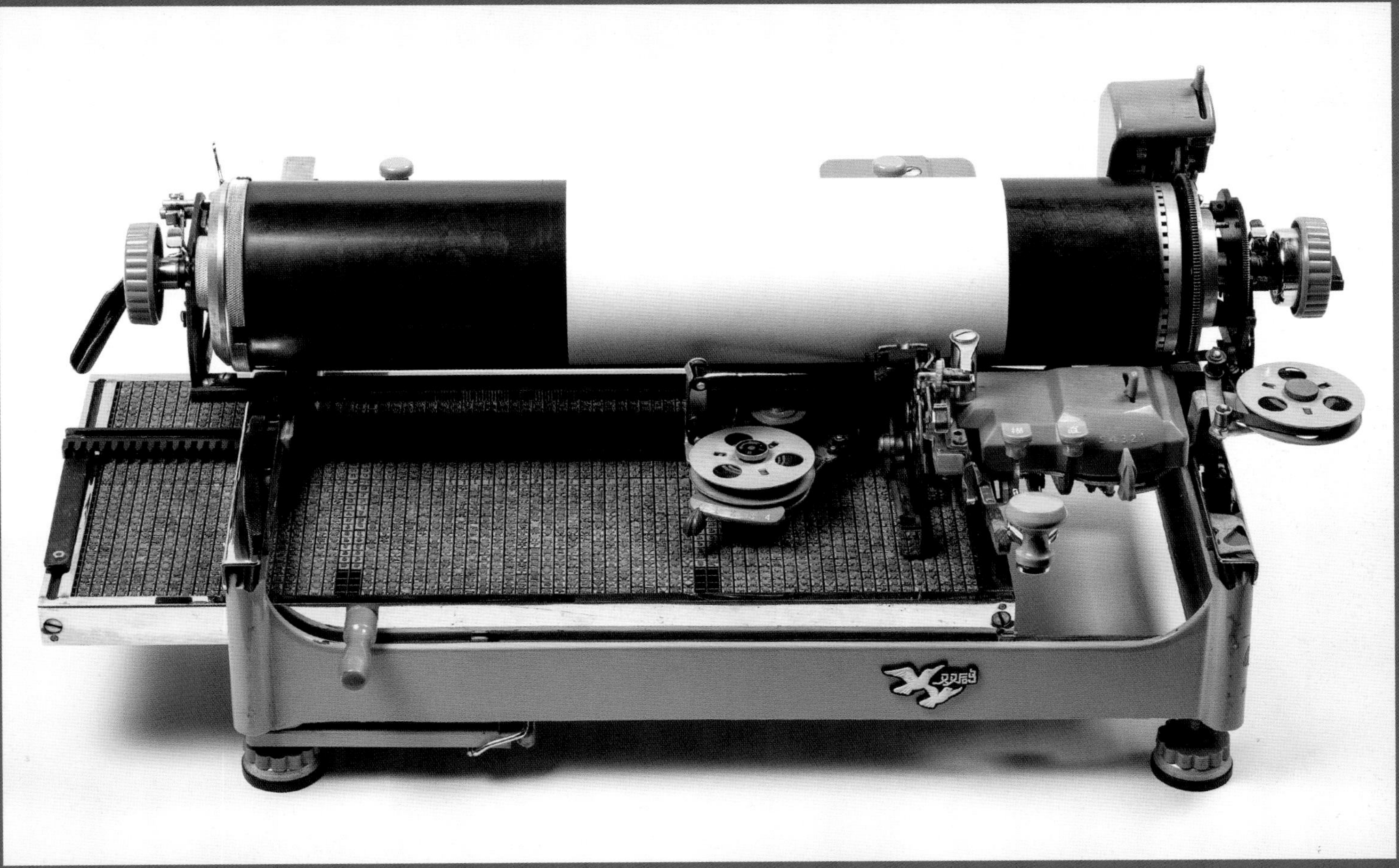

Double Pigeon Chinese typewriter. Shanghai (China), 1975.
British Library collection

4

COMMUNITIES OF WRITERS

EWAN CLAYTON

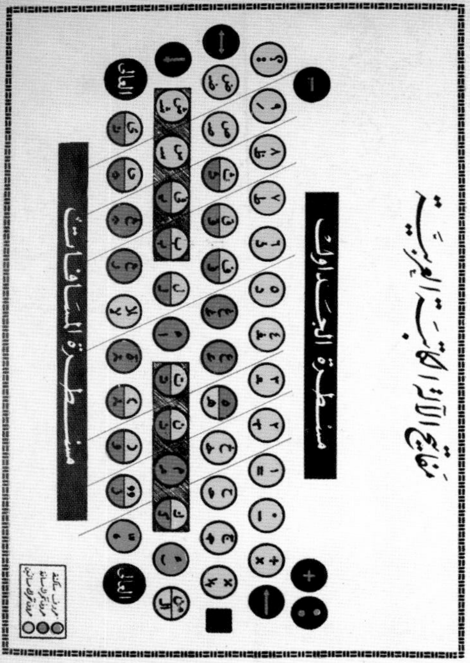

تطلب من دار مكتبة الحياة - بيروت

People engage with writing in many ways: as a skilled craft, a tool for a specific purpose and as a means of expression. In this chapter we present objects that show four ways of engaging with writing. But before we dive into the detail it might be useful to step back and look at the kind of skills that are on display here and what that says about writing itself and how it works.

We have looked at a number of writing systems, at the development of the roman alphabet, and the tools and materials that different writing systems use. But if we are to become functionally literate within our society there is one other skill associated with writing that we have to master. Writing never comes to us floating in the air; it is always materialised in some type of document. It might be as a book, the news on an electronic ticker tape running round a building, an address label, a supermarket receipt or a work of art. It will always be embedded in some kind of written artefact whose form we can usually hope to recognise. For convenience we can call these forms document genres: recognisable examples of a particular category of an object. Even at a distance most of us know what a birthday card or invitation should look like. One of the skills we have to learn if writing is to be useful is how to create and handle these objects; we need to understand the conventions and expectations that surround them. If writing systems and letters make up one side of the coin of writing, then the other is the world of documents themselves: genres of written artefacts and the communities that use them.

One can think of written objects as human bodies and writing symbols as the blood that circulates within them, animating them. It is these bodies that take writing out into the world and allow it to pass from hand to hand, to circulate, to be stored and consulted. Without these bodies writing has no real purchase on the world. One of the problems with the term 'information', which we have tried to avoid using here, is that it suggests writing is disembodied and has no specific material existence or containing structures, whereas it is precisely the details of how writing is embodied that can explain how it has particular effects in this or that case. Different kinds of bodies allow different kinds of interactions to happen. Even when embodied in the circuitry of a computer or stored in the Cloud writing is given certain physical properties and potentials by the specific context in which it is embedded.

Genres are intrinsically social. They are shaped by repeated actions of different individuals or communities over time, and they materialise aspects of a community's life. As material artefacts these written objects are also culture-bearing artefacts.

Different genres of documents can also be thought of as building communities in very particular ways. For while they may represent specific actions – a request for information, a promise – the fact is that from the moment of their conception that action was actually happening: they are life itself unfolding, they are an activity materialising itself. Take a document, such as a simple promissory note to repay the lender a sum of money; when it was being written back in the seventeenth century, it was alive. Banking was actually happening when it was being written; writing that document was doing banking. Human conventions and then organisations grew up around this repeated practice of writing. The organisation (banking) and the document were co-creating themselves; they were mutually instantiating each other.

Writing is also powerful because it originates and lands in our bodies; it is a somatic process. Writing might be thought of as lying inert on a bookshelf or good for one transaction only, but actually when reading and writing happen they physically embed themselves in our neurobiology with all that potential to interact with our energy and imagination, our desire for safety,

PREVIOUS PAGE *al-Uslūb al-sahīh fī al-ḍarb 'alá al-ālah al-kātibah al-'Arabīyah: 'ilmī 'amalī bi-ṭarīqat al-lams.* Printed book. Beirut, 1966. British Library: 14544.ee.60

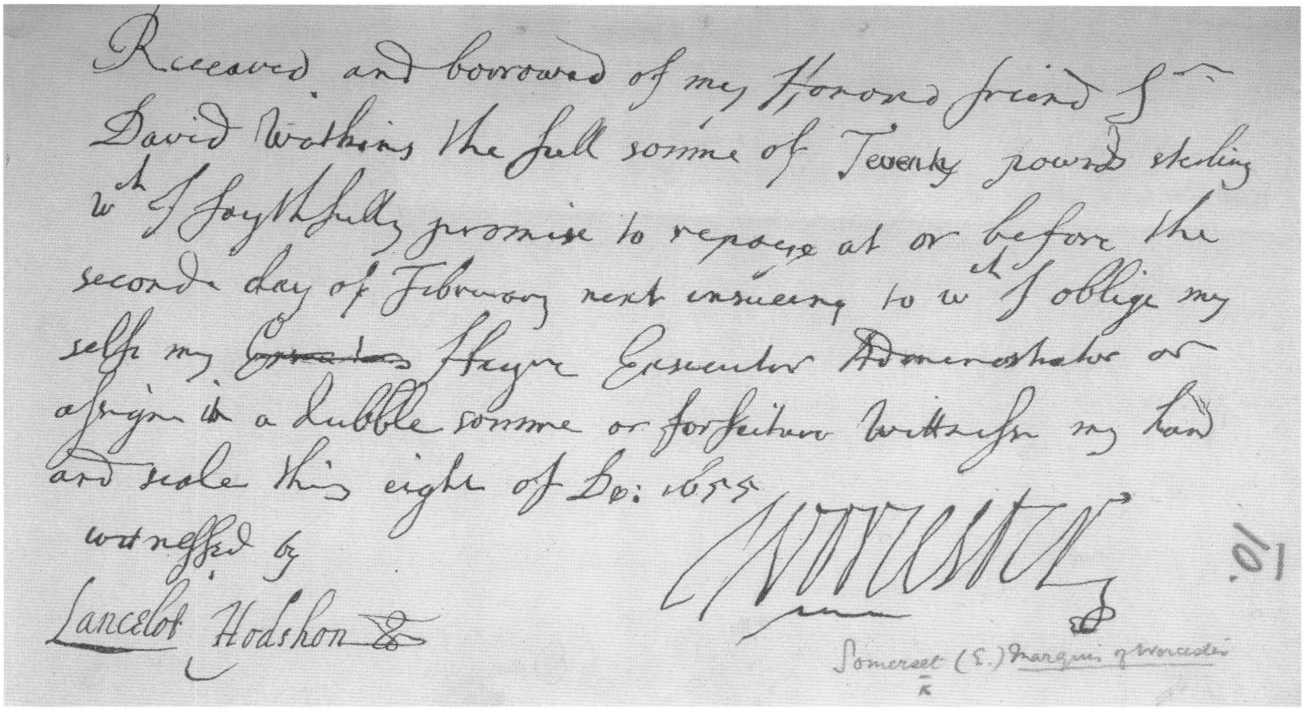
Received and borrowed of my Honored friend Sr David Watkins the full somme of Twenty pounds sterling wch I faythfully promise to repaye at or before the second day of February next ensuing to wch I oblige my selfe my ~~[illegible]~~ Heyre Executor Administrator or assigne in a dubble somme or forfeiture witnesse my hand and seale this eight of Dec: 1655

witnessed by

Lancelot Hodshon

Worcester

Somerset (E.) Marquis of Worcester

10

dignity, a sense of belonging, history and purpose. We use writing because we have discovered that it can be employed to bring order to our world and meaning into our lives and relationships. Writing and reading documents can also build our sense of self.

So far, writing systems, technologies and the documents themselves have been presented as three topics, but in fact they are completely interlocked with one another. The architecture and physical reality of a document, the technologies and materials from which they are made, and the human communities and conventions that build up around them are all mutually constitutive of one another. If you alter a factor in one area there will be a knock-on effect in another. That is why a change in the medium from paper to electronics can have such far-reaching effects. One illustration of how sensitive systems of documents can be to a wide variety of technological and behavioural factors comes from an outcome of the PARC ground-control operations room study that was mentioned in the previous chapter (p. 111). Following the first phase of the study the airport was knocked down and rebuilt. The team then went back in and filmed the same people, doing the same job; initially even the flight schedule was exactly the same. But there had been a shift in documentary procedures and shapes. It seemed a huge puzzle why this should be. The reason turned out to be that the chairs in the room had been replaced. The old chairs had wheels on them: you could scoot over and look out of a window or swivel across and glance at a colleague's screen. With the new fixed chair arrangement, like a lecture theatre, this was no longer possible. Information flows had been disrupted simply by changing the furniture. This is why it is helpful to think of documents and writing existing within ecologies and it exposes the many risks faced by large-scale public programmes of

ABOVE Edward Somerset (2nd Marquess of Worcester), promissory note for £20 received from Sir David Watkins, 1655. Lithographed facsimile, *c.*1840. British Library: Tab.436.a.5(10)

digital conversion without very careful understanding of how a current system is responsible for the way things are (rather than how it works in theory). Without this knowledge such schemes are likely to disturb the current order of things in unsuspected ways. It may also be one of the explanations for why digitisation has not yet yielded the gains in productivity that had been anticipated; instead we have a so-called 'productivity gap'.

Sometimes the work a document does can be invisible to workflow analysis. A number of years ago a company introduced a multitasking photocopying machine. Unexpectedly the paperwork around the production of a document went up considerably. The company did not realise that by allowing everything to be sent electronically it had cut out an important part of how the office was functioning. When you handed over the document in person not only did you collect a lot of information (how busy they were, could you trust the deadline, etc.), but you also had many other interactions as you carried the document to the print room – brief conversations, noticing who was in and out, etc. – all of which had come to play a role in the smooth operation of the workplace. All of these interactions had been stripped out by the simple action of sending the document electronically rather than hand delivering it.

Because the idea of genre is important to our functioning as literate citizens, this chapter looks at writing through the objects associated with several specific categories of writers: those who are learning to write, artists and designers, the note-taker, and the citizen. There are many more communities or interest groups that we could discuss: those connected with religion and the law, for instance. Considering communities carrying out particular tasks will help us see how the genre, tools and technologies, and all the various social structures that surround the written word, interact to create a play of constantly shifting forms.

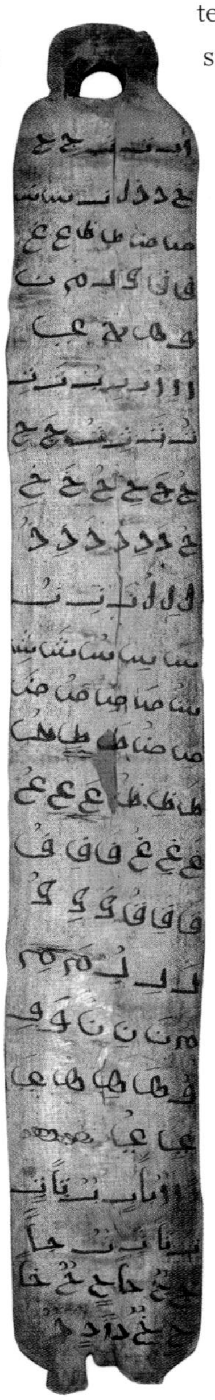

Learners

Writing is a skill that has to be acquired at a number of levels. We can study writing simply in terms of its shape: getting to know what the letters and characters look like. Writing is also a kinaesthetic skill: we need to understand the number, order and direction in which strokes are formed and become accomplished in making those movements. Writing has to be mastered so that it can become a purposeful tool of communication. How do we learn to create comprehensible messages or records? We may want to write poetry, too, or use writing to think, or simply to wonder at the world. And we can pursue writing as a means of personal aesthetic expression.

From time immemorial imitation has played a key role in learning how to write: a student copies a teacher's exemplar written on a wax tablet, slate, blackboard or slip of paper. Instruction can happen alongside the performance or it can come later. Quintilian, the Roman educator (b. *c.*AD 35), writes of teaching children to know the shapes by making them sets of ivory letters that they can play with and suggests learning how to trace incised letter shapes with one's finger. In East Asia characters are sometimes learnt, alongside work on paper, by classes using the whole arm to write in the air. This physical exercise builds up the writer's muscle memory for the character. In classical Chinese calligraphy it is the whole arm that writes (from the shoulder joint), not the fingers or the wrist. Different systems pose different challenges.

To be able to write Arabic one needs to learn twenty-nine letters and eight diacritical marks, but Arabic has had such a long history of writing by hand that it has developed up to four variants for each letter according to the position in which it falls in a word. Letters can have stand-alone forms, and forms for the beginning, middle or end of a word. This makes handwriting instruction manuals complex. There are about sixty shapes a child must master; this is the first stage of learning. Next one learns how letters are joined in different combinations, as Arabic is always written in a cursive style. Indeed the way letters join partly accounts for the adaptations of shape that letters have taken for various placements within a word.

Japanese children have one of the most complex writing systems to learn. In elementary school they practise *hiragana* and *katakana*, two syllabaries that are used for writing Japanese. But the Japanese system also borrows some characters from the Chinese and children study a few at a time in a prescribed order. They will have mastered 1,006 characters over their six years in the elementary school system. In addition, in the third year of school they are taught *kaisho*: characters written calligraphically with a brush, which are practised on special squared paper.

Since the 1950s the government of the People's Republic of China has limited the overall number of standard-use characters and promoted a simplified form of writing in order to encourage literacy. The principal modification was to reduce the number of strokes the characters contain. Standard lists were produced in 1956 and 1964. In 2013 the Chinese Ministry of Education ruled that calligraphy would now be a required course in primary and middle school. Because of the long unbroken tradition of teaching calligraphy in China, Chinese has strong conventions relating to stroke sequences, their number, order and direction. The sequence for each character is standardised. There is, in a sense, an

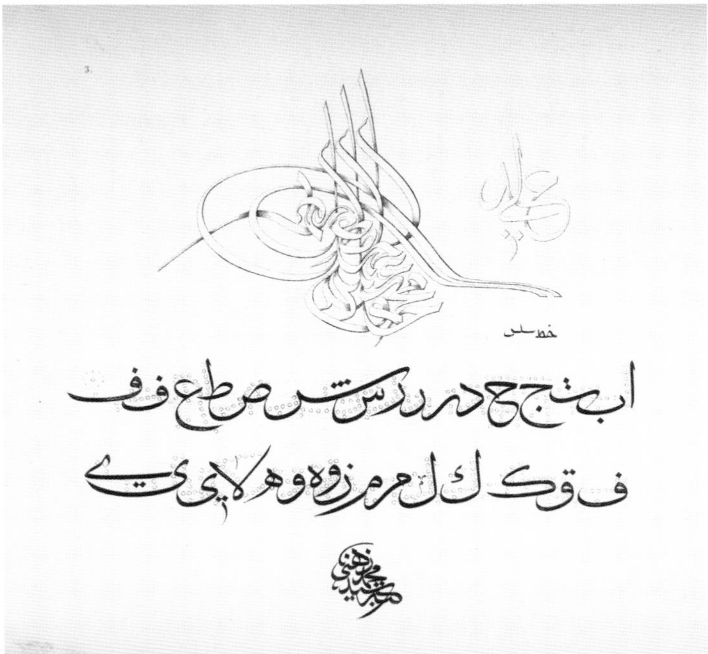

ABOVE Boys write verses from the Qur'an on their prayer boards in the madrasa of Sidi Abdulsalam. Zliten (Libya), 2007
BELOW Ottoman calligraphy manual. Engraved book. Istanbul, 1850s? British Library: HSL.74/671, Plate 3
OPPOSITE Qur'an board with Arabic character exercises. Wood. Somalia, 20th century. British Library: Or.16442

official system. Much the same is true for fine calligraphy in Arabic, Ottoman, Persian and Urdu.

By contrast, in the roman tradition an understanding of the number, order and direction of strokes, the *ductus* for formal calligraphic letters, has been lost (except for italic and *fraktur*). This happened because the printing press and movable type gradually replaced the genre of work in which the book script calligraphers in Europe were skilled – and their craft knowledge was rarely written down. Those involved in the twentieth-century calligraphic revival in Europe had to rediscover older sequences by careful analysis of historical manuscripts. It also means that there are varied stroke number, order and direction sequences even in European handwriting, especially where ligatures are involved.

Writing systems are always undergoing change. Learning to write is a lifelong process, as we change and the world around us also changes. Modern technology is having an impact in a variety of ways. In China and Japan there are increasing reports of character amnesia as more and more people write electronically using keypads on mobile phones and computers. Pinyin (literally 'spell sound') allows Chinese writers to spell out the sounds of Chinese characters in roman letters and then software converts the letter strings into characters. Bopomofo (or *Zhuyin fuhao*) is a system that does the same using a form of character-based shorthand. It means that people no longer need to write the characters every day.

In the USA the introduction of computer keyboard technology has raised the question as to whether learning cursive (joined-up) writing is useful any more. From 2010 onwards the US federal government's Core Curriculum for English no longer required the teaching of cursive writing; print script alone would suffice. In Europe Finland followed suit. Yet the newest computer software is progressively invested in handwriting recognition; as computing becomes miniaturised and as economies such as India and China become increasingly significant markets (for whom the keyboard can be unwieldy) it is likely that handwriting will cross over onto digital platforms as one of the main ways that we interact with the digital world.

It is only fair to point out that cursive writing as practised in the USA today is still an essentially looped nineteenth-century script with elaborate capital letter shapes that bear little relationship to printed capital letters. These scripts were developed by commercial penmen and then initially marketed as systems through business schools. In Britain, where there is no such clamour for change, almost a century of continuous handwriting reform has delivered a much simpler form of cursive writing and block capital letters.

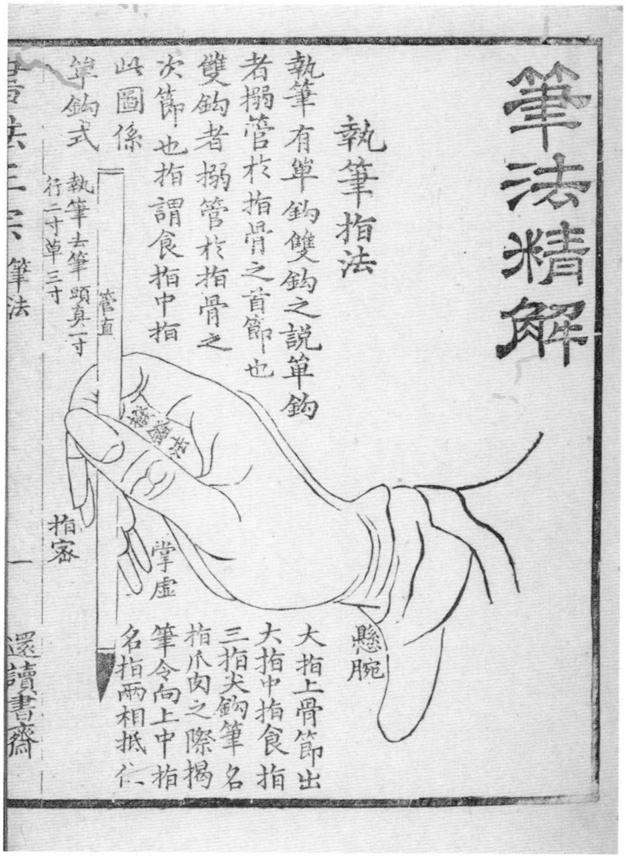

ABOVE Illustration of correct way to hold a brush. Xu Shixun, *Shu fa zheng xong*. Printed book. China, 1835. British Library: 15344.b.13, fol.6.

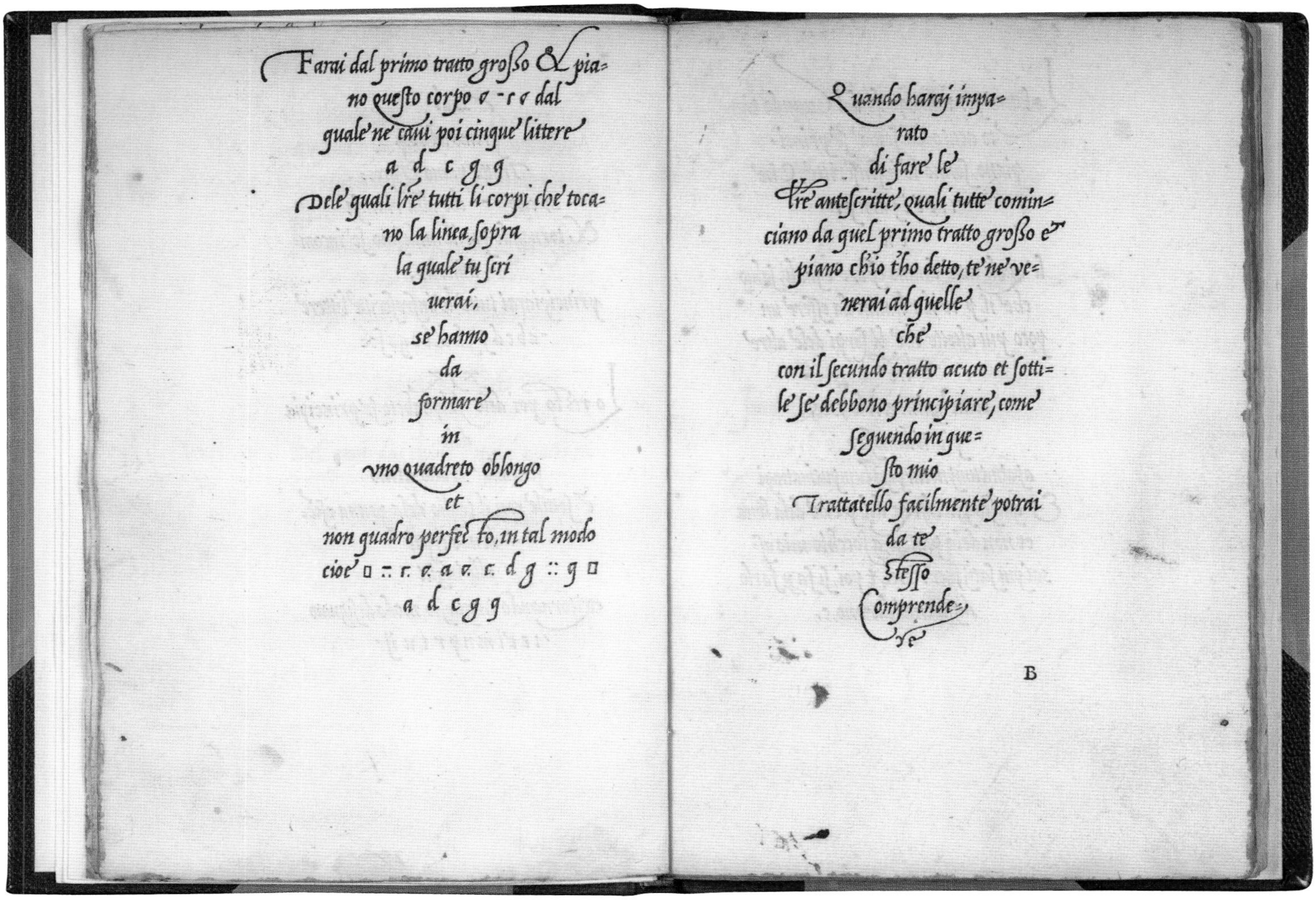
Farai dal primo tratto grosso & pia-
no questo corpo
quale ne caui poi cinque littere
a d c g q
Dele quali lre tutti li corpi che toca-
no la linea, sopra
la quale tu scri
uerai,
se hanno
da
formare
in
vno quadreto oblongo
et
non quadro perfetto, in tal modo
a d c g q
Quando harai impa-
rato
di fare le
lre antescritte, quali tutte comin-
ciano da quel primo tratto grosso &
piano ch'io t'ho detto, te ne ve-
nerai ad quelle
che
con il secundo tratto acuto et sotti-
le se debbono principiare, come
seguendo in que-
sto mio
Trattatello facilmente potrai
da te
stesso
comprende-
re
B

There has always been a strand of teachers who have been interested in applying theory to their practice. One of the most interesting can be seen in the Arabic tradition, where the rhomboid dot has been employed to organise a letter's proportion. However, as this became instrumental in transforming Arabic calligraphy as an art form, this example will be discussed in the section on artists and designers later in this chapter (see p. 131).

The earliest printed writing manual from Europe is dated to 1522 and was written by the Italian Ludovico degli Arrighi in Rome. He took the newly popular italic style of handwriting and showed a simple logic behind the shapes. Using four dots he asked the reader to imagine they form the corners of a parallelogram that slopes forwards. This provides the basic shape around which a letter can be written.

Printed manuals allowed the teaching of one writing master to spread. Previously a master's influence was confined to the pupils he taught, but now an exemplar could travel right across Europe; new models

ABOVE Ludovico degli Arrighi, *La Operina*. Engraved book. Rome, 1522. British Library: C.31.f.8(1)

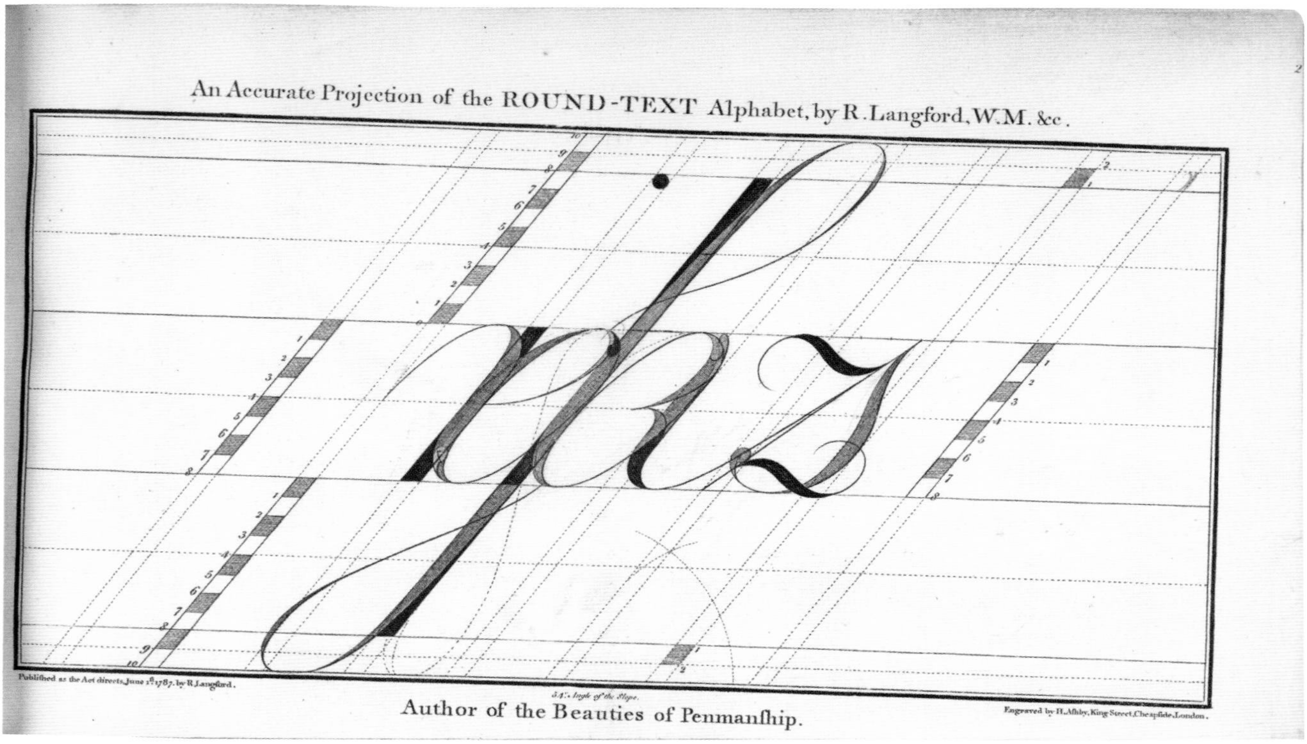

and standards were being set by the most popular books.

An Accurate Projection of the ROUND-TEXT Alphabet, by R. Langford, W.M. &c.
Author of the Beauties of Penmanship.

A generation later it was fellow Italian Giovanni Francesco Cresci, born in Milan *c.*1535, who set the pattern for the future with a slightly more rounded and cursive script that led ultimately to English round hand, the dominant hand in commerce in the eighteenth and early nineteenth centuries. In the eighteenth century clear structural analysis was applied to handwriting just as it was to type. The British understanding was typified by a diagram from Richard Langford titled 'An Accurate Projection of the Round-Text Alphabet', in his book *A Complete Set of Rules and Examples for Writing with Accuracy & Freedom* (London, 1787).

In the early nineteenth century a new way of conceiving penmanship became popular. Promoted by Joseph Carstairs (1783–1844), originally a tailor from Sunderland, it emphasised whole-arm movement. This movement comes from the shoulder joint. Carstairs recommended people begin to write by making patterns at least 4 inches (10 centimetres) high and allow their pens to travel to all four corners of the page. The emphasis here was placed on the human body, not simply the letter shape. The Carstairs system became popular in Europe and North America where it was picked up and promoted by the educator Benjamin Franklin Foster (1798–1868). Paradoxically, free shoulder movement is only possible if the arm and hand remain stiff and unmoving. To assist in this Carstairs, and teachers who followed him, sometimes bound the pen to the hand of the writer with ribbons, so that no other movement was possible. This was the era of the whalebone corset for women and stiffened collars for men, so handwriting, too, was being disciplined into what the American historian Tamara Plakins Thornton

ABOVE Richard Langford, *A Complete Set of Rules and Examples for Writing with Accuracy & Freedom*. Page cropped crookedly during a rebinding. Printed book. London: Published for the Author, 1787. British Library: 1322.m.55, fol. 3

describes as a technology of the self: 'pedagogy promised a good deal more than training in a particular skill. Its real product was not handwriting but men, men of a type compatible with a new social order.'[1]

In the mid-nineteenth century the new social and industrial order in Britain required greater clarity of form and practicality in handwriting. The Vere Foster Civil Service Hand copybooks were initially conceived as a philanthropic scheme to help Irish emigrants instruct themselves in writing before leaving for the USA, in order to assist with gaining employment. Vere Foster (1819–1900) eliminated the contrast between heavily weighted downstrokes and thin upstrokes in favour of strokes with an even thickness. He made the letters more upright. The scheme was endorsed by the British Prime Minister Lord Palmerston and endured in parts of the British Isles into the 1960s.

The present-day method of teaching handwriting in the UK has its roots in a report for the London County

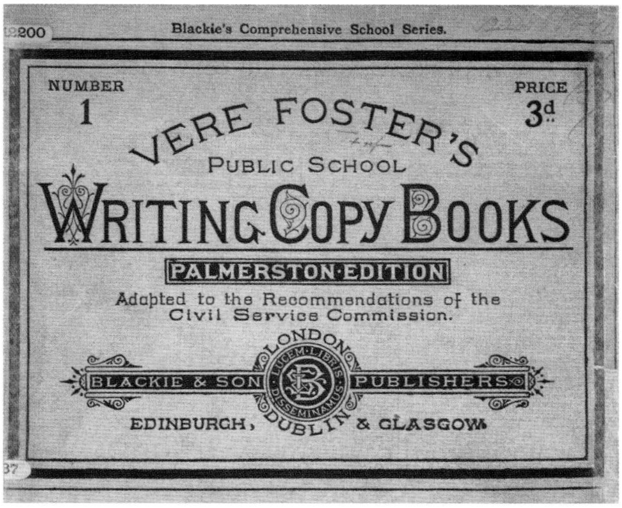

ABOVE *Vere Foster's Public School Writing Copy Books: Palmerston edition.* Printed book. Edinburgh & Glasgow: Blackie & Sons, 1881. British Library: 12200.bbb.20/37
BELOW Joseph Carstairs, *Lectures on the Art of Writing*, plate before p. 161. Printed book. 5th edn. London: J. Taylor, 1822. British Library: RB.23.a.23715

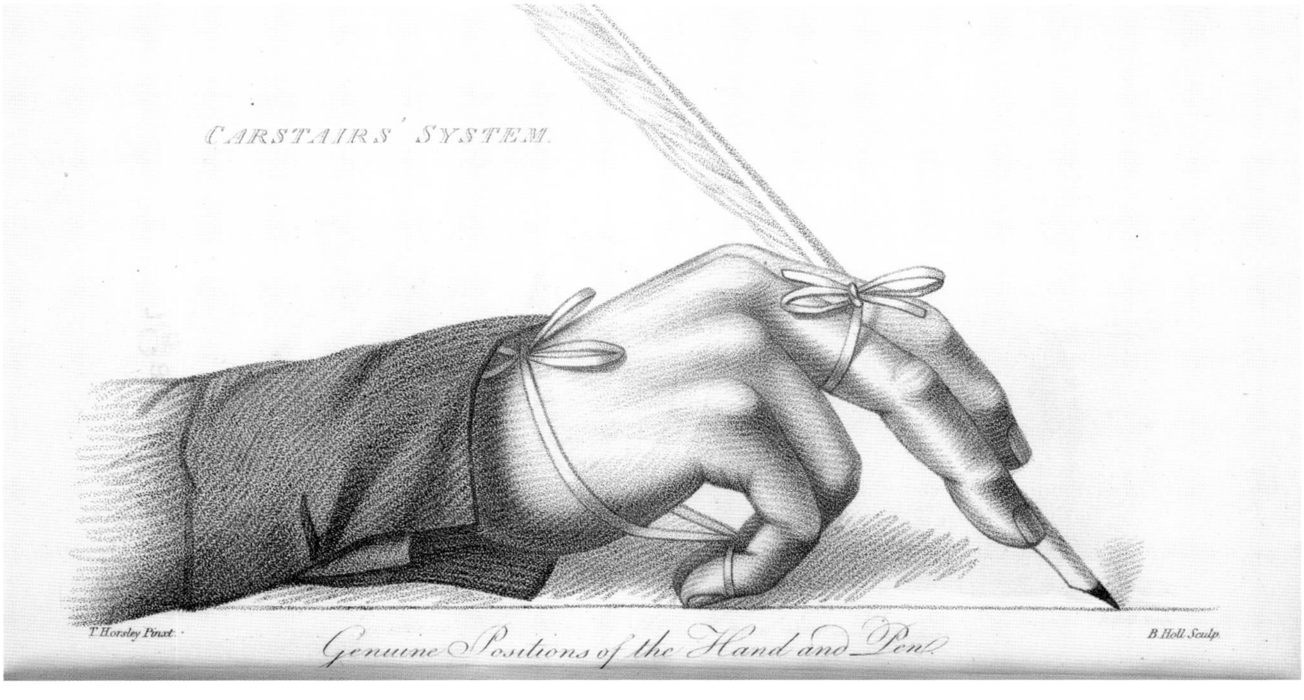

Council in 1906. It was presented by the calligrapher Edward Johnston (1872–1944), known today for his design of the London Transport type and logo. He recommended that students retrace the evolution of the roman letterform, starting with capitals on wax tablets (this idea gives us the block capitals we use today), and then follow their historical transformation into lower-case forms. Next, using a broad-edged pen they should try to write a basic lower-case print script that could mature into a running hand. Johnston's ideas were not sympathetically received, but in 1913 – much to his surprise – the LCC announced the adoption of a handwriting system they called 'print script'.

Johnston's ideas had been picked up by new educational theorists, however, who saw childhood as a developmental process. Children could not be expected to produce adult handwriting, since their neuro-muscular and cognitive development was not yet complete. Handwriting was an emergent process. Over time the child would find ways of joining up their letters and a unique script would evolve. And there were further justifications: not only were these simple shapes suited to the limited physiological development of the child, but a child could start to form the letters and express themselves in words the moment they began to learn. Furthermore, these letters were visually related to the letter shapes children saw when they read. 'Manuscript', as this system was later called in the USA, had reconceived handwriting 'as a means "to tell" rather than a motor habit'.[2] At school children learnt to write the day's date and record the weather, to order seeds for the classroom's window box, to make notices of all kinds: these were real tasks, not just penmanship exercises.

The only handwriting scheme Johnston directly endorsed was that of his pupil Marion Richardson (1892–1946), although the form in which we have it today does not include the revision she had intended to make before her untimely death. The new scheme

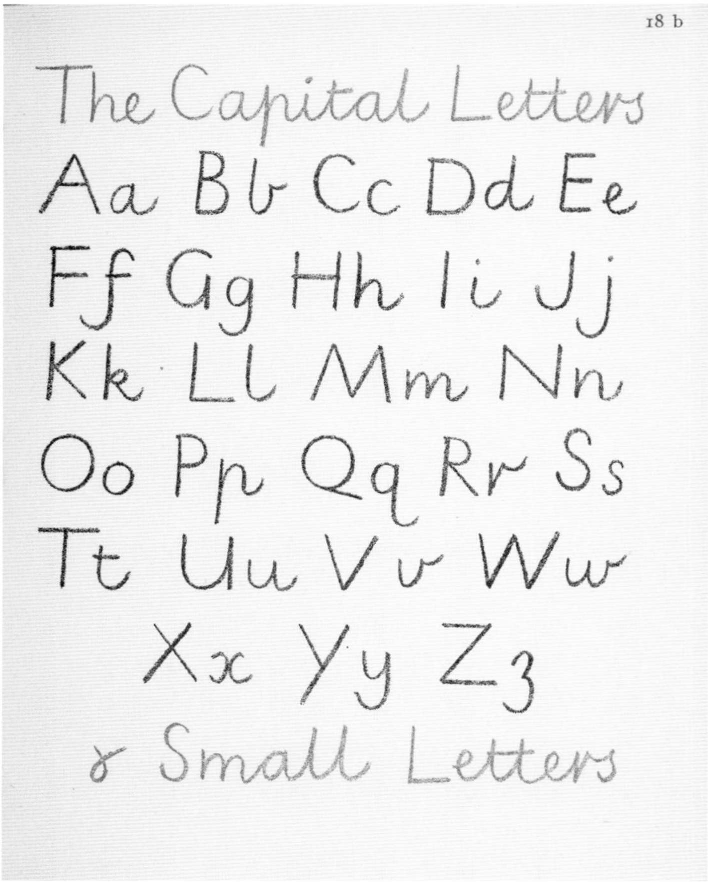

would have prioritised a different writing rhythm. Richardson called it an 'arcade' rhythm – echoing the arches of the **m** and **n** – in preference to the 'garlanded' rhythm we see in the letter **u**. Too many writers were forming **m** and **n** shapes that could not be told apart from the letter **u**. She was onto something for it is indeed the top part of a word that is used in word recognition. Preserving the forms in that upper area is something that makes a script intrinsically more legible. Simplified schemes like those in Richardson's copy-books are the origin of many of the handwriting models we use today.

Following the Second World War, the new Elizabethan age coincided with a revival of interest in

ABOVE Marion Richardson, *Writing & Writing Patterns.* Printed book. London: University of London Press, 1935. British Library: 7946.e.6, Book 1, p. 18b.

italic hands; they have provided the model for many British, European and North American handwriting programmes. One of the leading proponents of italic hands in the USA was Lloyd Reynolds (1902–1978). He taught English and art at Reed College in Portland, Oregon. It was there that Steve Jobs (1955–2011) discovered a love for well-designed lettering, a feature he would later ensure had a place on all his new Apple computers. For more detail about current ideas in handwriting education and research I recommend readers turn to Chapter 6 in this book.

Artists and designers

As well as performing a functional purpose writing has been seen as a form of art: a playground for human invention, ingenuity, wonder and skill. While some aim to meet the highest expectations of a society, others seek to challenge and reinvent, and whereas an artist may be free to choose where and how to express themselves, a designer always needs to communicate the particular brief that they have been given.

Within traditional calligraphy there have been limits on freedom imposed by the nature of the task. Before the arrival of printing calligraphers were responsible for passing on literature from one generation to another. If the work was not made to last and was not legible it failed in this task. It is only recently that calligraphy has been freed from this burden of legibility and able to explore its full graphic potential. In the examples of fine calligraphy we present here from Europe, Asia and Africa there is a broad consensus about what makes work interesting: an explicit sense of form and finish to the written strokes; careful balancing of space and weight; an overall awareness of pattern in which one can discern certain themes that both balance and contrast with each other; an understanding of deliberate proportion applied to the text block and the page; and finally, and perhaps most significantly, ease of movement.

Ideas have changed many times in history about what makes a beautiful form. Behind much Western art and writing lie notions that come from the Greeks. When Polykleitos, the Greek sculptor from the fifth century BC, wrote his famous *Canon* he declared that beauty comes from the proportion of one part to another and of all the parts to the whole. Similar ideas seem to have led the Greeks to think in a modular way about their alphabet (and design in general) and it has remained true of classic roman calligraphy through to modern times. The alphabet is not seen as a random collection of twenty-six letters but is conceived of as a whole system of interlocking proportions based on squares, rectangles and circles; these idealised proportions are often modified in practice but always with an idea of inner coherence guiding them.

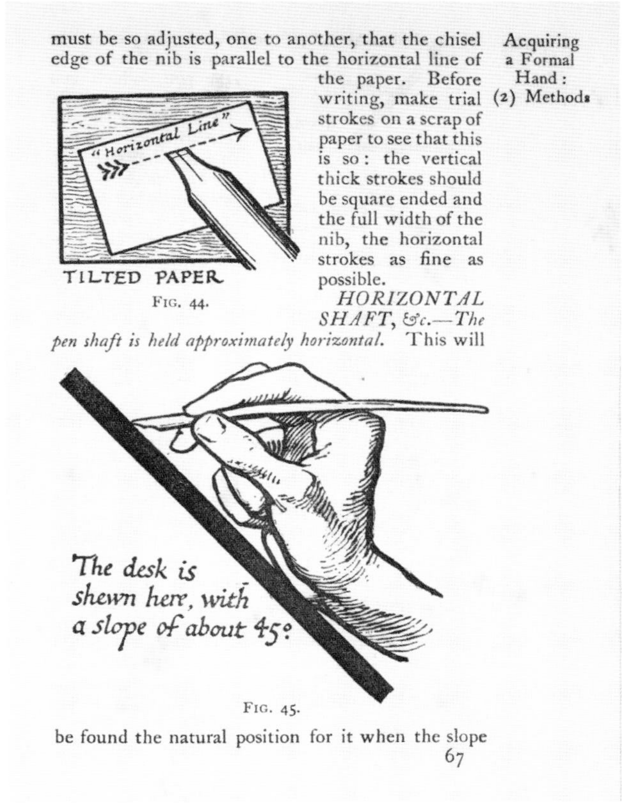
must be so adjusted, one to another, that the chisel edge of the nib is parallel to the horizontal line of the paper. Before writing, make trial strokes on a scrap of paper to see that this is so: the vertical thick strokes should be square ended and the full width of the nib, the horizontal strokes as fine as possible.

Acquiring a Formal Hand: (2) Methods

HORIZONTAL SHAFT, &c.—The pen shaft is held approximately horizontal. This will be found the natural position for it when the slope

67

ABOVE Edward Johnston, *Writing & Illuminating, & Lettering (Artistic Crafts Series)*. Printed book. London: John Hogg, 1906. British Library: 07942.e.1/5, p. 67

pudore: & operiantur
sicut diploide confusione sua
Confitebor dn̄o nimis in ore meo
& in medio multorum
laudabo eum
Qui astitit a dextris pauperis
ut saluam facer&
a persequentibus animā meā

PSALM̄ DAUID.

DIXIT DN̄S DN̄O MEO.

SEDE A DEXTRIS MEIS
Donec ponā inimicos tuos
scabellum pedum tuorum
Uirgam uirtutis tuę emitt& dn̄s

At the heart of the twentieth-century revival of calligraphy in Europe was the British calligrapher Edward Johnston, a self-educated man who studied calligraphy by going back into the manuscript collections of the British Museum. He realised that the historical writing tool for the manuscripts he consulted was an edged pen, which was different to the pointed pen that most people used for handwriting in his day. Through exacting study he re-created what was essentially a lost tradition. He began teaching writing, illuminating and lettering at the Central School of Arts and Crafts in London in 1899. In 1906 he published a handbook on the subject including chapters on calligraphy type, painted lettering and cut letters in stone. It was through this book and his teaching at the Royal College of Art that the revival spread.

The manuscript that inspired his basic calligraphic teaching hand (he called it his 'foundational hand') was the tenth-century *Ramsey Psalter*. Here we see letter shapes broadly similar to the letters we use in type today. The alphabet has an inner structural coherence: one can see the arches at the top of the **m** and **n** reflect the curve at the top of the **o**; the shape of the **o** can be seen also behind the **d** and **p**; the **u** is like an **n** rotated through 180 degrees. This hand is written with a consistent pen angle (the angle at which the nib is held in relation to the line one writes along), and at a letter height of about four nib widths. The clear sense of relationships existing between the form of one letter and another is harmonious. This hand was written by a Benedictine monk sometime in the 980s in a monastery in late Anglo-Saxon England. The script is freely written with an unselfconscious ease. There is no showing off and the letters sit together as one community echoing the values that underpinned St Benedict's rule of life. This was the model that lay behind Johnston's recommendation that we begin writing with a 'print' script and edged pen.

By strange coincidence of timing the scribe of the *Ramsey Psalter* was born in the same era as the key calligrapher for major developments in the Arab tradition. While the English monastic reformation was beginning in Anglo-Saxon England, in the city of Baghdad 'Alī Ibn Muqla (885/6–940), who had served as vizier to three Abbasid caliphs, was pining in prison. He had suffered grievously for his involvement in politics and he would die, perhaps by execution, on 20 July 940.

Ibn Muqla was a skilled calligrapher. When political rivals had his right hand cut off, legend says he continued to write with a pen fastened to his arm. In his mind he composed an overarching system of proportions for Arabic script, perhaps Pythagorean in inspiration. He took as its basic element the rhomboid dot, one of the simplest shapes a square-nibbed pen can make. On this, he built a system that resonated on all levels of Islamic philosophy and which in practice meant that an invisible grid of dots could be used to visualise related proportions across an alphabet of any current or future Arabic letterform. This allowed Arabic calligraphy to develop and to extend formal thinking even to cursive shapes, so that, to quote the celebrated German scholar Annemarie Schimmel, henceforth 'the perfection of a script is judged according to the relation of the letters to each other, not simply to their shapes'.[3] Ibn Muqla had invented a method of study and analysis that gave a rational and metaphysical basis to his calligraphic tradition. Other calligraphers, such as his follower Ibn al-Bawwāb (d. 1022), might bring more grace to his work, and later Yāqūt al-Mustaʿṣimī (d. 1298) would propose a different way to trim the pen, but this method is foundational for all future manifestations of formal Arabic calligraphy.

The first evidence for Arabic writing dates from the early sixth century. There was a simple everyday handwriting and more formal careful writing attributable to different cities. The formal writing style of many early

OPPOSITE Latin psalter, known as the *Ramsey Psalter.* Manuscript book (parchment). Winchester or Ramsey? (England), second quarter of 10th century.
British Library: Harley MS 2904, 144r

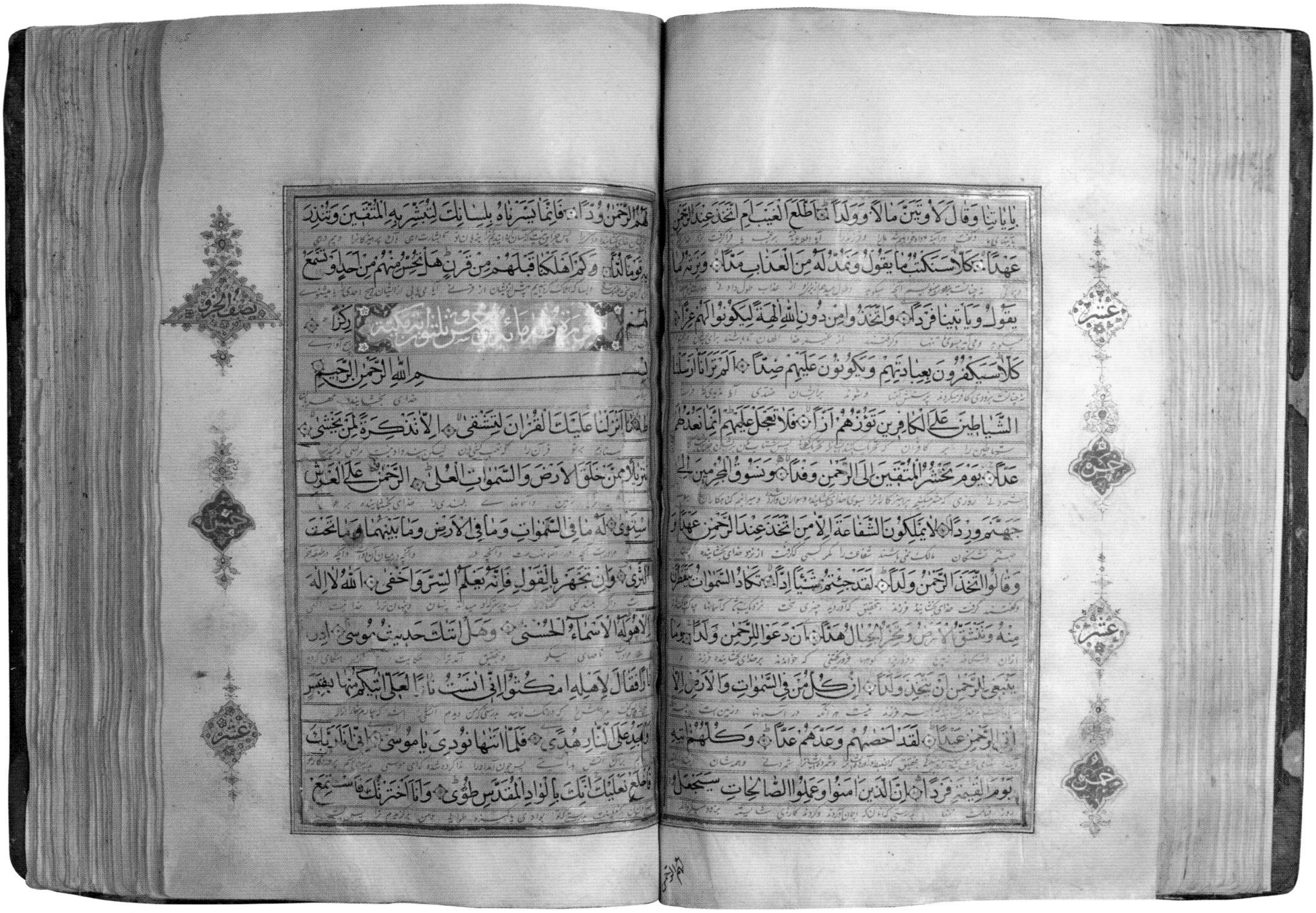

Qur'ans is called Kufic script, named after the Iraqi city of Kufa, and has a strong horizontal stress. It was applied to architecture, metalwork and ceramics, and flourished for many centuries; it still appears today in a rectangular form for decorative purposes. By the tenth century there were a number of cursive and chancery scripts that scholars group into six principal calligraphic varieties: *muhaqqaq* (originally the name for any careful script and a favourite hand for copying the Qur'ān); rihani (a smaller version of *muhaqqaq*); *naskh* (the main copyist's hand and the most widely used today); *thuluth* (a large display script, a favourite of the Ottomans and featuring in many architectural inscriptions); *tawqi'* (a light version of *thuluth* often adopted for official signatures and rising up along the line from right to left); and *riq'a* (a smaller more cursive version of *tawqi'* frequently employed for correspondence). These designations represent a rationalisation of a history that is complex and extends over many centuries. Four regionally attributed scripts can be added to the picture. The softer rounded *maghribi* styles come from North Africa and Spain. *Nasta'liq*, meanwhile, was the

ABOVE *Qur'an*. Manuscript book. Iran, 17th century. British Library: Or.13371, ff. 164v-165r
OPPOSITE *Ashkenazi Haggadah*. Manuscript book. Southern Germany, 143–70. British Library: Add MS 14762, fol.6v

עבדי לשנה הבאה בני חור
חורין
ורחצו כוס שני
נשתנה הלילה הזה מכל
הלילות שבכל הלילות אנו
אוכלים חמץ ומצה הלילה

ኦ ፡፡ ሪ ፡፡ ት ፡፡

ወጸውዖ፡እግዚአብሔር
ለሙሴ፡ወተናገሮ፡እም
ውስተ፡ደብተራ፡ዘመርጡ
ል፡፡ወይቤሎ፡በሎሙ፡
ለደቂቀ፡እስራኤል፡ወአይ
ድዖሙ፡እመቦ፡ዘአብአ፡
ብእሲ፡መባአ፡እምኔክ
ሙ፡ለእግዚአብሔር፡እ
ምእንስሳ፡ወእምኔ፡አልህ
ምት፡ወእምኔ፡አባግዕ፡፡
ታበውኡ፡መባአክሙ፡ለእ
ግዚአብሔር፡ለእመ፡ለሠ
ዊዕ፡መባኡ፡እምውስተ፡
አልህምት፡ተባዕተ፡ንጹ
ሐ፡ያመጽእ፡ኀበ፡ኆኅተ፡
ደብተራ፡ዘመርጡል፡ያበ
ውእ፡ስጥወ፡ቅድመ፡እግ
ዚአብሔር፡ወያንብር፡እ
ዴሁ፡ላዕለ፡ርእሱ፡ለዝክ
ቱ፡ላህም፡ዘአምጽአ፡ለሠ
ዊዕ፡ከመ፡ይስጠዎ፡ወይስ
ረ፡ሎቱ፡በእንቲአሁ፡ወይ
ጠብሕዎ፡ለውእቱ፡ላህም፡
ቅድመ፡እግዚአብሔር፡፡

ዘ ፡ ሌ ፡ ዋ ፡ ዊ ፡ ያ ፡ ን ፡

ወያመጽኡ፡ደቂቀ፡አሮን፡ደ
ሞ፡ለሊሆሙ፡ካህናት፡ወይ
ክዕውዎ፡ለደሙ፡ላዕለ፡
ምሥዋዕ፡አውዶ፡ዘኀበ፡
ኆኅተ፡ደብተራ፡ዘመርጡል
ወይወቅዕዎ፡ወይፌልጡ
መለያልዮ፡ዘዘዚአሁ፡ወ
ይወድዩ፡እሳተ፡ደቂቀ፡አሮ
ን፡ካህናት፡ላዕለ፡ምሥዋ
ዕ፡ወይዌጥሑ፡ደቂቀ፡አሮን
ካህናት፡ዘከተ፡ዘገመዱ፡
ወርእሶኒ፡ወሥብሐኒ፡ላዕ
ለ፡ዕፀው፡ወላዕለ፡እሳት፡ዘ
ውስተ፡ምሥዋዕ፡ወንዋየ፡
ውስጡ፡ወእገሪሁ፡የሐፅቡ፡
በማይ፡ወይወድዮ፡ካህን፡ኵ
ሎ፡ውስተ፡ምሥዋዕ፡ወመሥ
ዋዕት፡ውእቱ፡ዘቍርባን፡ወ
መዓዛ፡ሠናይ፡ለእግዚአብ
ሔር፡፡ወእመሰ፡እምኔ፡አባግ
ዕ፡ውእቱ፡መባኡ፡ለእግዚአ
ብሔር፡እመኒ፡በግዕ፡ወእመ
ኒ፡ማሕስእ፡ለሠዊዕ፡ተባዕቱ፡
ንጹሐ፡ያመጽእ፡ወይጠብኆ

invention of a fifteenth-century Persian calligrapher, Mīr 'Alī of Tabriz (c. 1360–1420). He dreamed of a flock of geese in flight and made his letters hang in the air while dropping slightly in the direction of travel. The late seventeenth-century Qur'an from Safavid Persia (Or 13371) shown on page 130 has its Arabic main text in *naskh* and the red interlinear Persian translation is in *nasta'liq*. Finally, two other styles, *divani* and *siyaqat*, were both important for official documents in the Ottoman Empire.

Hebrew also has many variations of script styles. In the illustration on page 133 we show a Haggadah that sets out the texts read at Passover. It dates from mid-fifteenth-century Germany. It is written on parchment from mid-fifteenth-century Germany in Ashkenazi square script and an Ashkenazi semi-cursive script. The illuminator adds his name in a colophon: Joel ben Simeon. In the illustration we see an example of how the scribe justifies his left-hand margin. Hebrew is written right to left. At the end of line two he creates an 'abstract' calligraphic symbol to justify the left-hand margin. It looks like a letter but it is not. In this manuscript all the diacritic vowel marks are composed of dashes as opposed to the usual dots and dashes.'

An Ethiopian manuscript from the fourteenth or fifteenth century (see opposite) contains eight books of the Old Testament and is written in the liturgical language of Ge'ez. Produced with a reed pen, the Ethiopic script sits in a matrix of space defined by lines scored into the vellum surface with a blunt point. The red decoration is reminiscent of Celtic interlaced ornament. In truth scholars today believe that one of the sources for this kind of work in insular manuscripts may have been books that reached Ireland with early Christian monastic influences from Egypt and other parts of Africa.

Stone inscriptions in southern Asia from the third century BC, such as the Ashoka Edicts written in

developed Brahmi and *kharoṣṭhī* script, show that writing had arrived in the Indian subcontinent several centuries earlier. Brahmi, most likely derived from Aramaic roots, would diversify into more than 200 variants. The northern branch includes Devanagari, Tibetan, Gurmukhī, Bengali, Gujarati and the Siddham script, which is still written for religious purposes in Japan. The southern branch leads us also to Sinhalese and Tamil as well as the scripts of Southeast Asia, including Thai, Khmer and Burmese. The majestic *Treatise on the Art of Politics*, in Gurmukhī script, was prepared for Mahārājā Ranjīt Singh (1780–1839) in the nineteenth century. The letters are written with strong, direct, confident penmanship using an edged pen.

A folding paper book containing the legend of a Buddhist monk, Phra Malai, who visited both heaven and hell, dates to 1857. It is written in sacred Khom script, which has affinities with Khmer; here it is used for Thai and Pali languages. Khom dates back to as early as the thirteenth century AD and was revered for an almost magical efficacy; it was popular for protective

OPPOSITE The Octateuch. Manuscript book. Ethiopia, 14th century. British Library: Or.480, fol. 88r
ABOVE *Treatise on the Art of Politics*. Manuscript book, produced for the Māhārajā Ranjīt Singh. India, 19th century. British Library: MS Hin D13a, fol. 1r

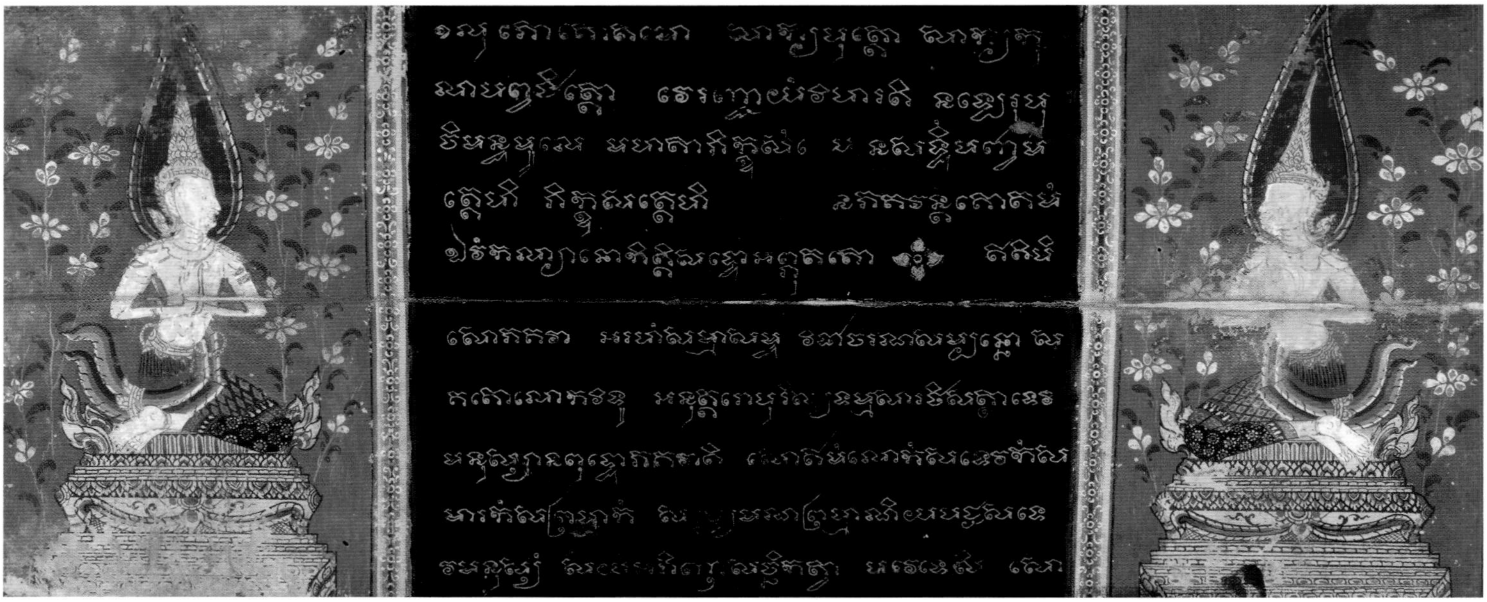

texts on amulets, tattoos and warriors' shirts. The scribe has written the angular script in gold ink on a polished, dyed background. The writing runs from left to right.

An album compiled in the nineteenth century shows extracts of work by famous Japanese calligraphers. The opening contains rare samples of the hands of Emperor Shōmu (701–756) and Empress Kōmyō (701–760) that date from *c.*750. In both the Islamic world and East Asia, collecting albums of calligraphy was a way to improve one's knowledge of fine writing but it also displayed a cultivated nature.

Communication in any calligraphic tradition comes not only through marks but also colour, surface, scent, sheen and movement. Yet discussing various artefacts from different calligraphic cultures is a sensitive task. One risks appropriating a system to one's own understandings, when each has such specific sensibilities as their basis. Nonetheless, one might hope that in encountering a calligraphic work from any tradition, because it originates in a physical and purposeful task, we may yet find that it stimulates a more vivid awareness of our own embodiment.

Following the development of printing with movable type in Mainz in the 1450s, this method of printing spread to other European cities. In the earliest printed books the letters are gothic in form; these volumes attempted to rival German handwritten, illuminated manuscripts. The same imitation of local forms happened when printing moved to Italy in the 1460s. The first books in roman upper- and lower-case types, printed by the Frenchman Nicolas Jenson (*c.*1420–1480) in Venice in 1470, took their cue from the Humanist calligraphy then practised in Padua and the surrounding Veneto region. It was in Venice again, thirty years later, that roman letters achieved a new peak of refinement in the work of the publisher-printer, Aldus Manutius (*c.*1451–1515). His *Hypnerotomachia Poliphili* from 1499 is the earliest example of roman book typography to show exceptional design in all its parts. The pattern set

ABOVE *Legend of Phra Malai* and other Buddhist texts. Manuscript folding book. Thailand, 1857. British Library: Or.14732.

OPPOSITE Calligraphy by Emperor Shōmu and Empress Kōmyō. Otekagami calligraphy album. Japan, 750–1650 (compiled 19th century). British Library: Or.12227, fol. 1r

聖武天皇 香散華
香散華而以供養極盡忠心後
復打金作棺盛師子皮以用起
塔尒時人民緣是善心壽終之後
光明皇后 時四部
時四部衆咸皆歡喜身意快然得未曾有
眉間光明照于東方万八千土皆如金色
從阿鼻獄上至有頂諸世界中六道衆生

elegi, Concupiui salutare tuū domine: et
lex tua meditatio mea est, Viuet anima
mea et laudabit te: et iudicia tua adiuua-
bunt me, Erraui sicut ouis que perijt
quere seruum tuum quia mādata tua
non sum oblitus, Gloria patri et. Anthia.

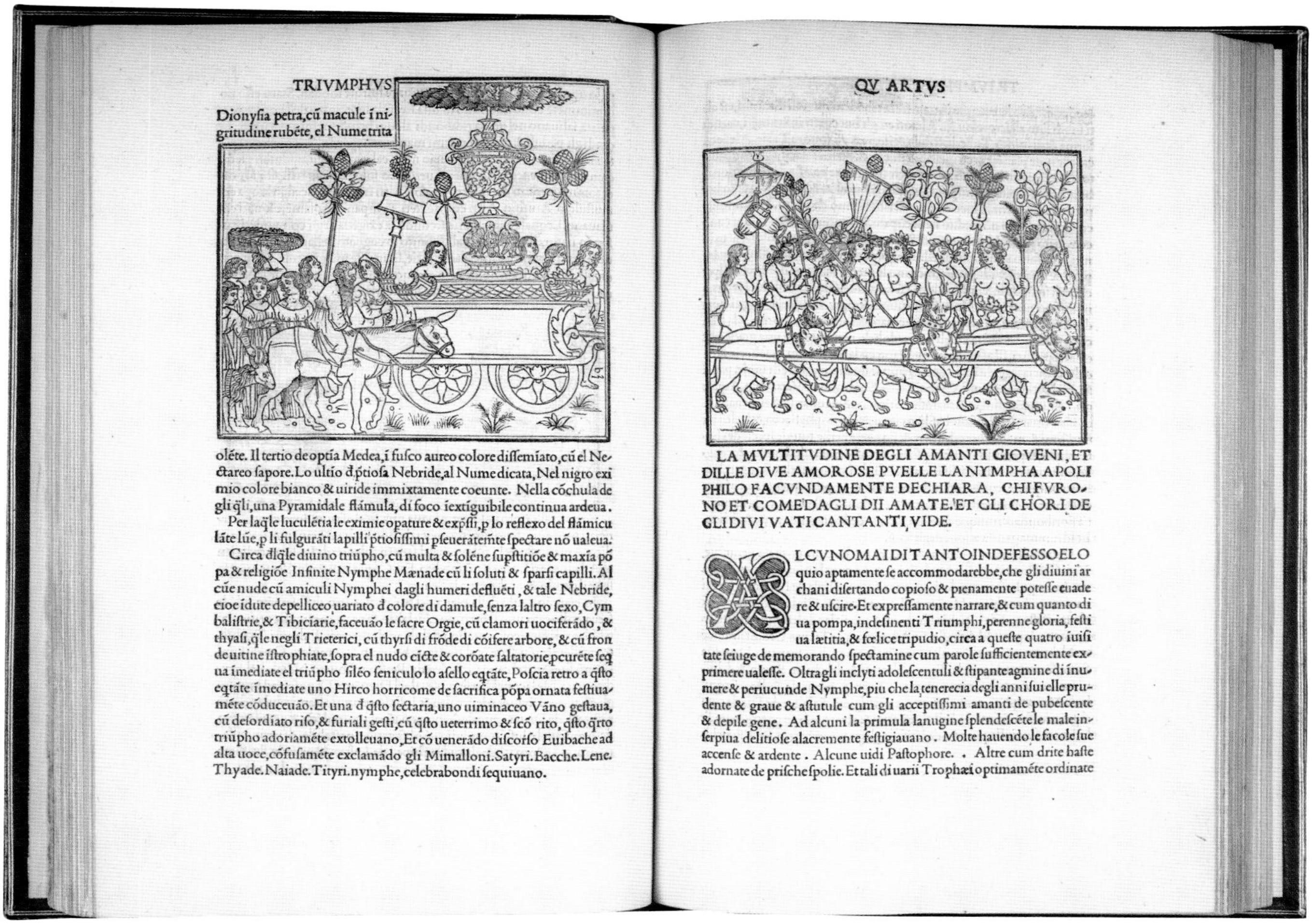

by Aldus established a standard that was followed through to the late seventeenth century. It was also Aldus who first used an italic letter in printed form.

In 1693 the French Académie des Sciences established a committee to study printed letterforms. The result was a series of plates (1695–1716), engraved by Louis Simonneau, showing idealised constructed letterforms in both Roman capitals (see page 71) and for lower-case roman and italic forms. These plates illustrate the perception of letter shapes shifting towards more upright counters and high contrast between thick and thin strokes. (Counters are the blank internal shapes of letterforms. In early type design they reflect the tilted axis that comes from writing letters with an edged pen held in a comfortably slanted position.) In this they were following the prevailing tendencies in European written and engraved roman lettering, which had developed in this direction since the mid-1550s.

In Britain the writing master John Baskerville (1707–1775) took note of these trends when he ventured into the world of printing in the mid-eighteenth century. He lived in an age that was consciously 'improving' all aspects of life. In his preface (1758) to *Paradise Lost* by John Milton he comments that he was 'an early admirer

OPPOSITE Latin psalter, known as the *Mainz Psalter*. Printed book. Mainz (Germany): Johannes Fust and Peter Schoeffer, 1457. British Library: G.12216, fol. 36v

ABOVE Francesco Colonna, *Hypnerotomachia Poliphili*. Printed book. Venice: Aldus Manutius, 1499. British Library: G.10564, fol. l ii r-l v r

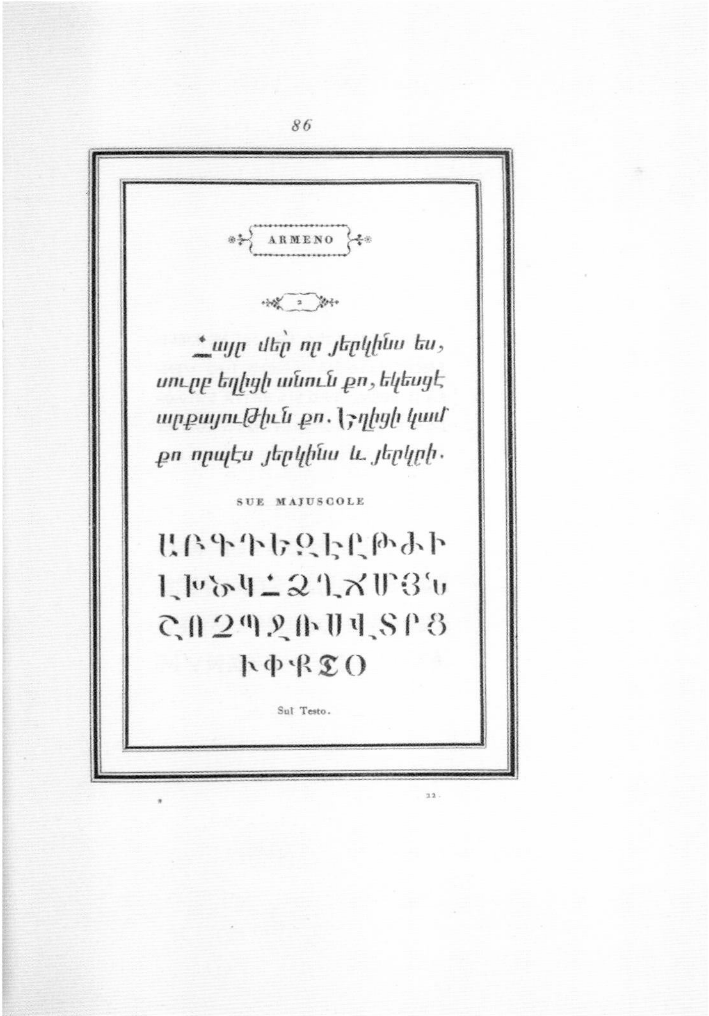
86

ARMENO

Հայր մեր որ յերկինս ես,
սուրբ եղիցի անուն քո, եկեսցէ
արքայութիւն քո. Եղիցին կամք
քո որպէս յերկինս և յերկրի.

SUE MAJUSCOLE

ԱԲԳԴԵԶԷԸԹԺԻ
ԼԽԾԿՀՁՂՃՄՅՆ
ՇՈՉՊՋՌՍՎՏՐՑ
ՒՓՔ[illegible]Օ

Sul Testo.

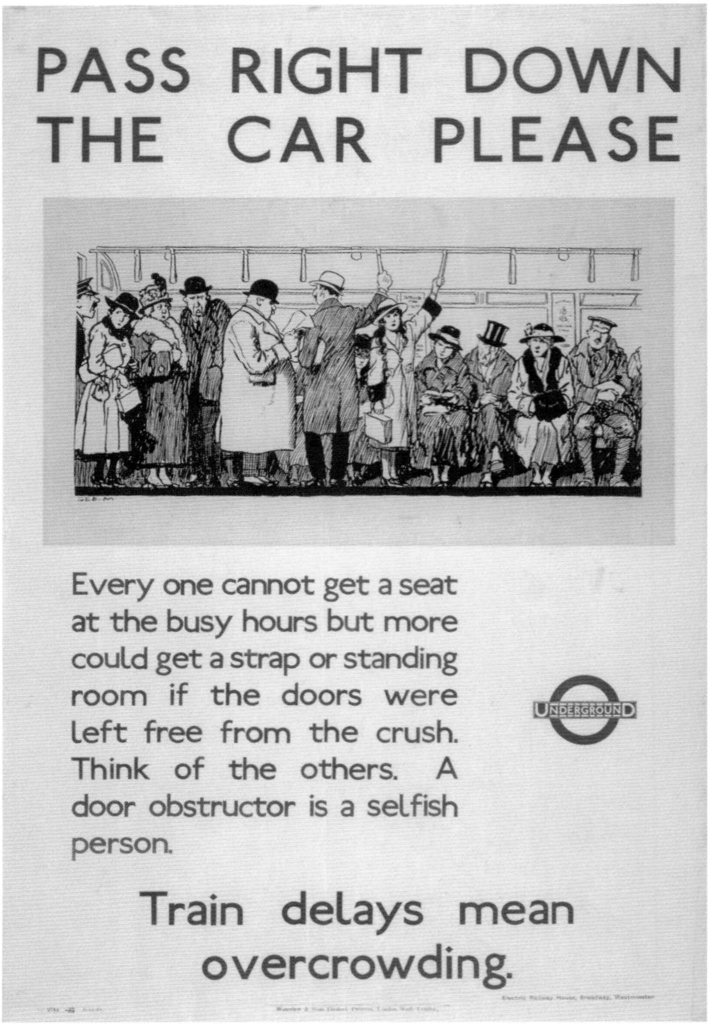

of the beauty of letters ... and desirous of contributing to the perfection of them'.[4] Now as one of Birmingham's great manufacturers he was also bringing his keen eye and experience in the japanning trade to bear on print. He cast new type designs, which were wider and with clearer contrasts between thick and thin strokes.

In addition, Baskerville re-engineered the printing plates of his presses, introduced a novel way of smoothing paper through a 'hot press' process and mixed a blacker ink. No part of the production process escaped his attention, and his books won him admirers from across Europe.

His work was built on by the Didot brothers in France and in Italy he inspired Giambattista Bodoni (1740–1813) to a lifetime's work in type design and printing. Bodoni's *Manuale Tipografico*, printed after his death by his widow in 1818, displays one of the greatest individual achievements in Western type design. He shows type specimens cast from matrices created from his own hand-carved punches in almost every size and weight imaginable. The

ABOVE Armenian types. Giambattista Bodoni, *Manuale tipografico*. Printed book. Parma (Italy): G. Bodoni, 1818. British Library: 59.c.19-20, vol. 2, p. 86

ABOVE Edward Johnston's sans-serif typeface. Poster designed by George Morrow. London: Underground Electric Railway Company Ltd., 1918

book encompasses 538 pages in two volumes and also contains his types for Greek, Hebrew, Russian, Arabic, Phoenician, Armenian, Coptic and Tibetan.

As printing technologies change, and new uses for type arrive, designers respond. One of the first designs for a type that effectively branded an organisation was Edward Johnston's design in 1916 for the London Electric Railway, the Underground. Johnston's block letters established the trend for sans-serifs, one of the most popular types of letter today.

Johnston's student Eric Gill (1882–1940) applied his master's thinking to his own type, Gill Sans, familiar to many from the BBC's logo. The BBC, facing many new demands for type across a variety of platforms, recently commissioned a proprietary typeface for its own use. 'Reith' was designed by the London-based type foundry Dalton Maag and began to be introduced by the BBC in 2017. The design process shows how far type design has changed over the last few decades but also how we still draw on deep roots. Designers wrote and drew letters with pencils and broad-edged pens, they consulted the British Library's *Ramsey Psalter*, they brainstormed the advantages and disadvantages of different typefaces, and then they evolved a type family of unseriffed and seriffed forms for the BBC's worldwide platforms.

Software enables designers to create digital masters for the letters, either working directly on the screen or from scanned-in drawings. The letters are generated by software that draws lines and curves between points placed by the designer on the letter's outline. One aims to do this with a spare economy of points, working simultaneously on designs for a lightweight and a heavyweight (bold) letter. Later, with these dimensions established, one can interpolate all the various weights in between.

In the six designers mentioned above (Jenson, Manutius, Baskerville, Bodoni, Johnston and Gill), we can see a community in dialogue across the centuries with one another. Each was aware of the significant achievements of the past yet keen to evolve new solutions for the problems of their day. Developments in the world of legible lettering have, on the whole, been guided by evolutionary rather than revolutionary principles as well as a sense of fellow feeling.

✧ ✧ ✧

Wordplay has exerted a fascination for artists across writing systems; it is not just the shapes of letters that can be played with but their arrangement as well. Rabanus Maurus (*c.*780–856) was a monk in Fulda, Germany, and a scholar and teacher. His poems on the cross are examples of elaborate spatial wordplay. He was following in a tradition that runs back to the Roman poet Ennius (239–169 BC) and forward to Guillaume Apollinaire (1880–1918) and the Concrete poets of the twentieth century. He completely broke with the usual convention of rendering poetry but relied on our sense of curiosity to puzzle out his meaning.

El Lissitzky's *Dlia golosa* (For the Voice) (1923) is a rendering of thirteen poems by the Russian Futurist Vladimir Mayakovsky (1893–1930) into typographic form for reading aloud. Lissitzky (1890–1941) was a key channel for the transference of some of the ideas of the Constructivists into graphic and typographic design. Of most significance was their use of the grid as an organising principle for multiple graphic elements, a principle they found in Picasso's handling of his cubist collages. It was the grid that would later help integrate type and photography in powerful graphic images.

In Chinese artist Xu Bing's (b. 1955) two volumes – *An Introduction to Square Word Calligraphy* and *Square Word Calligraphy Red Line Tracing Book* (1994–6) – what we think is one thing is turned into another. We believe we are looking at Chinese brush calligraphy, but in fact these are English words arranged as single 'characters'.

NATEPATRISSVMMIQVITELAFEROCIAFRANGIS
DAMIHIRITECRVCISVICTRICIACARMINAFARI
NĀCAELESTANIMALMITISVOLATOREIOHANNIS
TRANSPENETRANSAQVILAETVEROOMINEVIDIT
EOUMSOLĒVERBVMHAVSITINARCEPOLORVMHOC
GRATIASICQ;IOHANNIANTEOMNESVIVIDAFATV
DONATAVTQ;ART:HOMINISSIBISVMERETAVCTOR
SCRIPSERITATQE[illegible]PIODEVSVN:ETALM:
SĒPERCV̄PATREQI[illegible]ITAQVESALVSQVE
SITNATVSFACTVSQVECARODOMINATORINORBE
HVNCIEOHVNCVITVLVSREGĒDANTPONTIFICĒQ;
VTLEOQVIFORTISRETVLITCERTAMINEPREDAM
HOSTIĀETOBTVLERATSV̄MVSSERITESACERDOS
MẎSTICADONASVISCONSORTIB:OPTIMEDONANS
NEMPEDATORVMMYSTERIOSEPTEMETPIEPANVM
DATMARCVSSEPTESPSQVOQEVIVIDECANTV
OTVREGEMIVSTIECCEAGNV̄DAPIELVCAS
HOCSIGNATQ;FIDESDEIECCEAPONTIFICEQVE
DAT[illegible]RHEDOSQITOLLITCV̄[illegible]ES
FOR[illegible]MANVSETPARECCEDI[illegible]DIS
INBETHLEĒGENIT:MATREAMMIRABILISINFANS
IPSESATVSMARIAMVNDODITISSIMACVRAHVIC
NOBILISATQVEPVERPERSONAVETVSTADIERVM
QVIVENITDEEDOMDEBOSRAHICVESTECRVENTA
CALCATVRVSERATQVISOLVSTORCVLARAVCTOR
INCRVCEPENSAND:QVISVSTINETASTRASVPERN:
VTCRVXALMAFORETDIVINOHAECMVNEREDIVES
NĀSCRIBENSBENEMATHEVSDEDITORDINEPRIM:
QVIINFACIEFIRMATIVSHVNCABORGINEDAVID
PROGENITV̄ESSEHOMINEMSIGNAVITQ:MPIEVOTV̄
CVMMONSTRAVITINORDINESTIRPISFID:ABRAĀ
QVODGEN:HOCDEDERITPISTILLOFRAVDISINIQ:
EXPVLSONAMRITE[illegible]VSOMNERETEXTVM
CONTINETHOCVER[illegible]SCREDERESIGNVM
NEMPEDECETDVDVMCRISTVSQIANASCIERILLA
PROMISSVSSTIRPESTSALVATORMAXIMVSORBI

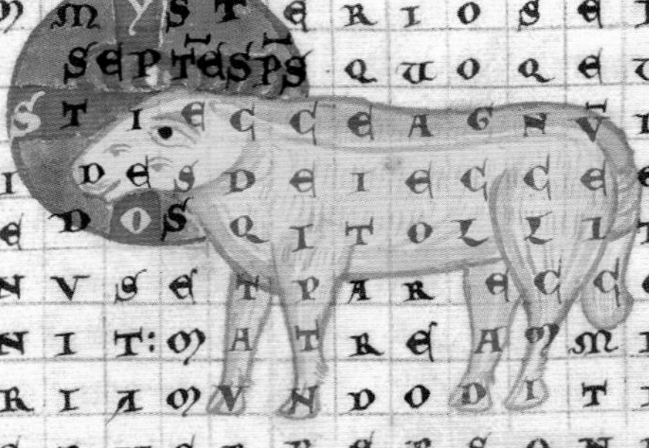

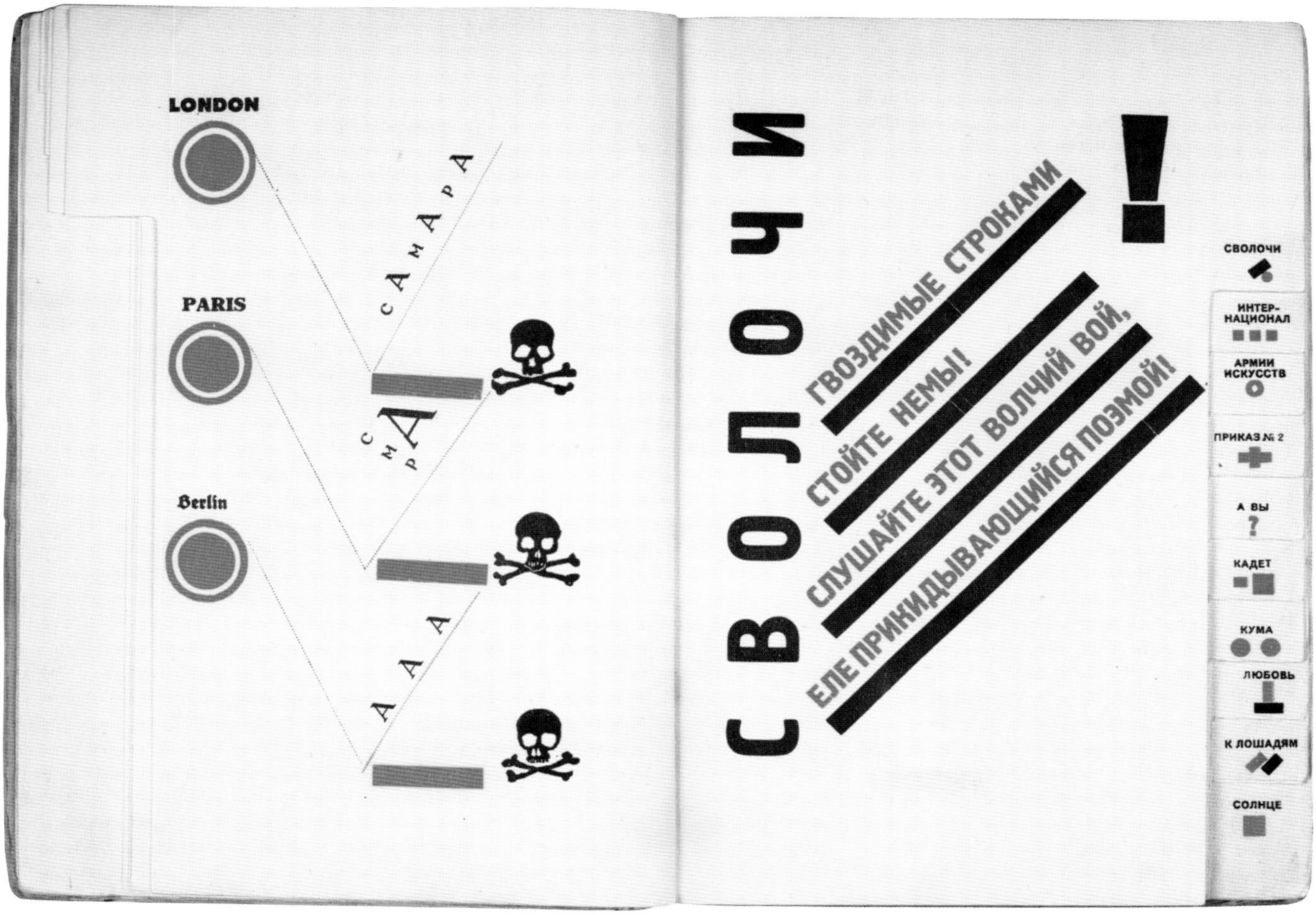

Xu Bing's work encourages us to question exactly what meaning we attribute to the writing, which oscillates between being a picture, a visual phenomenon and then something with a verbal meaning, and back again. In this respect it is a work of art that challenges not only our thinking about writing as a whole but also how we make sense of anything in the world about us. Is meaning fixed or does it change as we bring different visual cultural and conceptual frameworks into play? This work suggests things change. Text artists from Europe and the USA also exist in this boundary land but the 'market' places them firmly in 'art'.

There is one phenomenon we must consider before we leave this section on writing and creativity. Graffiti has always been with us but the big difference between then and now is who the populations of writers are and the available tools. In our own time what the media calls graffiti, but writers themselves simply call 'writing', has been a young person's practice. Authorities may bewail the costs to them in terms of cleaning up but 'writing' shows that centuries of campaigning for universal education has worked. For the first time in human history the majority of young people can write. Is it surprising that they will start to write what they want?

OPPOSITE Rabanus Maurus, *De Laudibus Sanctae Crucis*. Manuscript. Arnstein (Germany), 1170–80. British Library: Harley MS 3045, fol. 20v
ABOVE Vladimir Mayakovsky, *Dlia golosa*. Printed book. Berlin: Gosudarstvennoe izdatel'stvo, 1923. British Library: C.114.mm.33, pp. 6–7

ABOVE Xu Bing, 'Art for the people'. Banner with Square Word calligraphy. Museum of Modern Art (MoMA), New York, 1999

The other thing that has changed is the tools. The spray can writes easily on any surface and on a huge scale; it is a liberation. The marker pen has inks that are permanent, and again you can write on virtually anything. The energy behind 'writing' is the same energy that drove writing at its various points of origin: the desire to name and claim things, to belong, the excitement of display; for graffiti we can add the risk of performance. 'Writing' takes writing back to its roots.

Do aesthetics matter? They certainly matter in terms of our self worth: being able to pour our creativity into something, to produce something beautiful or ingenious, makes us feel good. For those who use these creations we sense the care and inventiveness invested in them and, by association, in ourselves too. The spot where beauty and function meet is a sweet one. The aesthetics behind the roman alphabet have grown over the years to create a set of letter shapes with a fine balance of unity and difference. The shapes have evolved to enable us to sustain our attention when reading. We have no shortage of information around us in the world today: so much in fact that it can be overwhelming. Aesthetics have been one of the tools that we have used to allow certain kinds of writing to call out to us and attract our attention. The writer Nicholas Carr has observed that with so much information surrounding us we remain faced by the problem we have had all along: how do we turn mere information into embodied wisdom?[5] The aesthetics have been one of the ways we developed to do this, to emphasise and relate one part of a text to another and above all to allow us to sustain our engagement with the text, if necessary for hours. Even the architecture of certain buildings or rooms, like the library for instance, helped us do this – as did the social codes around silence within the library. The aesthetics help us bring ourselves to the task of reading and writing with as full a human presence as possible.

Note-takers

Recording facts and figures, keeping lists, is one of the oldest functions that writing has had; it is also an area where, in recent years, some of the newest technologies have been brought to bear. By electronic means we can collect, store and analyse quantities of data that would have been unimaginable in the past. This is changing many aspects of our lives, from our politics to health (think of the Human Genome Project), and of our everyday experiences online. Note-taking can be carried out with different degrees of care. Notes can be made in the field under a variety of constraints ranging from the

location to time. Their legibility reflects the pressures affecting the writer, their individual skills and for whom they are writing. Strategies can involve using cursive handwriting, abbreviations and shorthand.

Methodical note-taking is apparent in a number of professional environments, and it also occurs in private manuscripts made with an eye to history. Sir Walter Raleigh's (1552–1618) notes, eventually published in his *History of the World* in 1614, were written while he was a prisoner in the Tower of London. They were copied out in a clear hand and include carefully drawn maps. There is a sense that this was a manuscript book in its own right, whether or not it would ever see publication. There is a similar feeling to a diary written by the Sultan Ahmad al-Salih Syamsuddin of Bone (ruled 1775–1812). The diary is written in Arabic and Bugis scripts: the Arabic written right to left, and Bugis left to right. The pages are carefully arranged and record political events, religious ceremonies, notable visitors and the births, deaths and marriages of the royal family.

Wolfgang Amadeus Mozart's handwritten record of his compositions, begun in 1784 and continuing until the year of his death in 1791, is also carefully planned; essentially it is a list. Each page contains five works in chronological order. On the left-hand page he noted the title, the instruments for which he scored the composition, and other details. On the other side of the page he ruled five sets of musical staves and here he wrote out the first few bars of each piece. Clearly he wanted a complete list of his compositions to survive. This is useful today because some of the pieces are lost; if they were ever found this list could help us identify them.

A marginal space gives a writer another degree of freedom. In medieval books the marginal drawings by

ABOVE eL Seed, *Perception*. Calligraffiti mural across fifty buildings in Manshiyat Naser, home to Cairo's garbage collectors. Written in Arabic, these words from St Athanasius read: 'Anyone who wants to see the sunlight clearly needs to wipe his eye first'. Cairo, 2016

Damiata is not Pelusium. but the next port of Nilus unto it towards the west. wch is also called Tanis. but this is not Tanis

c.30 wch Ezekiel calls Taphnes, Antonius, Thanis, & Egesippus Thamna l.4.

for that Tanais is adioyning to Gosen. the same wher Jeremy was stoned to death, & wch the hebrews call Soan. & hath also the name

Melr: guil: of Sais, & now Sibnit.

Pelusium. the scriptures call Sin, & Libna, saith Montanus. others take it for Caphtor. Castaldus & Sieglerus think it is Damiata. Ang: Curio saith y^t it is now Bilbin. Ortelius Tenesse: others, Belbais.

Babilon, the Arabians call Mazar. the Chaldeans Alchabyr. Joseph Lerussolin, the Hebrews Misraim. Cairo stood on the west side of it & are now become one Citty, saith Brochard.

Heliopolis, ther are too Citties of y^t name, the one on the edg of the inferior Egypt, the other surnamed metropolis standeth farther north, the scriptures call it On. gen. 41. Esai. 19. p: Mela l. 63. c. 9. & plinij l. 5. c. 9. call it Solis opidum. Melr: Guilandinus, calls it Bethsemes, Tyreus, Malber. the Arabeans, Bahalbeth. Simeon Sethi, Solis fons. Bethsemes. in Josua c. 15. 19. 21. kings, 1. 6. kings. 4. 14. par. 1. J. 2. 25. 28.

Memphis built by Apis saith Aristippus in y^e 1 booke of y^e Arcadien history, & therfore Aristeus argivus called it Sarapidis. & Apis was y^e third from Inachus.

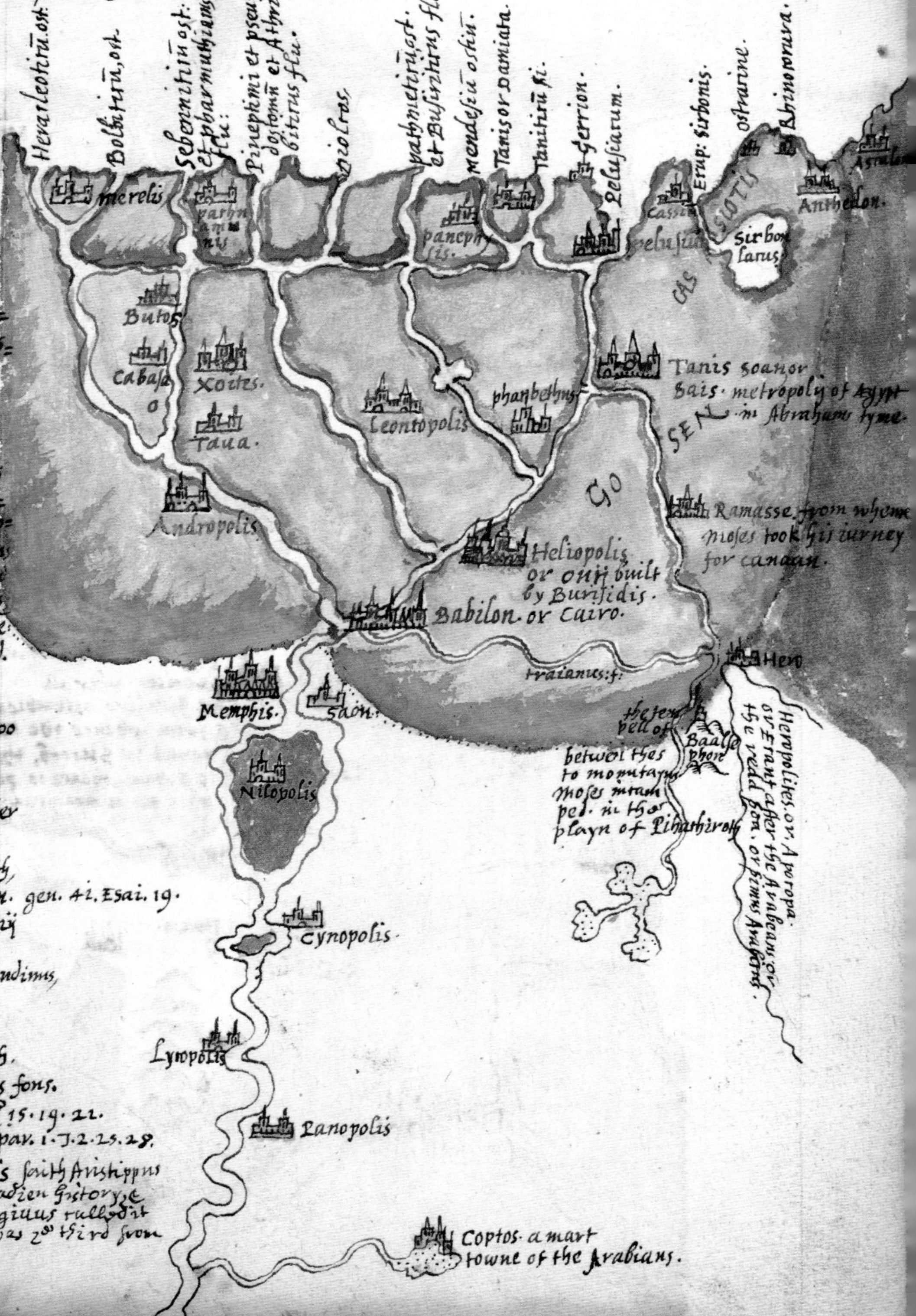

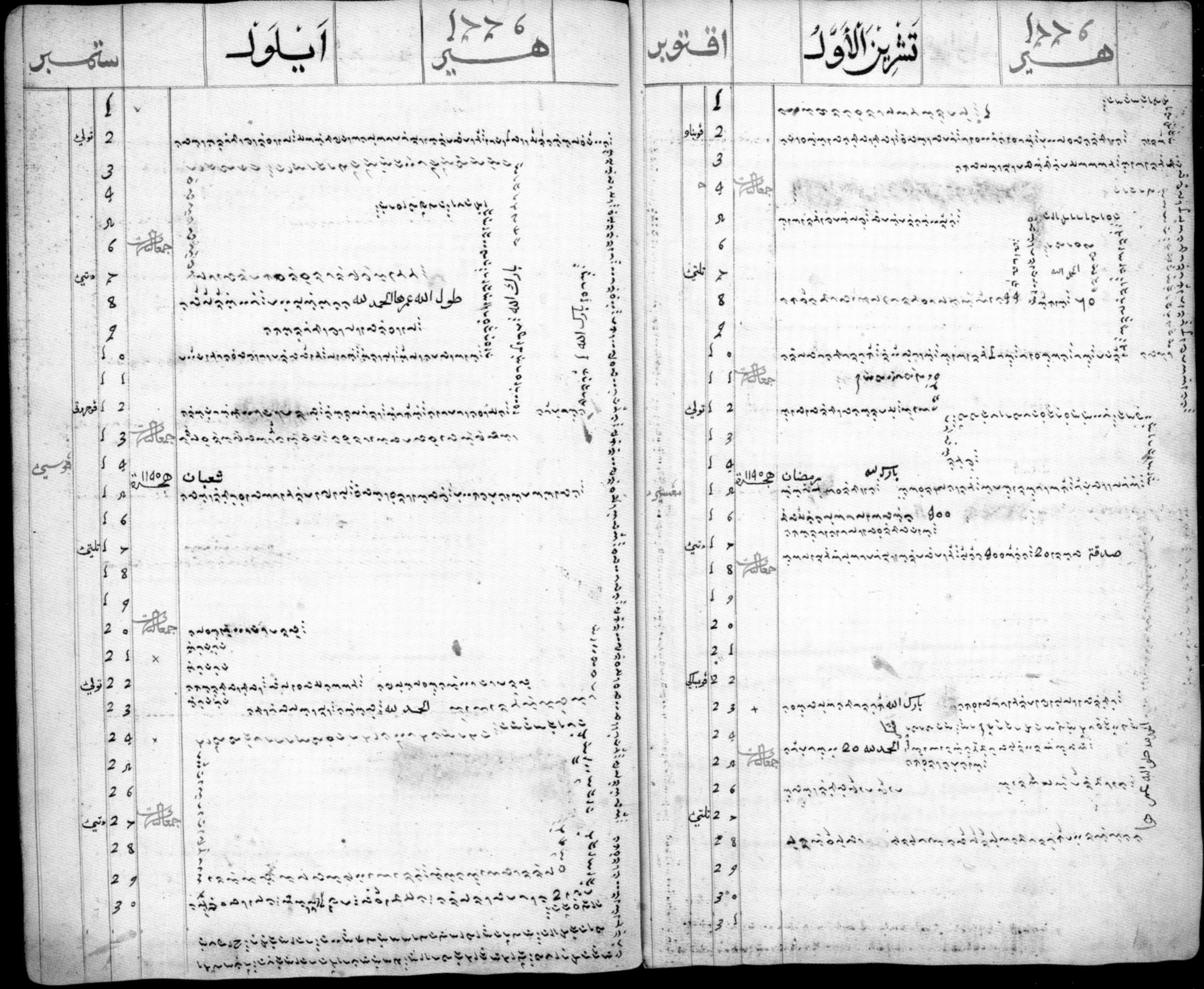

OPPOSITE Walter Raleigh, Commonplace book. Manuscript volume. London, *c.*1606–8. British Library: Add MS 57555, fol. 23r

ABOVE Sultan Ahmad al-Salih of Bone, Diary. Manuscript volume. Bone (Indonesia), 1775–95. British Library: Or.12354, ff. 17v-18r

illuminators often contain humour, satirising the text. There is something provisional about this space. The blank white page and its text block can be intimidating. When William Wordsworth began to write (in 1802) what would become his great autobiographical poem *The Prelude* (1850), he started on the last pages of his notebook as if to commence on the first would have been to make too definitive a statement. The poet Emily Dickinson (1830–1886) sometimes wrote poetry on informal scraps of paper. The paper, such as an old envelope, was already marked and so less intimidating, and sometimes the unusual shape of the paper actually helped form the line length and shape of the poem. The way a sheet of paper is filled can be telling. Oscar Wilde's original manuscript of *The Ballad of Reading Gaol* (1898), written while in prison, fills the entire page in minute writing. There are no margins. The paper was brought to him each morning and taken away at night.

Perhaps most carefully planned of all annotated manuscripts were the great glossed books of the Middle Ages, in which the pages were ruled with a variety of marginal spaces, some pre-filled with commentaries on the main text and others left blank for readers to add their own comments. These books were seen as a resource that would grow over time.

The East India Company minute book from 1663 is part of a sequence of minute books that show a cross section of administrative record keeping during the seventeenth and eighteenth centuries. The script is an early form of English round hand. The East India

ABOVE W. A. Mozart, *Verzeichnüss aller meiner Werke vom Monath febrario 1784 bis Monath [November] 1791*. Manuscript volume. Vienna?, 1784–91. British Library: Zweig MS 63, ff. 6v-7r
OPPOSITE East India Company, *Court of Committee minutes book for 1657–66*. Manuscript volume. London, 1657–66. British Library: IOR/B/26, fol.296r

A Court of Committees holden the XXth of February 1662.

Present.

Sr Thomas Chambrelan Governour
Sr William Rider Deputy.

Sr Andrew Riccard	Mr Christ Boone
Sr Jno Lewis.	Mr Peter Vandeput
Sr George Smith.	Mr Thomas Kendall
Sr Stephen White	Mr Francis Clarke
Arthur Ingram Esqr	Mr Robert Sant
Jno Bathurst Esqr	Mr Jno Mascall
Mauri Thompson Esqr	Mr Christ Willoughby
Mr Sam Barnardiston	Mr Thomas Canham

The Court had this day a long debate about disposeing of their Iron and Battery to the Royall Company but they came to noe resolucon.

[Mi]nister at ye Fort — It was Ordered that the remainder of the proceeds of the Callicoes sold by the Governour, which was given the Minister at the Fort by the Factors and sent home to buy him bookes, should be sent him in Rialls of 8t after the bookes are paid for.

[Tra]nsport. — **The** Transport of 1000li Subscription, of which 500li is paid by Mr Edward Sidcombe to Mr Christopher Boone, was this this day read in Court & allowed of.

Warrants were now signed for payment of.

100.00.00.	Percivall Angeir	21.00.00.	Henry Risbey
16.10.06.	Thomas Winter	10.03.06	Thomas Fend
1.19.00.	Mary Milton	56.05.06	Jno Watts.

500li Owners Coast Friggott.

26 24

Dec 11. 28

Inhibition by Moulds.

Moulds planted on broth in flasks Nov 30. Room temp. (cold weather)

Equal parts ~~[illegible]~~ mould broth and boiling agar mixed and filled into holes in an agar plate. After solid. surface flooded with blood agar containing haemolytic streptococci.

After 18 hours.

	Mould broth imbedded.	Inhibition of growth
1.	Inhibitor	Complete for 5 mm. round
2.	C Janiia Viridescens	Partial only over imbedded broth
3	Botrytis cinereum	Nil
4	Aspergillus fumigatus	Nil.
5	Penicillium	Complete for 7 mm around.
6	Sporotrichum	Nil.

Where inhibition of streptococcal growth then blood corpuscles preserved. Others laked.

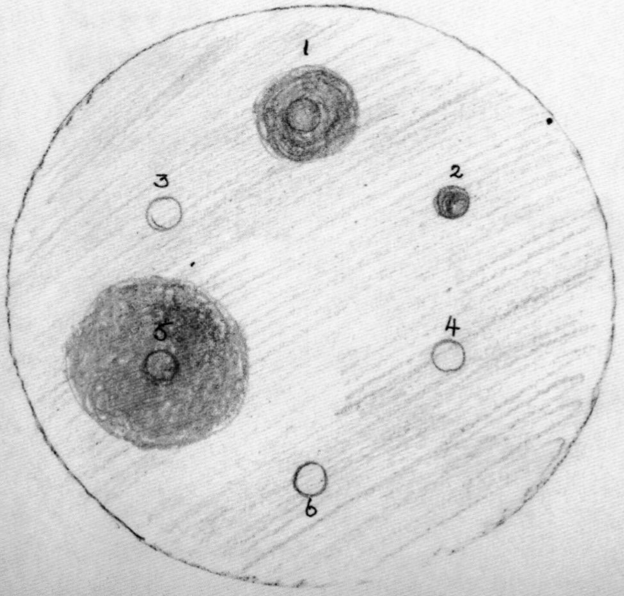

Company developed elaborate documentary systems to keep control over its ships and fort-like 'factories' in India. Eventually it maintained identical sets of records in India and London. Methodical record-keeping was vital for the growth of distributive organisations and governments across the globe.

Even after the invention of printing handwriting remained essential for first-hand reporting from the frontiers of science and exploration. Alexander Fleming's (1881–1955) notebooks of his research into penicillin are representative of many scientists' notebooks, from those of Sir Isaac Newton (1643–1727) back to Galileo's observations of Venus in 1610 and Leonardo da Vinci's recordings of his dissections of the human body from 1506.

Almost too poignant to look at is the journal of Captain Scott from his final expedition to the South Pole. Written on 29 March 1912 in his snowbound tent, the notes are in pencil. The 'but' on line two shows how the contact between the paper comes and goes; he was clearly finding it difficult to control his writing. Angularities (see 'are' in line three) and changes of scale indicate stiff fingers and the initial **p** in people in the last line is reminiscent of an intake of breath. Deep feelings seem to waver in his hand, arm and chest.

Since the days of the Greeks writers have made efforts to keep up with the speed of thoughts and the flow of speech. The most popular system from the ancient world was that of Marcus Tullius Tiro (d. *c.*4 BC). Tiro, once a slave to Cicero but later freed by him, invented a way of writing down Cicero's speeches. In his original system there were about 4,000 signs and abbreviations. By the Middle Ages this had almost quadrupled before the method fell out of favour. Shorthand writing was popular again in the British Isles in the seventeenth century. Thomas Shelton's (1600/01–*c.*1650) *Tachygraphy, the Most Exact and Compendious Method of Short and Swift Writing* was first published in

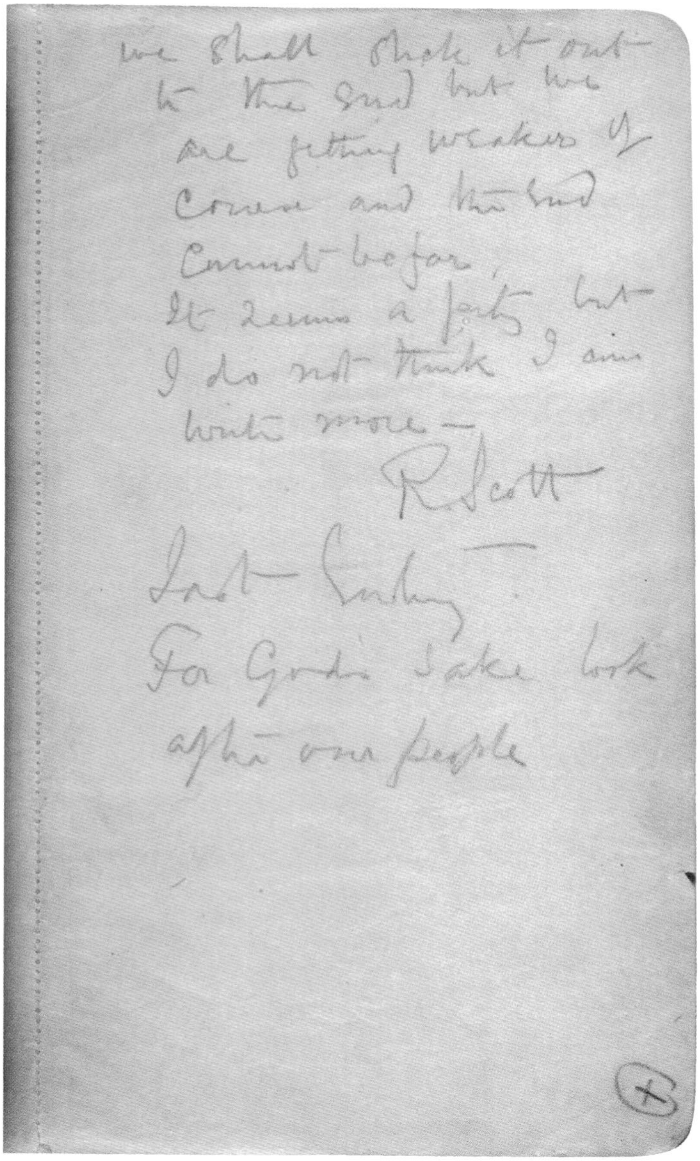
We shall stick it out
to the end but we
are getting weaker of
course and the end
cannot be far,
It seems a pity but
I do not think I can
write more –
R Scott
Last Entry
For God's sake look
after our people

OPPOSITE Alexander Fleming, Lab book. Manuscript volume. London, 1928. British Library: Add MS 56162, fol. 26r
ABOVE Captain Robert Falcon Scott, Terra Nova Antarctic diaries. Manuscript volume. Antarctica, 1912. British Library: Add MS 51035, fol. 39

London in 1628, and ran to numerous editions. Tachygraphy means 'speedy writing' in Greek. Shelton's system included abbreviated letterforms together with simple lines and curves. It was used by Sir Isaac Newton, Thomas Jefferson (1743–1826) and Samuel Pepys (1633–1703), who employed it in his famous diary.

In the nineteenth century Isaac Pitman (1813–1897) developed a new system of abbreviated marks that could be joined and written cursively. Vowels were added as small signs at different positions along the stems of consonants; there were also many signs for whole words. This system has proved of use to secretaries, the police and in journalism. It differentiated some marks through the application of pressure on the pen, reflecting the penmanship of that time. The fastest transcription rate recorded is 350 words a minute.

Inevitably mechanics were brought to bear on the problem, and a number of stenographic devices became common in workplaces and the court system. Today voice recognition software has launched a new era in the transcription of spoken language.

It is worth noting that transcription is not the only reason for writing something down. We ask writing to do many things for us and we do not always need it to be done quickly. Writing can also be used to carefully compile information, and the very act of writing can help to strengthen our memory. We can employ writing to make requests, as a form of art or meditation, to protest, to control, to create and express ourselves, or to mark out places as of special significance.

Citizens

Individual groups can use writing systems to reflect their cultural or religious identities. States may employ and change writing systems for their own political purposes: for nation building, for encouraging literacy or modernisation. Protesters can use writing against the state or for campaigning.

Almost as long as writing has existed, writing systems have been invented to better reflect the concerns of different groups. Among the Inuit of Northern Canada, Inuktitut-speakers have promoted the use of syllabics, originally adopted in the mid-nineteenth century from their Cree neighbours to the south. In 1976 the Language Commission of the Inuit Cultural Institute made it the co-official script for the Inuit languages along with roman script in Canada. The Vai script from Liberia was invented as early as the 1830s by Mọmọlu Duwalu Bukẹlẹ; it came to him in a dream. It remains in use in West Africa today.

Writing systems have themselves passed through phases of increased or receding popularity. One of the most dramatic transformations of script in the twentieth century was visited upon Hebrew. From being a script largely found in a scholarly or religious context it awoke to find itself at the heart of a modern state and had to adapt and diversify with astonishing speed. Another example of a revived letterform from the twentieth century is the revised Rovásírás medieval Hungarian runic writing of Szekély communities.

Working in the opposite direction some scripts have seen themselves displaced through moves to modernise a country. In the early twentieth century the most striking example was in Turkey. Following the dissolution of the Ottoman Empire the country's leader, Mustafa Kemal Atatürk (1881–1938), sought to turn the nation westwards and loosen its ties to its Middle Eastern past. Alongside language reforms a new roman-based alphabet was created of twenty-nine characters, and writing in Arabic was dropped. Atatürk toured the country himself explaining the nature of the reform and urging its immediate adoption. Atatürk's reforms from 1928 changed the course of the nation's history.

In 2018 we saw a similar reform of the alphabet in Kazakhstan, planned to be phased in over several years.

OPPOSITE Vai-language manuscript. Liberia, 1849. British Library: Add MS 17817A

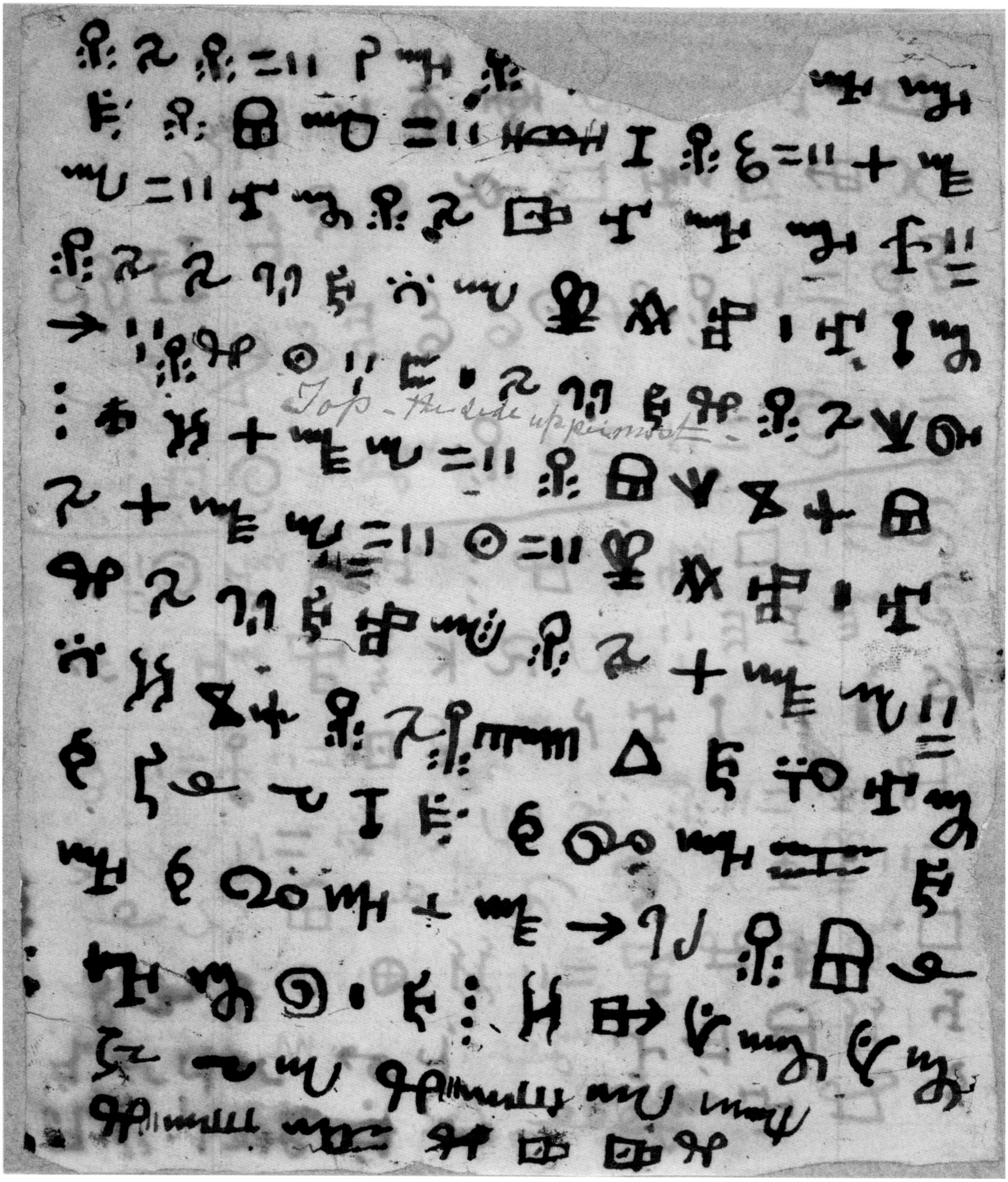
Top – the side uppermost –

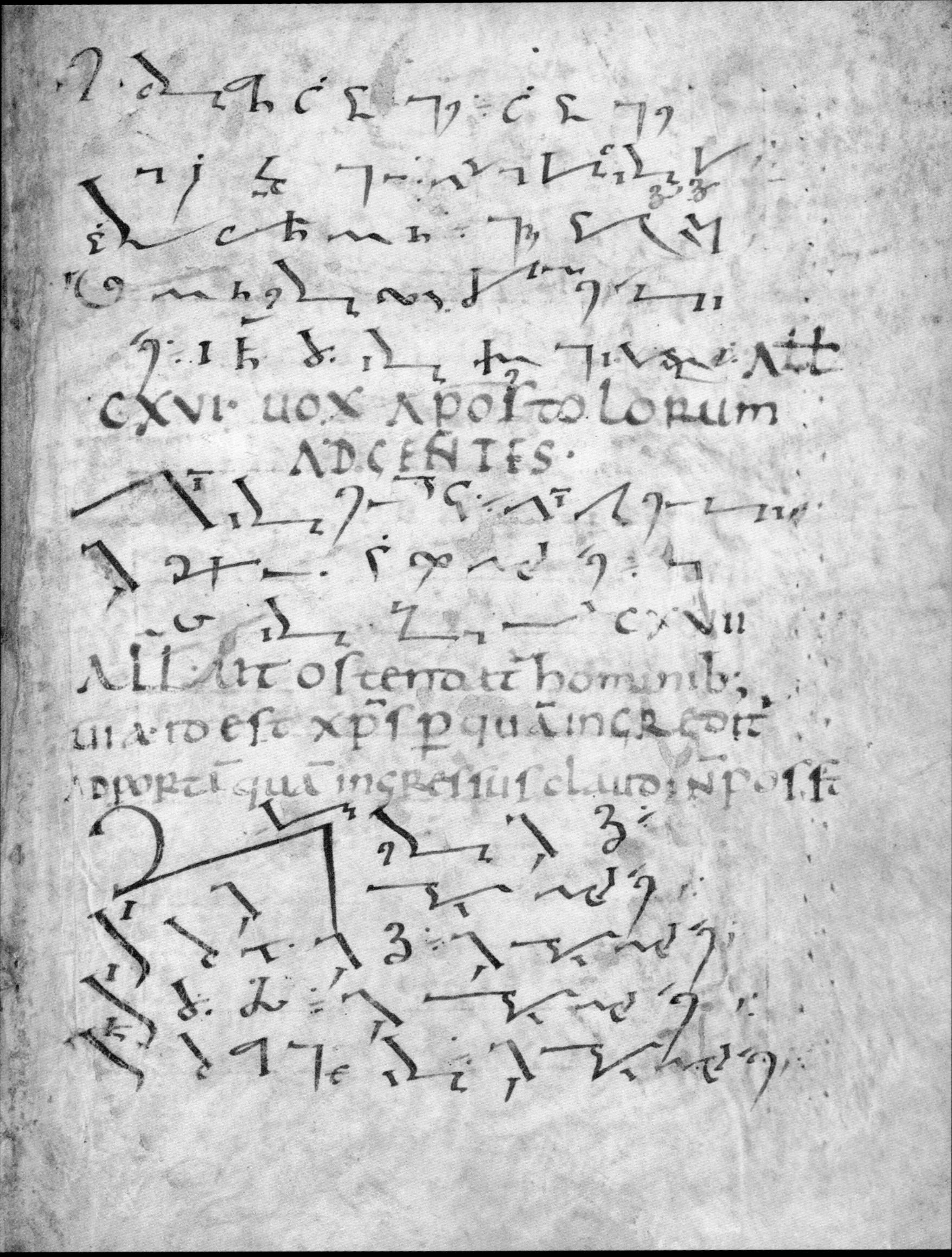

ABOVE Latin psalter in Tironian shorthand notes. Rheims (France), late 9th century. British Library: Add MS 9046, fol. 70r

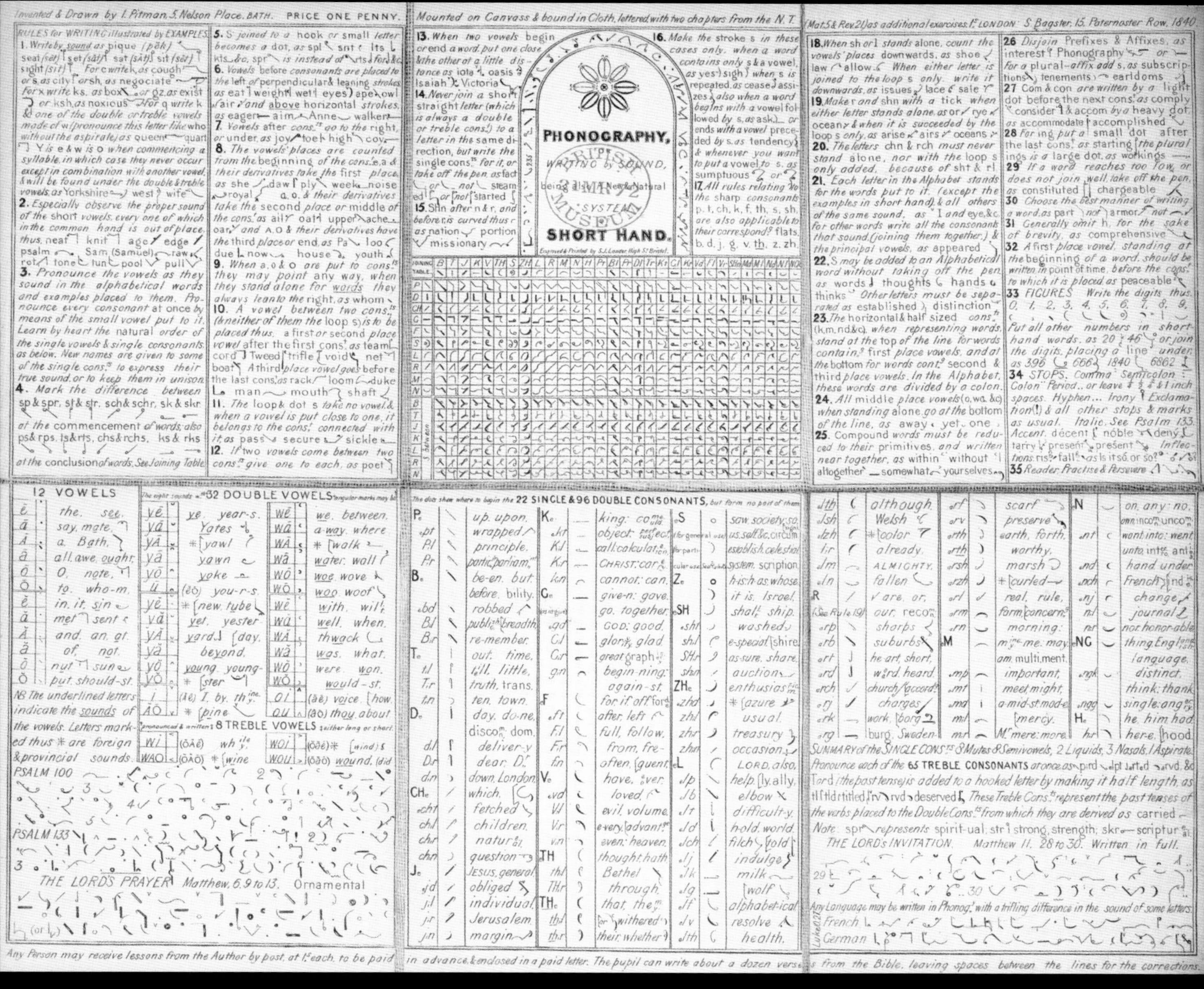

ABOVE Isaac Pitman, *Phonography: writing by sound*.
Printed pocket guide. London (England): I. Pitman, 1840.
British Library: 12991.a.4

Kazakh is a Turkic language and it has been written in a variety of roman transliterations as well as Arabic, but since the 1930s the principal system used was Cyrillic lettering. The new roman-based system attempts to turn away from this Soviet-era imposition and assert a different national identity. Meanwhile in Russia, which has an official day of Slavic Writing and Culture on 24 May (by coincidence the very day this sentence was written), the Cyrillic alphabet is regarded as an unofficial badge of nationhood. It became the official alphabet of Russia and its republics in 2002.

Just as writing can be co-opted by the state to its own purposes, so writing can give individuals and groups a voice against the prevailing order, a voice of protest that may be seen in public or disseminated in private. In the era of the Soviet Union Samizdat literature circulated beyond the range of the official censor and its appearance reflects this. In typescript or handwritten, using semi-professional presses or just carbon copies, the text was often blurred and the presentation nondescript.

From the beginning writing has been censored, books banned or burned, and individuals killed. Writing can be a dangerous business, something upon which people stake their lives. Graffiti may be thought by some to be a harmless and messy annoyance but in certain contexts such writing in a public space can be a

ABOVE Moawiya Sayasina, one of the schoolboys whose arrest for scribbling slogans sparked Syria's war in 2011. Seven years later he sits next to graffiti drawn on the wall of a schoolyard reading in Arabic 'Your turn, Doctor'. Rebel-held neighbourhood, Dar'a (Syria), 5 June 2018

powerful act. The children who wrote political slogans on walls in Dar'a in Syria, who were arrested and then tortured, and whose torture sparked the first protests of the Syrian civil war – what prompted them to do it? Had a culture of young people 'writing' spread across the globe? Did they understand that in this medium they had a voice? Perhaps this was the reason.

And then there are the official channels. Citizens can organise to vote. One of the posters written on a wall in Pompeii shows a candidate seeking favour with the electorate by sponsoring pairs of gladiators to fight in the Pompeian arena. 'Give me your vote' the poster pleads. In some countries one might march in procession carrying banners and wearing slogans on clothing, headbands and badges. Another form of protest is the petition with its collection of signatures or a petition with an online presence.

There is, and has always been, a relationship between writing and power: power for the good and the bad. There is a dark side to writing and documents. In National Socialist Germany, from the Olympic Games of 1936 onwards, calligraphy and the gothic letterform were consciously projected in Nazi propaganda, so that after the war this whole repertoire of forms became untouchable for the next generation of German designers. Without writing and its organisational power many of the mass genocides of the twentieth century could not have happened on the scale they did. The establishment and control of concentration camps and the gulag were facilitated through millions of written documents about victims and perpetrators alike. For all its supposed civilising force, writing is simply a tool for human beings; it has no moral force of its own.

Plato, back in fourth-century BC Athens, understood this. In his dialogue *The Phaedrus* (*c.*370 BC), produced just a few centuries after writing had arrived in Greece, he asks how writing can be kept alive and authentic? And he turns the focus back on us and asks how we develop opinions and what it means to search for whatever we might come to hold as a truth. This is a grounding human purpose to bear in mind as we turn now to consider writing and its future.

Focus Three

DEXTERITY AND DIVERSITY: A BILINGUAL LETTER FROM MOSUL

Michael James Erdman, PhD, Curator, Turkish and Turkic Collections

As Curator of Turkish and Turkic Collections, I deal frequently with works in multiple languages. These works are often written in languages that all use the same script – Russian and Kazakh; English and Turkish; Kurdish and Arabic – eliminating at least one intellectual hurdle for both the composer and the reader of the texts. This is why I find a collection of letters by Jeremiah Shamer, a book merchant from nineteenth-century Mosul, to be so interesting. Shamer composed his letters not only in two different languages, Arabic and Swadaya, but also in two different scripts. Swadaya is a dialect of neo-Aramaic still spoken in Iraq, Iran, the Caucasus and among diasporic communities. The Arabic of his letters is in a style known as *riq'a*, a speedy form of recording Arabic that requires minimal lifting of pen from paper, making the writing of correspondence as efficient and rapid as possible. His Swadaya, similarly, is in a hand that reveals a desire for speed, a departure from the ornate letterforms of Syriac manuscripts.

One of Shamer's letters concerns the sale and delivery of books, most of which were Christian literature by the saints of Mount Sinai and other centres of Syriac learning. The Arabic half speaks of his acquisition of various titles, while the Swadaya component relates to his sale of items (the same ones?) to an unnamed elder, a French Dominican priest resident in Mosul. Two things strike me about this text. The first is that Shamer was clearly versed enough in Arabic and Swadaya to write in both scripts with the speed and dexterity required for systems such as *riq'a*. This demands continual practice and is a testament not only to the multilingualism of the region, but also to Mesopotamia's multi-scriptual tradition. The second is that he evidently felt it important to switch scripts and languages part way through his letter. The reasons for this are not obvious, as the content of the text does not change drastically from one script to the next. Was the choice of writing in Swadaya in Syriac script a marker of identity; a demonstration of intellectual dexterity; or a crude form of encryption, protecting commercial information from those without a need to know?

These are questions for which we can only offer possibilities and conjectures, assumptions based on our own relationship to script and language. Shamer's letter reminds us of how personal a choice of writing system is. His fluidity in writing both the Arabic and Syriac scripts means that his selection was influenced by more than just skill. This brief composition brings to the fore all of the messages encoded in how we record our thoughts and feelings: our sense of belonging; our desires; and our wish to establish bonds, however tenuous, with particular people. We do not know if Jeremiah Shamer ever sold his books to the French Dominican, but we can be certain that he left his mark, however fragile, on the rich history of Middle Eastern writing.

OPPOSITE Jeremiah Shamer, commercial correspondence. Mosul (Iraq), 1881. British Library: Or.9326, fol. 37

الموصل تشرين ثاني شرقي ٨/٤١

سيدي العزيز

بعد السلام خطك المورخ تشرين اول ٢٦ وصل شكرنا الله تعالى على سلامتكم
وصحة مزاجكم : ماجاني منكم جواب مكاتيبي ٤ ما اعرف ما وصلوا
او يوجد سبب اخر واحد منهم اذكر عن ٩ كتب اشتريت من ورثة
شماس عبد الواحد اليعقوبي : وثاني اذكر فيه عن عن [illegible]
ورقتايه : والثالث داخله مكتوب ضمنه دفتر الكتب الذي جا لي
من جبل طور : والان يوجد كتاب ميامر مار افريم ومار يعقوب
سرياني ثمنه ٨٢ غرش وكتاب [illegible] لابن العبري ثمنه ليرا عثمانية ٣
كبرتيه ونظيف خط جيد وتمام ولوا احسن الموجود من اسقفي [illegible] في
جبل طور ويوجد كتب [illegible] من ضياع حوالي الموصل وجبل طور
وكم [illegible] الناطره ان كان تريد ارسل لي بخمس ٥٠ ليرا حتى اطلع
اشتري لك الله وكيل بدالك بقيمة التي اخذتهم لك والكتب يلزمني كل
يوم خرجية ٤ واحد لاكلي ثاني لامراتي : ثالث للمكاري
خادمي او ادي الذي يدور معي من قرية الى قرية : ربع اي [illegible]
[illegible]
[illegible]
[illegible]
[illegible]
[illegible]
[illegible]
[illegible]
[illegible]

5

THE FUTURE OF WRITING

EWAN CLAYTON

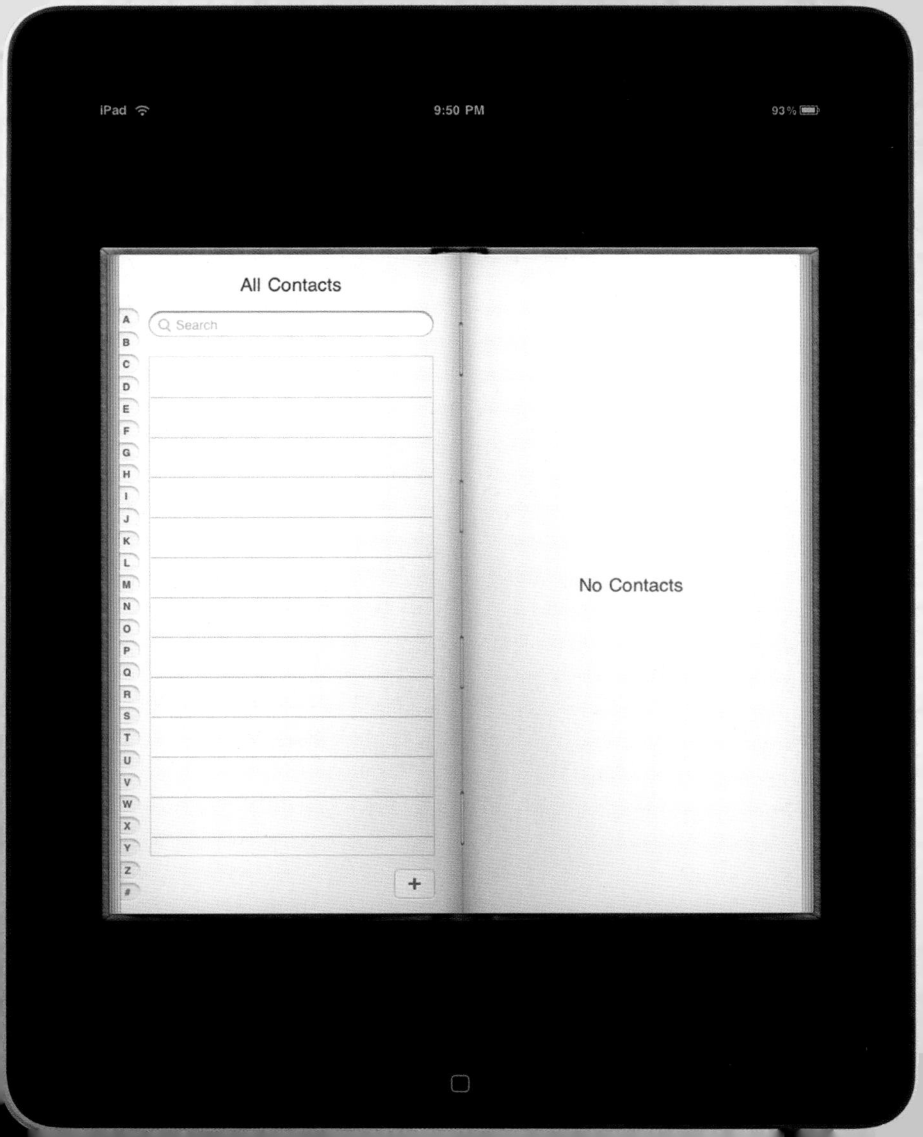
iPad
9:50 PM
93%
All Contacts
Search
A
B
C
D
E
F
G
H
I
J
K
L
M
N
O
P
Q
R
S
T
U
V
W
X
Y
Z
#
+
No Contacts

If the future, in some form, is already with us then the best we can say about it will come from the careful examination of the present moment. Often this examination involves forging a new language in which to talk about our experience of the obvious and everyday. To that end this chapter incorporates two conversations with professionals in the sphere of writing: David Levy, a computer scientist, writer and Professor in the Information School at the University of Washington, and Brody Neuenschwander, a calligrapher and text artist who lives and works in Bruges, Belgium. Both have a practice of engaging with new technologies in thoughtful ways and both also have a deep understanding of the roots of writing.

A detailed re-examination of one's experience is a characteristic feature of intellectual life from early times and often it precedes a forward movement in human thought. Frequently the trace of such activity in the written record is an upsurge of interest in grammar (the careful use of language). In Europe we see this during the Carolingian Renaissance of the eighth century and again in the early days of the Italian Renaissance. From the sixteenth century onwards we see traces in the handwritten notebooks kept by scholars and scientists, which valued first-hand experience and observations. In our own time programming languages, the mindfulness movement and other consciousness-raising exercises, the study of writing itself and the numerous articles about new information technology in the press could be understood as providing similar indications.

Our situation today, as we saw in the introduction to this book, is characterised by the development of more and more electronic means for sending and recording messages of various kinds, and this is affecting the majority of the world's writing systems. Meanwhile, we are experiencing a shift in the way media are being used. Commands can now be spoken to machines rather than typed into them. YouTube videos are replacing some kinds of instruction manuals. Biometric data is used in place of signatures. Podcasts and audio books edge into the role played by text in entertainment. And with a diminished role for handwriting in daily life 'character amnesia' has reportedly become a problem in China and Japan.

Careful use of language is necessary in the debates around these shifts. History tells us that we would be wise to avoid framing stories in black-and-white contrast. The detail is usually subtle and often it is the detail that matters. Tracking the fate of an iconic object like the book and posing simple binary choices in eye-catching headlines, such as 'e-books replace the book', has consequences. A decade ago we saw stories about the rise of electronic books: market share grew from a little over 1 per cent to 3 per cent in a year, but today sales have levelled off to around 23–25 per cent of market share. Leading bookshops in the UK no longer stock e-readers. In the meantime, libraries were closed and building plans restructured.

We may be about to make the same kind of mistakes around the presumed redundancy of handwriting. In 2010, in the USA, as the continued usefulness of handwriting (framed in opposition to keyboarding) in education was being questioned, the federal authorities issued new guidance in favour of dropping the teaching of joined-up, or cursive, writing and instead just teaching print script. In Europe this position was adopted by Finland in 2015. Yet, as discussed in earlier chapters, a rich ecology of writing tools and materials is useful. Also, electronic media themselves are moving towards handwriting as a new interface to take over from keyboards in areas where they are no longer a practical inputting device. Furthermore, evidence has recently suggested that for some tasks handwriting has an advantage over keyboarding (note-taking in lectures, for instance), producing better conceptual analysis of content and laying down longer-term memories.[1]

PREVIOUS PAGE A tablet computer displaying the contacts application

Stories matter in another way: they hint at how societies may be redefining areas of experience. As David Levy mentions in his interview in Tamara Plakins Thornton's *Handwriting in America: a Cultural History* (1996), she points out that a shift occurred in how people regarded handwriting when print culture finally became widespread in the late seventeenth century. In Europe handwriting came to be seen as personal, as opposed to print where everything looked identical. For the first time individuality and character became part of what people saw in the marks that they made upon a page. They started to collect autographs, the 'science' of graphology was invented and pure graphic gestures began to be appreciated as an expressive aspect of painting and drawing. Today, as Brody Neuenschwander notes in his interview, our feeling about handwriting may be shifting again. Certainly he is finding handwriting difficult to use in contemporary artwork: he perceives it as nostalgic rather than as the 'authentic' voice that it stood for even as little as a decade ago. It is these kinds of stories from the workplace that are interesting 'data' and it is this material from a scientist and an artist that the interviews in this chapter aim to reveal. They provide a model for our own self-reflection.

ABOVE Students taking notes using various media. Johannes Wolfang Goethe-University, Frankfurt (Germany), 2014

INTERVIEW: THE COMPUTER SCIENTIST

Professor David Levy is a computer scientist by training. He has also long been interested in the nature of written forms and documents and questions of how they are changing, or not, in the digital era. A key formative period for him was the two years he studied in London in the 1980s at the Roehampton Institute of Higher Education, where he learnt calligraphy and bookbinding as a counterweight to the world of artificial intelligence and computer science in which he was normally immersed. Today David is Professor in the Information School at the University of Washington. David and I ('Ewan' in the interview) first met in London and then worked together at the Palo Alto Research Center of the Xerox Corporation (PARC) in the 1990s.

EWAN: How do you define writing, David?

DAVID: Well, in the course I teach with Sandra Kroupa, the book arts librarian at the University of Washington Libraries, I do a session on the nature of writing where we discuss Denise Schmandt-Besserat's and Ignace Gelb's theories about the origins of writing. So we talk about writing emerging from counting or from pictures, and its relationship to spoken language. Then I do this exercise where I have students take out a piece of paper and write down their own definition of writing. I ask them to look at their definition and see what it includes and what it excludes. Every definition is going to have, at least implicitly, some kind of conception of what writing is – and what writing isn't.

I give them a list of things, of possible forms of writing, that are either going to be included or excluded. Would you include footprints in the sand, for example? Would you include an audio recording or a video? What about sign language?

I want my students to see that every attempt to define writing is a conceptual exercise, and it's also political because it's prioritising certain human activities and minimising others, and that's hugely important. Next I pull out various written definitions. I pull out the one from Gelb, as well as the one from the linguist Geoffrey Sampson, and show them that some traditional definitions of writing consider it to be very close to, almost a kind of transcription of, spoken language, whereas other definitions are much more abstract.

EWAN: What I'm hearing is that, in your work and your writing, you're deploying a number of different definitions according to how you're working.

DAVID: I'll give you two answers to that. One is, yes, that's exactly right and I'm much more interested, almost anthropologically, in the range of different definitions – not because I think any one of them is absolutely right, but because each one is, as I was just saying, a different social and political conceptualising of what's important. The other answer is that, actually, in my own work I don't need a definition of writing at all (as opposed to in my teaching where it's pedagogically useful to explore definitions).

And speaking of the politics involved in defining writing in a particular way, I think it's useful to say something about orality and literacy. In my course, we talk about the politics in the last 100-plus years involved in anthropologists and linguists trying to come to terms with the distinction between the so-called developed world and the less developed world. The original anthropological understanding was that we have both primitive people and sophisticated, modern people – people like us. But then people began to realise that this distinction was Eurocentric and racist, and scholars looked for another way to distinguish between these two kinds of societies. Maybe, they thought, what we're really talking about is a distinction between orality and literacy. But this turns out to be complicated too, because now you realise that whether a culture is literate or not depends on your definition of what writing is! And so we're back again realising that there is no single correct definition of writing, and that how you define it will have political consequences. It's pretty fascinating.

EWAN: I am thinking now about the shifts that are going on in writing practice at the moment. The things I notice are that various aspects of our lives that used to be handled by writing are being handled in other ways. For instance, biometric data is taking over from signatures and the audiovisual is moving into areas like instruction books. I'm thinking of YouTube videos, and also Alexa and voice commands on the computer. Although we're writing more than we've ever written, the things that we're writing seem to be beginning to change and shift. Then, of course, there's the whole issue of machine writing. There's been a lot in the news lately, for example, about all the data sharing that's been going on without people quite realising it. What's your view of the shift that's going on? How are you seeing change there?

DAVID: Well, first, just to underscore what you're saying, I think this is one of the most profound things that we have to wrestle with now: how as a result of new media and new technologies we have new kinds of 'writing' like those you just mentioned. It's the collection of biometric data, in ways to an extent that we've never had before, but it's also the replacement of certain earlier modes of personal communication, such as letter writing, by these newer modes. We now have so many other mechanisms by which some kind of personal communication can happen, from texting and social media to video and audio, and so on. It seems like there's a range of communicative functions that people engage in. Whether or not the actual range of those functions is changing, I think, is an open question. But it seems clear that some of these modes of communication are being transposed or translated into other, newer media.

EWAN: Yes, like storytelling became film.

DAVID: Exactly, that's a great example. Or advertising, which was first born in print media, was later realised in radio and television, and has now taken many new forms online.

One thing that seems to be true about this shift, that we still can't fully understand, is that many more choices are possible for realising any one communicative mode than existed before. Take personal communication. People do still write letters and they do still send greeting cards, even as they also use texting and social media to make personal contact. But we can now choose which technologies or media to use, and so the social meaning of our choices may be changing. In her book *Handwriting in America*, for example, Plakins Thornton made this point, that as the printing press established itself in the USA, writing by hand changed its social meaning. I suspect we are beginning to see handwriting again change its social meaning as we have so many opportunities to communicate via digital means.

But here's one very specific example that I've learnt over nearly twenty years of teaching with Sandra Kroupa, which has to do with the enduring but also changing nature of the book. Not so long ago, we went through a period when people were proclaiming or decrying the death of the book. That, of course, hasn't turned out to be true. But the very fact that there are now more choices for 'publication' has in some sense freed up the book to be many more things. And so there has been a tremendous explosion of different uses of the book format, the codex, in the book arts. The traditional, print-and-paper book has perhaps been dislodged from its pre-eminent cultural position, but this has liberated tremendous artistic creativity that is being poured into the book arts.

EWAN: The same is happening with calligraphy as well. It's being freed from the burden of legibility. I think Brody Neuenschwander will chip in on that when I have an interview with him.

DAVID: So to summarise, I do think we're seeing more choices for different communicative modes: a shift in the social meaning and uses of traditional forms, but the forms aren't going away. And along with this is a potential freeing, a kind of liberation, of some of those forms, now that they don't have to be locked into what were the previous, traditional modes of expression.

EWAN: What this makes me think of next, actually, is your book, *Mindful Tech* (2016), and why you wrote it and how that bears on writing itself, in terms of the way that people are handling new possibilities and the challenges that that is evoking, for you, in university work and in the lives of your students.

DAVID: Great. I would start by going back a bit earlier, to the time in the 1980s and 1990s when I was a researcher at Xerox PARC and I brought you in as a consultant over a number of summers. We were both excited to be exploring the transition from paper to digital formats. This is work that deeply influenced my book, *Scrolling Forward* (2001), and yours, *The Golden Thread* (2013).

During this time, I became interested in the effects that these new digital forms were having on society. People were beginning to talk regularly about information overload. I was beginning to worry that we were caught up in a kind of acceleration and a vast proliferation of information. This led me to be interested and concerned with slower and more contemplative ways of reading and writing, something that had earlier led me to study calligraphy and bookbinding at Roehampton, which is where you and I first met.

My concern about the effects of digital developments on acceleration and overload was also connected to my own deepening meditation practice, which also provides some of the background for my 'Mindful Tech' work. I began to feel that if people could slow down enough, and become more present with and aware of what they were actually doing when they were on their digital devices, that they might make some interesting discoveries that could potentially transform the way they were operating online. And that has in fact been the case. It's been thirteen years since I created a course called Information and Contemplation, which helps students to become more mindful and present in their use of digital devices, in the process noticing some of the impulses that are driving them to engage in unhealthy and ineffective ways. It's interesting: I first moved to London to study calligraphy because I wanted to slow down and get away from digital culture. But what I discovered over the years was that this slower, more contemplative mode of being could also help us to participate more effectively in digital culture.

It's been wonderful to watch as students have slowed down enough to observe the complexities of their engagement with digital media and the new modes of writing that these have made possible. Take texting, for example. On the face of it, this is a communication method that has extremely limited expressibility. But this hasn't stopped young people from trying to read important social cues from each text they receive.

For example, they might have texted their boyfriend or girlfriend, or someone might have texted them. How quickly did they get a response? Did they get a response right away? What was the punctuation? Was there a period [full stop] at the end? Was there a smiley or some other emoticon?

And I realised that although the communicative method was new, the social concerns were the same as in earlier eras. Before people had these online possibilities, the same anxieties, the same forms of social learning, were at work. Is so-and-so mad at me now? Are they still going to want to be my friend? How close friends are we? In an earlier era, these things would have been transacted in person. Maybe they would have been transacted, at least in part, on the phone. But what has seemed new is the speed and density of these questions. I came to realise that now, with young people having these devices, they were walking through a constant cloud of communicative interactions with their social community, throughout the day, even at night. Pinging one another. Am I okay, are you okay, how do you feel about me?

So my 'Mindful Tech' work has given me the pedagogical means to support people, of any age, in being observant of and reflective about their device use and the effects it is having on them. I'm able to help them see the extent to which their online behaviour is being driven by anxiety, by boredom, by envy, by anger and frustration, as well as, of course, by many positive emotions and intentions.

EWAN: Now I'm wondering about your use of writing as an academic and a thinker and what writing means to you, how you write, and what your writing is to you in your world as a tool for thinking. I know you're working on another book at the moment. What's your writing practice? What do you actually do? Where do you go? What do you use?

DAVID: First of all, writing is really important to me. But it's also really hard. So over the years I've discovered that I need to create the physical and emotional conditions that are conducive to writing. I have found that I write best in the morning. I go to my favourite coffee house here in Seattle. I bring my laptop and compose on it. I have a lot of materials that I'm using on my laptop but I may also have stacks of paper for whatever it is I'm working on at the time. The reason I go to a coffee house is I want that social sense of being with other people, but at the same time I put in my noise-cancelling headphones. I listen to Bach cantatas on my iPhone. There is something really uplifting about those cantatas, and the fact that they're being sung in German and I don't speak German means that I'm not distracted by the words. Typically, I will sit and work for anywhere from one to three hours and that's about as

ABOVE The writer Kingsley Amis at his desk, 1974. Photograph by Fay Godwin

much as I can do before I feel that I no longer have the mental acuity.

When I can afford the time, I will do this day after day. It becomes as regular a part of my day as meditation or having coffee or reading the *New York Times*. It means that on any given day, sometimes the writing is happening and sometimes it isn't, and sometimes I'm reconceptualising and taking notes. And when it's working, it puts me into a kind of wonderful contemplative state that is as precious to me as anything that I may or may not produce.

In fact, when I'm in such a state of engagement and connection, it feels like what I write, what I produce, is secondary to my state of being; it's almost a kind of prayerful state. It's one of the things I most deeply value. It's interesting because it is partly intellectual: I am thinking, I am at times writing and reading, but the mind is also open to possibilities and there's a kind of freedom to it. However, when I'm anxious, when I'm having concerns about where the writing is going or the book is going, it makes it impossible, basically, to enter into, or to stay in, such a state. I'm still, after all these years, after having written two books and now working on a third, trying to learn how to work with my own inner states around writing.

I realise as I say all of this that there is very much a parallel here with the work I'm trying to help students and others to do to gain clarity around the use of their devices and apps. I help them to see how their states of mind and body regularly drive the way they're actually operating online, and how they can potentially reconfigure their inner and outer conditions to work more effectively. I, too, am continually doing that work in relation to my own writing, so that I can write more effectively.

EWAN: I know it's an impossible question, but I've got to ask it. How do you see the future of writing?

DAVID: Yes, it's impossible! But since you ask, I'd like to start somewhere else. Before we get to where writing is going, I want to start with where we are going as a species. And then not so much predict where writing is going to go, but where I hope it will go. I'm actually pretty caught up right now in the political challenges we're facing in the USA, and indeed around the world. I'm referring, of course, to the rise of right-wing authoritarian leaders, the deep divisions between left and right, and the seeming impossibility of communicating sanely and responsibly about the vast challenges facing the planet.

Unless we can learn to communicate with one another in more authentic and compassionate and intelligent ways, I fear that we're going to keep going down, falling off this terrible cliff. I'm sure you know what I'm talking about. And all of this is being vastly exacerbated by social media and the way it's being used to deepen the divisions between us into warring tribes.

So we need to learn to speak and listen, in deeper ways, to one another. I think that those of us who are aghast at the current situation and genuinely want to help heal the liberal order are in some ways exacerbating the situation by further alienating others, in our anger and frustration. Shaming and name-calling – which is going on on both sides, of course – is no way to achieve greater harmony and reconciliation across our differences.

So perhaps what I'm getting at is that there are ethics of speaking and writing that transcend the particular modes and mechanisms of writing that we've touched on here. We need to recover, and to cultivate, more ethical forms of communication, in speech and in writing, whether online or in traditional media. In a paper a student wrote for my course this year, he quoted that famous line of Martin Buber's: 'all real living is meeting'.[2] This says to me that our deepest living, our greatest aliveness, is to be found in our actual relationships and engagement with one another, with the material world and with ourselves. Perhaps we need to cultivate this kind of understanding and to strive to achieve real 'meeting' on the deepest level. I think that unless we can bring the ethical dimension, explicitly, into education and into the cultural conversation so we can relate to one another differently, we're not going to be able to move beyond our warring tribal behaviours.

But what do I see, in terms of the future? Well, if we just extrapolate from where we are today, we're going to see increasing amounts of shallow, divisive, accelerated communication. We're going to see advertising, and other powerful forms of persuasion, continuing to manipulate people's attitudes and orientations to life, much of it tied to the baser aspects of our economic system, which is why we need to bring ethics to bear.

So when I think about the future of writing, my hope is that we can learn to communicate more ethically and responsibly. And as a thought exercise, I would ask where are the ethical and deeper forms of real engagement happening in reading and writing today? What can we learn from these cases? What conditions bring them about? In what ways are they dependent on the properties of the media in which they are occurring? And most importantly, how can these instances inspire us as models for how we might write in the future? So that writing can be the great gift to the world that, at its best, it has always been.

EWAN: And one final question. Do the aesthetics of writing matter?

DAVID: Of course they do!

EWAN: Why would they matter? Why don't we just want the most effective and efficient means of communication possible?

DAVID: Because there's a whole dimension of our lives that is not simply instrumental. From an instrumental point of view, yes, we want the fastest, the cheapest, the most efficient way to be in touch with one another. But there's this whole other dimension of human experience, which is our sense of being fully alive and loving one another and the world. And there's beauty and there's awe and there's reverence and all of those qualities. Let's recall William Morris and his concern for beauty as a necessary ingredient in a healthy society. I would hate to live in a kind of technocratic world in which we were simply solving problems by figuring out the most efficient way to be: I think it would be the death of our deepest humanity.

INTERVIEW: THE ARTIST

Brody Neuenschwander is a calligrapher and text artist, who describes his career as one long effort to understand the essence of calligraphy, first in Western culture and then extending to other cultures and their scripts. He does not practise Arabic, Chinese and Japanese calligraphy, but he has studied the three languages and their traditions of writing in the hope of enriching his understanding of roman letters (Brody refers to them as Latin letters in his interview).

At the same time, and almost from the beginning of his career, he started to ask questions about the relationship of calligraphy to contemporary art.

In an email he sent in preparation for this interview he wrote:

> Would I stay in the comfort zone of the traditional Latin letters (roman, medieval and Renaissance) that formed the core of my schooling as a calligrapher in London in the early 80s? Or would I find the courage (and insights) to challenge the separation of art and craft typical

> of English calligraphy since its revival in the early twentieth century? It was astonishing to learn that the creation of an entirely new artistic genre, text art, by artists such as Picasso, Duchamp and Marinetti, nearly coincided with the publication of Edward Johnston's *Writing & Illuminating & Lettering* (1906). Johnston and his colleagues in the Arts and Crafts movement were not aware of these new developments, but I could hardly afford the same nostalgic luxury.

Brody is continuing to explore both these themes in a series of films that are being made by Dox Productions, London, for Arte and the BBC to coincide with this exhibition and publication. This three-part documentary will look at the origins of writing worldwide, the development of the great traditions of calligraphy in China, the Islamic world and the West, and the influence of print and digital technologies on the future of writing and calligraphy.

EWAN: One of the themes that has come up in preparing this book has been shifts in the definition of one area of writing against another. I know that one shift you are experiencing as an artist is in the meaning that we read into handwriting.

BRODY: The changes in the practice and meaning of handwriting present me with a real artistic dilemma. It is frustrating to watch handwriting lose its validity as a way of representing my presence, my voice, in a work of art. If you look at text art through the twentieth century, handwriting was used by countless artists to say 'this is my voice, these are my thoughts'. We can't really say that any more, because there is already nostalgia attached to virtually every kind of handwriting.

Artists in the twentieth century also used typewriters and then typewriter fonts to represent their presence, while more formal fonts were used to suggest the voice of authority. The typewriter has also passed into the realm of nostalgia. The revolution in font design that came with desktop publishing has completely shifted the aesthetics of what writing looks like. What's done by hand looks like it's in the past. I'm struggling with that a great deal, because I worked with a variety of odd tools that make splatters, irregular marks and rough lines in order to add expressive energy to my writing. And now I find even this type of handwriting/calligraphy trickling through my fingers and disappearing into the sand.

What was the point of all that calligraphic research? I suppose I wanted to take the energy of Jackson Pollock and fuse it to writing, to visual language. Pollock seemed to me so full of unrealised potential (from a calligrapher's point of view). If you dribble paint with a stick, you will tend to make the same movements over and over again. The interest in his work is not its graphic invention, but the different kinds of linear density and pattern. If, however, you use a similar gesture to write words, even if they all are illegible, the command given by each letter in sequence means that you do more interesting movements. So the graphics would be, by nature, richer than what would come from an automatic process without writing.

Hans-Joachim Burgert (a twentieth-century artist and influential writer on calligraphy from Berlin) helped me to understand this. He pushed me to ask what writing and calligraphy would be if they were not a craft (that is, have no function). Burgert did not believe that calligraphy could be a fine art: for him the medium of line and surface was too limited in its freedom for that. But he gave me a language by which I could analyse Pollock and Chinese calligraphy and Arabic calligraphy all using the same formal terms. This helped me to see how much more could be done than either the calligraphers or the artists were doing.

The next paradigm shift for me came by working

with film director Peter Greenaway. For *Prospero's Books* (1991) he asked me to create a visually exciting form of a Shakespearian script that would charm the camera. To anyone viewing the film this script will seem correctly historical. But the writing in the film actually becomes a contemporary aesthetic, a contemporary artistic product, with a really strong conceptual foundation. By moving an historical script to a film screen it gained in artistic power and meaning. Now, I'm not the artist there, Greenaway is the artist, but it made me realise that a medium shift could save my calligraphy. Pen and ink on paper are historically correct; they carry historical associations. Something had to give and this was achieved by moving the calligraphy to the screen.

ABOVE Brody Neuenschwander, *At this stage it is necessary to develop a new graphic language that attempts to lay bare my soul.* Gouache on Rives BFK paper, written with a pointed sable brush. 2018

EWAN: In the last few years you have been working with installations too?

BRODY: Yes, all sorts, and it is starting to wear me out physically. My energy is starting to show its limits these days, because all the projects are so different one from another. One is architectural, using laser-cut steel, another is ceramic, another is a textile, another is a video, another is a performance. I think that I've been maybe a little too manic in looking for all the different ways calligraphy can be anything but writing on paper.

EWAN: Have you found a home in any of those media? Film seems the obvious one there.

BRODY: I never learnt the editing software. And I think that that would be a really good thing to do because, as long as I have to rely on a technician who knows the software, I don't have the freedom that I have, say, in Photoshop. I feel freer in Photoshop than with practically any analogue tool. There are certain limitations there; analogue tools have them as well. The commissions keep coming for metal, laser work, architecture, textiles, and so on. These all require a medium shift. I usually start on paper, then scan my work in, change it on screen with a stylus and Wacom tablet, and create vector files that are sent to the factory for laser cutting, weaving or whatever. And then somebody else builds or mounts the thing.

I think the future of calligraphy will, for the most part, be a future OFF paper. We will perhaps learn it on paper, using traditional tools. But my work is rarely delivered to the client on paper: in metal, bronze, glass, textile, ceramics, on walls, any place but paper. It often goes through a digitising process before the final product is made.

EWAN: So, could you give us an idea of some of the kinds of projects that you've undertaken?

BRODY: Well, yes. In Bruges we have quite a tradition of public lettering and most of that was in stone. And at a certain point the public authorities wanted some sort

ABOVE Vivian Wu in *The Pillow Book*, a film directed by Peter Greenaway, 1996

of dedicatory texts not in stone and they commissioned me to do a pair of gates. These were laser cut in Corten steel and allowed to rust to a radiant patina. These gates led to another set of gates, and then another, so I now have three nice big gates in Bruges. The first set was strictly geometric, as I was feeling my way forward with the new technology. The second gates use a calligraphic line, with very good results. The third gates use very simple typography. I find that the stricter forms of typography relate well to the architecture and are a natural way of using the laser technology. After the third set of gates I encased an entire chapel in laser-cut words. That was very complicated because of the size of the building and the vast amount of vectoring that had to be done.

I now give the vector work to my students, so I can skip that. The chapel project led to another large project for the same client (a convent in Flanders). This is a commission to do the railings around a new cemetery containing the names of all the sisters from over the last 300 years. For practical considerations this will be done in typography. With 500 names to be vectored, any kind of script would simply take so much time and be too expensive. Legibility would also suffer. So I think a simple sans-serif font would probably be best.

EWAN: So, if it's okay, I'd love to jump back for a moment in the conversation because the name Peter Greenaway will flicker on the page for people. And although I know the story, it would be worthwhile, just briefly, saying what you learnt from that collaboration.

BRODY: What I didn't learn from Ann Camp [Brody's calligraphy teacher] and Burgert, I learnt from Greenaway and Donald [the calligrapher Donald Jackson was Brody's first employer; see page 97 for an example of his work]. Quite simply, Peter taught me to think conceptually about what we were doing; to realise that the message of the work of art could function on many levels – levels of form, association, intuition and idea – and that the job of the artist is not simply to choose a medium, like letters, and do something nice with letters, which is what calligraphers almost universally do, but to think the project through and bring in meaning on all these levels. Calligraphy might be the solution, but it cannot be a choice simply because one likes calligraphy. Typography will work better in some cases. Choices of material and scale are also important in the process of creating text art. In this way Peter broke my tie to calligraphy and made me a better calligrapher at the same time.

EWAN: You mentioned Ann Camp, Donald Jackson and Burgert. What did you learn from those three individuals who have been important to you?

BRODY: From Ann I learnt to think clearly about the shapes of letters [laughs] and to carry a thought through. From Donald I learnt about play, spontaneity, embodiment, and a way of mocking things up for the client quickly. He taught me quite a lot about the business of calligraphy, as I did him! From Burgert I learnt a formal language, which allowed me to compare Western scripts with Arabic and Chinese scripts and to describe what I was seeing in those scripts. What does Arabic script have that Latin scripts do not? Burgert gave me a language to analyse this question and I've used it ever since. These are questions that a calligrapher in the Johnstonian tradition would not ask. The page in Johnston's book where he shows twenty-six **a**'s, only one of which is made correctly, always drove me mad. Instead, I propose twenty-six different **a**'s, all of which are made correctly. The more variation, the better. The harmony of an alphabet according to the Western tradition is not the same as the harmony of a fully developed graphic language.

This has been a wonderful revelation. Recently I have started to do fusion writing in an effort to move away from my explosive gestural writing. It seemed like the time to make a change and go back to something slower and more deliberate. It wasn't just that I felt that I was flying off the rails with all those Pollockian gestures. It was also because it takes so little time to fill a large sheet or canvas with gestural writing ... and then what do you do the rest of the day?

I thought I would have to find some way of slowing down. And Burgert was always a critic of speed. He always felt that if you're going too fast, you can't really think, even at the intuitive level of thinking. You can't really think the formal relationships through. Again, this would be the criticism that I was applying to Pollock. You can't think the formal relationships through, so you wind up with things that are usually either monotonous or just badly formed. By slowing down and making deliberate decisions to fuse different kinds of writing, which you can only do when you're working calmly, it becomes possible to think what might be taken from Kufic here and from the *Yellow Submarine* record covers of the 1960s there, from Art Deco here or from Gothic there, or even going back to something formal like a roman capital. That could happen only at a slower pace. It entails a risk every time, because the slower you go, the more hours you put into a work, and the greater the loss if you screw it up.

EWAN: That's fascinating. Risk, is that important to you in your work?

BRODY: Oh, that's the whole thing for me, I think. I've been walking on coals my whole life [laughs]. It would be wise not to do that, but it's just the nature of the beast. Even with thousands of somebody else's money riding on it, I'm still willing (or foolish enough) to take the brush, address the wall, make the mark without having thought much about it all. My process is to react to something, not to sit in a chair, figure it out and then execute it. I prefer to take the white piece of paper, make it a little less white and then move on.

I am using a fine, pointed brush these days: very fine kolinsky sable. And I'm really pleased with the results because I think they give me back some of that ... I don't know if other people see this ... freshness and the contemporary feeling that I felt I was losing. I'm going to pretend that I'm ahead of the curve here, making a fusion from Islamic, Chinese, Latin and other scripts. It's still English, it's still Latin script, but it's becoming what the English language is becoming in a place like Nigeria. It's no longer the possession of the English speakers. The Latin alphabet, of course, is not the possession of those who invented it. But I like the idea that fusion would suggest a sort of awareness of what's going on in other cultures. We're all fusing all the time now.

I want to say one more thing about the relevance of this cross-pollination and fusion. There was only one moment when I was doing calligraphy and had no inclination to ask myself what calligraphy meant, whether it was valuable, worth doing. That moment was during a performance called *A Brush with Silence*.

A Brush with Silence brings twelve to fifteen calligraphers from different traditions together in one large space. Chinese, Japanese, Arabic, Hebrew, Latin, Greek, English, Cyrillic, Thai, Hindi, Tibetan, whatever we can find really. Each writer, dressed in white, sits at a spot-lit table in the darkened space and simply writes. I always ask them to write a text of importance to them and to their culture and I ask them to eliminate all the fireworks. This is not about showing off fancy penmanship; this is about a good, beautiful, noble script without colour, written with dignity. And everybody remains silent. The public is asked to keep silent, so they simply move from table to table and see the different scripts

being written. It is astonishing to see how the public reacts to this. They are so intensely silent and focused on the work of the calligraphers. The children are silent and focused. People go out the door and phone their friends to say, 'You have to come and see this.'

After we did *A Brush with Silence* the first time (I can still get quite emotional about this) I realised it was not about the calligraphy. It was about all the calligraphers together, symbolising all the people together, at peace with each other. How beautiful.

Suddenly it all fell into place. Calligraphy is important because writing remains a marker of each society; one of the most highly recognisable markers, in fact. When you pass a shop front with Chinese writing on it you know it's a Chinese restaurant. Islamic writing or Arabic writing immediately suggests the culture. We don't have to know what it says. We know the shapes. Cyrillic script is instantly recognisable, as is Hindi. These scripts are badges for their cultures on the international stage. When we bring them all together in peace and stillness it is a dignified, deeply human statement of tolerance and respect. When people see this it gives them hope again.

Suddenly *A Brush with Silence* is catching. We've done it seven times, and now we're going to do it in Moscow in July, in Poland and Paris in October. *A Brush with Silence* is my message to the world.

✧ ✧ ✧

ABOVE Tashi Mannox at Brody Neuenschwander's *A Brush with Silence* installation. The Round Church, Cambridge, 2018

These interviews could spread across professions and maybe they will. It would be revealing to post the experience of an office worker, an accountant (the electronic spreadsheet was revolutionary), a school child, diplomat, shopworker, social calligrapher, journalist and lawyer. It would be great to host one big conversation about our experience of writing, not driven by the hype of a new product or a media story, but reflecting on actual lived experience, now, in the early twenty-first century. One thing seems clear: whatever the future, and whatever changes the new technologies bring, our present technology already requires us to think about a new ethic of communication, maybe a new rhetoric also.

In preparing this chapter each interviewee let me know how they wanted to be presented to the reader by sending me an email. Then we had a recorded 'Zoom' conversation over the Internet. During the next forty-eight hours the audio tape was typed up and sent back to the interviewee to look over. It was apparent that speech is a lot looser than writing. Sentences were interrupted by other thoughts; at times it was difficult to make sense of the typed-up text. Using new tools requires new ways of working, new self-disciplines, in this case new ways of speaking for writing. And of course technologies are changing all the time: old ones are being updated and new ones launched. Are we ever now fully on top of them? James Williams, author of *Stand Out of Our Light: Freedom and Resistance in the Attention Economy* (2018), has described this experience as living on a 'treadmill of incompetence'.[3] There is no doubt that learning to write is a lifelong process. The evidence of change in the historical record is so insistent over the last 2,000 years that it would seem to indicate it ever was so.

✧ ✧ ✧

So what will the future of writing look like, what will we write? How will we write it, will it disappear? Predictions are difficult and technology is moving fast. One thing we can say from reading the different contributions to this book is that there is a consensus among our authors that writing is here to stay; new technologies seldom totally displace the old technologies, but rather they add choices.

Handwriting, too, has a future even if in times to come our tools look rather different. They may include smart pens, other movement and tracking software in normal or augmented reality, electronic and smart paper we can fold or scroll, and a huge range of surfaces that might become available to be written upon. Calligraphy also has an exciting new future now that it can move seamlessly into the digital world by being scanned or filmed. It can be translated into a number of different materials, be used on an architectural scale or be developed as a performance art: we see this potential in the many short video clips one can find on Instagram. So much has already changed. On our screens today we write in light! Images can thus be instantly changed or coloured: this would be a land of enchantment to the painter of the illuminated manuscript.

Type design is also evolving; drawn letters and characters are scanned and vectorised. Although this has led to some typefaces being built of standard components in a way that makes them more uniform and perhaps more bland than in the past, there has been a resurgence of interest in the area. Families of type are now designed to be global in scope, ranging from roman letters to Japanese and Thai. They have to work at many different scales and across a variety of media and platforms. They may also have families of symbols and emojis associated with them. Emojis are particularly interesting. Short messaging systems have become a place for experimenting with a new type of hybrid writing system. First we used emoticons and now emojis: almost like determinatives to help untangle the ambiguities of the format and lend nuance to a brief message. In future type will probably also become animated and personalised.

Social media is a phenomenon whose implication we are only now beginning to grasp. As we have seen all media have always been social but the difference today is that they place large numbers of users in almost instant communication, and at the same time they open them to social persuasion and statistical analysis. In the hands of corporations with global ambitions, national states and other alliances, individuals can become subject to goals that may be beyond their individual grasp and interest. Many voices point to a new kind of attention that is helpful and perhaps necessary when handling these media. In this chapter David Levy has spoken about how he handles this with his students at the University of Washington. The language of attention, presence and meeting is perhaps one of the new windows through which we can view this subject.

All these media, materials and tools, these drives to communicate, record, name, claim, make accessible and storytell, all the institutions that surround the written word and give structure to our individual lives, make up an ecology of writing. Writing goes forward on a number of levels and at different scales. What keeps it all alive and changing is the human imagination and, quite literally, our bodies. We/they make marks by pressing, printing, painting, scratching, inking and tracing forms that carry a numinous history themselves: the record of those parts of the ecology from which they emerged. Mostly they evolve slowly over time but at other moments change seems revolutionary as some community or individual is galvanised into a deep response to a changed environment of human thought or circumstance. Travelling as we now are through one of those moments, we wonder 'is the writing on the wall' for writing? No, writing is bigger than that, it is as big and as multifarious as we can imagine. We should not allow our dreams to be downsized by any one particular passing technology.

Finally I am reminded, each time I cross the floor and climb the stairs of a great library to meet the curators with whom I am working, of all those dreams that a place like a library contains. I am grateful to those who care for these fruits of our imagination, born from the years each one of us spends learning to be competent members of a literate community.

ABOVE People at work in the public spaces of the British Library, London, around the King's Tower.

6

HANDWRITING NOW AND IN THE FUTURE

ANGELA WEBB

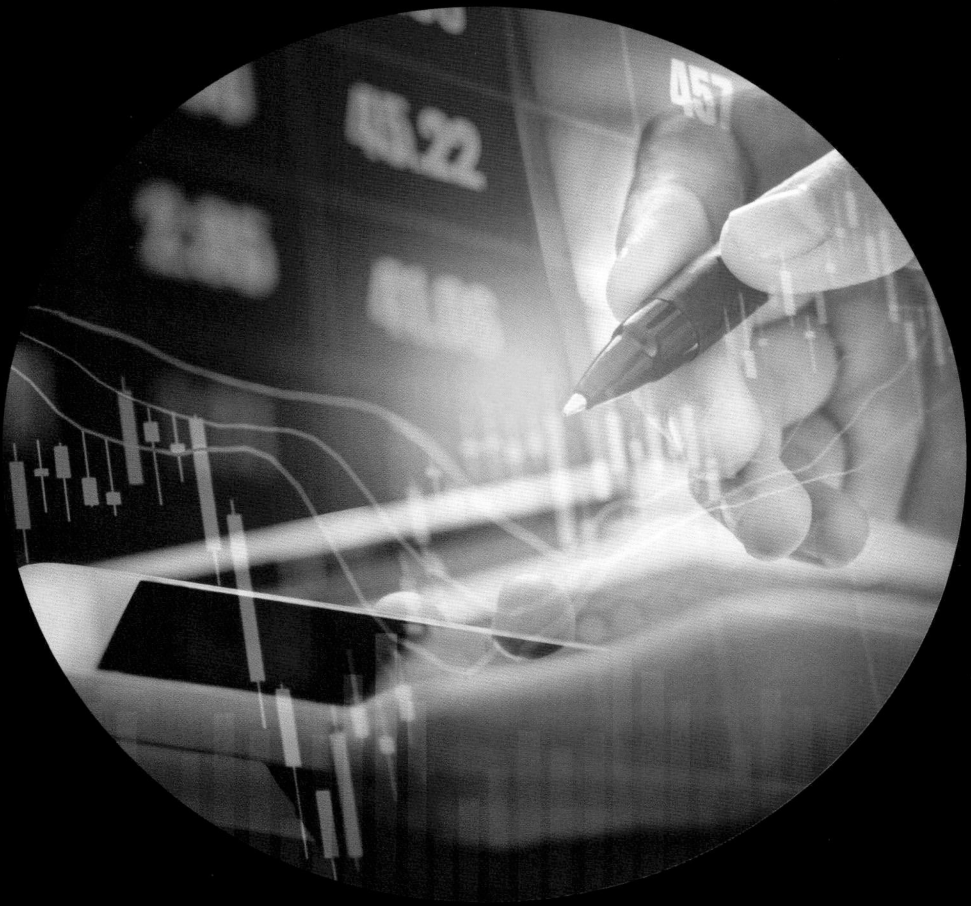
457
45.22

The term 'writing' is used to describe both the process of putting symbolic marks onto a surface and the product of what is written, as in 'a piece of writing': the former is dynamic, the latter a completed act. Looking back through history we have many examples of the product, as this exhibition illustrates, such as indentations on clay, carved hieroglyphs on stone, symbols painted on parchment or on paper with ink. They are lasting traces of the writer's intentions. However, it is harder for us when looking at this evidence to glean much knowledge of the process by which those symbols were produced – how the hand delivered what the eye can see – or begin to understand what was going on in the brains of the writers. We can only speculate how they acquired their art. Were they following some prescribed style or form literally 'to the letter', or were they free to 'ad lib', to make it up as they went along? Were their forms consistent in shape and scale? What were the writers' physical capabilities? Were they selected for their particular dexterity? How important to them was the visual impact of what they wrote: the aesthetic? Was it as important as the messages to be communicated? We just cannot tell. Neither can we know how these ancient writers refined their writing skill. Were they schooled in their art by a tutor or did they simply copy what they had observed others doing? Did they practise writing so as to become more proficient? Many of these questions from the distant past remain, to a large extent, unanswerable.

However, things have changed, particularly within the last 100 years. Today the process of writing has become something we are better able to evaluate. This has come about partly through informed observation but also, to an even larger extent, through the use of highly developed tools. Electronic ways of analysing script have only comparatively recently become available and are still evolving with ever-increasing speed and accuracy. We could question why we should be interested in understanding more about how we write but one argument could be that since writing has become more universally attainable, a skill for the masses, like reading, the need to enhance acquisition of the skill for a wider population has driven a desire to gain more knowledge about what is involved in producing text by hand. Whatever our motivation, we are now in the privileged position of being able to analyse to a high level of detail how we handwrite and, as a result, optimise the proficiency of all writers.

OPPOSITE Rudolf Laban with his notation system on a board
PREVIOUS PAGE Writing on a smart phone using a digital pen

MEASURING THE PROCESS OF WRITING

Describing the physical act

Two different approaches for assessing the physical aspect of writing have been utilised. The first seeks to measure the biomechanics of the writer in terms of the skeletal, muscular, nervous and sensory systems of the body. This kind of understanding draws upon sports science for its framework and is influenced by what research in that field can tell us about the learning and refining of writing as a motor skill. The 'bible' for motor learning, written by Richard Schmidt and Tim Lee, has been updated over several decades to reflect research findings.[1] This approach has relevance to handwriting because of the skill's substantial motor component, although it does not serve to capture all of its elements. A second approach has been to focus less on the physical make-up and competences of the writer, but more on the qualities of the movements themselves, looking at the spatial, temporal and force components of the actions as well as their fluidity of delivery. Objective measures of the nature of the movements used to produce written traces provide us with a different way of evaluating the proficiency of the writer. If the movements are slow and ponderous, for example, or if they are faltering and lack fluency, the impact on the handwriting will be apparent. One such system of movement analysis, Kinetography Laban, was devised in 1928 by the Hungarian dance theorist and teacher, Rudolf Laban (1879–1958), whose studies of human actions provided the intellectual foundation for the development of central European modern dance.[2] This motion notation system allowed observers to record all forms of human movement. The Laban system was, in a way, 'alphabetic' in that symbols represented movement components through which the patterns within each action could be 'spelt out', in a manner not dissimilar to writing an alphabetic text.

While Laban never set out specifically to measure the movements of writing, his system did provide a platform from which judgements of movements could be made because it could describe in detail how and which particular parts of the body were moving. It served also to record the velocity and force of individual movements as well as their fluency: all factors critical to handwriting. I mention it here as an example of an early means of documenting the process of a motoric skill through observation and skilled human analysis. This technique pre-dates the adoption of electronic tools available today, but the additional use of film and later video recordings of people handwriting could, in turn, allow filmed movement sequences to be analysed using Laban's system. Although these provided useful evidence for learning purposes, there are obvious limitations to what is visible to the naked eye, namely, that visual observations alone cannot describe all levels of a process as complex as handwriting. The next stage in assessment was to develop tools for measuring underlying elements that might be less obvious.

Electronic tools for measuring handwriting

Innovative as Kinetography Laban was at the time, it was never an exact science and unsurprisingly it has been superseded by the introduction of new technologies that provide a more scientific analysis. Arguably the most significant revolution in this field has been the development of the digitiser or graphic tablet, which, together with software programs of increasing variety and complexity designed to be used with it, can yield data on a number of different measures. This invention has contributed enormously to our understanding of the ergonomics of handwriting and helps us to interpret handwriting 'behaviours' with greater accuracy.

If we examine the range of handwriting factors measurable using this type of technology we can see how its potential takes us far beyond where we have been in the past. For example, data on spatial, temporal and force elements are widely collected using this method. Typical examples of these measures are stroke length, azimuth (pen angle), stroke velocity and pen pressure.[3] Objective readings can give evidence of specific levels of competency. Software has been developed showing how fluent the text production is by tracking the movements of both the eye and the pen.[4] Other programs can provide information on when, how and where the pen is moving but also when it is not moving, that is, when and where the writer pauses. Interestingly, by measuring the pattern of pausing during a written assignment, and by calculating the proportion of time the pen spends off the page, how frequent those pauses are and where they occur in the text, information can be gleaned on the automaticity of transcription at any given time.[5] Pause analysis can also indicate the degree to which other factors, such as spelling difficulties, constrain the writing.[6] There is even software that charts the pathway of the pen when it is not on the page but up in the air, showing the degree of the motor and spatial control of the writer.[7] One further type of analysis relates to the fluency of the handwriting movements. This research demonstrates how the writer's performance may vary according to context and environmental circumstances, and the extent to which fluid performance may be compromised by non-writing, such as cognitive and emotional, factors. Christian Marquardt illustrates this point by showing how a five-year-old who can draw circles smoothly and without hesitation when pattern-making becomes awkward and dysfluent when writing the **O** at the start of his name.[8]

Being able to measure the writing process with this degree of detail and accuracy has obvious advantages, particularly for the nascent writer. Not only can it help to identify general levels of efficiency but, in the case of someone less proficient, it can also highlight which aspect or aspects of the skill may be causing problems. This enables intervention planning to be sensitive. I will elaborate on the topic of handwriting difficulties later in the chapter, but the role of technology in diagnosing anomalies and as a tool for researching the handwriting process has been significant.

One final type of measurement tool to mention here provides information on what is happening in the brain when different writing tasks are performed. Scanning using magnetic resonance imaging (MRI), or functional MRI (fMRI), or encephalography (EEG), gives us a window into the workings of the brain during writing (and other tasks) and can show both the incidence and location of neural activation during the activity. This revolutionary tool has the potential to extend the parameters of our knowledge of process in even greater ways.[9] Furthermore, it can now demonstrate the possibility of altering the patterns of neural response (after certain interventions) and achieving lasting neuro-plastic change.[10] The importance of this for teaching need not be spelt out.

The complex nature of handwriting

Handwriting is frequently assumed to be purely a motor skill, similar to other physical skills such as throwing a ball, threading a needle, knitting or juggling, and in that case dexterity or good hand–eye coordination would be the only requirements for mastering it. This view is partially true as handwriting has a significant motor component to it, possibly accounting for around 70 per cent, but as we shall see later, there is a lot more to writing than appears on the surface. Handwriting is often also described purely in terms of hand function, relating to strength and agility in the wrist, hand and fingers without any acknowledgement of how the rest of the body might contribute. A more accurate description would include the whole body, not just the hand. For example, for the hand and arm to be free to be fluent, the core of the body must be controlled and stable. To achieve this stability, muscles in the trunk, pelvis and shoulder girdles have to work hard to maintain good posture. Physical therapists sometimes use the mantra 'no mobility without stability', showing how crucial it is for the whole body to be under control.

Postural stability is particularly important for the writing of alphabetic scripts, which are delivered horizontally and must flow smoothly across the page (in whichever direction), but it impacts also on the production of ideographic characters, hieroglyphs and other symbols where it may appear that the emphasis of movement is focused on the fingers with short, jabbing gestures.

Because of its high motor content the basic teaching approach for physical skills is appropriate also in the teaching of handwriting. Typically, three clear phases can be identified. The first, sometimes referred to as the 'cognitive' phase, focuses on imparting the basic movements of the skill. In handwriting this is when letterforms are taught. The second phase, termed the 'associative' phase, is when the skill is refined through practice, and for the handwriter this is when the writing increases in accuracy and consistency. The third and final phase, the 'autonomous' phase, is where high levels of automaticity are achieved so that the movements can be performed fluently and with a minimum of conscious thought.[11] Becoming automatic allows the writer to focus on the content of what he or she wants to express and less on the nuts and bolts of how the symbols are delivered to the page. Where handwriting requires undue thought, attention is diverted away from what are considered to be the 'higher order' processes of composing, planning and editing text.[12] Although individual differences in physical make-up and movement ability mean that the rate of progress through the different phases may vary, being aware of the framework can assist teachers to impart skills, such as handwriting, which have a motor component.

Another misconception about motor skills is that they involve only physical elements – muscle strength, agility, flexibility and coordination – but there are other subtle systems at work in the body to produce movements, such as those involving the sensory systems. Feedback from our muscles when we are in motion (kinaesthesia), an understanding of our position in space (proprioception) and the ability to maintain balance (vestibular) all affect the production of movement, together with visual monitoring. All are skills that have an impact on performance. In no place are these components more at work than in the production of handwritten symbols.

Having shown how handwriting has much in common with other motor skills, it is also important to recognise that it is greatly more complex than the rest and encompasses additional elements that make it unique. As well as the motor, perceptual, visual and sensory systems, cognitive components come into play, especially when learning the conventions of each specific writing system. All systems vary in terms of directional and spatial rules. This includes hieroglyphs, ideographic characters and alphabetic script. Knowledge of written conventions and the linguistic constraints of each particular orthography (spelling patterns) require important cognitive input,[13] and understanding the significance of, as well as being able to 'see' and reproduce, the spatial organisation of letters and words on the page is dependent upon keen visual perceptual skills.[14] In terms of script acquisition, acknowledging the niceties and making the rules or conventions explicit can enhance a child's ability to assimilate them.

All these different aspects of writing play a significant part. However, the contribution of one often-overlooked component is language. Handwriting is a form of language and thus language is the medium through which it communicates. The American psychologist, Virginia Berninger, describes the four pillars of linguistic skill as 'language by ear' (listening), 'language by mouth' (speaking), 'language by eye' (reading) and 'language by hand' (writing) in order to illustrate how language underlies and unites these four abilities.[15] As a child matures, these systems evolve, not in discrete sequential stages, but rather in parallel and overlapping waves, the mastery of each occurring along a continuous trajectory while influenced by other forms of language. Knowing how the various language systems develop and interrelate helps to shape our understanding of how a writer's performance is affected by competence in all the systems, particularly with oral language where the 'inner voice' contributes by preparing what is to be written down.[16] Some research studies have shown that linguistic competence is a key factor underpinning learning to write and that children with a good command of oral language are more likely to be proficient writers if these elements are in place.[17] Conversely, there is research which shows that those with developmental language disorders often struggle with handwriting.[18] All these component skills – motor, sensory, perceptual, visual, cognitive, linguistic – are integral to the performance of handwriting in every writing system, be they alphabetic or not.

Communicating is core to writing, even if only with oneself, as in the recording of a personal diary or journal. For example, it is assumed that the purpose of writing something is that someone can read it and share the writer's thoughts; it has the intention of reaching an audience. We could become expert jugglers or knitters, and although it might be enjoyable to show off our skills to others, our proficiency in performing them is not dependent upon that. Handwriting also has the facility for leaving a lasting visible trace, unlike the spoken word, and as a result it allows what is written to survive over time, in some cases long enough to be revisited after very extended periods. Without these traces we would not be able to appreciate much of the content of this current exhibition or marvel at the skill of the script producers.

Handwriting as a taught skill

Another core characteristic of the language of handwriting is that, like reading, it involves a highly sophisticated system of symbols as its mode. This is, again, common to ideographic qualities in some Asian languages, the hieroglyphs of the Maya or Egyptians, and alphabetic scripts. They share the fact that the symbols are not naturally determined nor their meanings universally understood. Therefore, in each case, the system used has to be explained and taught. A young child left unaccompanied in a desert with a ball would probably lift, kick, throw, roll or bounce it without guidance; given a stick he would perhaps make marks in the sand, patterns or pictures, but without specific instruction, the symbols that represent and communicate our language in whatever form could not be performed. This crucial element means that the teaching of any handwriting system is an essential part of the system's survival.

Seen opposite are examples of handwriting by two ten-year-old boys, one taught, one untaught. The boy in the top example has had consistent tuition and practice since he was five years old; the other has never been effectively taught, having been left to copy the symbols for himself without ever learning either the essence of

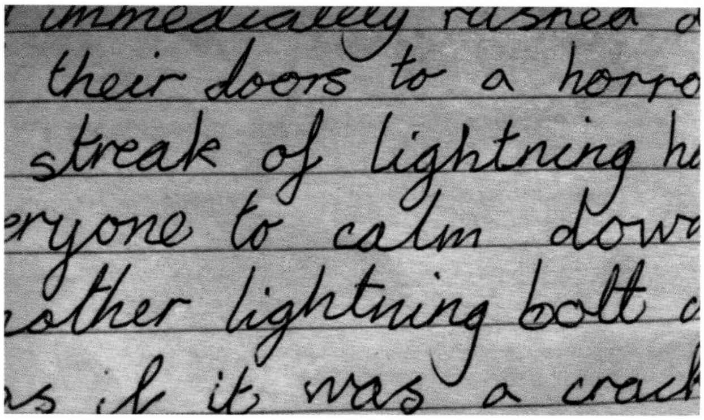

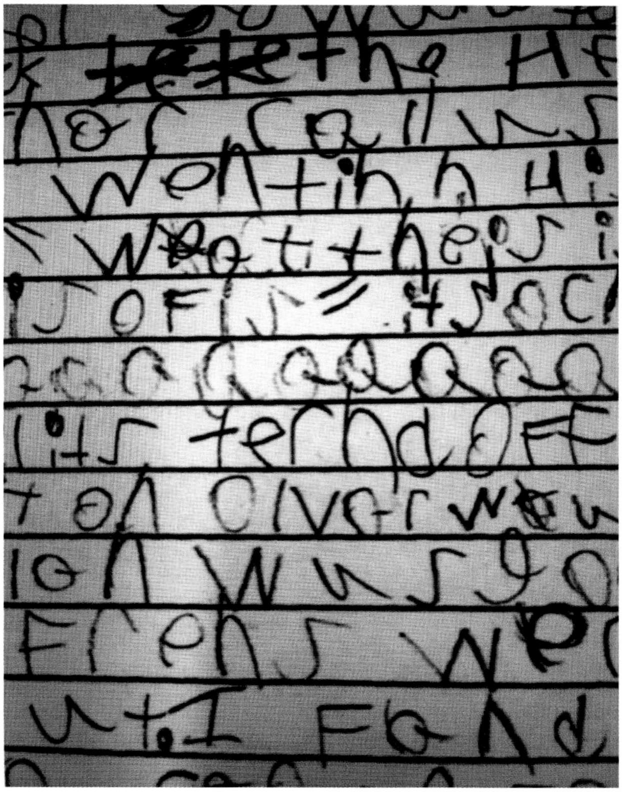

ABOVE Samples of handwriting from two ten-year-old boys, showing taught writing (above) and untaught writing (below)

their shape or the ideal movements for forming them. The difference is marked. Had the second boy had the benefit of being shown how the letters were composed of the different lines – vertical, horizontal, diagonal, curved – and taught the correct movement sequences for forming them, his output would have been transformed.

The mechanisms through which handwriting is delivered

Several psychologists have attempted to describe or model how we write by hand and most have failed because of the extreme complexity of the task. However, the Dutch psychologist, Gerard van Galen, constructed a model in 1991 to explain the mechanisms and processing for writing to be produced by hand. This has endured over time and is still considered by many to be the most comprehensive description of the writing process of an alphabetic script.[19]

Set out in cascade form from the top to the bottom, the seven individual units in van Galen's model are sequential, that is, each part happens after the one before. The timeframes within which the steps occur are so minute that in skilled writers the activity appears as a single continuous stream. However, a more detailed analysis can detect a series of discrete processes within the whole, some conceptual, some linguistic, later moving into the motor domain. At the start, the writer has to have an intention to write and an idea of the purpose of the task. He or she will have made a decision to set something in writing, be that jotting down a quick personal note, signing a birthday card or writing the chapter of a book. That decision activates all the subsequent actions. First, as the ideas come into mind, the writer must put those thoughts into words. Either consciously or subconsciously vocabulary is selected that encapsulates the meaning to be communicated. This 'idea-into-words' process is often referred to as 'translation' and triggers the writing event. Also involved in this part of the process are decisions about how best to deliver the intended meaning – what language to use, how to structure and organise it – in short, 'composing' the piece. Composition, described by the *Shorter Oxford Dictionary* as 'the putting together or assembling of parts into words', encompasses the crafting of words, phrases and sentences to convey meaning in the way that the author intends, and it is highly demanding of intellectual resources. The crafting stage also requires the writer to address syntax, that is, to make sure that grammatical structures are correct and to consider the organisation, unity and cohesion of the text if the task is to produce something longer or more exacting.

All the steps so far described occur internally and take place before words are set down on the page. As these generated ideas, encapsulated in language and crafted into meaningful units, come to be transcribed onto the page, a wholly new set of processes comes into play. First, the spelling of each word must either be constructed using phonic ('sound') mechanisms or be retrieved as a whole unit from memory. These spelling units are held in a memory store (sometimes called the 'orthographic buffer') ready to be accessed. It was for many years believed that spelt words were recalled either at single-letter or at whole-word level. However, studies by the French psychologist, Sonya Kandel, and her colleagues have shown that retrieval can also happen at intermediate levels of syllables or orthographic (spelling) clusters.[20] Irrespective of the level of recall, each letter or combination of letters in sequence must be selected and matched to the visual letterforms (or 'allographs'). For these letters to be performed with the writing implement, the exact allographs (forms of the letters, e.g. 'g', 'g' or 'G') must be selected from a visual memory store and the movements for forming them must be mapped on to the motor, or 'kinaesthetic', memory. Production is smoother and quicker if these motor patterns are established and practised so that they are readily accessible when needed. During the motor delivery of the text, the writer must invoke movement control of the strokes performed so that the letters are the correct size and slant, and appropriate spacing is observed. In addition, force control ensures that the correct pressure from the writing implement is applied to the writing surface and maintained. All these details require minute muscular adjustments, involving both postural control (engaging the large groups of muscles throughout the body) and the manipulation of the digits entailing more fine control. The entirety of this seven-step process, from ideation to execution, happens each time we handwrite, although we are probably never conscious of the complexity of the sequence of steps or of the detailed coordination needed to achieve them.

Setting out van Galen's steps of handwriting in this way helps to raise awareness of how complex it is to write by hand and highlights how each unit contributes to the overall production of the text. It serves to demonstrate how, if a writer experiences impairment in any one of the steps involved, the whole process will be disrupted, impacting on the smooth delivery of the text. It can also go some way to explaining the need for the handwriting process to become automatised (as far as possible) so that focus is not diverted away from the essence of the activity.

Is it critical to master handwriting, and what are the benefits?

Given all that has been described in this chapter about the complexity of the handwriting process it is hardly surprising that, as the use of technological alternatives became ubiquitous, people began to ask whether writing by hand was still worthwhile. After all, if by pressing a sequence of keys on a keyboard or speaking into a microphone we could produce legible and neat text simply, quickly and relatively effort-free, why would we want to handwrite? Most of us would agree that fewer adults handwrite on a daily basis than did even five or ten years ago. Our regular writing diet currently consists mainly of texting, keyboarding, touch-screen technology and voice activation. Handwriting is reserved for the occasional personal letter or the odd scribbled note. This observation alone could lead us to believe that handwriting is no longer relevant in our lives and that its demise is imminent.

This point of view was prolific around the turn of the twenty-first century, not just in the UK, Europe and the USA but all across the literate world. The general assumption was that handwriting was dying. To learn more, surveys were conducted to gather data, first on current practice in schools and next to gauge popular and professional attitudes. These were followed by questionnaires on the competence and confidence of teachers to deliver handwriting in their schools. What emerged from these exploratory moves was unexpected. In terms of current practice it was found that children spend up to 60 per cent of the school day on pen and paper tasks, even at primary level.[21] Additionally, it was still the medium through which a child's knowledge, understanding and ability were measured, through spelling and knowledge tests and school and public exams.[22] Furthermore, only 10 to 17 per cent of secondary school students were found to be using technology for schoolwork on a daily basis.[23] So, the message here was that handwriting was still very much alive and active. Popular attitudes canvassed by YouGov found that 94 per cent of adults and 91 per cent of children felt that it was still important to be able to write by hand, and 86 per cent of business managers expected job applicants to be able to handwrite as well as use a keyboard.[24] Professional attitudes were surprisingly similar when surveyed. While 85 per cent of teachers rated handwriting as very important (and as important as reading), two-thirds of them had had no initial training in how to teach handwriting and less than 50 per cent had received any in-service support. It would appear that uncertainty over the future of handwriting might have had negative consequences in terms of skilling teachers, with the inevitable knock-on effect on children.

While we were waking up to the fact that the imminent death predicted did not seem to be happening, several research projects were conducted in the first decade of the new millennium to examine what, if any, were the benefits of writing by hand. The majority of the studies contrasted handwritten delivery of school and university assignments with oral delivery or the use of a computer keyboard. Interestingly, the results of most of the research published found overwhelmingly in favour of handwriting as the mode most likely to support learning, and the strength and consistency of the findings took some by surprise. In brief, what emerged was evidence that the physical connectivity of pen on paper seems to confer benefits to learning, in terms of higher compositional quality and in stimulating written creativity.[25] Other studies highlighted the importance of proficiency: a lack of fluency in handwriting was found to constrain writing quality by limiting resources for higher-order processes.[26] Producing enough text also correlated with the composition quality of the written content: the more words children wrote, the greater was the richness of language and depth of the stories they created.[27] Conversely, interventions to improve children's handwriting quality and quantity resulted in improved written text on similar measures.[28] Benefits were also recorded in terms of fact recall, where students who handwrote notes in a lecture retained more content on subsequent testing than those whose notes were keyboard recorded.[29] In 2012 a US summit entitled 'Handwriting in the 21st Century' was convened to examine evidence into the benefits of handwriting. Here research was presented on a number of topics. Specifically cited was the impact of writing by hand on the development of reading, showing how the forming of individual letters stimulated neural activity in areas required for sound–symbol correspondence.[30] Also presented was the effect on writing in its widest sense,[31] in the development of language,[32] and in critical thinking.[33] The influence of handwriting was not confined to literacy but was found across all academic subjects.[34] In short, it has been suggested that it provides a foundation for higher-order processing.[35] Since the publication of these studies work has continued to be conducted and findings appear to point in a similar direction.

All the benefits outlined above relate to learning and cognitive development. However, there is anecdotal evidence of numerous other ways in which handwriting helps us. These include benefits to health, particularly to mental health and wellbeing where being able to articulate feelings through the hand seems to be soothing and has therapeutic impact. Handwriting has also a personal element, enabling us to express our individuality. Most of us consciously adopt a particular style, usually during adolescence, which reflects how we choose to present to the world, how we want others to perceive us. And there are practical benefits as well; handwriting is cognitively and materially accessible and relatively inexpensive.[36] It is also safe. As one nine-year-old recently said, 'You can't hack handwriting!'

What we need to take from all this evidence is that, despite adult use of the pen being in possible decline, handwriting has clear implications for education and if it were not to survive the impact on children's learning would be considerable.

How can we help those who struggle to handwrite?

Given what we know about the complexity of handwriting, it is hardly surprising that there are large numbers of children who experience difficulty mastering it. It has been estimated that approximately 10 to 34 per cent of young people of school age cannot handwrite well enough to fulfil their potential in the classroom.[37] In the UK, where levels are measured during the last year of primary school when children are aged ten to eleven years, a fifth of girls and a third of boys are found to enter secondary school unable to fulfil curricula demand in terms of written assignments.[38] While one must always be cautious of prevalence figures, it still remains the case that there are many who experience problems.

In order to address the issue and provide effective intervention it is essential that the nature of the difficulty is identified and understood, but with such a multifaceted skill problems may occur in one or more quite different areas. No two children present with identical profiles. It may help to look first at what we expect competent handwriters to be able to do. The essence of successful handwriting is seven-fold: it should be legible, neat, comfortably delivered, fluent, fast, able to be performed with the minimum of conscious effort and able to be sustained over time if the task demands.[39] Where these goals are achieved, handwriting develops as a functional tool for recording, communicating and storing ideas through language and carries all the advantages outlined above. Where this level of competence is not achieved, however, considerable frustration and distress is experienced, not only for the young people themselves but also for their parents and teachers, and providing some form of support or intervention becomes a priority.

A not unnatural response to evaluating handwriting competence is to look at the script. But the focus of this chapter has been to examine the process of writing, so I would argue that the traditional approach of just correcting the errors on the page has little effect for the child, especially where the issue is severe. That is not to play down the value of good teaching, but many of those who experience problems do so irrespective of how well they have been taught in class. The obstacles lie much deeper. One source of confusion may be the variability of handwriting performance from child to child. For some children the letters and joining strokes are wrongly formed and the handwriting tends to feature spatial or directional errors suggesting impairment in the linking perception and action. For others, the handwriting is untidy or hard to read, indicating a more isolated problem of motor control. Here, writing may be produced slowly and requires undue effort, while discomfort and fatigue are also frequently reported.[40] Conversely, the writer may rush and produce careless errors, affecting legibility. It is also true that problems can be experienced in any one or in several of these areas. Simply placing children in 'handwriting groups' and giving them extra practice may well not help (that is, the blanket approach is not the answer). Each individual will bring his or her own specific cocktail of performance to the table and a personalised intervention plan will yield the best results.

Because the writing process is a dynamic system it means that a breakdown in any of the component skills within it will have an impact on the efficient production of the whole. A more informed approach, therefore, is to seek to identify the areas responsible for the specific locus of weakness and to target intervention accordingly. For intervention to be most effective, accurate assessment of the child's problem has to be the starting point. There are a number of assessment instruments available to teachers and psychologists (for example, DASH) that provide data showing the norms for any particular population.[41] In this way the severity of the deviation from the norm can be quantified. Tests that measure handwriting speed and levels of legibility can be most useful both for identification of the difficulty and also for quantifying improvements after intervention.[42]

Some clinicians have offered a framework for classifying the difficulties, referring to impairment or

weaknesses in the type of processing rather than by seeking errors in the product. For example, using the overall term 'developmental dysgraphia' (that is, disturbance in the ability to write), Anne O'Hare suggests three possible categories to consider: the first, 'motor', describes children whose difficulty results from poor motor coordination; the second, 'visuo-spatial', relates to those who experience weaknesses of visual perception; the third, 'language', describes those who may have linguistic impairments that impact on their ability to perform.[43] This approach to classifying the origins of the problem can be of more use to parents and teachers than those that focus on errors in the handwritten script alone. To take this further, if it were to be found on assessment that a child has poor motor coordination, perhaps meeting the criteria for developmental coordination disorder, some physical therapies to improve movement ability might make an impact. If, on the other hand, visual-motor impairments were identified, targeted therapies in this area would be more appropriate. Again, if the difficulties were found to be more associated with language, intervention in this domain would be recommended. More detailed diagnosis would lead to more targeted and, hopefully, more successful remediation.

Working on the underlying competencies contributing to handwriting can also relieve a struggling child from the burden of failure.[44] The reluctance to write that

ABOVE A five-year-old child using a giant peg board

so often accompanies a handwriting problem is as significant an issue to address as any physical impairment. Remotivating disaffected children and providing the right kind of support can rekindle the enjoyment of writing and thus is a vital step. Attractive apparatus can be used that strengthens the required motor and perceptual skills without the child putting pencil to paper, and particular exercises link the activities directly with the handwriting elements to be improved. This approach is also novel for the child and is more likely to engage his or her interest. One example is the giant pegboard and pegs (see opposite) through which the child can gain understanding of the lines comprising the various letterforms by actually making them. The physical contact with the materials strengthens the relevant parts of the hand and arm. In addition, the patterns constructed can be transferred onto paper to be turned into letter strokes and letterforms and children are encouraged to use specific spatial and directional language to direct motor activity and to cement concepts.

The future of handwriting in a digital age

The final task of this chapter is to consider where society will take handwriting in the future and how it will sit alongside alternative modes for producing text. Any attempt to predict the future must do so with reference both to the past and to the present. Our thinking on the role of handwriting and its possible survival (or demise) has been found to fall into three clear phases. In the first, around the turn of the twenty-first century when technological advances were growing rapidly, there was an assumption that it was only a matter of years before the handwritten piece would be consigned to the grave, as has been discussed earlier. This followed a second phase which gave rise to a wealth of research studies conducted to explore the value, if any, of handwriting. Not only did this phase have the advantage of identifying the benefits, it also filled many educationalists with zeal in the fight to preserve it. A wave of almost 'Luddite' enthusiasm ensued in some camps in which modern technologies were not used for fear that they would replace and expedite the death of a beloved friend. There is no doubt that the evidence showing handwriting's unique role in learning and cognitive development is powerful, but we have to be realistic about what society does and will value. This takes us into a third phase where we recognise that handwriting and technology can exist side by side. We cannot turn back the clock.

For that reason I believe that we should be brave and reconceptualise writing by hand for the future, modifying our attitudes towards it. It seems unlikely that it will retain the dominant position it has enjoyed for so long, yet clearly it still contributes something extraordinary. Perhaps the first step is to differentiate in our minds between handwriting as an art form and handwriting as a functional tool. The artistic form focuses on the aesthetics and is exemplified in calligraphy, with all the beauty and cultural hinterland that brings. In contrast, the functional tool activates or supports a range of different cognitive processes and stimulates creativity in writing. There does not have to be a conflict here; I believe that handwriting can be both of these things as long as we do not confuse what each contributes. For example, young people will enjoy learning to produce attractive flowing script and indulge the movements involved. Equally, they need to know whether we expect them to produce perfectly formed and aesthetically beautiful handwriting in their day-to-day assignments or whether it is acceptable to compromise on neatness in order to increase productivity under time constraints, as in an exam. We should educate children to the purpose of the writing in any particular context. Next, if we conceive handwriting as a functional tool it is essential to clarify what aspects of handwriting are fundamental to the task. I would suggest that legibility is core, as are fluency and comfort and also speed (if we want to get enough down to achieve good grades). Automaticity has been shown to be key so that the writer does not have to divert essential resources away from the higher processing required for structuring high-quality text. All these elements have been identified as significant factors in the research cited.

One further point I believe to be relevant is that we should move away from a binary attitude: one that asks whether we should promote handwriting or keyboarding as a technical alternative. Why, at a time of so many additional technologies, should we limit ourselves to one or even two modes of transcribing? After all, a QWERTY keyboard must surely be outdated, and the likelihood of it surviving beyond the next few years must be extremely low. Young people should be both free and skilled to use a number of different methods for delivering text and to be able to engage with the many new ones being developed. They will have a toolbox full of options, of which handwriting will be one, each beneficial for specific purposes. The key issue will be to ensure that a range of delivery mechanisms and styles are taught so

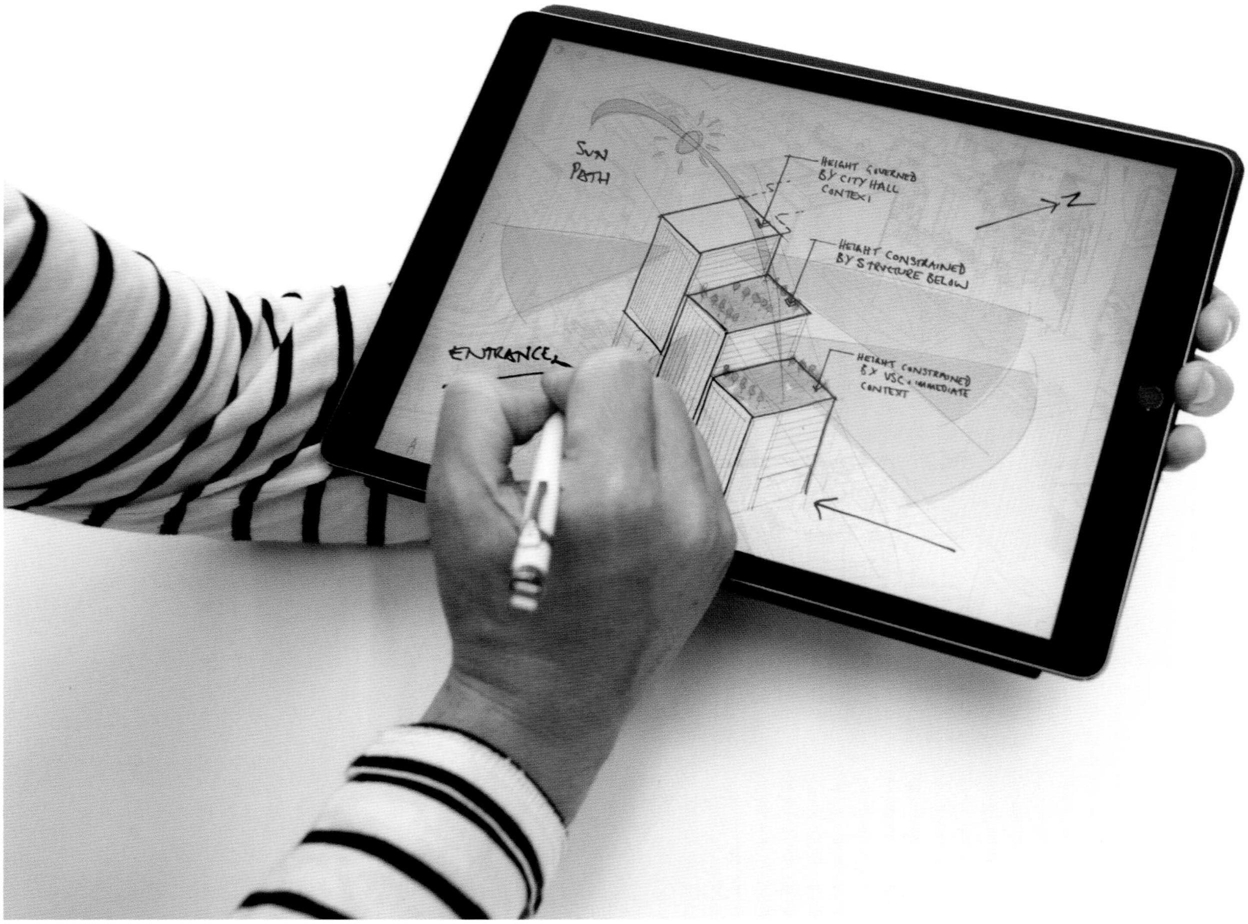

ABOVE An architect designing on a graphics tablet

that transcription can be as automatic as possible. Children will then need to learn how to select the best tools for each task: handwriting for personal letters and note-taking, for example, and keyboarding for longer assignments. Virginia Berninger[45] talks about developing 'hybrid writers': writers who can print in simple letters for reading or for annotating and produce joined-up script that perhaps supports spelling, but who can also use a keyboard, record into voice-activated software, employ swipe-screen technology and perform on a digitiser tablet, all with equal ease. Why not? They will be born to it and will soon out-skill their teachers in nearly every respect.

My final word on handwriting in the future relates to human–machine interaction and how we develop tools that harness the best from both sides. New technologies will be invented that deliver, in miraculous ways, the essence of human talent. While their digital efficiency can only be marvelled at, the benefits of the human input also should not be underestimated; the relationship has, I believe, to be symbiotic. Take, as an example, an architect designing a building. He or she can draw and write on a tablet surface using the stylus of choice and the resulting images can be transformed by the software, first into 3-D drawings and then into models. This way, the personal, creative advantages of the human connection through the graphic skills can be maximised, with all the advantages of digitisation. The delivery can also gain from the new wave of writing implements – stylus, sensitive pen, finger – and the merits of handwritten form are retained.

The impact of this relationship has to be bi-directional. The image on page 190 is an example of how handwriting can enhance digitised delivery. The opposite is also true; we can derive benefits for handwriting through tablets, smartphones, whiteboards, digitisers and sensitive pens by the accessibility of different devices and for the motivational factors that can engage children readily. Software programs can provide scientific measurement, as described earlier, and are proving essential both for the diagnosis of handwriting difficulties and for research. There may be practical issues to address during the development of these different approaches (such as how we can make writing easier on a slippery surface) but these are mechanical problems that can easily be resolved.

These few examples give just a flavour of where developments may be taking us. There is obviously more to come. The road ahead is unknown but all the evidence to date suggests that handwriting will still be very much part of the journey.

Focus Four

A 2,000-YEAR-OLD HOMEWORK BOOK

Peter Toth

The British Library holds one of the largest collections of written documents in the world. As intriguing as any lavishly elaborated treasures are those average or sometimes rather poor-looking items that give insight into the everyday life of ordinary people centuries and even millennia ago.

The library's collection of ancient manuscripts, with thousands of inscribed papyrus, parchment and pottery pieces from between the third century BC and the eighth century AD, is exceptionally rich in such documents. Owing to the hot climate of Egypt, writing materials of the most diverse kinds survived in the sand to preserve fragments of people's personal lives that are unknown from anywhere else before the modern era.

One of these hidden treasures, from almost 2,000 years ago, is a little notebook from the second century AD that preserves a complete homework book of a schoolchild. It is a set of two wooden tablets hollowed out in the middle and filled with wax to be inscribed with a metal stylus and smoothed with its flat end. The two holes on the top edges served as binding holes for strings to attach the tablets together, whereas those on the botttom were to bind the booklet shut when transported. Inside this neatly designed wooden notebook, so similar in size and shape to our Kindle or Nook readers, are the writing exercises of a primary-school pupil from Egypt.

After the conquest of Egypt by Alexander the Great in the fourth century BC, Greek became the official language of the Egyptian administration; everyone seeking a career had to learn to read and write it. The first part of this booklet (lower image, opposite) shows us how this was achieved. At the top of the tablet, written parallel to the long side, are two lines of a maxim (*Accept advice from someone wise / it is not right to believe every friend of yours*). These lines are written in the neat handwriting of the schoolmaster to be copied by the child at home. Below, the pupil tries hard to complete the homework, but misses the first letter (**C**) and runs over the right margin with the **N**. He tries once more below, but the first letter is forgotten again and, although he does not run over this time, his last line becomes so narrow that the squeezed letters hang below the lines. On the opposite side (upper image, opposite), we see the teacher's hand again. On the left he has copied a multiplication table for the child from 1 × 1 to 3 × 10. On the right he has put a selection of two-syllable words starting with 'th-' for the pupil to practise reading by recognising syllables.

Literacy, numeracy and handwriting exercises are all together in this handy little booklet, which, in addition to preserving a rather nicely kept homework book of an unknown child from two millennia ago, also foreshadows a great revolution in the history of writing when books like this would completely replace the ever-present scrolls.

OPPOSITE Set of two Greek wax tablets. Egypt, 2nd century AD. British Library: Add MS 34186

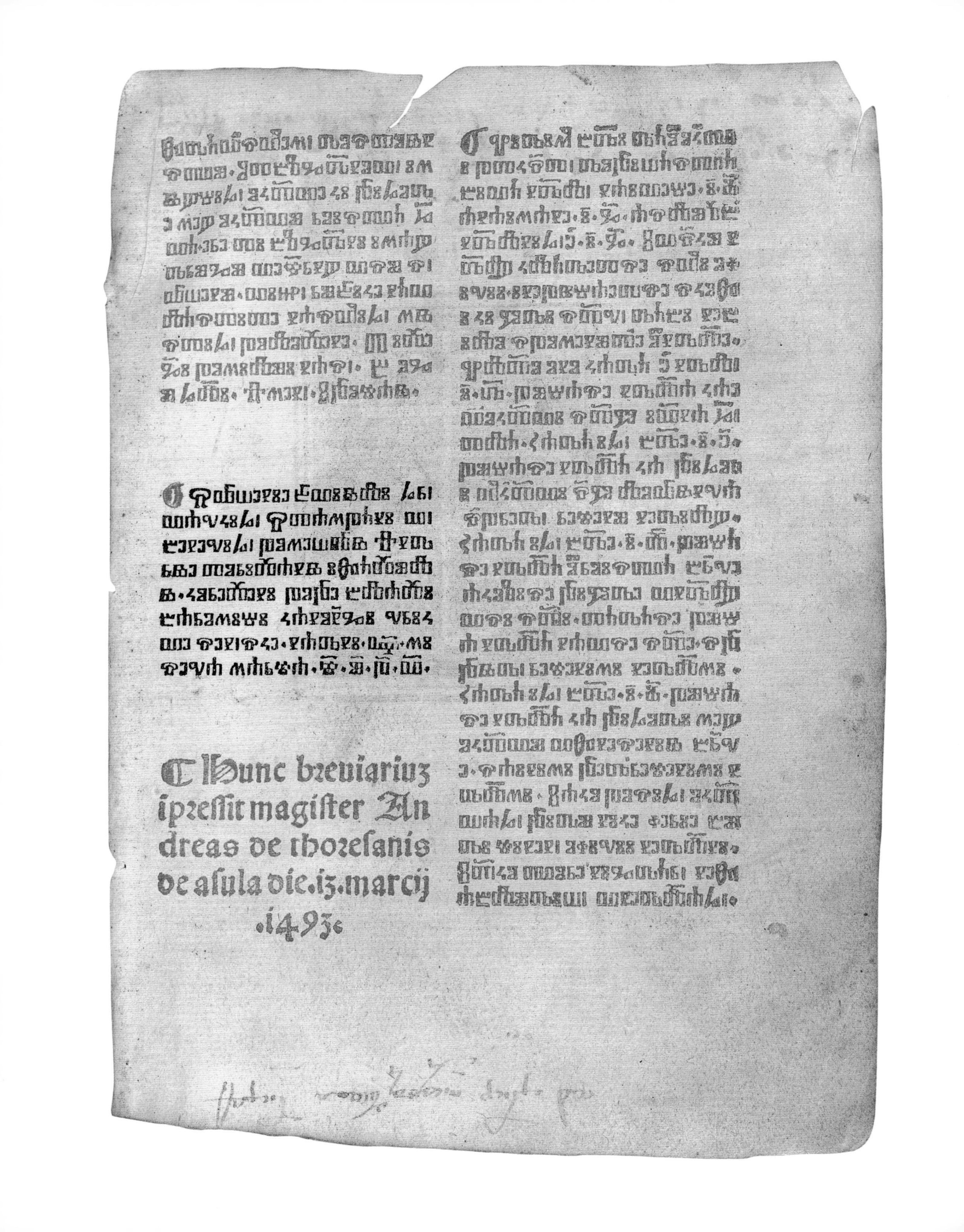

[illegible]

[illegible]

[illegible]

Hunc breviariuz
ipressit magister An
dreas de thoresanis
de asula die .iz. marcij
.1493.

[illegible]

WRITING AND THE COLLECTIONS OF THE BRITISH LIBRARY

Adrian S. Edwards

The British Library is one of the world's largest repositories of the written word. There are thought to be well in excess of 150 million items in its care, although this figure certainly encompasses formats that often feature little or no writing, such as photographs, engravings, drawings, paintings and audio or video files. Official estimates suggest that a further 3 million items are currently being added each year. These range from archived websites and e-journals, through medieval manuscripts and literary papers, to paperback novels and antiquarian printed books. With the exception of the earliest scripts from the Middle East and the Americas, most of the world's writing systems appear to be fairly well represented in the collection. In fact, research for the library's 2019 exhibition on writing has shown that the oldest written items held are not the Chinese oracle bones as previously thought (*c.*1300–1050 BC), but a group of Ancient Egyptian stelae and *shabtis* (*c.*1600–1200 BC), which arrived with the archive of the nineteenth-century photography pioneer William Henry Fox Talbot (1800–1877). As the custodian of such a wide range of written materials, the British Library is therefore an appropriate venue in which to explore the phenomenon of writing in all its forms.

OPPOSITE Old Church Slavonic Breviary, in the Glagolitic alphabet. Printed book. Venice: Andreas Torresanus, 1493. British Library: IA.21702
ABOVE Late Period Ancient Egyptian *shabti* figure. Egypt, 664–332 BC. British Library: Talbot Shabti 2

Development of the collection

The library was founded in its present form in 1973 following the implementation of the British Library Act in the UK. The origins of its collections, however, go back much further as a number of existing repositories were brought together to form the new institution. The most extensive of these were the collections of three departments from the British Museum: Printed Books (including the National Reference Library of Science and Invention), Manuscripts, and Oriental Books & Manuscripts. These in turn incorporated books and manuscripts originally collected between the sixteenth and nineteenth centuries by Sir Hans Sloane, Sir Robert Cotton, Robert and Edward Harley, Thomas Grenville and King George III, alongside England's principal royal library formed under a succession of monarchs from Edward IV (1442–1483) to George II (1683–1760). The holdings of the National Central Library were also included from the outset and, nine years later, these were joined by the library and archival records of the India Office. Each of these was full of examples of handwritten and printed texts from the Western world; in addition, the British Museum and India Office collections were also particularly rich in writing systems from Asia.

Since its establishment the British Library has continued the British Museum's aim of taking a broad approach to collecting written texts from all around the world, reflecting the library's ambition to be seen as a major international research resource and cultural institution. The right to claim one copy of every printed book, magazine, newspaper, map and music score published or distributed in the UK was also transferred from the British Museum. But changes in the nature of publishing have led to an increasing focus away from print towards electronic media. This was reflected in law when the Legal Deposit Libraries (Non-Print Works) Regulations of 2013 extended the library's collecting responsibilities within Britain to encompass digital publications and UK websites. Funding is still available to collect heritage materials in print and manuscript, but inevitably most writing entering the collection today is received in the form of digital bytes, mirroring the changes that have been happening to writing in the wider world.

Survey and highlights

The ancient Egyptian artefacts and the oracle bones mentioned above are not typical of the library's holdings. Outline descriptions of the kinds of materials held in much larger numbers can be found on the website and in numerous print publications, and full catalogues are freely accessible via the Internet. The following survey is therefore limited to a few highlights selected to demonstrate the breadth of resources available to researchers investigating the history of writing.

Writing systems

By far the largest percentage of texts in the library is written with alphabets, broadly defined as phonetic scripts that separately indicate their consonants and vowels. Of these, the roman alphabet, as used for English, Latin, French, German and Spanish, constitutes the most substantial part. Other alphabets represented include Greek (particularly from the third century BC onwards), Cyrillic, Old Church Slavonic and Glagolitic, Armenian, Georgian, Coptic, vertical Mongolian and Manchu, and Korean Hangul. Each of these categories can encapsulate a great deal of variation in their character sets and also in the shapes of individual letters. The library's holdings of materials that document how the letters of the roman alphabet have been shaped in Britain over the past two millennia are, for example, probably unparalleled. They range from medieval manuscript forms (uncials, half-uncials, early gothic cursives, etc.), through typefaces designed for print, to specialist adaptations such as shorthands and the large 'Egyptian' display letters of Victorian advertisements.

Besides these alphabetical texts, researchers can also find examples of *abjads* (where only consonants are generally written), *abugidas* (where most shapes denote both a consonant and its inherent vowel), syllabaries (where each character denotes an entire syllable), and systems that might be categorised as being logographic in origin (symbols that indicate meaning, perhaps with added features to suggest pronunciation). The main *abjads* represented are the Arabic script (as used for Arabic, Persian and Ottoman Turkish) and Hebrew, although numerous other languages ranging from Aramaic to Sogdian can also be found. *Abugidas* are primarily associated with South and Southeast Asia, and the library's historical connection with the East India Company and the British government in India has resulted in especially rich collections associated with these regions. They include texts in Devanagari (Hindi, Nepali, Marathi, etc.), Bengali-Assamese, Gujarati, Gurmukhī, Kannada, Malayalam, Odia, Tamil, Telugu, Tibetan, Burmese, Khmer, Thai, Javanese and Bugis, among others. But *abugidas* from other regions are also

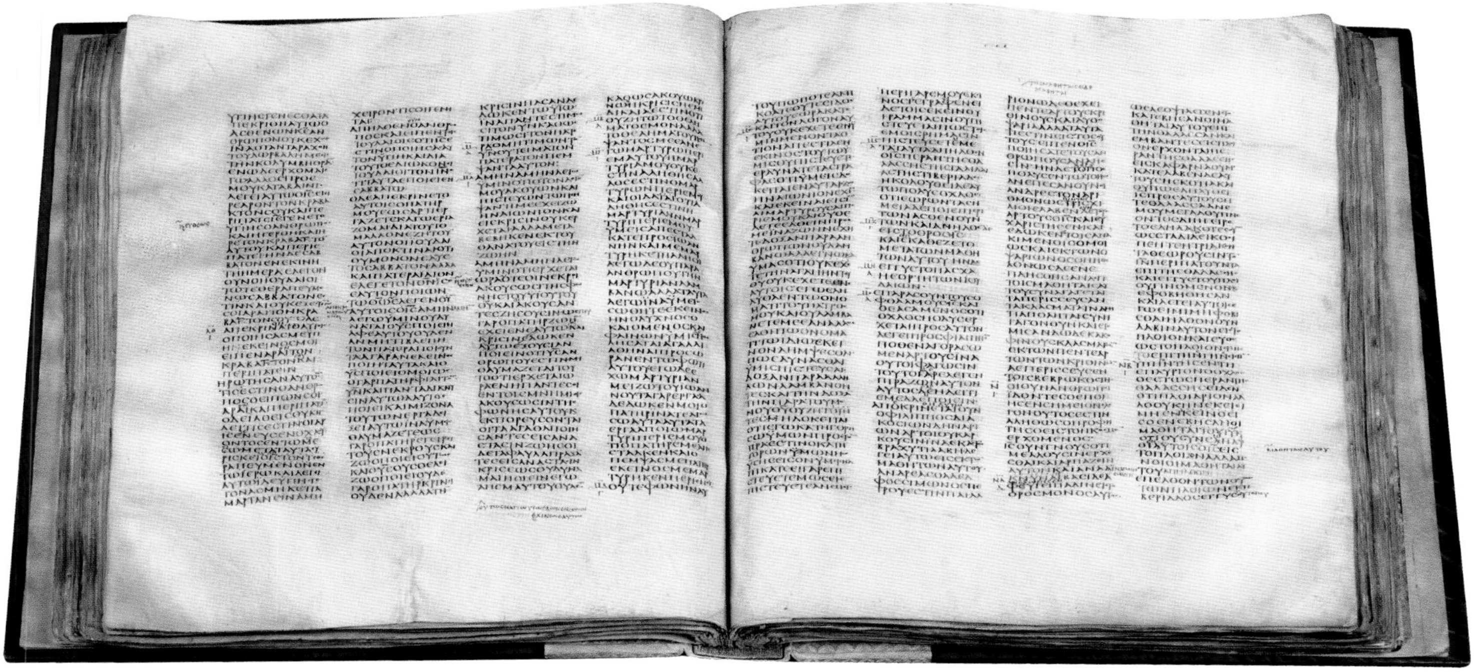

present in the form of Ethiopic and Tocharian. The best represented among the different types of syllabaries are the two *kana* scripts of Japan, but there are also small numbers of syllabic texts from North America (particularly in Cherokee, Cree, Ojibwe and Inuktitut) and West Africa (Vai). Systems with their origins in logography are primarily represented by Chinese characters, including their adaptations for Korean (*hanja*), Japanese (*kanji*) and, historically, Vietnamese (*chữ nôm*). The library in fact has well over 3,000 years of material written in Chinese characters, by far the longest continuous chronological span of any of its varied collections.

Handwriting

Collection development at the British Library has focused primarily on handwritten, printed and – in recent years – digital writing, although there are also small but significant numbers of other formats, such as typescripts and incised palm leaves. Holdings of manuscript and typescript items are notoriously difficult to count owing to the fact that some are described collectively while others are listed leaf by leaf. As of March 2018, the British Library's online catalogue of manuscripts and archives contained 2,441,447 entries. Behind this figure there is a huge amount of diversity in terms of writing traditions from around the world. The bulk of the documents will have been written using either a brush or a pen with ink, most often on paper or parchment (including parchment of the finest quality known as vellum). Highlights from among the twenty-four centuries of manuscript materials in the collection range from the largest segment of the *Codex Sinaiticus* (fourth century AD; in the Greek alphabet), through the *Lindisfarne Gospels* (eighth century; in the roman alphabet), to twenty-four volumes of the *Yongle Dadian*

ABOVE Greek Bible, known as the *Codex Sinaiticus*. Manuscript book (parchment). North-central Israel?, 4th century. British Library: Add MS 43725, ff. 249v-250

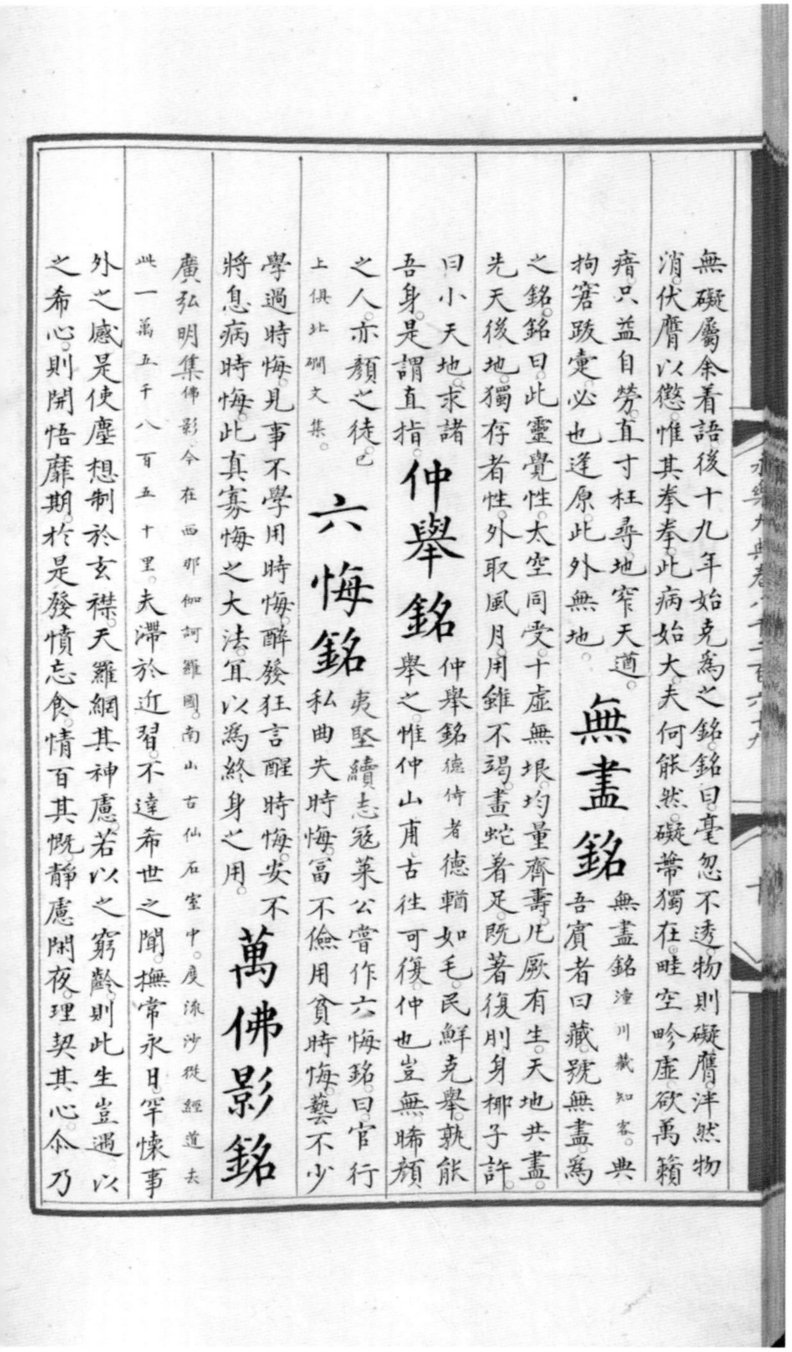

ABOVE *Yongle Dadian*. Manuscript. China, 1562–72. British Library: Or.11272, fol. 36v

(1562–72; in Chinese characters). These high-status texts written by the best calligraphers are supported by examples of everyday correspondence, personal notes and diaries, institutional or governmental archives, and – as we enter the modern period – increasing numbers of handwritten and typescript drafts that relate to works intended for publication. All these categories of material continue to be acquired today, although a fair proportion of literary, scientific and political archives switched to typescript during the course of the twentieth century and are now in part being received in the form of digital files of emails, word-processed documents and spreadsheets.

Alongside these handwritten works on paper and parchment, the library is custodian of some 4,000 Egyptian *ostraca*: everyday ink inscriptions in Greek or Demotic made on broken pieces of pottery or stone. These are accompanied by thousands of ancient papyrus rolls, codices and fragments, written in Greek, Latin or Coptic, usually with reed pens and ink. But not all historical texts in the collection comprise ink or pigments laid onto a surface using a pen or a brush. Texts on palm leaves – most often created by incising with a sharp stylus and then rubbing a mixture of oil and soot or lampblack into the shallow cuts – have long been common in parts of South and Southeast Asia, and the library has a varied collection of these. There are also a few Graeco-Roman wax tablets from Egypt, where a stylus has been used to write directly onto a surface layer of beeswax, generally with the expectation that the text would later be erased and the tablet repeatedly reused. To these can be added small numbers of texts incised into metal surfaces, some of which were created in the Roman Empire and others in early modern India. And finally, of course, there are the 484 oracle bone pieces from Shang-dynasty China, each with early forms of Chinese characters carved into their surface.

Printed writing

The earliest printed writing was created using wooden blocks in a process known as xylography. The technology seems to have developed first in East Asia, and some of the library's Japanese woodblock printed texts, for example, date from the eighth century. But the oldest complete surviving book produced in this way to which a firm date can be ascribed is a Chinese version of the Buddhist *Diamond Sutra*, whose colophon tells us that the printers finished their work on 11 May 868. Other early examples in the library are in Korean *hanja* or in Tibetan. Beyond East Asia block-printed texts are found first in the Middle East, where the technology was employed in medieval Egypt to create paper amulets, and later in Europe, where illustrated works known as 'block books' were produced along the Rhine Valley in the period around 1450 to 1480. The library has long been known for its strong collection of some thirty-five of these block books, but the discovery of three medieval Arabic woodblock prints is very recent and others may yet be identified.

The concept of printing with 'movable type' was also developed in East Asia. The earliest type of this kind was made from wood or clay, and seems to have been of limited application. It is not always clear whether some of the texts now in the British Library were created using woodblocks or movable type. It is however certain that printers in Korea were already utilising movable type cast from metal by the end of the fourteenth century. The library holds around fifty early Korean works printed in this way, among them *The Collected Commentaries on the 'Spring and Autumn Annals'* (1434). The technology of printing with metal movable type spread across East Asia, but scholarly opinion remains divided about whether it influenced the parallel, but later, development in Europe. This began at Mainz, Germany, in the 1450s, when Johannes Gutenberg (*c.*1400–1468) – or workshops in some way associated with him – produced a series of documents culminating in a Bible, a papal indulgence and a Latin grammar. These first European printed texts are in Latin, but by the end of the century works were being printed in around a dozen other languages also using the roman alphabet, as well as in Greek, Hebrew and Glagolitic. The British Library is a major repository for these fifteenth-century Western printed books known as *incunabula*, holding some 12,500 items in 10,390 editions. The collection includes two complete Gutenberg Bibles, twenty-nine volumes printed by the Venetian master Aldus Manutius (active 1495–1515) and seventy-nine volumes printed in England under the auspices of William Caxton (*c.*1422–1492). Over the

ABOVE Book of Revelation. Block book (fragment). Germany, c.1468. British Library: IB.16, fol. 1r

course of the sixteenth century European printers created the type needed to print Arabic, Syriac and Cyrillic, and took their technology to continents further afield beginning with the Americas (Mexico, 1539), South Asia (Goa, 1556) and Southeast Asia (Manila, 1593).

By the end of the nineteenth century all of the world's most widespread writing systems could be printed using metal movable type and it is possible to follow most, if not all, of these developments through the library's collections. Texts printed in this way range from world-class treasures to everyday ephemeral matter, the latter encompassing handbills, newspapers, political pamphlets and advertisements. Some of these are very poorly produced indeed, but they constitute vital evidence of how writing was used in past generations for communication and the sharing of ideas, public or private record, and for entertainment. The numbers of publications containing samples of printed writing – whether created with movable type or with one of the methods developed since the early nineteenth century, such as lithography – are enormous. A report run from the British Library's main online catalogue at the end of March 2018 found 15,756,786 monographs and 853,449 serial titles (including newspapers). This is, however, only part of the picture, as all of the 70 million patent specifications and a great deal of the music and cartographic collections also feature substantial amounts of printed text.

Digital writing

Although hard copy or 'analogue' publishing appears to be holding its own for the time being, from a librarian's perspective it also seems likely that electronic publishing is here to stay and will soon squeeze print publications into a minority share of the contemporary book market. Significant numbers of traditional hard-copy publications are still received by the British Library: 72,859 UK monographs and 120,221 UK serial parts were received through legal deposit in 2017/18, for example, but just two years earlier these figures had been significantly higher at 97,759 and 162,622 respectively. On the other hand, full-scale legal deposit arrangements are now working well for electronic publications in Britain, and the most recent figures show that receipts of e-media are beginning to outstrip receipts for their printed counterparts: 142,045 UK e-monographs and 105,795 UK e-serial parts in 2017/18. An increasing number of new works in Britain are issued in digital format only, but there are nevertheless plenty of titles that continue to be published simultaneously on paper and as an e-book. In these cases the law requires the library to choose which format it wishes to receive through legal deposit: it can claim only one. The migration from print to electronic is therefore being managed on a publisher-by-publisher basis, often beginning with academic and scientific publishers. In parallel thousands of public websites hosted on the UK web domain are regularly archived through a process known as 'web harvesting', and there are licensing arrangements in place that provide researchers with access to digital publications created overseas. The purchase (and indeed receipt through donation) of current and antiquarian printed publications from overseas does of course continue as the library seeks to maintain its position as a world-class research collection.

Secondary sources

Libraries contain not only primary texts that can be examined as evidence of writing in itself, but also extensive amounts of secondary literature: that is, published research about the past, present and future development and use of writing around the world. In the British Library some of these books, articles and theses relate specifically to forms of writing for which no original examples exist in the collection, such as Maya glyphs or the cuneiforms of ancient Mesopotamia. More generally, there is a wide range of literature relating to ciphers, cryptography and the process of decipherment; this includes discussions of scripts that remain undeciphered, such as Linear A from Crete, Rongorongo of Rapa Nui and the Harappan script of the Indus Valley. The inclusion of the UK's National Sound Archive within the British Library also means that researchers have access to audio interviews with calligraphers (as part of the *Crafts Lives* project) and with creative writers, some of whom discuss their relationship to the activity of writing itself.

Custodianship

With such wide-ranging collections of international significance comes the combined responsibility of ensuring their preservation while at the same time providing access. The British Library aims to preserve all these texts for future generations, and therefore takes great care in how they are repaired, stabilised and stored. Items are catalogued, which helps with their security and allows them to be discovered by researchers. Out-of-copyright materials are increasingly digitised from cover to cover, which generates high-quality images accessible from anywhere via the online catalogues. The writing within these digitised images is in turn enhanced through the application of optical character recognition (OCR) software, which enables researchers to trawl quickly through extensive pieces of text looking for the occurrence of their desired words or phrases. In some cases these large digital datasets of writing (both the images and the associated OCR text files) are freely available to download, which encourages reuse by the scholarly community and creative industries. Digitisation also helps to protect the original documents from unnecessary handling and facilitates a more considered approach to making them available, whether to researchers in the library's reading rooms or to the general public through its programme of exhibitions. This latter now comprises onsite and touring shows, alongside a busy schedule of individual loans to exhibitions run by other cultural institutions in the UK and abroad.

Writing: Making Your Mark

The British Library's 2019 exhibition on writing has given curators an opportunity to consider the collections in a new light. Treasures such as the *Diamond Sutra* and the *Lindisfarne Gospels* have often been displayed in the public galleries before, but rarely has the focus been so centrally on how they help tell the wider story of the development of writing. It has also been an opportunity to demonstrate the research and cultural value of everyday items, such as school copybooks, advertisements and business letters, in what we hope to be an enjoyable way. Although many of the stories we tell in the gallery are new, others may be familiar to visitors from textbooks and television documentaries. However, there is nothing so rewarding as being in the presence of original historical documents and, perhaps, seeing something that no one else seems to have spotted. With this exhibition, we hope to underline the richness of the collections as a resource for anyone researching the evolution of writing, and above all to inspire visitors to think about their own engagement with this amazing invention.

NOTES

INTRODUCTION

1. Baines, *Visual and Written Culture*, pp. 64–75.
2. For headline figure see National Literacy Trust website: https://literacytrust.org.uk/parents-and-families/adult-literacy/. For the detailed breakdown across the UK (2011) see references at: https://literacytrust.org.uk/information/what-is-literacy, accessed 11/08/18.
3. https://wearesocial.com/us/blog/2018/01/global-digital-report-2018, accessed 11/08/18.
4. World Economic Forum website: https://www.weforum.org/agenda/2018/05/what-happens-in-an-internet-minute-in-2018, accessed 11/08/18.
5. Italic type makes its first appearance for a complete book in an edition of Virgil printed by the Venetian publisher Aldus Manutius in 1501.
6. Coulmas, *The Writing Systems of the World*, p. 2.
7. DeFrancis, *Visible Speech*, p. 5; Gelb, *A Study*, p. 12.

CHAPTER 1

1. Robinson, *Cracking the Egyptian Code*, p. 237.
2. DeFrancis, *Visible Speech*, p. 4.
3. De Saussure, *General Linguistics*, p. 111.
4. Quoted in Duhoux, Palaima and Bennet, *Problems*, p. 26.
5. Ventris, 'A note', p. 200.
6. Quoted in Robinson, *The Man Who Deciphered Linear B*, p. 14.
7. Quoted in Mead and Modley, 'Communication', p. 58.
8. Robinson, *The Story of Writing*, p. 8.

CHAPTER 2

1. In personal correspondence, February 1983.
2. Johnston, *Writing & Illuminating, and Lettering* (1906), p. 416.
3. In the colophon of the Virgil published by Aldus Manutius in 1501.
4. Quoted from report of the *Histoire de l'Académie royale des Sciences* (1699) in Jammes, 'Académisme et Typographie', pp. 72 and 73.
5. Quoted from the introduction (*Avis*) to Fournier's quarto type specimen, *Modèles des Caractères de l'Imprimerie* (1742) in Hutt, *Fournier, the Compleat Typographer*, p. 29.
6. Quoted from Baskerville's own letter to the President of the French Royal Academy of Sciences (undated, ?1773) in Pardoe, *John Baskerville of Birmingham*, p. 131.
7. Quoted from anonymous letter now in Birmingham Assay Office (undated, ?1776) in Pardoe, *John Baskerville of Birmingham*, p. 140.
8. Quoted from Fournier's *Manuel typographique*, Vol. II (1768) in Hutt, *Fournier, the Compleat Typographer*, p. 47.
9. Quoted from Richard Austin's introduction to his *Imperial Letter Foundry Specimen of Types* (Shoreditch, London, 1819), unpaginated, in James Mosley, *Typefoundry* blog, 'Richard Austin', 14 February 2007: typefoundry.blogspot.com/2007/02/scotch-roman.html, accessed 6/9/18.

CHAPTER 3

1. Fisher, 'Ink', p. 68.
2. Shinoda, 'Sumi infinity', p. 79.
3. *Manchester Guardian*, 3 October 1840, front page.
4. Ishikawa, *Taction*, p. 1.
5. Schmandt-Besserat, *When Writing Met Art*, pp. 63–86.
6. Suchman, 'Centers of Coordination', pp. 41–62.
7. For more on conversation analysis see Goodwin and Heritage, 'Conversation analysis', pp. 283–307.

FOCUS 2

1. Mao's words from 'On Coalition Government' (24 April 1945) quoted on cover of Double Pigeon typewriter manual, produced in Shanghai, *c.*1964–1975. British Library collection. English translation by author.

CHAPTER 4

1. Thornton, *Handwriting in America: A Cultural History*, p. 43.
2. Ibid. p. 172.
3. Schimmel, *Calligraphy and Islamic Culture*, pp. 18–19.
4. Baskerville, 'The Preface', opening page (unpaginated).
5. See Carr, 'The Information by James Gleick: review'.

CHAPTER 5

1. Mueller and Oppenheimer, 'The pen is mightier'.
2. Buber, *I and Thou*, p. 11.
3. Williams, *Stand Out of Our Light*, p. 23.

CHAPTER 6

1. Schmidt and Lee, *Motor Control*.
2. Hutchinson Guest, *Labanotation*, pp. 15, 29.
3. Alamargot et al., 'Eye and pen: a new device to study the reading during writing', pp. 287–99.
4. *Ibid.*
5. See, for example, Prunty et al., 'An examination of writing pauses'.
6. Sumner, Connelly and Barnett, 'Children with dyslexia are slow writers because they pause more often', pp. 1–18.
7. Rosenblum, Parush and Weiss, 'The in air phenomenon', pp. 933–54.
8. Marquardt and Mai, 'A computational procedure for movement analysis in handwriting', pp. 39–45.
9. See, for example, James, 'How printing practice affects letter perception'; and Zwicker et al., 'Smaller cerebellar growth and poorer neurodevelopmental outcomes in very preterm infants'.
10. Izadi-Najafabadi et al., 'Participation of children with developmental coordination disorder'.
11. Schmidt et al., *Motor Control and Learning*.
12. Galbraith, Van Waes and Torrance, *Writing and Cognition*.
13. Apel, Wolter and Masterton, 'Effects of phonotactic and orthotactic probabilities during fast mapping', pp. 21–42.
14. Chu, 'The effects of visual perceptual dysfunction on the development and performance of handwriting skills', pp. 42–55.
15. Berninger, 'Development of language by hand and its connections with language by ear, mouth, and eye', pp. 65–84.
16. Chenoweth and Hayes, 'Fluency in writing', pp. 80–98.
17. Myhill, 'Becoming a designer: trajectories of linguistic development'.
18. Dockrell, 'Causes of delays and difficulties in the production of written text'.
19. Van Galen, 'Handwriting: issues for a psychomotor theory', pp. 165–91.
20. Kandel and Valdois, 'The effect of orthographic regularity on children's handwriting production', p. 17; Kandel and Valdois, 'French and Spanish-speaking children use different visual and motor units during spelling acquisition', pp. 531–61.
21. McMaster and Roberts, 'Handwriting in 2015: a main occupation for primary school-aged children', pp. 38–50; Rosenblum, Weiss and Parush, 'Handwriting evaluation for developmental dysgraphia: process versus product', pp. 433–58.
22. *National Curriculum Assessment* 2014.
23. Department for Education (DfE), www.DfE.education.gov.uk/statistics; Marquardt et al., 'Learning handwriting at school – a teachers' survey', pp. 82–9.
24. *YouGov*, 2014, cdn.yougov.com/cumulus_uploads/document/2epvuor52x/YG-Archive.
25. Berninger et al., 'Treatment of handwriting problems in beginning writers', pp. 652–66; Jones and Christensen, 'Relationship between automaticity in handwriting and students' ability to generate written text', pp. 1–6; Webb, 'The relationship between handwriting and written composition'.
26. Connelly and Hurst, 'The influence of handwriting fluency on writing quality', pp. 5–57; Christensen, 'The role of orthographic-motor integration in the production of creative and well-structured written text', pp. 441–53; Christensen, 'The critical role handwriting plays in the ability to produce high-quality written text'; Bourdin and Fayol, 'Is graphic activity cognitively costly?', pp. 183–96.
27. Webb, 'The relationship between handwriting and written composition'.
28. Jones and Christensen, 'Relationship between automaticity in handwriting and students' ability to generate written text', pp. 1–6.
29. Mueller and Oppenheimer, 'The pen is mightier', pp. 1159–68.
30. Berninger, *Past, Present, and Future Contributions of Cognitive Writing Research*; James, 'How printing practice affects letter perception'.
31. Berninger, *Past, Present, and Future Contributions of Cognitive Writing Research*; Graham and Santangelo, 'A meta-analysis of the effectiveness of teaching handwriting'.

32. National Governors Association Center for Best Practices, *Common Core State Standards for English Language Arts.*
33. Peverly and Sumowski, 'What variables predict quality of text notes', pp. 104–17.
34. Case-Smith et al., 'Effect of a coteaching handwriting program for first graders', pp. 396–405; Anthony, Yang and Koedinger, 'The benefits of handwritten input for students learning algebra', pp. 521–3.
35. Berninger, *Past, Present, and Future Contributions of Cognitive Writing Research*; Peverly and Sumowski, 'What variables predict quality of text notes', pp. 104–17; Christensen, 'The role of orthographic-motor integration in the production of creative and well-structured written text', pp. 441–53.
36. Wollscheid, Sjaastad and Tømte, 'The impact of digital devices vs. pen (cil) and paper on primary school students' writing skills', pp. 19–35.
37. Rosenblum, Weiss and Parush, 'Handwriting evaluation for developmental dysgraphia: process versus product', pp. 433–58; Smits-Engelsman, Niemeijer and van Galen, 'Fine motor deficiencies in children diagnosed as DCD', pp. 161–82.
38. Department for Education (DfE), *Key Stage 2 SATS results.*
39. Department for Education and Employment (DfEE), *Developing Early Writing.*
40. Case-Smith and Weintraub, 'Hand function and developmental coordination disorder'.
41. Barnett et al., *Detailed Assessment of Speed of Handwriting.*
42. *Ibid.*
43. O'Hare, 'Dysgraphia and dyscalculia'.
44. Zwicker, 'Effectiveness of occupational therapy in remediating handwriting difficulties in primary students'.
45. Berninger et al., 'Early development of language by hand'.

BIBLIOGRAPHY

INTRODUCTION

Baines, John, *Visual and Written Culture in Ancient Egypt* (Oxford: Oxford University Press, 2007)

Coulmas, Florian, *The Writing Systems of the World* (Oxford: Blackwell, 1989)

–, *Writing Systems: An Introduction to their Linguistic Analysis* (Cambridge: Cambridge University Press, 2003)

Daniels, Peter T., *An Exploration of Writing* (Sheffield: Equinox Publishing, 2018)

DeFrancis, John, *Visible Speech: The Diverse Oneness of Writing Systems* (Honolulu: University of Hawaii Press, 1989)

Gaur, Albertine, *A History of Writing*, revised edn (London: British Library, 1992)

Gelb, Ignace J., *A Study of Writing* (Chicago and London: Chicago University Press, 1963)

Sampson, Geoffrey, *Writing Systems* (Stanford, CA: Stanford University Press, 1985)

CHAPTER 1. THE ORIGINS OF WRITING

Clayton, Ewan, *The Golden Thread: The Story of Writing* (London: Atlantic Books, 2013)

Coe, Michael D., *Breaking the Maya Code*, second edn (London: Thames & Hudson, 1999)

Daniels, Peter T. and Bright, W. (eds), *The World's Writing Systems* (New York: Oxford University Press, 1996)

–, *An Exploration of Writing* (Sheffield: Equinox Publishing, 2018)

Darnell, John Coleman (ed.), *Two Early Alphabetic Inscriptions from the Wadi El-Hol* (Boston, MA: American Schools of Oriental Research, 2006)

DeFrancis, John, *Visible Speech: The Diverse Oneness of Writing Systems* (Honolulu: Hawaii University Press, 1989)

Duhoux, Yves, Palaima, Thomas G. and Bennet, John (eds), *Problems in Decipherment* (Louvain: Peeters, 1989)

Gardiner, Alan, 'The Egyptian origin of the Semitic alphabet', *Journal of Egyptian Archaeology*, 3 (1916), pp. 1–6

Harris, Roy, *The Origin of Writing* (London: Duckworth, 1986)

Houston, Stephen D. (ed.), *The First Writing: Script Invention as History and Process* (New York: Cambridge University Press, 2004)

Mead, Margaret and Modley, Rudolf, 'Communication among all people, everywhere', *Natural History*, 77:7 (1968), pp. 56–63

Pope, Maurice, *The Story of Decipherment: From Egyptian Hieroglyphs to Maya Script*, second edn (London: Thames & Hudson, 1999)

Robinson, Andrew, *Cracking the Egyptian Code: The Revolutionary Life of Jean-François Champollion* (London: Thames & Hudson, 2012)

–, *Lost Languages: The Enigma of the World's Undeciphered Scripts*, second edn (London: Thames & Hudson, 2002)

–, *The Man Who Deciphered Linear B: The Story of Michael Ventris* (London: Thames & Hudson, 2002)

–, *The Story of Writing: Alphabets, Hieroglyphs and Pictograms*, second edn (London: Thames & Hudson, 2007)

–, *Writing and Script: A Very Short Introduction* (Oxford: Oxford University Press, 2009)

de Saussure, Ferdinand, *Course in General Linguistics*, trans. Roy Harris (London: Duckworth, 1983)

Schmandt-Besserat, Denise, *Before Writing: From Counting to Cuneiform*, Vol. 1 (Austin, TX: University of Texas Press, 1992)

Trustees of the British Museum, with an introduction by J. Hooker, *Reading the Past*, includes 'Cuneiform', 'Egyptian Hieroglyphs', 'Linear B and Related Scripts', 'The Early Alphabet', 'Greek Inscriptions' and 'Etruscan' (London: British Museum Press, 1990)

Unger, J. Marshall, *Ideogram: Chinese Characters and the Myth of Disembodied Meaning* (Honolulu: Hawaii University Press, 2004)

Ventris, Michael, 'A note on decipherment methods', *Antiquity*, 27 (1953), pp. 200–6

CHAPTER 2. THE ROMAN ALPHABET

Beaujon, Paul (Beatrice Warde), 'The "Garamond" types, XVI and XVII century sources considered', article in *The Fleuron*, Vol. V (London: Curwen Press, 1926)

–, (ed.) in facsimile, *The 1621 Specimen of Jean Jannon, Paris and Sedan, Designer and Engraver of the Caractères de l'Université now owned by the Imprimerie Nationale* (Paris: Librairie Ancienne Honoré Champion, 1927)

Bischoff, Bernhard, *Latin Palaeography: Antiquity and*

the Middle Ages, translated by Dáibhí Ó Cróinín and David Ganz (Cambridge: Cambridge University Press, 1990)

Bishop, T.A.M., *English Caroline Minuscule* (Oxford: Oxford University Press, 1971)

Blumenthal, Joseph, *Art of the Printed Book, 1455–1955* (New York: Pierpont Morgan Library, 1984)

Bowman, Alan K. and Thomas, J. David, *Vindolanda: The Latin Writing Tablets* (London: Society for the Promotion of Roman Studies, 1983)

Boyle, Leonard E., *Medieval Latin Palaeography: A Bibliographical Introduction* (Toronto: University of Toronto Press, 1984)

Brown, Michelle P., *A Guide to Western Historical Scripts from Antiquity to 1600* (London: British Library, 1990)

–, *The Lindisfarne Gospels: Society, Spirituality and the Scribe* (London: British Library, 2003)

Carter, Harry, *A View of Early Typography up to about 1600* (Oxford: Oxford University Press, 1969. Reprinted with an introduction by James Mosley, London: Hyphen Press, 2002)

Carter, Sebastian, *Twentieth Century Type Designers* (London and New York: W. W. Norton and Company, 1995)

Catich, Edward, *The Trajan Inscription in Rome* (Davenport, IA: Catfish Press, 1961)

–, *The Origin of the Serif: Brush Writing and Roman Letters* (Davenport, IA: Catfish Press, 1968, and Davenport, IA: St Ambrose University, 1992)

Chappell, Warren and Bringhurst, Robert, *A Short History of the Printed Word* (Vancouver: Hartley & Marks, 1999)

Clayton, Ewan, *Edward Johnston: Lettering and Life* (Ditchling: Ditchling Museum, 2007)

–, *The Golden Thread: The Story of Writing* (London: Atlantic Books, 2013)

–, 'John Baskerville the Writing Master', article in Caroline Archer-Parré and Malcolm Dick, *John Baskerville: Art and Industry in the Enlightenment* (Liverpool: Liverpool University Press, 2017)

De Hamel, Christopher, *The Book: A History of the Bible* (London, Phaidon, 2001)

De la Mare, Albinia C., *The Handwriting of Italian Humanists*, Vol. I (Oxford: Oxford University Press, 1973)

Dowding, Geoffrey, *An Introduction to the History of Printing Types* (London and New Castle, DE: British Library and Oak Knoll Press, 1998) Fairbank, Alfred J. and Wolpe, Berthold, *Renaissance Handwriting* (London: Faber & Faber, 1960)

Gordon, Arthur, *Latin Epigraphy* (Berkeley, CA and London: University of California Press, 1983)

Harling, Robert, *The Letter Forms and Type Designs of Eric Gill* (Westerham, Kent: Westerham Press, 1979)

Heal, Sir Ambrose, *The English Writing-Masters and Their Copy-books* (Cambridge: Cambridge University Press, 1931)

Howes, Justin, *Johnston's Underground Type* (London: Capital Transport, 2000)

Hutt, Allen, *Fournier, the Compleat Typographer* (London: Frederick Muller, 1972)

Jammes, André, 'Académisme et typographie: the making of the romain du roi', article in the *Journal of the Printing Historical Society*, No. 1 (London: Printing Historical Society, 1965)

Johnson, A.F., *Type Designs: Their History and Development* (London: Grafton and Co, 1959)

Johnston, Alastair, *Transitional Faces: The Lives and Work of Richard Austin, Type-cutter, and Richard Turner Austin, Wood-engraver* (Berkeley, CA: Poltroon Press, 2013)

Johnston, Edward, *Writing & Illuminating, & Lettering* (London: John Hogg, 1906 and many reprints and new editions since)

Knight, Stan, *Historical Scripts* (New Castle, DE: Oak Knoll Press, 2003)

–, *Historical Types* (New Castle, DE: Oak Knoll Press, 2012)

Lowe, E.A. (ed.), *Codices Latini Antiquiores: A Palaeographical Guide to Latin Manuscripts Prior to the Ninth Century*, 11 vols plus supplement (Oxford: Clarendon, 1934–72)

–, *English Uncial* (Oxford: Clarendon Press, 1960)

Morison, Stanley, 'Early Humanistic Script and the First Roman Type', article in *The Library*, Fourth Series, Vol. 24, Nos 1 and 2 (Oxford, The Bibliographical Society, 1943)

–, *Four Centuries of Fine Printing* (London: Ernest Benn, 1949)

–, *On Type Designs: Past and Present* (London: Ernest Benn, 1962)

Mosley, James, *The Nymph and the Grot: The Revival of the Sanserif Letter* (London: Friends of St Brides Library, 1999)

Osley, Arthur S., 'The Origins of Italic Type', article in

Calligraphy and Palaeography (London: Faber & Faber, 1965)
Pardoe, F.E., *John Baskerville of Birmingham: Letter-founder and Printer* (London: Frederick Muller, 1975)
Parkes, Malcolm B., *English Cursive Book Hands, 1250–1500* (Ilkley: Scolar Press, 1969)
Steinburg, S.H., *Five Hundred Years of Printing* (London and New Castle DE: British Library and Oak Knoll Press, 1996)
Tschichold, Jan, *The New Typography*, translated by Ruari McLean (London and Berkeley, CA: University of California Press, 1998)
Ullman, B.L., *Ancient Writing and its Influence* (Cambridge, MA: MIT Press, 1969)
–, *The Origin and Development of Humanistic Script* (Rome: Edizioni di Storia e Letteratura, 1974)
Updike, Daniel Berkeley, *Printing Types: Their History, Forms, and Use* (Cambridge, MA: Harvard University Press, 1922, second edn 1937. Many reprints since)
Vervliet, Hendrik, *The Palaeotypography of the French Renaissance* (Leiden and Boston: Brill, 2008)
–, *French Renaissance Printing Types: A Conspectus* (London and New Castle DE: The Bibliographical Society/The Printing Historical Society and Oak Knoll Press, 2010)

FOCUS 1. CAXTON'S FIRST PRINTING OF *THE CANTERBURY TALES*

British Library, *Catalogue of Books Printed in the XVth Century Now in the British Library (BMC). Part 11: England* ('t Goy-Houten: Hes & De Graaf, 2007)
Hellinga, Lotte, *Caxton in Focus: The Beginning of Printing in England* (London: British Library, 1982)

CHAPTER 3. WRITING TOOLS AND MATERIALS

Baines, Phil and Haslam, Andrew, *Type and Typography*, second edn (London: Lawrence King, 2005)
Barrett, Timothy, *Japanese Papermaking: Traditions, Tools, Techniques* (New York: Weatherhill, 1984)
Berman, Brenda and Stirling, Annet, *Heavens Above: Incisive Letterwork: Brenda Berman & Annet Stirling* (Fowey: Ian Grant, 2005)
Bigelow, Charles and Day, D., 'Digital Typography', *Scientific American* Vol. 248:2 (August 1983), pp. 94–105
–, and Ruggles, L. (eds), 'The computer and the hand in type design', *Visible Language*, XIX (1985), pp. 5–9
Bierbrier, M.L. (ed.), *Papyrus: Structure and Usage* (London: British Museum Press, 1986)
Bodoni, Giambattista, *Manuale tipographico del cavaliere Giambattista Bodoni* (Parma: Presso la vedova, 1818)
Clayton, Ewan, 'John Baskerville the Writing Master: calligraphy and type in the seventeenth and eighteenth centuries', in Caroline Archer-Parré and Malcolm Dick, *John Baskerville: Art and Industry in the Enlightenment* (Liverpool: Liverpool University Press, 2017), pp. 113–32
–, 'Workplaces for writing', in Michael Gullick, *Pen in Hand: Medieval Scribal Portraits, Colophons and Tools* (Walkern: Red Gull Press, 2006), pp. 1–17
Cooley, Alison E., *The Cambridge Manual of Latin Epigraphy* (Cambridge: Cambridge University Press, 2012)
Davies, M., *The Gutenberg Bible* (London: Pomegranate/British Library, 1997)
Fisher, M. Thérèse, 'Ink', in C.M. Lamb (ed.), *The Calligrapher's Handbook* (London: Faber and Faber 1956), pp. 65–74
Fournier, Pierre-Simon, *Manuel typographique*, Vols I and II (Paris: Barbou, 1764–6)
Gaur, Albertine, *Writing Materials of the East* (London: British Library, 1979)
Gleick, James, *The Information* (London: Fourth Estate, 2011)
Goodwin, Charles and Heritage, John, 'Conversation analysis', in *Annual Review of Anthropology*, Vol. 19 (1990), pp. 283–307
Gullick, Michael, *Pen in Hand: Medieval Scribal Portraits, Colophons and Tools* (Walkern: Red Gull Press, 2006) Hazeldine, Gillian, *Contemporary Calligraphy: How To Use Formal Scripts Today* (London: Hale, 2011)
Hunter, David, *Papermaking: History and Technique of an Ancient Craft* (New York: Dover, 1978)
Hutton, Dorothy, 'Pigments and media', in H. Child (ed.), *The Calligrapher's Handbook* (London: A&C Black, 1985), pp. 45–56
Ingmire, Thomas, *Codicii* (San Francisco, CA: Scriptorium of St Francis, 2003)
Ishikawa, Kyuyo, *Taction: The Drama of the Stylus in*

Oriental Calligraphy (Kyoto: International House Press, 2011)
Jackson, Donald, 'Gilding', in H. Child (ed.), *The Calligrapher's Handbook* (London: A&C Black, 1985), pp. 177–97
–, 'Preparation of quills and reeds', in H. Child (ed.), *The Calligrapher's Handbook* (London: A&C Black, 1985), pp. 15–36
Ja'far, Mustafa, *Arabic Script: Naskh Script for Beginners* (London: British Museum Press, 2002)
Johnston, Edward, *Formal Penmanship and Other Papers*, ed. Heather Child (London: Lund Humphries, 1971)
–, *Writing & Illuminating, & Lettering* (London: Hogg 1906, later editions Pitman, A&C Black, Dover)
Lei Lei, Qu, *Chinese Script: Standard Script for Beginners* (London: British Museum Press, 2004)
Lyons, Martyn, *A History of Reading and Writing in the Western World* (New York and London: Palgrave Macmillan 2010)
Mansour, Nassar, *Sacred Script Muhaqqaq in Islamic Calligraphy* (New York and London: I. B. Tauris, 2011)
McWilliams, Mary and Roxburgh, David J., *Traces of the Calligrapher: Islamic Calligraphy in Practice, c. 1600–1900* (Houston, TX: Museum of Fine Arts, 2007)
Monro, Alexander, *The Paper Trail* (London: Allen Lane, 2014)
Ogborn, Miles, *Indian Ink: Script and Print in the Making of the East India Company* (Chicago, IL and London: University of Chicago, 2007)
Osley, Arthur S., *Scribes and Sources* (London: Faber & Faber, 1980)
Pardoe, F.E., *John Baskerville of Birmingham: Letter-founder and Printer* (London: Frederick Muller, 1975)
Petroski, Henry, *The Pencil: A History* (New York: Knopf, 2002)
Reynolds, Lloyd J., 'Notes on movement involving touch', in Arthur S. Osley (ed.), *Calligraphy and Paleography* (London: Faber & Faber, 1965), pp. 197–206
Schmandt-Besserat, Denise, *When Writing Met Art: From Symbol to Story* (Austin, TX: University of Texas Press, 2007)
Seipel, Wilfried (ed.), *Der Turmbau zu Babel: Ursprung und Vielhaft von Sprache und Schrift: eine Ausstellung des Kunsthistorischen Museums Wien für die Europäische Kulturhauptstadt Graz 2003* (Milano: Skira, 2003)
Senefelder, Alois, *The Invention of Lithography*, trans. J. Muller (New York: Fuch & Lang, 1911)
Shinoda, Toko, 'Sumi infinity', *Kateigaho International Edition*, trans. E. Seidensticker (Tokyo: Kateigaho, Autumn 2003), pp. 72–87
Smith, Douglas K. and Alexander, Robert C., *Fumbling the Future: How Xerox Invented, and Then Ignored, the First Personal Computer* (Lincoln, NE: iUniverse, 1999)
Somerville, Sam, 'Parchment and vellum', in H. Child (ed.), *The Calligrapher's Handbook* (London: A&C Black, 1985), pp. 59–83
Steinberg, Jonathan, *Fountain Pens: Their History and Art* (New York: Universe, 2002
Steinberg, S.H., *Five Hundred Years of Printing* (London: Faber & Faber, 1959)
Suchman, Lucy, 'Centers of Coordination: a case study and some themes' in L.B. Resnick, R. Säljö, C. Pontecorvo and B. Burge (eds), *Discourse, Tools, and Reasoning: Essays on Situated Cognition* (Berlin: Springer-Verlag, 1997), pp. 41–62
Twyman, Michael, *Printing 1770–1970* (London: Eyre and Spottiswoode, 1970)

FOCUS 2. THE DOUBLE PIGEON CHINESE TYPEWRITER

Mullaney, Thomas S., *The Chinese Typewriter: A Global History of the Information Age* (Cambridge, MA: MIT Press, 2017)
Reed, Christopher A., *Gutenberg in Shanghai* (Vancouver: University of British Columbia Press, 2005)

CHAPTER 4. COMMUNITIES OF WRITERS

Allworth, Edward, *Nationalities of the Soviet East: Publications and Writing Systems: A Bibliographical Directory and Transliteration Tables for Iranian-and Turkic-Language Publications, 1818–1945, Located in U.S. Libraries* (New York: Columbia University Press, 1971)
Barrass, Gordon S., *The Art of Calligraphy in Modern China* (London: British Museum Press, 2002)
Baskerville, John, 'The Preface' in John Milton, *Paradise Lost* (London: J. and R. Tonson, 1758)
Benson, John H., *The First Writing Book: The Operina of 1523 Ludovico degli Arrighi* (New Haven, CT and

London: Yale University Press, 1954)
Billeter, Jean François, *The Chinese Art of Writing* (New York: Skira Rizzoli, 1990)
Camille, Michael, *Image on the Edge: The Margins of Medieval Art* (London: Reaktion Books, 1992)
Carr, Nicholas, 'The Information by James Gleick: review', https://www.thedailybeast.com/the-information-by-james-gleick-review-by-nicholas-carr, accessed 28/08/2018
Clayton, Ewan (ed.), *Edward Johnston: Lettering and Life* (Ditchling: Ditchling Museum, 2007)
DeFrancis, John, *The Chinese Language: Fact and Fantasy* (Honolulu: University of Hawaii Press, 1984)
Edgren, J.S., 'The history of the book in China', in Michael F. Suarez, S.J. and H.R. Woudhuysen (eds), *The Oxford Companion to the Book* (Oxford: Oxford University Press, 2010), pp. 353–65
Hanebutt-Benz, Eva-Maria, Glass, Dagmar and Roper, Geoffrey (eds), *Middle Eastern Languages and the Print Revolution: A Cross-Cultural Encounter: A Catalogue and Companion to the Exhibition* (Westhofen: WVA-Verlag Skulima, 2002)
Howes, Justin, *Johnston's Underground Type* (London: Capital Transport, 2000)
Johnston, Priscilla, *Edward Johnston* (London: Faber & Faber, 1959)
Kornicki, P.F., 'The history of the book in Japan', in Michael F. Suarez, S.J. and H.R. Woudhuysen (eds), *The Oxford Companion to the Book* (Oxford: Oxford University Press, 2010), pp. 375–85
Lewis, Geoffrey, *The Turkish Language Reform: A Catastrophic Success* (Oxford and New York: Oxford University Press, 1999)
McDermott, Joseph P., *A Social History of the Chinese Book: Books and Literati Culture in Late Imperial China* (Hong Kong: Hong Kong University Press, 2006)
McKillop, Beth, 'The history of the book in Korea', in Michael F. Suarez, S.J. and H.R. Woudhuysen (eds), *The Oxford Companion to the Book* (Oxford: Oxford University Press, 2010), pp. 366–73
McWilliams, M. and Roxburgh, D., *Traces of the Calligrapher: Islamic Calligraphy in Practice, c.1600–1900* (Houston, TX: Museum of Fine Art, 2007)
Ogborn, Miles, *Indian Ink: Script and Print in the Making of the East India Company* (Chicago, IL and London: University of Chicago, 2007)
Omniglot: The Online Encyclopedia of Writing Systems and Languages, http://omniglot.com/, accessed 8/9/18
Porter, Venetia, *World into Art: Artists of the Modern Middle East* (London: British Museum Press, 2006)
Roper, Geoffrey (ed.), *Historical Aspects of Printing and Publishing in Languages of the Middle East: Papers from the Third Symposium on the History of Printing and Publishing in the Languages and Countries of the Middle East, University of Leipzig, September 2008* (Leiden and Boston, MA: Brill, 2014)
–, (ed.), *The History of the Book in the Middle East* (Burlington, VT: Ashgate, 2013)
Sadgrove, Philip (ed.), *History of Printing and Publishing in the Languages and Countries of the Middle East* (Oxford: Oxford University Press, 2004)
Schimmel, Annemarie, *Calligraphy and Islamic Culture* (London: I. B. Tauris, 1990)
Thornton, Tamara Plakins, *Handwriting in America: A Cultural History* (New Haven, CT and London: Yale University Press, 1996)
Tsien, Tsuen-hsuin, *Written on Bamboo and Silk*, second edn (Chicago, IL: University of Chicago Press, 2004)
Turner, Fred, *From Counter Culture to Cyberculture* (Chicago, IL: University of Chicago Press, 2006)
Whalley, Joyce Irene, *English Handwriting, 1540–1853* (London: Her Majesty's Stationery Office, 1969)
Xu, Bing, *XuBing: cong Tianshudao Di shu XuBing: Book from the Sky to Book from the Ground* (Taipei: The Eslite Corp., 2014)

FOCUS 3. DEXTERITY AND DIVERSITY: A BILINGUAL LETTER FROM MOSUL

Nājī Zayn al-Dīn, Musawwar al-khatt al-'arabī (Baghdād: Matbū'āt al-mujamma' al-'Ilmī al-'irāqī, 1968)

CHAPTER 5. THE FUTURE OF WRITING

Borgman, Albert, *Holding On To Reality: The Nature of Information at the Turn of the Millennium* (Chicago, IL: University of Chicago Press, 1999)
Buber, Martin, *I and Thou* (New York: Charles Scribner's Sons, 1958)
Burgert, Hans-Joachim, *The Calligraphic Line: Thoughts on the Art of Writing* (Berlin: Burgertpresse, 1989)

Chartier, Roger, *The Order of Books* (Stanford, CA: Stanford University Press, 1994)
Clayton, Ewan, *The Golden Thread: The Story of Writing* (London: Atlantic, 2013)
Ellul, Jacques, *The Technological Society* (New York: Vintage Books, 1964)
Gelb, Ignace J., *A Study of Writing* (Cambridge: Cambridge University Press, 1963)
Levy, David, *Mindful Tech: How to Bring Balance to Our Digital Lives* (New Haven, CT and London: Yale University Press, 2016)
–, *Scrolling Forward: Making Sense of Documents in the Digital Age* (New York: Arcade, 2001)
MacCarthy, Fiona, *William Morris: A Life For Our Time* (London: Faber & Faber, 1994)
Marinetti, Filippo Tommaso, 'Destruction of syntax – imagination without strings – words in freedom' (1913), in Umbro Apollonio (ed.), *Futurist Manifestos* (New York: The Viking Press, 1973), pp. 95–106
Milne, Esther, *Letters, Postcards, Email: Technologies of Presence* (New York and London: Routledge, 2010)
Mueller, Pam and Oppenheimer, Daniel, 'The pen is mightier than the keyboard: advantages of longhand over laptop note taking', *Psychological Science*, 25:6 (2014), pp. 1159–68
Neuenschwander, Brody, *Textasy* (Ghent: Imschoot, 2006)
Sasson, Rosemary, *Handwriting in the Twentieth Century* (London and New York: Routledge, 1999)
Schmandt-Besserat, Denise, *Before Writing: From Counting to Cuneiform* (Austin, TX: University of Texas Press, 1992)
Thornton, Tamara Plakins, *Handwriting in America: A Cultural History* (New Haven, CT and London: Yale University Press, 1996)
Williams, James, *Stand Out of Our Light: Freedom and Resistance in the Attention Economy* (Cambridge: Cambridge University Press, 2018)

CHAPTER 6. HANDWRITING: ITS RELEVANCE NOW AND IN THE FUTURE

Alamargot, D., Chesnet, D., Dansac, C. and Ros, C., 'Eye and pen: a new device to study the reading during writing', *Behavior Research Methods, Instruments and Computers*, 38:2 (2006), pp. 287–99
–, Dansac, C., Chesnet, D. and Fayol, M., 'Parallel processing before and after pauses: a combined analysis of graphomotor and eye movements during procedural text production', in M. Torrance, L. Van Waes and D. Galbraith (eds), *Studies in Writing and Cognition: Research Applications* (Oxford: Elsevier, 2007), pp. 13–29
Anthony, L., Yang, J. and Koedinger, K.R., 'The benefits of handwritten input for students learning algebra', *Artificial Intelligence in Education*, 7 (2007), pp. 521–3
Apel, K., Wolter, J. and Masterton, J., 'Effects of phonotactic and orthotactic probabilities during fast mapping on 5-year-olds' learning to spell', *Developmental Neuropsychology*, 29 (2006), pp. 21–42
Barnett, A., Henderson, S.E., Scheib, B. and Schulz, C., *Detailed Assessment of Speed of Handwriting* (Cambridge: Pearson Education, 2007)
Berninger, V. W., 'Development of language by hand and its connections with language by ear, mouth, and eye', *Topics in Language Disorders*, 20:4 (2000), pp. 65–84
–, Abbott, R.D., Jones, J., Wolf, B.J., Gould, L., Anderson-Youngstrom, M. and Apel, K., 'Early development of language by hand: composing, reading, listening, and speaking connections; three letter-writing modes; and fast mapping in spelling', *Developmental Neuropsychology*, 29: 1 (2006), pp. 61–92.
–, (ed.), *Past, Present, and Future Contributions of Cognitive Writing Research to Cognitive Psychology* (New York and Hove: Psychology Press, 2012)
–, Vaughan, K.B., Abbott, R.D., Abbott, S.P., Rogan, L.W., Brooks, A., Reed, E. and Graham, S., 'Treatment of handwriting problems in beginning writers: transfer from handwriting to composition', *Journal of Educational Psychology*, 89:4 (1997), pp. 652–66
Bourdin, B. and Fayol, M., 'Is graphic activity cognitively costly? A developmental approach', *Reading and Writing*, 13 (2000), pp. 183–96
Case-Smith, J., Holland, T., Lane, A. and White, S., 'Effect of a coteaching handwriting program for first graders: one group pretest–postest design', *American Journal of Occupational Therapy*, 66:4 (2012), pp. 396–405
–, and Weintraub, N., 'Hand function and developmental coordination disorder', in S.A.

Cermak and D. Larkin (eds), *Developmental Coordination Disorder* (Albany, NY: Delmar Thomson Learning, 2002), pp. 157–71

Chenoweth, N.A. and Hayes, J.R., 'Fluency in writing: generating text in
L1 and L2', *Written Communication*, 18 (2001), pp. 80–98

Christensen, C.A., 'The critical role handwriting plays in the ability to produce high-quality written text', in R. Beard, D. Myhill, J. Riley and M. Nystrand (eds), *The Handbook of Writing Development* (London: Sage Publishers, 2009), pp. 284–99

–, 'The role of orthographic-motor integration in the production of creative and well-structured written text for students in secondary school', *Educational Psychology*, 25:5 (2005),
pp. 441–53

Chu, S., 'The effects of visual perceptual dysfunction on the development and performance of handwriting skills', *Handwriting Today*, 2 (2000), pp. 42–55

Connelly, V. and Hurst, G., 'The influence of handwriting fluency on writing quality in later primary and early secondary education', *Handwriting Today*, 2 (2001), pp. 5–57

Department for Employment and Education (DfEE), *Developing Early Writing*, DfES Publications, 2001, http://www.dfes.gov.uk/achievingsuccess, accessed 8/9/18

Department for Education (DfE), 2014, http://www.DfE.education.gov.uk/statistics, accessed 8/9/18

–, *Key Stage 2 SATS results*, DfE, 2018, https://schoolsweek.co.uk/key-stage-2-sats-results-2018-64-achieve-expected-standard/, accessed 8/9/18

Dockrell, J., 'Causes of delays and difficulties in the production of written text', in R. Beard, D. Myhill, M. Nystrand and J. Riley (eds), *The Sage Handbook of Writing Development* (London: Sage, 2009), pp. 489–505

Galbraith, D., Van Waes, L. and Torrance, M., *Writing and Cognition: Research Applications* (Amsterdam: Elsevier, 2007)

Graham, S. and Santangelo, T., 'A meta-analysis of the effectiveness of teaching handwriting', *Handwriting in the 21st Century* (Washington, DC: US Educational Summit, 2012), https://www.hw21summit.com/media/zb/hw21/files/H2948_HW_Summit_White_Paper_eVersion.pdf, accessed 8/9/2018

Hutchinson Guest, Ann, *Labanotation or Kinetography Laban: The System of Analyzing and Recording Movement* (New York: Theatre Arts Books, 1954)

Izadi-Najafabadi, S., Ryan, N., Ghafooripoor, G., Gill, K. and Zwicker,
J.G., 'Participation of children with developmental coordination disorder', *Research in developmental disabilities* (2018), in press.

James, K.H., 'How printing practice affects letter perception: an educational cognitive neuroscience perspective', *Handwriting in the 21st Century* (Washington, DC: US Educational Summit, 2012), https://www.hw21summit.com/media/zb/hw21/files/H2948_HW_Summit_White_Paper_eVersion.pdf, accessed 8/9/18

Jones, D. and Christensen, C.A., 'Relationship between automaticity in handwriting and students' ability to generate written text', *Journal of Educational Psychology*, 91 (1999),
pp. 1–6

Kandel, S. and Valdois, S., 'The effect of orthographic regularity on children's handwriting production', *Current Psychology Letters*, 17:3 (2005), pp. 1–11

–, 'French and Spanish-speaking children use different visual and motor units during spelling acquisition', *Language & Cognitive Processes*, 21:5 (2006), pp. 531–61

Marquardt, Christian, Meyer, Diaz M., Schneider, Manuela and Hilgemann, René, 'Learning handwriting at school – a teachers' survey on actual problems and future options', *Trends in Neuroscience and Education*, 5(3) (2016), pp. 82–9

–, and Mai, N., 'A computational procedure for movement analysis in handwriting', *Journal of Neuroscience Methods*, 52:1 (1994), pp. 39–45

McMaster, E. and Roberts, T., 'Handwriting in 2015: a main occupation for primary school-aged children in the classroom?', *Journal of Occupational Therapy, Schools, & Early Intervention*, 9:1 (2016), pp. 38–50

Mueller, Pam and Oppenheimer, Daniel, 'The pen is mightier than the keyboard: advantages of longhand over laptop note taking', *Psychological Science*, 25:6, (2014), pp. 1159–68

Myhill, D., 'Becoming a designer: trajectories of linguistic development', in R. Beard, D. Myhill, J. Riley and M. Nystrand (eds), *The Sage Handbook of Writing Development* (London: Sage, 2009)

National Curriculum Assessment, UK, 2014 https://

www.gov.uk/government/collections/national-curriculum, accessed 8/9/18
National Governors Association Center for Best Practices, Council of Chief State School Officers, *Common Core State Standards for English Language Arts*, Appendix A (Washington DC, 2010) http://www.corestandards.org/assets/Appendix_A.pdf, accessed 8/9/18
National Literacy Trust, *Young People's Writing in 2011: Findings from the National Literacy Trust's Annual Literacy Survey*, 2012, www.literacytrust.org.uk/, accessed 8/9/18
O'Hare, A., 'Dysgraphia and dyscalculia', in K. Whitmore, H. Hart and G. Willens (eds), *A Neurodevelopmental Approach to Specific Learning Disorders* (London: Mac Keith Press, 1999)
Peverly, S.T. and Sumowski, J.F., 'What variables predict quality of text notes and are text notes related to performance on different types of tests?', *Applied Cognitive Psychology*, 26:1 (2012), pp. 104–17
Prunty, M.M., Barnett, A.L., Wilmut, K. and Plumb, M.S., 'An examination of writing pauses in the handwriting of children with developmental coordination disorder', *Research in Developmental Disabilities*, 35:11 (2014), pp. 2894–905
Rosenblum, S., Parush, S. and Weiss, P.L., 'The in air phenomenon: temporal and spatial correlates of the handwriting process', *Perceptual & Motor Skills*, 96:3, (2003), pp. 933–54
–, Weiss, P. and Parush, S., 'Handwriting evaluation for developmental dysgraphia: process versus product', *Reading & Writing: An Interdisciplinary Journal*, 17 (2004), pp. 433–58
Schmidt, R.A. and Lee, T.D., *Motor Control and Learning* (Champaign, IL: Human Kinetics, 2011)
Schmidt, R.A., Lee, T., Winstein, C., Wulf, G., and Zelaznik, H., *Motor Control and Learning, 6th Edition* (Champaign, IL: Human Kinetics, 2018)
Shorter Oxford Dictionary, sixth edn (Oxford: Oxford University Press, 2007)
Smits-Engelsman, B.C., Niemeijer, A.S. and van Galen, G.P., 'Fine motor deficiencies in children diagnosed as DCD based on poor grapho-motor ability', *Human Movement Science*, 20:1 (2001), pp. 161–82
Sumner, E., Connelly, V. and Barnett, A.L., 'Children with dyslexia are slow writers because they pause more often and not because they are slow at handwriting execution', *Reading & Writing: An Interdisciplinary Journal*, 10:6 (2012), pp. 1–18
Van Galen, G.P., 'Handwriting: issues for a psychomotor theory', *Human Movement Science*, 10 (1991), pp. 165–91
Webb, Angela, 'The relationship between handwriting and written composition in children with developmental coordination disorder', PhD thesis, University College London, 2013
Wollscheid, S., Sjaastad, J. and Tømte, C., 'The impact of digital devices vs. pen (cil) and paper on primary school students' writing skills – a research review', *Computers & Education*, 95 (2016), pp. 19–35
YouGov, 2014, cdn.yougov.com/cumulus_uploads/document/2epvuor52x/YG-Archive, accessed 8/9/18
Zwicker, J.G., 'Effectiveness of occupational therapy in remediating handwriting difficulties in primary students: cognitive versus multisensory interventions', MA thesis, University of Victoria, Canada, 2005
–, J.G., Miller, S.P., Grunau, R.E., Chau, V., Brant, R., Studholme, C. and Tam, E.W. (2016), 'Smaller cerebellar growth and poorer neurodevelopmental outcomes in very preterm infants exposed to neonatal morphine', *The Journal of Pediatrics*, 172, pp. 81–7
–, and Izadi-Najafabadi, S., 'Brain changes associated with CO-OP intervention for children with DCD', *Presentation to DCD UK conference* (London: Brunel University, 2018)

FOCUS 4. A 2,000-YEAR-OLD HOMEWORK BOOK

Brashear W.M., 'A Trifle', *Zeitschrift für Papyrologie und Epigraphik* 86 (1991), pp. 231–2
Kenyon F.G., 'Two Greek school tablets', *Journal of Hellenic Studies* 29 (1909), pp. 29–40: 39–40
For tablets and papyri in the BL, see https://www.bl.uk/help/find-papyri, and in general https://www.trismegistos.org

AFTERWORD: WRITING AND THE COLLECTIONS OF THE BRITISH LIBRARY

Attar, Karen (ed.), 'British Library', in CILIP Rare Books and Special Collections Group, *Directory of*

Rare Books and Special Collections in the United Kingdom and the Republic of Ireland, third edn (London: Facet Publishing, 2016)

British Library, *Annual Report and Accounts 2016/17* (London: British Library, 2017) and online at http://www.bl.uk/aboutus/annrep/index.html, accessed 8/9/18

–, *Living Knowledge: The British Library 2015–2023* (London: British Library, 2015) and online at https://www.bl.uk/projects/living-knowledge-the-british-library-2015-2023, accessed 8/9/18

Harris, Phil R., *A History of the British Museum Library, 1753–1973* (London: British Library, 1998)

Nixon, Margaret, A.E., *The British Library: Guide to the Catalogues and Indexes of the Department of Manuscripts*, third revd edn (London: British Library, 1998)

Omniglot: The Online Encyclopedia of Writing Systems and Languages, http://omniglot.com/, accessed 8/9/18

ILLUSTRATION CREDITS

All images © The British Library Board except the following:
(a=above, b=below, l=left, r=right)

8 © The Trustees of the British Museum; **23** Patrick Cabrol/Centre de Préhistoire du Pech Merle/akg-images; **24** © The Trustees of the British Museum; **25b** Metropolitan Museum of Art, New York; **28** © The Trustees of the British Museum; **30** © Ashmolean Museum, University of Oxford; **33**, **35**, **36**, **37** © The Trustees of the British Museum; **43** Biblioteca Apostolica Vaticana; **44a** © The Trustees of the British Museum; **44b** National Geographic Image Collection/Alamy Stock Photo; **47** Biblioteca Apostolica Vaticana; **63l** Archiv des Bistums Augsburg; **77b** Courtesy James Mosley; **83a** © The Trustees of the British Museum; **85** Metropolitan Museum of Art, New York; **86b** © The Trustees of the British Museum; **87** © Flavia Soprani/Dreamstime.com; **88** © Khaled Eladewy/Dreamstime.com; **90**, **91** Courtesy Ewan Clayton; **99** Photo Stokes Photo Ltd, courtesy of the Crafts Council; **109a** Courtesy Ewan Clayton; **110** Cardiff Council Flat Holm Project; **123a** Charles O. Cecil/Alamy Stock Photo; **140r** © TfL from the London Transport Museum; **144** © Xu Bing Studio; **145** © eL Seed; **156** Mohamad Abazeed/AFP/Getty Images; **161** Jim Goldstein/Alamy Stock Photo; **163** Thomas Lohnes/Getty Images; **171** © Brody Neuenschwander; **172** © Mark Noad, Letter Exchange; **175** AF Archive/Alamy Stock Photo; **179** © Sarinya Pinngam/Dreamstime.com; **180** Mary Evans/SZ Photo/Scherl; **185**, **191**, **192** Courtesy Angela Webb.

INDEX

Introductory Note
To indicate an illustration, the number span is in *italic*.
E.g. motion notation systems *178–80*

FOLLOWING PAGE The Kabuki actor Ichikawa Danjūrō VI, woodcut by Toyokuni Utagawa, from *Yakusha Konote Kashiwa* (*Actors among the Garden Oaks*), Edo, 1803. 16104.a.39, Plate 2

三升